The Discourse of News Values

The Discourse of News Values

HOW NEWS ORGANIZATIONS CREATE NEWSWORTHINESS

MONIKA BEDNAREK AND HELEN CAPLE

OXFORD
UNIVERSITY PRESS

Oxford University Press is a department of the University of Oxford. It furthers
the University's objective of excellence in research, scholarship, and education
by publishing worldwide. Oxford is a registered trade mark of Oxford University
Press in the UK and certain other countries.

Published in the United States of America by Oxford University Press
198 Madison Avenue, New York, NY 10016, United States of America.

© Monika Bednarek & Helen Caple 2017

All rights reserved. No part of this publication may be reproduced, stored in
a retrieval system, or transmitted, in any form or by any means, without the
prior permission in writing of Oxford University Press, or as expressly permitted
by law, by license, or under terms agreed with the appropriate reproduction
rights organization. Inquiries concerning reproduction outside the scope of the
above should be sent to the Rights Department, Oxford University Press, at the
address above.

You must not circulate this work in any other form
and you must impose this same condition on any acquirer.

Library of Congress Cataloging-in-Publication Data
Names: Bednarek, Monika, 1977– author. | Caple, Helen, author.
Title: The discourse of news values : how news organizations create
newsworthiness / Monika Bednarek and Helen Caple.
Description: New York : Oxford University Press, [2017] | Includes
bibliographical references and index.
Identifiers: LCCN 2016024098 (print) | LCCN 2016038876 (ebook) |
ISBN 9780190653941 (pbk. : alk. paper) | ISBN 9780190653934 (cloth : alk. paper) |
ISBN 9780190653958 (pdf) | ISBN 9780190653965 (ebook) |
ISBN 9780190653972 (online resource)
Subjects: LCSH: Journalism—Language. | Discourse analysis.
Classification: LCC PN4783 .B43 20107 (print) | LCC PN4783 (ebook) |
DDC 070.4—dc23 LC record available at https://lccn.loc.gov/2016024098

Contents

List of tables ix
List of figures xi
Acknowledgements xv

1. Introduction 1

    1.1. The discourse of news values 1

    1.2. Why study news values? 4

    1.3. Key terms 6

    1.4. Corpus-assisted multimodal discourse analysis 8

    1.5. Summary and overview of chapters 22

Part I THEORY

2. News values 27

    2.1. Journalism/communications studies 27

    2.2. Linguistics 36

    2.3. A new approach to news values 39

3. Discursive news values analysis 49

    3.1. The discursive construction of news values 49

    3.2. Our list and labels 53

    3.3. Conceptualizing news values 56

    3.4. Context-dependency, preferred meaning, and the target audience 67

    3.5. Example analysis and concluding remarks 68

Part II ANALYTICAL FRAMEWORKS

4. Language and news values   77

    4.1. Introduction   77

    4.2. Towards an inventory of linguistic resources   78

    4.3. Combining news values and example analysis   102

    4.4. Summary   104

5. Visuals and news values   107

    5.1. Introduction   107

    5.2. The relationship between images and news values   108

    5.3. Visual resources in images   110

    5.4. Other semiotic resources constructing news values   124

    5.5. Front-page news: An example analysis   127

    5.6. Concluding remarks   132

Part III EMPIRICAL ANALYSIS

6. What is newsworthy about cyclists?   137

    6.1. Introduction   137

    6.2. The corpus   138

    6.3. Analysis of 'typical' news values   144

    6.4. Analysis of news values around cyclists   151

    6.5. Summary and conclusion   164

7. Images, news values, and Facebook   171

    7.1. Introduction   171

    7.2. Social media and news feeds   172

    7.3. Data and methodology   173

    7.4. Results   179

    7.5. Conclusion   193

8. 'All the news that's fit to share': News values in 'most shared' news   195

    8.1. Introduction   195

    8.2. Data and methodology   197

8.3. Verbal patterns 203

8.4. Visual patterns 216

8.5. Visual-verbal patterns 218

8.6. Conclusion 223

Part IV   EXTENSIONS

9. Discursive news values analysis as an opportunity for diachronic and cross-cultural research 229

    9.1. *Salacious Fiends* and *News from the Dead*: Diachronic research 229

    9.2. *El terror yihadista, Terroralarm, terrordramat*: Cross-cultural research 237

    9.3. Concluding remarks 246

10. Reflections 249

    10.1. *From little things, big things grow* (chapter 1) 249

    10.2. Surveying the field: *It's a jungle out there* (chapter 2) 250

    10.3. Situating our own approach to news values: *Which corner of the jungle do we inhabit?* (chapter 3) 250

    10.4. The *discourse* of news values (chapters 4 and 5) 252

    10.5. Case study 1: 'Pedalling' a critical, topic-based approach to DNVA (chapter 6) 253

    10.6. Case study 2: DNVA and the digital disrupters of social media (chapter 7) 253

    10.7. Case study 3: Combining DNVA and CAMDA (chapter 8) 254

    10.8. *Xīnwén jiàzhí, arzeshe khabari, Khabari Iqdaar* (chapter 9) 256

    10.9. Concluding remarks 257

Appendix 259
References 283
Index 299

List of tables

2.1	Galtung and Ruge's (1965) news values	29
2.2	Bell's threefold categorization	40
2.3	Dimensions of news values	43
3.1	Key verbs used by linguists	50
3.2	The lost boy of Syria, 16 February 2014	52
3.3	News values and their definitions in DNVA	55
3.4	News values construction in example (3)	71
4.1	Linguistic resources for establishing news values	79
4.2	Example analysis of three lead paragraphs	103
5.1	News values in figure 5.17	131
6.1	Newspapers included in the corpus	139
6.2	UK sub-corpus	142
6.3	Australian sub-corpus	142
6.4	US sub-corpus	143
6.5	Most 'prototypical' news items about cycling (ProtAnt)	146
6.6	Least 'prototypical' news items about cycling (ProtAnt)	149
6.7	Collocates for *cyclist* in top 50 (MI3, T-score, LL, and range)	154
6.8	The spread of collocates across CyCo publications (MI3)	155
6.9	Nominal phrases containing *old*	156
6.10	Collocates for *cyclists* in top 50 (MI3, T-score, LL, and range)	157
6.11	Grouping cyclists with other road users	161
6.12	The role of cyclists	165
7.1	News media organizations sampled for the social media case study	175
7.2	General information regarding the makeup of the Facebook Corpus	180
7.3	News values constructed in the Facebook Corpus	183
7.4	The most common clusterings involving Eliteness, Personalization, and Proximity	183
7.5	The construction of Aesthetic Appeal in the Facebook Corpus	187

7.6	Total number of news values constructed according to country/region	189
8.1	Lexical words across at least four headlines and OPs	204
8.2	Other lexical words	204
8.3	Additional word forms	205
8.4	Sources constructed as elite	206
8.5	The construction of Proximity (*city, American, US, state, New*)	209
8.6	The construction of Timeliness (*Monday, Saturday, last, night*)	211
8.7	Tendencies in the construction of news values in headlines and opening paragraphs	214
8.8	Tendencies in the construction of Negativity and Positivity	214
8.9	Combining news values	215
8.10	The construction of news values in the image corpus (72 images)	216
8.11	Negativity/Positivity and the construction of Personalization and Eliteness	217
8.12	Correlation in the construction of news values across semiotic modes (out of a total of 72 stories that include both language and image)	219
9.1	Selected examples from *The Washington Post* (1877–1907)	232
9.2	The use of photography in *The Sydney Morning Herald* during the first half of the twentieth century	236
9.3	A sample of reporting on the Sydney siege (December 2014) from around the world	238
A4.1	Inventory of linguistic devices that often construct newsworthiness in English-language news	260
A5.1	Inventory of visual devices that often construct newsworthiness in English-language news	268
A6.1	Frequencies of search terms	272
A6.2	Top 50 collocates of *cyclist* (sorted according to MI3, T-score, LL, and range)	273
A6.3	Top 50 5L-5R collocates of *cyclists* (sorted according to MI3, T-score, LL, and range)	274
A6.4	Variants to refer to people who use a bicycle	274
A6.5	Analysis of patterns for *drivers/motorists and cyclists; cyclists and drivers/motorists*	275
A6.6	Analysis of patterns for the most frequent clusters for *cyclists and pedestrians/pedestrians and cyclists*	276
A8.1	URLs of items in the Shared News Corpus	276
A8.2	Types that occur across at least four Hs/OPs in the SNC	282

List of figures

1.1 A news photograph of migrants walking through Slovenia (*The Atlantic*, published and accessed on 26 October 2015) 2
1.2 Zones of analysis 10
1.3 Zones of analysis with examples 11
1.4 Example of a partial word cloud (from chapter 6) 13
1.5 Example of a GraphColl network (from chapter 6) 14
1.6 Sorted concordances 16
1.7 Visual resources comprising image content 18
1.8 Visual resources comprising composition 20
1.9 Visual resources comprising technical affordances 21
3.1 Possible subcategories for Timeliness 56
3.2 Geographical Proximity with respect to a Brisbane target audience 63
3.3 Geographical and cultural Proximity—a topology 63
3.4 Timeliness as a cline 65
3.5 Front page of the *New York Post*, 2 November 2014 69
5.1 The construction of Aesthetic Appeal in news imagery 111
5.2 The typical behaviour, clothing, and regalia associated with 'football' 112
5.3 (Stereo)typical portrayals of Australian and British football fans 112
5.4 Constructions of Eliteness 113
5.5 The construal of Eliteness through attributes associated with the represented participants 114
5.6 The construction of Eliteness in relation to man-made structures 115
5.7 Low camera angle reinforcing Negativity 116
5.8 Reporting of a tropical cyclone in the Australian news media 118
5.9 The media scrum and the construction of Eliteness, Positivity, and Negativity 119
5.10 The construction of Personalization in news imagery 121
5.11 The construction of Proximity in news imagery 122
5.12 The construction of Superlativeness in news imagery 122

5.13	The construction of Timeliness in news imagery	123
5.14	The construction of Unexpectedness in news imagery	124
5.15	The use of all caps in front-page headlines in the popular press	125
5.16	Front-page news: 'PARIS TERROR', *New York Post*, 14 November 2014, p. 1	126
5.17	Front-page news: 'TERROR HITS OUR HEART', *The West Australian*, 16 December 2014, p. 1	129
6.1	Situating the case study	137
6.2	Wordsmith word cloud (default settings, with stoplist)	144
6.3	Wordsmith plot for *cyclist/cyclists* (dispersion: 0.751)	152
6.4	Sketch Engine frequency distribution over concordance positions (granularity 100)	152
6.5	5L-5R collocates of *cyclist* (MI3 ≥ 9, min. frequency = 2)	153
6.6	GraphColl network (*cyclists, more*; MI3 ≥ 17, min. frequency = 2)	158
6.7	The construction of Superlativeness around *cyclists*	159
6.8	GraphColl visualization (*cyclists, not*; MI3 ≥ 16, min. frequency = 2)	160
6.9	Concordances for *injured* as modifier of CYCLIST	162
6.10	The verb collocate DIE + *cyclists*	163
6.11	Selected concordances for DIE as collocate of *cyclist*	164
7.1	Situating the case study	171
7.2	Layout of story posts and tweets on Facebook and Twitter and the corresponding website	174
7.3	The constructed week sampling method	176
7.4	Cues used to determine eligibility for inclusion in the data collection	177
7.5	The relational database user interface alongside the analysed image	178
7.6	The clusterings of Eliteness and Personalization with Proximity	184
7.7	The construction of Negativity, Impact, Personalization (and Superlativeness)	186
7.8	The construction of the news value Aesthetic Appeal in the Facebook Corpus	188
7.9	The use of stock photography in the Facebook Corpus	191
8.1	Images and headlines appearing in the most shared news on Facebook	195
8.2	Zones of analysis	198
8.3	Layout of the first screen of a story page on the CNN website; labelled according to Djonov and Knox (2014: 176-178)	199
8.4	A screen shot of the MS Access Database	200
8.5	The construction of 'possible' Proximity across words and image	201
8.6	The construction of 'possible' Eliteness across words and images	202
8.7	The construction of Personalization and Negativity/Positivity	217
8.8	The construction of Superlativeness through the depiction of extreme emotions	217

8.9	The construal (and reinforcement) of the news value Eliteness across headline, image, and opening paragraph 220	
8.10	Clash in valence between image and verbal text 221	
9.1	German tabloid headline about the November 2015 attacks in Paris, 15 November 2015, p. 1 245	

Acknowledgements

Most chapters of this research monograph were co-authored through a collaborative process—the exceptions are chapters 4 and 6 (written by Monika Bednarek) and chapters 5 and 7 (written by Helen Caple), although we did provide feedback on each other's chapter drafts.

There are a number of colleagues and institutions that have been instrumental in assisting us throughout the production of this book. We would like to acknowledge and thank them all most sincerely here (and in no particular order). First, we are grateful to Hallie Stebbins for commissioning the book and to the whole Oxford University Press production team for seeing the manuscript through to publication. We would also like to thank the anonymous reviewers who gave us invaluable feedback on earlier draft chapters of the manuscript.

Much of the groundwork for the beginnings of this book was undertaken in 2013 during our respective Visiting Fellowships with the Reuters Institute for the Study of Journalism (RISJ), University of Oxford. We are immensely grateful for this opportunity. We would also like to thank the Director David Levy and the then Director of Research Robert G. Picard, as well as all of the journalist fellows, for the valuable conversations we had at RISJ in relation to news values. We are also grateful that RISJ gave permission for us to reprint parts of our working paper *Delving into the Discourse: Approaches to News Values in Journalism Studies and Beyond* (2013) in chapter 2 of this book.

Chapter 8 is an output of the ARC Linkage Project grant *Sharing News Online: Analysing the Significance of a Social Media Phenomenon* (LP 140100148), in which Monika Bednarek participated. We are grateful to the industry partners Andrew Hunter, Hal Crawford, and Domagoj Filipovic from Share Wars and Mi9 and to the other project members Tim Dwyer, Fiona Martin, and James Curran for helpful discussions and access to ShareWars's Likeable Engine. We also want to thank three research assistants who compiled the data for this chapter, Joel Nothman, Samuel Luke, and Penelope Thomas—in particular Joel Nothman who acted as expert Data Mining consultant. Special thanks also to Laurence Anthony, of Waseda University, Japan, who created a visualization of text-image relations for the findings in chapter 8 (available at www.newsvaluesanalysis.com).

Helen Caple would like to thank the University of New South Wales for financial support through the School of the Arts and Media Research Grant Scheme. Monika Bednarek is grateful for funding provided through a University of Sydney Bridging Grant, which funded the image collection for chapter 8 as well as general research assistance throughout 2015, which was expertly provided by Samuel Luke. She also wants to extend her gratitude to the Freiburg Institute for Advanced Studies (FRIAS), University of Freiburg, Germany, for awarding her an FCFP External Senior Fellowship, which enabled her to put the final touches to the book manuscript in the second half of 2015.

For assistance with the translation of the news articles analysed in chapter 9, we would like to acknowledge the expertise of Pernille Day (Swedish), Audrey Deheinzelin (French), and Beatrice Quiroz (Spanish and Portuguese). Copyright for all material analysed in this book remains with the original authors.

Over the last three years, our ideas for discursive news values analysis have been tested on a number of audiences and have been refined through discussion with colleagues. We are grateful for the feedback we have received from these colleagues. Thank you in particular to Charlotte Hommerberg for organizing and funding our lecture tour to Sweden, to Martin Engebretsen for our stay in Norway, and to Theo van Leeuwen for meeting with us to discuss thorny theoretical issues. We also extend our gratitude to colleagues and research students who attended the News Discourse Research Group at the University of Sydney in 2015, and who participated in lively debate around our shared interests in the analysis of news discourse. Students in our undergraduate and postgraduate classes on media discourse and journalism also helped us in clarifying our approach, not only through their questions and feedback but also through their own application of discursive news values analysis in their assignments.

Finally, we would like to express our love and gratitude to our families and friends who continue to encourage and support us.

The Discourse of News Values

1

Introduction

1.1 The discourse of news values

This book is about words, images, and the construction of newsworthiness. By way of introduction, consider these three news items:

(1)
Women feature in only 7 per cent of sports programming in Australia, representing a backwards step compared to a decade ago and highlighting a significant gender gap in a country where sport is king, a new report shows. (http://abc.net.au, published and accessed on 13 April 2015)

(2)
Captain Adriano Binacchi, who manned the stranded, [sic] Carnival Spirit, is officially the world's most non-plussed sea captain. His ship took on 6–10m swells, but in taking questions from media his overall attitude seemed to be "no big deal".
When asked if facing such violent sea conditions is rare he replied:
"Not really, it's not my first time."
Were there any injuries sustained on board?
"No injuries, just some minor sea sickness."
Damage to the ship?
"What damage? Maybe some glass window panes. Minor things." (http://theguardian.com/au, published and accessed on 22 April 2015)[1]

(3)
News photograph in figure 1.1 on page 2.

In this book we are interested in how such verbal and visual texts provide an answer to the putative audience question *how is this news?* In other words, how do semiotic

Figure 1.1 A news photograph of migrants walking through Slovenia (*The Atlantic* photo: Jeff J. Mitchell/Getty Images).

(meaning-making) devices justify the newsworthiness of reported events or issues? Let's look at example (1) first: This item mentions that the reported issue concerns the country in which the audience lives (*in Australia*), that it is negative (*a backwards step*) and of a large scale (*a significant gender gap*), and that it has only just come to light (*a new report shows*). In fact, if we read on, we realize that this item refers to a report published in 2010 (*Towards a Level Playing Field: Sport and Gender in Australian Media*) and therefore somewhat artificially constructs it as new or recent information.

Moving on to example (2), this is unusual in that it includes a news worker's interview questions in addition to the interviewee's answers. These questions appear designed to elicit statements that the event was unusual (*rare*) and had negative effects (*injuries, damage*), but such answers are not provided by the interviewee. Neither does he construct the event as of a large scale; on the contrary, he uses the adjective *minor* several times (*minor sea sickness, minor things*). This makes it difficult for the news worker to use his quotes to construct the event as newsworthy in terms of unusuality and major negative consequences. Rather, the news worker turns the captain (and the interview) into a newsworthy story—the captain is evaluated as *officially the world's most non-plussed sea captain* and an unexpected contrast is established between the size of the waves (*6-10m swells*) and his attitude (*no big deal*). Both of these examples show how news workers skilfully manipulate linguistic resources to construct events as newsworthy.

In example (3), a long line of people (the caption tells viewers that they are migrants) are depicted walking through farmland along a raised bank. The fact that the image frame crops out both the beginning and the end of this line of people suggests that their size or scale cannot be fully accounted for in this one image, or may even be beyond reckoning. Here visual resources have been manipulated to construct this happening as newsworthy (i.e. of extremely large scale or scope). In all three examples, semiotic resources are hence used to establish events as newsworthy, persuading the audience that an item is worthy of being published as news and worthy of their attention.

This book is about how news organizations—metaphorically speaking—'sell' the news to us **as news** through verbal and visual resources, through what we might call the discourse of news values. News values are those values that have been recognized in the literature as defining newsworthiness. These include those constructed through discourse in examples (1), (2), and (3): Proximity (nearness to the audience), Negativity, Superlativeness (large scale/scope), Timeliness (e.g. recency, newness), and Unexpectedness (e.g. unusuality) as well as others. We will provide a comprehensive definition, a full overview and explanation of these news values in chapters 2 and 3.

We need to point out here that the term (*news*) *values* is sometimes used by news organizations themselves, for example, on their websites. Thus, the websites bbc.co.uk and ap.org (*Associated Press*) each have a section called 'our values' (*BBC*) or 'news values & principles' (*AP*). Sometimes similar values are included in sections labelled 'standards and ethics' (*The New York Times*) or in a code of practice (*Al Jazeera*).[2] The types of values or standards that these news organizations profess to the world include:

- trust, independence, impartiality, honesty, focus on audience, quality and value for money, creativity, respect, diversity, team spirit (*BBC*);
- truth, speed, accuracy, preciseness, honesty, integrity, fairness, independence, transparency, ethical behaviour, careful/unbiased/unaltered, transmitted in many ways (*AP*);
- truth, fairness, impartiality, transparency, integrity, accuracy, independence (*NYT*);
- truth, factuality, accuracy, clarity, honesty, courage, fairness, impartiality, balance, independence, credibility, diversity, respect of audience, transparency, diversity, support of colleagues (*AJ*).

Such journalistic values are also mentioned in introductions to newswriting (e.g. Bender et al. 2009: 136-139), and some academics use the term *news values* to discuss them (e.g. Fuller 1996; Palmer 1998; Johnson and Kelly 2003). These values are clearly important for journalism, but it is also clear that they are very different to the 'newsworthiness values' that we have introduced in relation to examples (1)-(3) above. They are examples of moral-ethical (e.g. truth, impartiality, honesty, fairness) and commercial values (e.g. speed, access via multiple platforms). We have analysed elsewhere how news organizations create value for themselves through referencing these in marketing and publicity material (Bednarek and Caple 2015).[3] Such values can also be constructed through semiotic resources in news products—for example, via speech/dressing styles, signature music, or set design (van Leeuwen 1984, 1989, 2006b; Bell and van Leeuwen 1994), but they are not the focus of this book. As mentioned earlier and further explained in chapter 2, when we use the term *news values* we refer solely to 'newsworthiness' values. Our goal is to introduce readers to how we can systematically analyse how these news values are constructed discursively, that is, through verbal and visual resources. The shorthand that we use for our approach is *discursive news values analysis*, or DNVA.

1.2 Why study news values?

The key areas of enquiry that inform our research in this book are media linguistics, corpus linguistics, discourse analysis, multimodality, and social semiotics, with a focus on the professional context of journalism. We aim to provide new insights into journalistic texts as social and semiotic practice, which can inform how we teach and learn about such texts in first and additional language contexts (i.e. media literacy) as well as how we teach students to create such texts (i.e. journalism education). We are also interested in making a contribution to research, offering a new perspective on how to study news discourse.

There is a wealth of insightful linguistic research on news discourse, for example, on ideology (e.g. van Dijk 1988a, b; Fowler 1991; Richardson 2007; Baker et al. 2013a), audience design (e.g. Bell 1991; Jucker 1992), register and genre (e.g. White 1997; Biber et al. 1999; Lukin 2010; Smith and Higgins 2013), newsroom practice (e.g. Cotter 2010; Perrin 2013), or the socio-historic development of news discourse (e.g. Conboy 2010; Facchinetti et al. 2012)—to name but a few topics. New introductions to news discourse are also published (e.g. Bednarek and Caple 2012a; Busà 2014). All this illustrates the continuing importance and relevance of the semiotic practices of journalism today. However, the concept of news values has not figured prominently in most of these studies (see chapter 2). While the body of research on news values is vast and diverse, this exists mostly within non-linguistic disciplines such as journalism and communications studies, which lack a systematic analysis of verbal and visual text.

But why should we study news values? As this book hopes to illustrate, DNVA aims to have both descriptive and explanatory potential, and means to answer a range of questions about news practice. This includes questions around the conventionalized resources or rhetoric of newsworthiness: DNVA can offer insights into what semiotic resources are repeatedly employed to establish particular news values (Bednarek and Caple 2014). In this way, DNVA can identify common practices, conventions, and clichés of news reporting and offer insights into news as semiotic practice, either at a particular point in time or across news cycles (Potts et al. 2015). Moving beyond this micro level of semiotic construction, it is also possible to use this type of analysis to explore if particular topics—such as indigenous news actors, asylum seekers/refugees, marriage equality, or climate change—are associated with specific news values. Such repeated associations may then have ideological implications, and DNVA can thus be used as a tool for critical discourse analysis (for further discussion of the critical potential of DNVA, see Bednarek and Caple 2014). Again, it is possible to undertake such analysis diachronically and across cultures. The aim here is to see if specific news values are emphasized, rare, or absent in reporting on particular topics or events, and in how far this is constrained by the event itself.

Further, DNVA can be used to analyse the packaging of news **as** news, for example in combination with attribution analysis (Bednarek 2016a). Such analysis makes it possible to see how news values are integrated and structured in the form of consumable news products and whether audience members engage with the voice and authority of the news organization or of sources (Bednarek and Caple 2012a: 214). Also in relation to packaging news, DNVA can be applied to examine the role that different (verbal/visual) components play—whether or not they reinforce, complement, or contradict each other—and to identify un/successful practices for multimodal news stories. This fits with research interests in intersemiotic relations (Caple 2013a). All of the above types of analyses can be undertaken in relation to particular news outlets or outputs, including but not limited to differences between the so-called popular and quality press.[4] Such analyses can also bring in the notion of audience positioning, as each news outlet will have their own target audience.

Last, but not least, there are potential applications in journalism education: By analysing how news professionals construct newsworthy stories we can make explicit the tacit knowledge and experience that such professionals have and provide insights into contemporary journalistic norms and practices. Journalism students can then be made aware of these practices, for instance by deconstructing actual news stories for their construction of news values before constructing their own multimodal journalistic texts (Caple and Bednarek 2016). In so doing, students gain a fuller understanding of what news discourse is and how newsworthiness is created through different semiotic resources.

DNVA has been an ongoing research interest for both authors for a number of years. Bednarek and Caple (2012a, b) are our earliest joint publications on this—one is an introduction which we use with our students (2012a), while the other is an example analysis of one environmental online news story (2012b). We have explored the role of corpus linguistics in DNVA using small and large corpora (Bednarek and Caple 2014; Potts et al. 2015; Bednarek 2016c). At the same time, Caple has been the lead researcher in publications where we focus on visual DNVA (Caple 2013a; Caple and Bednarek 2016). While most of this research focuses on print/online news, Bednarek (2016a) has started exploring broadcast news.

This cumulative research experience has led us to the conclusion that the discursive approach to news values analysis deserves book-length treatment, where it can be more fully explored and accounted for.

1.3 Key terms

Before providing further information on the approaches that we will use in this book, it is necessary to briefly introduce some key terms: *news*, *discourse*, *multimodality*, and *corpus linguistics*.

1.3.1 NEWS

In everyday usage, the word *news* is frequently used to refer to new information. We might ask each other if there is any *news* or check our Facebook *news*feed. Here the source of the information (friends, family, or strangers), its domain (public/private), and the type of information (gossip, opinion, announcement, or cartoon) can vary. In this sense, the words *news* and *newsworthy* can be used to refer to new information presented in personal narratives or casual conversation (Sidnell 2010: 228). In other broad uses, the term *news* has been applied to all discourse around a particular hashtag including tweets by bloggers and activists (Papacharissi and Oliveira 2012). In such and similar approaches, *news* becomes a broad concept that appears simply to refer to new content. Sometimes, the term *news* is used to refer to language as used in a newspaper and may include both editorials (opinion) and reportage—as is the case with Biber et al.'s (1999) news register, for instance.

In this book, we use *news* (and *newsworthy*) in a more specific way, as it relates to news reports disseminated by news organizations. As Fuller (1996: 6) states, most journalists would agree that 'news is a report of what a news organisation has learned about matters of some significance or interest to the specific community that news organisation serves'. Such a definition also brings into focus the notion of target audience (the specific community that a news organization serves). As will become evident throughout the book, we argue that news values are dependent on target audiences and other contextual factors.

In relation to news, we also talk about reported events, broadcast news, and time and place of publication. When we use the term *event*, we use it as a cover term for events, issues, and happenings, including elements or aspects of these. For example, when we talk about how events are constructed as newsworthy, this includes the event's news actors or its location. Broadcast news may include audio and video published online or through podcasts, not just on radio or television. Thus, *publication* is used in a broad sense to cover the publication or transmission of stories online, on mobile devices, in print, on the radio, or on television. Similarly, when we talk about *published* stories, we also mean broadcast stories.

In sum, this book is concerned with news reporting, including but not limited to hard news, soft news, and research news.[5] We do not deal with other journalistic texts such as advice, opinion, reader emails, interviews, or quizzes. As fully explored elsewhere (Bednarek and Caple 2012a), news reporting exhibits unique semiotic characteristics, for example, particular genre structures, uses of visuals, and lexical and syntactic features (e.g. nominalization, evidentiality). In this book, we focus on exploring the semiotic resources of news discourse for their potential to construct news values, rather than providing a general introduction to these unique features.

1.3.2 DISCOURSE AND MULTIMODALITY

Definitions of *discourse* are plentiful and have been discussed in different disciplines (e.g. Baker 2006: 3-5). One key distinction that is made in linguistics is between discourse as language in use and 'a more Foucauldian perspective, where discourses are seen as ways of looking at the world, of constructing objects and concepts in certain ways, of representing reality in other words, with attendant consequences for power relations' (Baker and McEnery 2015: 4-5). We align ourselves with the first perspective on discourse (language in use), but consider *discourse* as multimodal. Strictly speaking, texts that are 'multimodal' combine two or more modalities (e.g. visual, aural), whereas 'multi-semiotic' texts combine two or more semiotic (meaning-making) systems such as image or language (O'Halloran 2008). However, the term *multimodal* has typically been employed to mean both. We will follow this convention in relation to both the adjective *multimodal* and the noun *multimodality*. Further, we use the term *semiotic mode* to refer to meaning-making systems (image, language), while the term *semiotic resource* is used to refer to linguistic devices and visual techniques. Thus, multimodality can be defined as 'the combination of different semiotic modes—for example, language and music—in a communicative artefact or event' (van Leeuwen 2005: 281).

Our multimodal approach distinguishes us from other researchers who only include language in the analysis of news discourse. But a multimodal perspective is clearly useful when considering today's news:

> By now, newspaper discourse cannot be viewed and studied exclusively or mostly as a monolithic verbal text; on the contrary, it is the multi-faceted polyhedron whereby image, image-caption, headline, column, lay-out, and positioning in the (web-)page simultaneously contribute to the meaning-making process of the piece in a compositional way. Thus, the 'news piece' has turned into a 'news package' that calls for a holistic interpretation in order to be fully grasped. (Facchinetti 2012: 183)

We are also interested in how such multimodal discourse is actually put to use and how it contributes to the construction of news. Hence, when we use the noun *discourse* and its derived adverb *discursively* we refer to semiotic resources in use—for instance, the use of specific linguistic or visual devices (see chapters 4 and 5). In sum, our definition of discourse borrows from Halliday (1985) who states that text 'may be either spoken or written, or indeed any other medium of expression that we like to think of' (Halliday 1985: 10), and Halliday and Hasan (1976), who define text as 'a unit of language in use' (Halliday and Hasan 1976: 1).

1.3.3 CORPUS LINGUISTICS

Corpus linguistics is an empirical approach to the analysis of linguistic data that makes use of computer technologies to analyse computerized collections of text (corpora), which are often carefully designed and of considerable size. A corpus linguistic investigation usually focuses on language use and typicality (repeated patterns), and may combine quantitative with qualitative analysis. In addition to developing a set of new techniques for the analysis of language, corpus linguistics has also developed new theoretical positions and concepts. It thus combines a methodological innovation with a particular approach to language (Lee 2007: 87). Introductions to corpus linguistics abound and include Hunston (2002), Baker (2006), McEnery et al. (2006), and McEnery and Hardie (2012). In sum, researchers taking a corpus linguistic approach analyse an electronic data set (corpus) with the help of computer software and using specific techniques, concepts, and tools developed in corpus linguistics. We will introduce the main corpus linguistic techniques we use in this book in section 1.4.2.1.

1.4 Corpus-assisted multimodal discourse analysis

1.4.1 A NEW TOPOLOGY FOR SITUATING RESEARCH

While the primary goal of this book is to introduce readers to DNVA, another goal is to promote research that brings together multimodality, discourse analysis, and corpus linguistics—a combination of approaches that we have termed 'corpus-assisted multimodal discourse analysis (CAMDA)' (Bednarek and Caple 2014: 151).

The field of research that examines multimodality is vast (O'Halloran and Smith 2011), as are the approaches to multimodal discourse analysis. In a general sense, multimodal discourse analysis attempts to provide an 'integral and coherent picture of multimodal communication and all its resources, and all of the ways in which these are integrated' (van Leeuwen 2015: 108). The strand of multimodal discourse analysis that we are most aligned with is that of social semiotics (e.g. Kress and van Leeuwen 2001, 2006; van Leeuwen 2005), although we do not apply its metafunctional approach here (but see Caple 2013a).[6] In a more specific sense, multimodal analysis can be combined with particular approaches to the analysis of discourse, such as critical discourse analysis (e.g. Machin and Mayr 2012; Machin 2013; Djonov and Zhao 2014). Other notable work that combines multimodality with discourse analysis includes contributions to Chouliaraki (2012), which examine the multimodality of new media discourse, including convergence journalism and social networking sites.

Discourse analysis and corpus linguistics have also developed a fruitful relationship over the last 25 years (Baker and McEnery 2015: 6-8). This includes corpus linguistic research on discourse phenomena or discourse types as well as studies that combine in-depth discourse analysis with corpus linguistic techniques.[7] It includes both studies that are critical of analysed texts (combining corpus linguistics and critical discourse analysis, e.g. Mautner 2000; Baker et al. 2008) and those that are not (e.g. corpus-assisted discourse studies, see Partington et al. 2013). However, only a few studies bring multimodality into the mix (e.g. Adolphs and Carter 2013; Bednarek 2015).

As yet, studies that combine all three—multimodality, discourse analysis, and corpus linguistics—are rare. This is not surprising because such a combination of approaches is a highly complex undertaking. As will become clear, corpus-assisted multimodal discourse analysis involves a series of challenges that need to be negotiated before the analysis can proceed. News discourse, especially that which is rendered in the digital media of tablets and smart phones, is packaged in a complex verbal-visual display of images, graphics, typography, words, and navigational elements that guide the reader both within and away from the story page (e.g. through hyperlinks). Such multimodal richness leads to questions regarding what actually constitutes a multimodal analysis, and what should be the point of departure for the analysis. If readers (and researchers) engage with both the verbal and visual elements of a news story together, should the analyst treat the unit of analysis as a verbal-visual complex from the outset? Or is it possible for the analyst to separate out each semiotic mode (e.g. language, image) from its co-text and analyse each in isolation? How can corpus linguistics, which focuses on patterns **across** texts, be combined with multimodal discourse analysis, which focuses on patterns and relations between semiotic modes, often **within** texts? These are important methodological questions and need to be addressed in relation to both the context of analysis and the research paradigm being deployed.[8]

We see the value in a range of approaches to corpus-assisted multimodal discourse analysis, depending on the type of research question the analyst poses and the type of data being examined. We have developed a topology (figure 1.2) which maps the choices for both semiotic mode (horizontal axis) and unit of analysis (vertical axis). We use the term topology here in analogy to Martin and Matthiessen (1991) to refer to scalar rather than categorical distinctions which are typically represented in taxonomies. That is, these distinctions are best considered as clines, scales, or continuums. This topology shows four 'zones of analysis' where choices are made regarding the focus of analysis at any particular stage in the research process, allowing researchers to situate their research project in the most appropriate zone at each stage. Such an approach is useful whether the analysis is multimodal or not, corpus-assisted or not.

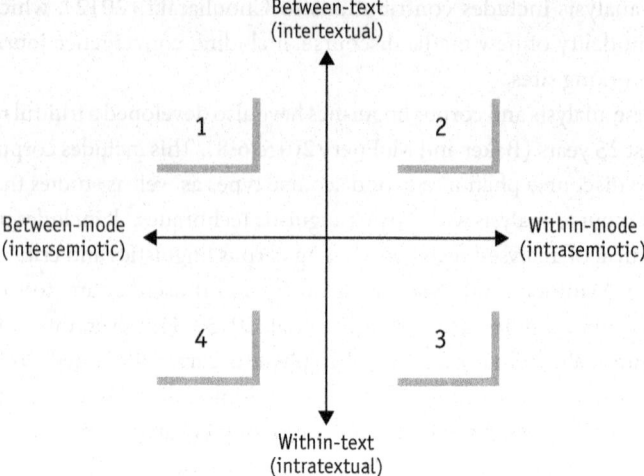

Figure 1.2 Zones of analysis.

In relation to news values analysis, a researcher might ask, for example, how are news values discursively constructed in press photographs? Here the analyst is interested in understanding how a particular semiotic mode (image) construes news values. Such mono-modal analysis would be located in the right-hand side of the topology in figure 1.2 (i.e. staying within-mode), and could examine the construction of news values in a photograph used within one text (and be situated in zone 3) or could examine the construction of news values in photographs used across a range of texts (and be situated in zone 2). One could then repeat this study with a different semiotic mode such as language and compare the results, bringing in a multimodal component through comparison of verbal and visual texts.

Researchers interested in how different semiotic modes combine to make meaning would locate their analyses in the left-hand side of the topology in figure 1.2 (between-mode/intersemiotic). In relation to news values analysis, the research question could be: How is newsworthiness constructed through the combination of semiotic modes? Such analyses could examine the contributions of both verbal and visual resources to the meaning of a single text (zone 4), or across a number of texts (zone 1).

Another way of viewing this topology is to consider the bottom half of the topology (zones 3 and 4) as concerning itself with logogenesis (Halliday and Matthiessen 1999: 17-18), the unfolding of meaning in text over time. Such analysis of logogenesis could either stay within-mode (e.g. looking at patterns of meaning as they unfold across a verbal text) or examining relations between-modes (e.g. how language and image co-contribute to the meaning of a particular text). Here issues such as discourse semantics or cohesion might be the focus of attention.

In contrast, the top half of the topology in figure 1.2 (zones 1 and 2) is more interested in looking at patterns across a number of texts, where generalizations may be made about a particular language variety, looking for example at headline writing styles (within-mode, i.e. zone 2), or looking at how headlines and lead images interact with each other on digital news story pages (between-mode, i.e. zone 1).

Analyses located in different zones can also be combined: for example, one might analyse the unfolding of meaning (logogenesis) across a number of texts in order to make generalizations about the structure of a particular genre. This would combine zones 2 and 3 (if the analysis stays focused on one mode) or zones 1 and 4 (if the analysis considers more than one mode). As a summary, figure 1.3 repeats the topology with example analyses.

In our previous studies on news values, we have not yet used this topology to situate our research, but our data have ranged from one online news story (Bednarek and Caple 2012b) to analysis of a 9.65 million word corpus (Potts et al. 2015). Some analyses focused on images only (e.g. Caple 2013a), some only on language (e.g. Bednarek 2016a), and some combined analysis of both semiotic modes (e.g. Bednarek and Caple 2012a, b).

In this book, our empirical analyses are both within-mode and between-mode, and focus on between-text analysis: chapter 6 presents a corpus linguistic analysis of news about cyclists/cycling (zone 2, language); chapter 7 analyses images disseminated by news organizations via social media (zone 2, image). Chapter 8 analyses language and photographs in a corpus of news stories shared via Facebook, first analysing each semiotic mode separately (zone 2) before bringing them together (zone 1). Since we do not focus much on the development of meaning within texts or logogenesis, we could call this type of analysis 'intertextual' CAMDA. We do not want to prescribe this as the only way of undertaking CAMDA, but rather encourage researchers to come up with different ways of doing so. In particular, we see the need to develop achievable and feasible approaches to the combination of

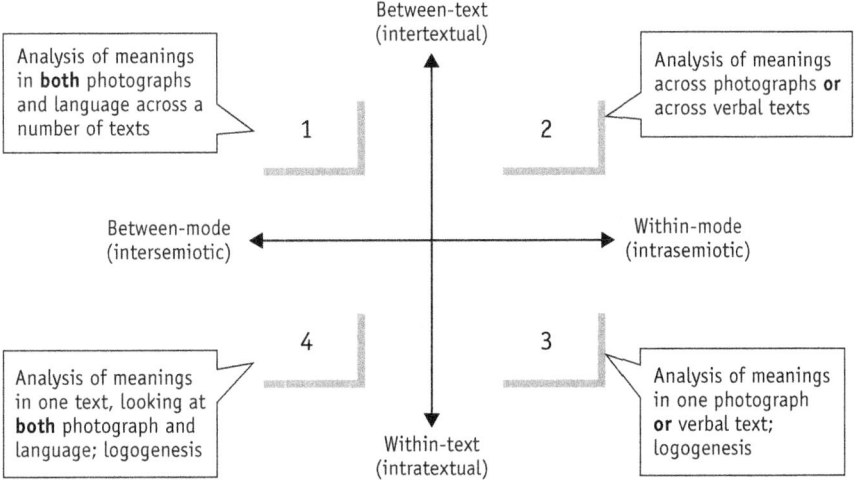

Figure 1.3 Zones of analysis with examples.

between-text (intertextual) and within-text (intratextual) analysis, while also bringing together analysis of different semiotic modes. One of the outcomes of this book, we hope, is that other researchers will come up with creative ideas for such a combination of approaches.

1.4.2 CONCEPTS, TECHNIQUES, AND TOOLS

In this section we introduce the key concepts, techniques, and tools that we apply in this book, starting with corpus linguistic analysis before moving on to visual analysis, and concluding with a brief mention of the tools (technologies) used in both.

1.4.2.1 Concepts and techniques for corpus linguistic analysis
A key component of CAMDA is corpus linguistic analysis (see section 1.3). In prior research on news values, corpus techniques such as lemma/word/n-gram frequency, key words/parts-of-speech/semantic tags, and collocation have been used in different ways (Bednarek and Caple 2012b, 2014; Potts et al. 2015; Bednarek 2016c). Rather than repeating here what we say about these techniques there, we point interested researchers to these publications for further detail. In this section we briefly introduce the main corpus techniques we use in this book, without discussing debates around them (see e.g. McEnery and Hardie 2012; Hunston 2013).

FREQUENCY, KEYWORDS, AND RANGE
Most corpus linguistic software programs, such as Wordsmith (Scott 2015), permit automatic frequency analysis, producing a list of items in a corpus together with the frequency with which each item occurs (frequency lists). One can distinguish between the frequency of *types* (different word forms) and *tokens* (all instances). For example, a corpus with 300,000 tokens may contain only 14,000 types, since many tokens will be repeated. Items in a frequency list can be lemmas (WALK), word forms (*walk, walks, walked, walking*) or longer structures (*I walked*). These longer structures are often called *n*-grams, referring to recurring combinations of *n*-words, for example, bigrams (two words, e.g. *of the, you know*) or trigrams (three words, e.g. *at the end, you know that*). In any frequency list, grammatical words tend to be the most frequent and therefore fill the top of the list. It is possible to exclude such words by using what is called a *stop list*—a list of words that are ignored when compiling the frequency list. The stop list that we use in this book is a default English list with 174 entries.[9] Frequency lists can be visualized in the form of *word clouds* where a larger size of a word represents a higher frequency (figure 1.4).

Further, some corpus software allows users to sort items in a frequency list according to their distribution within or across files, which is also referred to as their *dispersion* (e.g. Gries 2008) or *range* (e.g. Nation and Waring 1997). In this book we use the term *range* to refer to the distribution of instances across individual corpus files, identifying in how many corpus texts an item occurs. This is important

Figure 1.4 Example of a partial word cloud (from chapter 6).

because some items with a relatively high frequency may only occur in a few texts in a corpus. Analysis of range—sometimes called consistency analysis—is useful for identifying the core features of a language variety (Bednarek 2012) and for analysing similarity more generally (Taylor 2013).

Frequencies can also be compared across two corpora, for instance, through automatic keywords analysis. Here, the software compares the frequencies of items in one corpus (the node, target, or study corpus) with their frequencies in a second corpus which provides a baseline (the reference corpus). The calculation takes into account the different sizes of the corpora and applies statistical tests—most often log likelihood (LL; G2). This test tells us if the difference between two corpora is statistically significant by providing a log likelihood value which corresponds to a particular *p*-value. A *p*-value of 0.05 (G2 = 3.84) means that we can be 95% confident that the results are not due to chance.[10] A keywords list then is a list of items that are, statistically speaking, unusually frequent or unusually infrequent in the target corpus when compared to the reference corpus.

We also use a new software tool called ProtAnt (Anthony and Baker 2015a). This tool uses keywords to calculate which texts in a corpus are most and least prototypical of the corpus as a whole, when compared to a reference corpus.[11] To do so, ProtAnt first compiles a list of keywords for a corpus and then calculates how many of these keywords occur in each corpus file, ranking the files by the number of keywords they contain (Anthony and Baker 2015b: 278). Thus, the top ranked corpus texts will contain the most keywords (prototypical), while the lowest ranked corpus texts will contain the least keywords (atypical). The assumption behind this technique is that 'a text which contains a greater number of keywords from the corpus as a whole is also likely to be a more central or typical text in that corpus' (Anthony and Baker 2015b: 277). The primary motivation for this tool is to allow researchers to systematically identify texts for qualitative analysis—that is, as a down-sampling technique. It can also be used to identify what are the most 'typical' news values that are constructed in a corpus, which is the way we use it in chapter 6.

COLLOCATION AND COLLOCATIONAL NETWORKS

Another important corpus linguistic concept is that of collocation, which refers to the non-random association of words. It has been observed that some words 'go together', as it were—that is, they frequently occur in the vicinity of each other. Collocation analysis usually proceeds by taking a word (the *node*) and identifying which other words typically co-occur in a given co-textual span. These co-occurring words are called *collocates*. For example, *oh, sake, knows, thank, my*, and *bless* are all collocates of *god* in British English. Typically, researchers examine a span of four or five words to the left and to the right of the node. Collocates can be grouped according to their meaning. Thus, some word forms co-occur with attitudinally negative collocates and are said to have a *negative semantic prosody* (Louw 1993). In addition, one can identify collocational networks (i.e. networks of collocates). For instance, *spend* is a collocate of the node *time* and itself collocates with *money*, which in turn collocates with *pay* (Brezina et al. 2015: 152-153). Such networks can be visualized using GraphColl (Baker and McEnery 2015; Brezina et al. 2015), as seen in figure 1.5. Each circle represents a word and the length of lines between words represents collocational strength (the shorter the stronger). Thus, we can see that *more* is a collocate of the node *cyclists* and itself collocates strongly with *than* and *people* (in the corpus described in chapter 6).

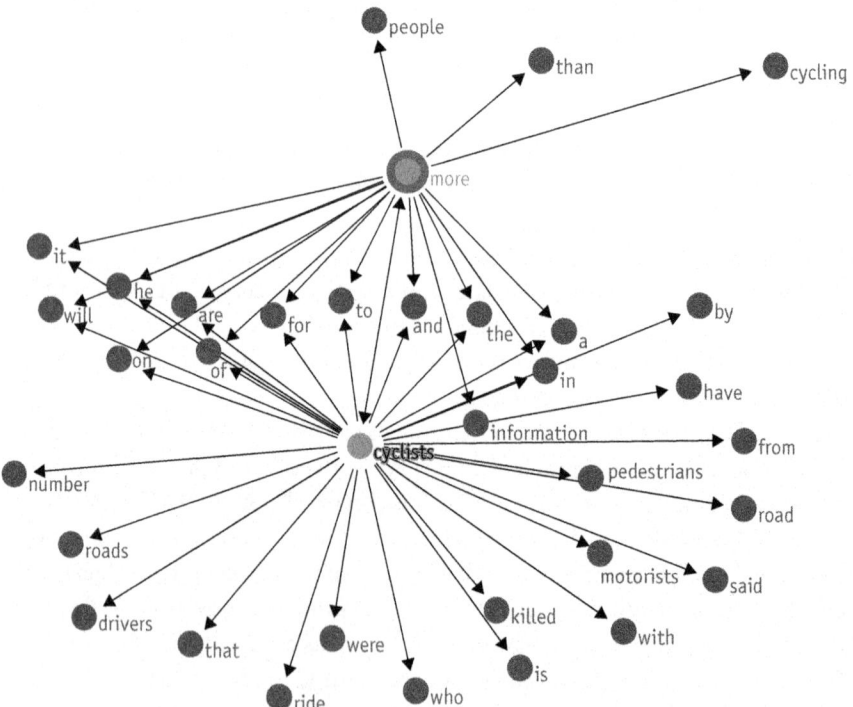

Figure 1.5 Example of a GraphColl network (from chapter 6).

Collocates are automatically identified by most software tools using an in-built statistical collocation measure, with different statistics producing different results.[12] Most association measures identify collocates by comparing how often they are expected to co-occur with the node with how often they actually occur (Brezina et al. 2015: 144). Unless otherwise stated, we generally use the MI3 statistic, a span of five words on each side of the node (5L:5R), with a minimum frequency threshold of two, and do not calculate collocations across sentence breaks (when using Wordsmith). MI3 (Daille 1995) is the cubed variant of the mutual information statistic, which reduces its low frequency bias—it gives more weight to observed frequencies and ranks frequently occurring (typical) collocations much higher than those that are uncommon (Brezina et al. 2015: 159–160). Other collocation measures that we will refer to are log likelihood and *t*-score.[13]

SEMANTIC TAGS AND WORD SKETCHES

In addition to identifying word frequencies and word associations, corpus linguistic programs (taggers or parsers) can categorize words according to their likely meaning or grammatical function. For example, the UCREL Semantic Analysis System (USAS) tags words as belonging to particular semantic fields (Archer, Wilson, and Rayson 2002). Each semantic tag stands for a semantic field such as 'Emotional Actions, States & Processes' or 'Time', with further subdivisions. For example, the items *recent, latest, new* might be tagged as belonging to the semantic field 'Time: Old, new and young; age'. With a tagged corpus, it becomes possible to create frequency lists of tags or word-tag combinations, for instance, focusing on analysis of the most frequent semantic tags in a corpus.

Sketch Engine's (Kilgarriff et al. 2014) word sketches bring together collocation analysis with grammatical analysis, by producing collocates for a node and grouping these collocates according to their grammatical relations (e.g. object of, subject of, modifier). In other words, Sketch Engine automatically identifies collocates as well as their likely grammatical relationship with the node (https://www.sketchengine.co.uk/word-sketch/).[14] In addition to simple word sketches for one lemma, Sketch Engine provides a functionality called word sketch differences, which allows the comparison of collocates for different lemmas or word forms by showing their shared and unshared collocates. In chapter 6 we use this functionality for identifying common collocates of the singular (*cyclist*) and plural forms (*cyclists*) of the same lemma, focusing on similarity (Taylor 2013) rather than difference.

CONCORDANCES AND SEARCH TERMS

The final technique to introduce here is concordancing—producing all occurrences for a particular search term (the node), together with its surrounding text (co-text). Concordancing is particularly useful for qualitative analysis, as the co-text can be expanded, and because concordances can automatically be sorted in

```
 1      better facilities that separate bicycles from automobile traffic. Memphis already has 51 miles of bike lanes, with other
 2      . So far in 2009, there have been 16 pedestrian fatalities in Memphis, already surpassing last year's total by three. y three.
 3      traffic-safety advocacy group Transportation for America ranked Memphis as the fifth most dangerous city in the country for
 4      , but the National Complete Streets Coalition's recent ranking of Memphis as the fifth most dangerous city for pedestrians
 5      the flowers showing off their beautiful colors in Overton Park, Memphis' bicycle culture appeared also to be in full bloom. m.
 6      than through art, film, music and performance?" Because Memphis' bicycle culture continues to expand its boundaries,
 7      protected bike lanes, or "greenlanes," in Memphis. Downtown Memphis Commission president Paul Morris, who is
 8      attractive place for people to live and work," said Downtown Memphis Commission President Paul Morris, who is
 9      safety, maintenance Syd Lerner, executive director of Greater Memphis Greenline, and Bill Jurgens, director of Oasis Bike
10      for the entire 13.34-mile stretch. A local group known as Greater Memphis Greenline was organized to promote the project. Last
11      . The pilot project, which will begin upon the conclusion of the Memphis in May International Festival, is among more than
12      added. The Green Lane project will start after the conclusion of Memphis in May, the annual event that shuts off traffic along
13      line through swampy forests and a sweeping cross-section of Memphis is on track to be converted this year into a biking and
14      2013 TN Bike Summit at Rhodes College. Local advocates believe Memphis is the ideal location for the big meeting. "Memphis
15      . The task force is currently working in conjunction with the Memphis Metropolitan Planning Organization to develop a
16      and multi-use paths will be placed over the next 20 years? The Memphis Metropolitan Planning Organization is forming a
17      start to dust off their bikes again after a record-breaking winter, Memphis police officers at Tillman Station wanted to remind
18      to criminals. Masson said conservancy officials have met with Memphis police officials and will meet with residents to
19      who work there. "We're really going to miss this place," said Memphis resident Barbara Scott, who says she visits the shop
20      say, because it enhances the accessibility to Shelby Farms for Memphis residents. Officials with the Shelby Farms Park
21      than academic. With 56 miles of bike lanes already installed in Memphis streets, local governments and private groups are
22      pilot project that officials hope will become a model for making Memphis streets more bike- and pedestrian-friendly. The grass
23      of Cory Horton. Horton, who was a founding member of the Memphis Thunder Racing Team in the spring of 2003, was killed
24      the text, "3 Feet - It's the Law." The signs were installed by the Memphis Thunder Triathlon Racing Team in partnership with the
25      a beautiful day for the bikers to ride from Memorial Park in East Memphis to Midtown, and then back to the cemetery for a
26      said he'll offer another, safer way for bikers to get from East Memphis to Shelby Farms. He wants to create a bike route on
27      , Southaven and Olive Branch. The plan, to be overseen by the Memphis Urban Area Metropolitan Planning Organization (MPO),
28      - Citizens views sought on bicycle , walking routes The Memphis Urban Area Planning Organization will hold public
29      daughter maneuver her first bicycle, Margaret Edwards of East Memphis was nervous as Maggie rode with one hand on the
30      . Last year, Tennessee ranked 26th. Now it's 17th. Last year, Memphis was selected by Bicycling magazine as the "Most
31      Country Club. He was airlifted to the Regional Medical Center at Memphis, where he died a short time later. The woman driving
32      10 a.m. The cyclist was flown to the Regional Medical Center at Memphis, where he underwent surgery and was listed in
33                                  'Green lanes' to enhance cycling Memphis will install 15 miles of protected bicycle lanes that
34      friendly in a test project set to start in three months, the city of Memphis will reserve two lanes of a mile-plus stretch of
35      become the eyes and ears of the community." In a city like Memphis with a high crime rate, more bicycle riders can serve
```

Figure 1.6 Sorted concordances.

different ways. For instance, figure 1.6 shows 35 sample concordance lines of the word *Memphis* sorted alphabetically according to the right (again using the corpus described in chapter 6).

Sorted concordances are particularly helpful for the identification of patterns, or recurring linguistic practices. Concordances can be produced for single word forms (e.g. *cyclist*) or combinations of word forms (e.g. *bike rider, cyclist death*) and * can be used as a wildcard to stand for one or more characters (e.g. a search for *cyclist** retrieves concordances for *cyclist, cyclists, cyclist's, cyclista, cyclistist*). A tool like Wordsmith also provides advanced search options such as the introduction of 'context words'. Using this function we can produce concordances for *cyclist* occurring in the co-text of *old* within five words to the left or right. Wordsmith can further calculate recurring 'clusters' for a given search term. These clusters are based on the concordance lines and are patterns of repeated phraseology within five words. Clusters can consist of two or more words (e.g. *cyclist deaths, cyclist was killed, death of a cyclist*).

In addition, some corpus tools offer information on the position of a search term in text files, showing if it occurs at the beginning, middle, end, or throughout the file. For instance, Wordsmith provides users with a dispersion *plot* (a visualization) and a dispersion value, which indicates the extent of uniformity of a search term's distribution. Generally, the dispersion value lies between 0 and 1, and the closer the value is to 1, the more uniform the dispersion.[15] Further, Sketch Engine allows users to view the distributional graph of concordances, which shows the distribution of the search word across parts (slices) of the corpus.[16]

1.4.2.2 Concepts and techniques for visual analysis

Some of the terms that we draw on in this book for the analysis of images are borrowed from Kress and van Leeuwen (2006), although we use them somewhat differently and always with a focus on news values. Other concepts come from the work of Caple (2013a), especially regarding the relationship between compositional balance and aesthetic appeal. Additional terms are taken from technical handbooks on the workings of camera equipment. As with our previous research on the construction of news values in images (Caple and Bednarek 2016), we continue here to examine images in terms of their **content** (what is depicted in the image) and in terms of their **capture** (also glossed as 'camera technique'). The latter involves two strands of analysis: that of the composition of the image (how the information is arranged in the image frame) alongside analysis of technical affordances (e.g. shutter speed, aperture).

CONTENT: REPRESENTED PARTICIPANTS, ATTRIBUTES, ACTIVITY SEQUENCE, SETTING

In examining image content, we look primarily for who or what is represented: the *represented participant*. In Kress and van Leeuwen's (2006: 48) terms, represented participants are:

> the participants who constitute the subject matter of the communication; that is, the people, places and things (including abstract 'things') represented in and by the . . . image, the participants about whom or which we are . . . producing images.

This allows us to identify who, where, or what is the subject matter of the image, be it a widely known famous politician, sports person, landmark or landscape, or an ordinary member of the public, or a victim of a negative happening.

We examine the different parts that constitute the represented participant, which in the case of people includes clothing or uniform, jewellery, medals, badges, equipment, and other regalia that they may be wearing, holding, or using. We label these *attributes* ('Possessive Attributes' in Kress and van Leeuwen's [2006: 50] terms). An examination of attributes can help us to further distinguish what kind of person is being represented in an image (e.g. whether it is a regular police officer or a police commissioner).

We also take into consideration the activities the represented participants are engaged in. A person, for example, may be photographed being, thinking, or feeling (e.g. posing for the camera as in a portrait shot with neutral, positive, or negative facial expression and direct or indirect eye contact). People may also be photographed doing something, depicted as '"agents", the doers of that action' (van Leeuwen 2008: 142), for example, firing a gun. They could be depicted as '"patients", the people to whom the action is done' (van Leeuwen 2008: 142), for example, being fired at; and they may be photographed saying something or listening to something/someone, where eye-contact, gesture, and body language can help to decode whether they are speaking or listening. We gloss analysis of such activities and the roles that represented participants play in them as *activity sequence*. Analysis of activity sequences can tell us more about what kinds of represented participants images depict and what they are doing (e.g. police arresting suspects).

We also examine the context or environment, glossed as *setting*, in which the represented participants are depicted (e.g. a court room, a government building, a lab, a person's living room). This may be non-existent (e.g. in an extreme close-up shot of a person's face), or maximally identifiable (e.g. in a very wide angle shot), or somewhere in-between. The setting tells us where a news event takes place and may further help us to identify the kinds of people and activity sequences they are engaged in—for instance, a person who is represented in a laboratory as filling a test tube with a syringe is most likely interpreted as a scientist engaged in some experiment. Figure 1.7 illustrates the visual resources we examine in relation to image content.

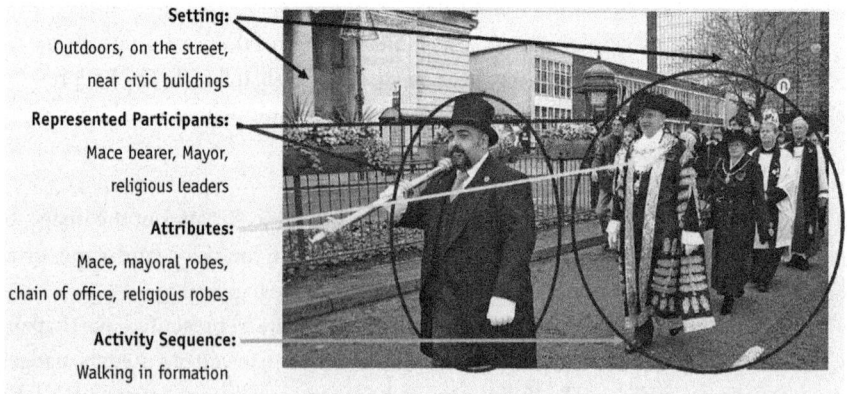

Figure 1.7 Visual resources comprising image content (*BBC News* photo: Tarek Chowdhury).

CAPTURE: COMPOSITION AND TECHNICAL AFFORDANCES
One strand of analysis in relation to image capture involves analysis of how the content is arranged in the image frame, which we gloss as *composition*.

Composition: Salience, shot length, cropping, angle, dynamic asymmetry, interrupted symmetry Represented participants may be placed towards the front of the image frame or moved backwards in the image frame. These are aspects of *salience* that can impact both on how the depicted elements relate to each other and on how closely or distantly viewers of the image relate to the image content. *Shot length* works in a similar way to salience in impacting on how closely or distantly viewers relate to image content. A long shot creates maximal disconnection between audience and represented participants (*'distanciation'* in van Leeuwen's [2008: 141] terms), but at the same time includes the setting in the image, thus informing audiences of where the depicted activity sequence is taking place. At the other end of the scale, an extreme close-up eliminates the setting completely, but demands maximal engagement between audience and image content.

The concept of *cropping* an image relates closely to salience and shot length, as it also tells us something about what has been included or excluded from an image.[17] A photograph may show us, for example, a politician speaking from a lectern. However, the audience that her gaze and gestures are directed towards may be excluded from the image. By cropping out the audience, the image is focusing our attention on the politician and possibly aspects of her facial expression, gestures, and body language. Cropping is also used in the image in example (3), given at the beginning of this chapter. We know that the heads at the front of the image are attached to torsos and legs and we are able to fill in this missing information. Cropping of this sort tells us that the size or scale of the event taking place in the image extends beyond what the image has captured.

Another concept that tells us about how information is arranged within the image frame is camera *angle* (horizontal and vertical). Represented participants may be photographed from eye-level, from a low angle (looking up towards the represented participants), from a high angle (looking down on the represented participants), or from a frontal (face on) or oblique (from the side) angle.

Two further concepts concerning composition are *dynamic asymmetry* and *interrupted symmetry* (Caple 2013a). Dynamic asymmetry involves the use of the diagonal axis in composing an image and establishes unequal relations between represented participants. When the main represented participants are placed in the bottom left of the image frame, these may be counterbalanced by other participants (usually less salient) placed in the top right corner of the frame and vice versa. Equally, the remainder of the image frame may be left empty. In a symmetrically balanced image, all represented participants are shown in equal relation to each other (e.g. a line of soldiers on parade). Interrupted symmetry entails a slight 'defect' or flaw in the symmetry (e.g. if one of the soldiers was looking the wrong way), which

Figure 1.8 Visual resources comprising composition (*The Telegraph* photo: Getty Images).

interrupts rather than completely destroys the symmetrical balance of the composition. Figure 1.8 illustrates aspects of composition.

Technical affordances: Movement, focus, noise The second strand of analysis in relation to image capture involves analysis of the effects of camera settings on image content, for example, whether all elements in the frame are in focus or not, whether all elements in the frame are well lit or not, whether elements are blurred or show movement, or whether they are static, frozen in time and space. We gloss this aspect of analysis as *technical affordances*.

While the researcher is not expected to know what shutter speed, aperture, or ISO was selected in image capture, she can familiarize herself with the effects that such camera settings have on image capture.[18] A slow shutter speed, for example, can result in a blurring effect around moving objects. Thus, water can be made to look silky or smooth through the use of a slow shutter speed. The sense of movement in an athlete running or jumping can be enhanced by using a slow shutter speed combined with a panning action (moving the camera in sync with the movement of the subject) and a flash. A high shutter speed freezes action. It allows the viewer to see in great detail aspects of movement that she would not ordinarily be able to see with the naked eye, for example, the shape of a water droplet or the contortions of the musculature of a diver performing an acrobatic dive. We gloss this as *movement*.

Depth of field, or how much of the image content is in focus, is an aspect of image capture that can be manipulated through changing the aperture in the camera settings. A drastically reduced depth of field will result in only a very narrow area of an image being in focus or sharp, and will blur the rest of the image. Maximizing the depth of field ensures that all elements in the image frame are in focus. We gloss this as *focus*.

Finally, a very high ISO (which is useful in very low lighting conditions and when a fast shutter speed is needed) will result in a very grainy effect in an image.

Figure 1.9 Visual resources comprising technical affordances (*The Guardian* photo: David Clapp/Getty Images).

A very low ISO will produce a clean, sharp, high-quality image. We gloss this effect as *noise*. Aspects of technical affordances are illustrated in figure 1.9.

1.4.2.3 Tools/technologies

As has become apparent in section 1.4.2.1, we use both classic and new corpus linguistic tools in our analysis, namely Wordsmith (Scott 2015), Sketch Engine (Kilgarriff et al. 2014), ProtAnt (Anthony and Baker 2015a), and GraphColl (Brezina et al. 2015). These tools allow us to undertake analysis of word/n-gram frequency, keywords and prototypicality, range, collocation and collocational networks, word sketches, and concordancing. In addition, we use UAM Corpus Tool (O'Donnell 2015), a software program that can be used for computer-assisted manual annotation, 'where a human annotates the text in terms of patterns that generally computers cannot recognize' (O'Donnell 2007). This tool allows the researcher to upload texts, to create annotation schemes (e.g. valence: negative, positive, or neutral/ambiguous), and annotate either the whole text or segments of the text accordingly, coding each sentence in turn if desired. It also allows complex queries and automatic processing of the annotated text data, for instance, producing all text segments that were annotated in a particular way or providing comparative numbers and statistics (e.g. 55 of 99 texts are coded as negative, 17 as positive, and 27 as neutral/ambiguous).

Further, we make use of a relational database (Microsoft Office Access) following an approach first applied in Caple (2009). We use this for the analysis of images and to bring the analysis of language and photographs together. While the initial design, construction, and manual population of database fields are time-consuming, it is a very efficient way of collating the analysis of a large data set (e.g. 1,100 images in the case study in chapter 7). The subsequent ability to query the inputted data is where the benefits of a database become clear. The query function works with the data that has been entered to not only show raw totals (e.g. how many instances of Negativity are present in the data?) but also to show any number of combinations of results. Complex questions can very easily be posed, such as: Which news values are likely to be combined with Negativity and across how many items? Where our analysis spans both words and images (in chapter 8) we can ask questions like: Do items that construct Negativity in the verbal text also construct Negativity in the visual text? Chapters 7 and 8 provide more details on the databases created for the case studies.

1.5 Summary and overview of chapters

In sum, this book brings together DNVA and CAMDA to explore the ways in which news values are constructed through the words and images that constitute journalistic discourse. The key features of this book are that it:

- is interdisciplinary and multi-methodological, bringing together corpus linguistics and multimodal discourse analysis in analysing the news media;
- explores how the news is 'sold' (made newsworthy) to audiences through the semiotic modes of language and image;
- provides comprehensive analytical frameworks for the systematic analysis of multimodal news discourse, which can be used by other researchers in their own subsequent explorations;
- combines in-depth theoretical discussion with manifold analyses of authentic news discourse (language and images) from around the English-speaking world, including three chapters dedicated to new empirical case studies.

In this chapter we have provided a first introduction to DNVA and outlined the key terms, concepts, and techniques that we use in this book. Readers unfamiliar with these approaches are advised to refer back to these sections when engaging with later chapters. Chapters 2 and 3 now provide an overview of the ways in which news values have been conceptualized in linguistics and other disciplines and outline our own approach (DNVA). Chapters 4 and 5 then describe the linguistic and visual resources that can be used to establish news values, providing comprehensive analytical frameworks. Chapters 6 to 8 present three new empirical studies. While chapter 6 illustrates how DNVA can be applied in the analysis of one particular topic (cyclists/cycling), both chapters 7 and 8 focus on a range of different topics but have in common that they explore news in the context of social media. In an era where the new media have created a period of instability and digital disruption for journalism and its business models, where clickability, likeability, and shareability have become crucial considerations in a new 'attention economy' (boyd 2012), and where technological advances have caused 'dramatic change in news making and news writing' (Facchinetti 2012: 152), it is crucial to analyse news reporting in this context. Chapter 7 examines the construction of news values in stories that news organizations post to their own Facebook feeds. Chapter 8 focuses on news values in news items that are widely shared by Facebook users. Chapter 9 then describes and illustrates two key areas for future research: diachronic and cross-cultural studies. Finally, chapter 10 revisits and reflects on each of the previous chapters.

Notes

1. http://www.theguardian.com/australia-news/live/2015/apr/22/nsw-storms-wild-winds-and-flooding-as-sydney-weather-brings-chaos-rolling-report#block-5536dcd3e4b0e90b560ce55b, accessed 22 April 2015.
2. These sections are available at http://www.news.com.au/more-information; http://www.bbc.co.uk/aboutthebbc/insidethebbc/whoweare/mission_and_values; http://www.ap.org/company/news-values; http://www.nytco.com/who-we-are/culture/standards-and-ethics/; http://www.aljazeera.com/aboutus/2006/11/2008525185733692771.html, all accessed 30 September 2015.
3. Self-references can also be used to create value for a news organization, for example, crafting an image of itself as an investigative newspaper or watchdog (Marchi 2013).
4. See Conboy (2006: 15–16) on tabloid news values, and Bednarek (2006a) on evaluation in UK tabloids and broadsheets.
5. Hard news has been classified as time-bound (Bell 1991), negative (Ungerer 1997), or destabilizing (Feez et al. 2008) in contrast to timeless (Bell 1991), positive (Ungerer 1997), or stabilizing (Feez et al. 2008) soft news. Soft news has also been connected to human interest or entertainment (Bender et al. 2009: 134), or hard news is contrasted with human interest rather than soft news (Piazza and Haarman 2011). In our experience, the suggested criteria cannot always be consistently applied. However, this book does not focus on news genre analysis or the linguistic differences between different kinds of news reporting.
6. Such a metafunctional approach assumes that semiotic modes fulfil three major functions: an 'ideational' function, wherein they represent the world around and inside us; an 'interpersonal' function, wherein they enact social relations; and a 'textual' function, wherein message entities or 'texts' attempt to present a coherent whole (Kress and van Leeuwen 2006: 15).
7. A bibliography is maintained by Costas Gabrielatos at http://www.gabrielatos.com/CLDA-Biblio.htm, accessed 30 September 2015.
8. Another challenge concerns the management of researcher subjectivity or bias, since corpus and discourse analyses are subject to variation depending on a range of factors (Marchi and Taylor 2009; Baker and McEnery 2015). To manage subjectivity, researchers can adopt the principles of transparency and consistency (Baker 2009: 83), as we have aimed to do in this book.
9. 'Default English stopwords list', downloaded from http://www.ranks.nl/stopwords/, accessed 12 November 2015.
10. See further http://ucrel.lancs.ac.uk/llwizard.html, accessed 13 November 2015.
11. Since ProtAnt works with UTF-8 encoded text files, all files were first converted into UTF-8 using EncodeAnt (Anthony 2014).
12. Debates about collocation revolve around criteria for identifying collocates, such as distance, frequency, exclusivity, directionality, dispersion, and type-token distribution (Brezina et al. 2015).
13. While the MI3 statistic measures collocation strength, these two scores measure the confidence with which one can claim that there is a non-random association between two word

forms (McEnery et al. 2006: 57; Brezina et al. 2015: 161). The *t*-score subtracts expected occurrences from observed occurrences and divides the results by the standard deviation (Hunston 2002: 70). The log likelihood formula compares the number of times two words occur together with how often they occur without each other, also taking into account when neither is the case (Dunning 2008). The top collocations produced with the *t*-score tend to consist of high-frequency pairs (Hunston 2002: 74; McEnery et al. 2006: 57), often function words, while both MI3 and log likelihood provide a mixture of high-frequency function and lower-frequency content words (Baker 2006: 102).

14. The statistic used by Sketch Engine to produce word sketches is logDice (Rychlý 2008). This measure is based on the Dice coefficient and takes into account the frequencies of the node, of the collocate, and of the collocation within a particular grammatical pattern (Baker et al. 2013a: 37). See further http://trac.sketchengine.co.uk/raw-attachment/wiki/SkE/DocsIndex/ske-stat.pdf, accessed 9 December 2015.
15. http://lexically.net/downloads/version7/HTML/index.html?plotdispersionvalue.htm, accessed 8 January 2016.
16. See https://www.sketchengine.co.uk/concordance/, accessed 9 December 2015.
17. By *cropping*, we mean the way in which the image content has been framed and thus presented to audiences. A more appropriate term might be *framing*. However, since Kress and van Leeuwen (2006: 177) already use the term *framing* to mean something quite different, we have opted for the term *cropping* to avoid confusion.
18. Shutter speed controls the length of time that light is allowed to make contact with the image sensors in the camera, by opening and closing the curtains (shutter) at the film plane. Lenses on a camera contain a diaphragm through which the light passes. The opening of the diaphragm (the aperture) can be made larger or smaller and determines the amount of focused light passing through the lens. ISO stands for *International Standards Organisation* and in photography it indicates levels of sensitivity to light. A low ISO (100), for example, means less sensitive to light and would be used under normal or bright lighting conditions to produce very clean/sharp high-quality images. High ISO (e.g. 3,200) means highly sensitive to light and would be used when lighting conditions are very poor, resulting in very grainy images that may appear less sharp. Fuller explanations of the technical aspects of camera settings can be found at any number of online photography sites, for example, http://www.all-things-photography.com/iso-settings/, accessed 22 March 2016.

Part I

THEORY

2

News values

In chapter 1 we briefly introduced news values in the sense of 'newsworthiness values' (i.e. those values that have been recognized in the literature as defining newsworthiness). However, the literature on news values is in fact vast, and the label *news values* has been used in many different ways. In 2013 we undertook an extensive cross-disciplinary review of the ways in which news values have been conceptualized in linguistics and other disciplines (Caple and Bednarek 2013).[1] We draw on this review here, without going into all the details presented in this publication. We start with a discussion of research in journalism/communications studies, before providing an overview of linguistic research. We also introduce our own discursive approach to news values analysis in this chapter, although the following chapters will offer further elaboration.

2.1 Journalism/communications studies

Walter Lippmann ([1922] 1965: 223) is widely acknowledged as the first person to suggest attributes or conventions for the selection of news items to be published; however, the most cited work is that of Galtung and Ruge (1965). Most of the research since the 1960s, including that in linguistics (e.g. Richardson 2007; Smith and Higgins 2013), has used their work as the starting point. Since this has therefore become the dominant conceptualization of news values in journalism/communications studies (Hoskins and O'Loughlin 2007: 31), we will devote some space here to explaining this approach. Note that Galtung and Ruge (1965) use the term *news factors*, which have subsequently come to be called *news values*, with the two terms being synonymous for most researchers.

2.1.1 THE FOUNDATIONS OF NEWS VALUES RESEARCH: GALTUNG AND RUGE (1965)

The approach to news values posited by Galtung and Ruge (1965) is firmly centred on how events become news. They suggest that twelve 'news factors' are at play any time an event is considered worthy of reporting as 'news'. The news factors that Galtung and Ruge propose are based on 'common-sense perception psychology' (66), created through analogy to radio wave signals. They include: Frequency, Threshold, Unambiguity, Meaningfulness, Consonance, Unexpectedness, Continuity, and Composition. These first eight factors are to be read as 'culture-free', solely based on perception, whereas the remaining four factors are 'culture-bound'. These are: Reference to elite nations, Reference to elite people, Reference to persons, and Reference to something negative. Table 2.1 provides Galtung and Ruge's explanations for each news value.

In talking about these news factors, Galtung and Ruge (1965: 65) propose a 'chain of news communication' that involves processes of selection, distortion, and replication. From this, they hypothesize that the more an event satisfies the criteria/news factors, the more likely that it will be registered as news (selection); once selected, what makes the event newsworthy according to the factors will be accentuated (distortion); and finally, that selection and distortion will be repeated at all steps in the chain from event to reader (replication). Thus, they present two further hypotheses. The first is the Additivity Hypothesis that 'the higher the total score of an event, the higher the probability that it will become news, and even make headlines' (Galtung and Ruge 1965: 71). They do not test this hypothesis since, as they claim, it is 'almost too simple to mention' (71). The second is the Complementarity Hypothesis, wherein an event low on one dimension or news factor will have to be high on another 'complementary' dimension to make it into the news. To test their assumptions, Galtung and Ruge carry out content analysis on press cuttings in the form of 'news story, editorial, article (reportage, interview) or letter to the editor' (74). This analysis involves the coding of a unit (press clipping) according to the presence or absence of various items, for instance, the presence/absence of elites (nations and people), and whether the 'mode' was 'negative', 'positive', or 'neutral' (74). The focus of the coding is on things and contexts—what is reported on and where? For example, they code each cutting for 'whether it reports something "negative" (something is destroyed, disrupted, torn down) or something "positive" (something is built up, constructed, put together)' and for people 'whether they are seen in a context that is negative or positive' (Galtung and Ruge 1965: 77). From their analysis, Galtung and Ruge tentatively conclude that 'there is probably such a phenomenon as *complementarity of news factors*' (1965: 80, italics in original), although they suggest that more research is needed.

There are a number of comments that are worth making from our perspective as discourse analysts in relation to this classic research. First, Galtung and Ruge squarely focus on events, as they seem to suggest that an event 'either possesses them [news factors] or does not possess them' (Galtung and Ruge 1965: 71). Thus, it appears that the events themselves are somehow invested with newsworthiness or that news factors/values are inherent in events, which is somewhat problematic

Table 2.1 **Galtung and Ruge's (1965) news values**

News value	Definition/explanation (all italics in original)
Frequency	'the more similar the frequency of the event is to the frequency of the news medium, the more probable that it will be recorded as news by that news medium' (66)
Threshold	'the bigger … the more violent [the event is] the bigger the headlines it will make' (66) 'there is a threshold the event will have to pass before it will be recorded at all' (66)
Unambiguity	'the less ambiguity the more the event will be noticed' (66) 'an event with a clear interpretation, free from ambiguities in its meaning, is preferred' (66)
Meaningfulness	'interpretable within the cultural framework of the listener or reader' (66–67) 'there has to be *cultural proximity*' (67) '*relevance*: an event may happen in a culturally distant place but still be loaded with meaning in terms of what it may imply for the reader or listener' (67)
Consonance	'*The more consonant the signal is with the mental image of what one expects to find, the more probable that it will be recorded as worth listening to*' (65) 'the word "expects" can and should be given both its cognitive interpretation as "predicts" and its normative interpretation as "wants"' (67)
Unexpectedness	'It is the unexpected *within the meaningful and the consonant* that is brought to one's attention, and by "unexpected" we simply mean essentially two things: *unexpected* or *rare*' (67)
Continuity	'once something has hit the headlines and been defined as "news", then it will *continue* to be defined as news for some time' (67)
Composition	'the desire to present a "balanced" whole' (67)—offering a range of news items within a newspaper or news broadcast
Reference to elite nations	'*The more the event concerns elite nations, the more probable that it will become a news item*' (68)
Reference to elite people	'*The more the event concerns elite people, the more probable that it will become a news item*' (68)
Reference to persons	'*The more the event can be seen in personal terms, as due to the action of specific individuals, the more probable that it will become a news item*' (68)
Reference to something negative	'*The more negative the event in its consequences, the more probable that it will become a news item*' (68)

(see further chapter 3). Galtung and Ruge have indeed been criticized for focusing on events as if they were endowed with epistemological qualities that infuse them with newsworthiness (see Harcup and O'Neill 2001: 265).

Second, the news values/factors relate to very different aspects, including apparent properties of reported events as well as the process of gathering and producing news (Bell 1991: 156). For instance, the news factor 'composition' relates to the mix of different types of news in a news publication (a newspaper, a bulletin), whereas the news factor 'threshold' relates to the scope or scale of an event, and the news factor 'continuity' relates to the news agenda. For us, it is important to either distinguish clearly between these different aspects if the term *news values* is to be used for all of them (as Bell 1991 does), or—our preferred solution—to apply the term *news values* in a more narrowly defined sense (see section 2.3.1).

Third, Galtung and Ruge distinguish 'selection' from 'distortion' and 'replication', and argue that the news media may accentuate newsworthiness. This means that the 'cumulative effects of the factors should be considerable and produce an image of the world different from "what really happened"' (Galtung and Ruge 1965: 71). This idea suggests that the image of the world in the news is one that has been constructed (or 'distorted') through discourse. However, rather than theorizing this discursive construction, Galtung and Ruge direct their focus onto how to relate the news factors to each other in quantifying the newsworthiness of events.

Finally, Galtung and Ruge's analysis of different journalistic texts examines content rather than linguistic or semiotic construction. This is understandable, since the disciplinary background of this research is not in linguistics or social semiotics, but it does mean that there is much room here for a contribution to the literature on news values that focuses on semiotic resources.

2.1.2 THE UPTAKE OF NEWS VALUES IN JOURNALISM/ COMMUNICATIONS STUDIES

Galtung and Ruge's research has been held up as the 'foundation study of news values' (Bell 1991: 155), the earliest attempt to provide a systematic definition of newsworthiness (Palmer 1998: 378), an innovative study (Allan 1999: 63), and as 'a classic social science answer to the question "what is news?"' (Tunstall 1970: 20). Many researchers have indeed applied (and misapplied) their approach (see the account by Hjarvard 1995), but at the same time, their work has been widely criticized and revised over the years. One criticism relates to its limited data—only assessing certain types of content from four Norwegian newspapers. The suggested news factors/values may thus not apply equally to other types of news, although Bell (1991: 155) argues that they 'have been found valid and enlightening for a wide range of news types in many countries'. Related criticism concerns the culture-free/-bound nature of Galtung and Ruge's news factors and/or their universality (Masterton 2005; Robie 2006; Guo 2012).

One of the first to comprehensively challenge Galtung and Ruge's study was Tunstall (1971). He points to limitations in relation to the specificity of the topic of study while ignoring the day-to-day coverage of other issues; that the news items originated almost exclusively through news agencies; that fundamental aspects of news presentation are neglected; and that the study ignores the visual aspect altogether. At the same time, Tunstall also signalled an 'unusual strength' of Galtung and Ruge's study: that their 'coherent set of hypotheses' had the potential for application in a wide range of news contexts (1971: 21–22). That this has turned out to be the case is evident in the vast body of research that has applied Galtung and Ruge since. We provide a brief discussion of this uptake in the following sections, focusing on some of the key issues arising from the review in Caple and Bednarek (2013).

2.1.2.1 News values and events

Many researchers follow Galtung and Ruge (1965) in taking events as a starting point (e.g. Schulz 1982; Shoemaker et al. 1991). News values are widely conceived of as selection criteria that are applied to the 'event' that has taken place and whether it is to be selected for investigation by a journalist. In some of these approaches, news values are not only talked about in terms of selection criteria but also as properties, qualities, or aspects of events.[2] For instance, Machin and Niblock (2006: 27) talk about 'the inherent qualities of a specific event or issue'. Palmer (2000: 31) also takes the event as the departure point. For him, 'news value consists of that aspect of an event which is in accordance with the timeliness, interest, importance, etc., of the event's relationship to its context' (Palmer 2000: 33). The same criticism that has been levelled at Galtung and Ruge also applies here (see section 2.1.1). A basic problem in talking about an event's news value or its newsworthy properties is that (i) it treats events as monolithic; (ii) it assumes newsworthiness can easily be objectively determined and that events are either newsworthy or not; and (iii) it seemingly ignores human intervention (social cognition and discursive mediation).

A related problem is that some of this research does not clearly distinguish between the terms *event* and *story* (news item). To give but one example, when Conley and Lamble (2006) discuss a flood event, it is unclear if they see the news value of Impact as a property of the event (the floods) or the story (the news report about the floods): 'The floods had a multi-faceted impact, which is the most common criterion for assessing a news story . . . the bigger the impact, the bigger the story. If a story has no presumed "impact", its newsworthiness might be limited' (Conley and Lamble 2006: 43). It is, of course, possible to conceive news values as selection criteria that are applied **first** to the 'event' that has taken place and whether it is to be selected for investigation by a journalist, and **second** to the 'story' as it competes with other stories to be selected for publication in the limited spaces of print newspapers and TV/radio bulletins. But such definitions do become particularly problematic when (i) news values seem to be 'inherent' in events or (ii) events and stories are conflated in the discussion.

2.1.2.2 News values and the different aspects of the news process

Many researchers also follow Galtung and Ruge (1965) in applying the term *news values* to very different aspects of the news process. To give just one example, Harcup and O'Neill's (2001: 279) 'contemporary set of news values' includes news values relating to the event and actors reported in news stories (*the power elite, celebrity, entertainment, surprise, bad news, good news, magnitude, relevance*) as well as news values relating to news attention/coverage (*follow-up*) and a news organization's particular preferences or political stance (*newspaper agenda*). More generally, an examination of the various 'news values' that have been posited by a wide range of researchers since 1965 (collated in Caple and Bednarek 2013) shows that there is research that focuses, inter alia, on events, stories, journalistic practice, the news agenda, or business models/market conditions.

Some of the suggested news values concern apparent qualities of the reported event or the people involved in the event. These include Negativity, Impact, Timeliness, Proximity, and Eliteness. Other researchers take into consideration elements of journalistic practice, which have little to do with the reported event. These include considerations of style, the structure of the story, and the clarity of the construction of the information. Such values may be glossed as Unambiguity, Simplification, Brevity, and Clarity. Similarly, aspects that concern balance between content or fit with the current news agenda are also classified as news values. Some researchers include factors relating to business models or economic conditions, although others quarantine these from consideration as 'news values'. For example, Brighton and Foy (2007: 29) include 'External influences' as one of their 'new news values', while O'Neill and Harcup (2008: 171) see 'occupational routines, budgets, the market, and ideology, as well as wider global cultural, economic and political considerations' as other factors at play in the news process. Going even further, Machin and Niblock (2006: 141) challenge sociological accounts of news values for failing to account for strategic market awareness and claim that 'audience targeting is a news value criterion'.

When a term is used in such different ways in the literature, it may to some extent become diffuse, potentially confusing, and lose some of its worth as an important theoretical concept. We can question whether it is actually useful to use the label *news values* for all of the different aspects that it has been applied to. It also becomes particularly important to clarify how the term is used in a particular publication and to delineate its scope—something we will do in section 2.3.

2.1.2.3 The nature or status of news values

Another problematic issue, which is related to the above discussion, concerns the nature or status of news values. Are news values the values that journalists hold, the selection criteria that they apply, the perceived qualities of material events, or values that can be discovered in published news stories? Montgomery (2007: 10) notes that 'the epistemological status of the "factors" [news values] is somewhat ambiguous'.

Most commonly, news values are perceived of as existing externally to the news story text, for instance, as 'routine and highly regulated procedures' (Golding and Elliot 1979: 114), as systems of criteria central to the decision-making process as to what will or will not be selected as news (Westerståhl and Johansson 1994: 71; Palmer 2000: 45). We could call this a 'social' perspective on news values, as it talks about news values being 'used' or 'applied' in the social practices of journalism. We have also seen in section 2.1.2.1 that news values may be regarded as properties or qualities of events that happened—a 'material' perspective that seems to apply the concept of news values to material reality. Finally, news values are also considered as values existing in the minds of journalists (Palmer 2000: 45; Donsbach 2004; Kepplinger and Ehmig 2006: 27; Schultz 2007: 190; Harrison 2010: 248; Strömbäck et al. 2012: 719). We could call this a 'cognitive' perspective on news values.

At the same time, much news values analysis uses content analysis to identify news values. Here, it seems that news values are approached as the values that can be discovered in published news items, even as they are simultaneously considered as selection criteria or event properties. Thus, Harrison (2006: 136) summarizes news value analysis as 'a form of **content-based** research which makes judgements about the production process by attempting to identify the way in which a "property of an event . . . increases its chance of becoming "news"'' (Harrison 2006: 136, bold added).[3] In a different vein, Staab (1990) proposes that in writing news stories, journalists can 'stress aspects of the actual event and therefore stress different news factors and, as a consequence, give a different meaning and emphasis to the event and the corresponding news story' (Staab 1990: 429). This is reminiscent of Galtung and Ruge's idea of 'distortion'. A focus on the writing, or discourse, that journalists produce might be regarded as a 'discursive' perspective.

While we contend that news values do have these different dimensions (social, material, cognitive, discursive) and can thus be approached from different perspectives, it is problematic when the perspective remains unclear or dimensions are conflated. O'Neill and Harcup's point that news values research 'sometimes blurs distinctions between news *selection* and news *treatment*' (O'Neill and Harcup 2008: 171, italics in original) is just one example of such a conflation.

2.1.2.4 Lists and labels

Several researchers have produced new lists of news values, as an alternative to those from Galtung and Ruge (1965). For the main part, authors point to the outdatedness or limited applicability—especially in the twenty-first century—of Galtung and Ruge's approach. This includes researchers such as Hoskins and O'Loughlin (2007) and Brighton and Foy (2007), who aim to address the transformations that have taken place in the news landscape, for example, in relation to live and continuous television news coverage, new media platforms, and shifts in the relationship between providers and consumers of news. Most researchers, however, do not fully justify why the need to propose new lists has arisen, nor do they explain how the new lists differ significantly from the old ones or why a particular label was chosen. In fact, many lists, including Brighton and Foy's 'new' (2007: 25) and Harcup and O'Neill's 'contemporary' (2001: 279) news values still demonstrate considerable overlap with 'traditional' news values.

In general, there is much overlap between the different lists of news values that have been published, as the review in Caple and Bednarek (2013) illustrates.[4] Just to take one news value, Eliteness, as an example, the explanations/definitions from 11 different sets of researchers are almost identical: the common assumption is that there is an element of eliteness (high status) in persons, nations, or organizations. The main differences occur in the naming/labelling of this news value as Eliteness, Celebrity, Status, Prominence, Worth, or Power. Since we do not see much point in adding to the proliferation of terms that now exist for news values, we will not introduce any new labels in this book and will justify in chapter 3 both which news values we investigate and why we chose a particular label.

2.1.2.5 News values and images

A final point to be made in relation to news values research in journalism/communications studies is the neglect of images (see further Caple 2013a).[5] This has only been noted by a few researchers (e.g. Rössler et al. 2011), and Tunstall (1971: 21) is the only researcher to criticize Galtung and Ruge (1965) for ignoring the visual.

An early semiotic approach is evident in Hall's (1973) writing on press photography. For him, there are two levels of signification of news. In relation to images, this involves the formal news value of the photographic sign—that is, the elaboration of the photograph and text in terms of the professional ideology of news (Hall 1973: 179). Formal news values as expressed in the press photograph include the unexpected, dramatic, recent event concerning a person of high status. The second level of signification is the ideological level of connoted themes and interpretations. Here, we can see parallels with Barthes's (1977) conceptualizations of denotation and connotation.

In contrast, for most of those who have dealt with news values and press photography, the focus remains on the selection process and content analysis. Thus, the concept of visualization and the availability of images have been listed as selection criteria (see Rössler et al. 2011: 417). For instance, Harcup and O'Neill (2001: 274) have a subcategory within their news value of 'entertainment' which is labelled 'picture opportunities'. They comment that 'if a story provided a good picture opportunity then it was often included even when there was little obvious intrinsic newsworthiness' (Harcup and O'Neill 2001: 274) and also mention stories 'with a good picture' (276). However, it remains unclear how to define such a 'good picture', and it is also somewhat problematic to talk about newsworthiness as being 'obvious' or 'intrinsic'.

Some researchers apply 'traditional' news values to press photography, as in Singletary and Lamb's (1984: 108) analysis of award-winning press photography in the United States, which found that the photos 'typically focused on a narrow range of those values'. These were Timeliness, Proximity, and Conflict in the case of news photos, and Proximity and Human Interest in feature photos. Only a few researchers have attempted to compile a list of news values that specifically relate to press photography. Craig's (1994) study of the use of press photographs in two Australian publications, *The West Australian* (a Perth-based metropolitan newspaper) and *The Australian* (a national newspaper), detects five news values at work in press photographs: Reference to Elite Persons, Composition, Personalization, Negativity, and Conflict/Dramatization. More recently, researchers have proposed a set of 'image-inherent news factors' (Rössler et al. 2011: 417). Their catalogue of photo news factors includes *Damage, Violence/Aggression, Controversy, Celebrities, Unexpectedness, Emotions, Execution and Technique*, and *Sexuality/Eroticism*. These photo news factors are defined as 'selection criteria' and are said to determine whether the images are 'worth publishing' (417). In relation to the existing work on news values and news photography, what is clearly missing are conceptualizations of exactly how the meaning of news images contributes to newsworthiness—for example, in terms of their aesthetic appeal (see Caple 2013a).

2.1.2.6 Interim conclusion

Before we hone in on research on news values in linguistics, it may be useful to provide an interim conclusion. It seems fair to say that researchers in journalism/communications studies usually consider news values as a production technique—news values are criteria that news workers use to systematize and determine what will be investigated or reported. News values are seen as the key drivers in the news process, which 'influence selection' (McQuail 2005: 310), 'drive' coverage, and 'dominate' practice (see O'Neill and Harcup 2008). Conley and Lamble (2006) put it particularly strongly:

> News values will **determine** whether stories are to be pursued. They will **determine** whether, if pursued, they will then be published. They will **determine**, if published, where the stories will be placed in news presentation. Having been placed, new [*sic*] values will **determine** to what extent the public will read them. (Conley and Lamble 2006: 42, bold added)

From our perspective as discourse analysts this seems to imply that news values are pre- and therefore a-textual, whereas we see a clear value in analysing how they are actually constructed **through discourse** (see examples 1-3 in chapter 1). We have also pointed to a number of aspects that need clarification. It is important to keep these in mind because they will inform our own conceptualization of news values in this chapter and the next. But before we introduce our approach below, it is necessary to briefly review research on news values in linguistics.

2.2 Linguistics

Most linguistic research on news discourse does not appear to be very interested in analysing or discussing news values at length, perhaps because they are not seen as relevant for linguistic analysis, but as lying outside the text. On the other hand, linguists such as Bell (1991: 76), Durant and Lambrou (2009: 89), and Smith and Higgins (2013: 1) have pointed out that a key component of a journalist's craft and a primary function of news discourse is to establish the newsworthiness of reported events. Nevertheless, much linguistic research does not mention news values at all or if it does, mentions them only in passing because the focus is on other aspects.

Where news values are mentioned, definitions from journalism/communications studies are usually taken on without questioning them (though see Montgomery's [2007: 10–11] discussion of the epistemological status of news values). Such studies often examine particular aspects of journalism, such as the relation between advert and news story (Ungerer 2004), narrativization and human interest in war reporting (Piazza and Haarman 2011), the construction of nature (Goatly 2002), or the representation of Muslims (Baker et al. 2013a), rather than being devoted to a close examination of news values. Even where researchers do pay attention to news values in more detail (P. Bell 1997; Ungerer 1997; ben-Aaron 2003, 2005; Jaworski et al. 2003; Bednarek 2006a; Smith and Higgins 2013), they usually follow established definitions, mostly citing key readings such as Galtung and Ruge (1965), van Dijk (1988a), and Bell (1991). Nevertheless, a handful of linguists have tried to come up with their own conceptualization of news values, with three broad approaches to be distinguished, which we have called *practice-based, cognitive*, and *discursive* (Caple and Bednarek 2013).

2.2.1 PRACTICE-BASED RESEARCH

The practice-based approach, which includes ethnographic newsroom research, is represented by Allan Bell and Colleen Cotter, who both draw on their professional background as journalists.[6] Bell in particular has been very influential in linguistics. Textbooks and other introductions to news discourse largely tend to follow his conceptualization when explaining news values (e.g. Durant and Lambrou 2009: 88; Smith and Higgins 2013) and it has also influenced our own work in the past (e.g. Bednarek 2006a; Caple 2009). In brief, Bell draws on journalism studies to describe news values as 'the—often unconscious—criteria by which newsworkers make their professional judgements as they process stories' (Bell 1991: 155).

For Bell, news values mould, control, or 'drive the way news stories are gathered, structured and presented' (Bell 1991: 247), with news values leading to events being framed in a particular way (e.g. Bell 1991: 169). As far as the coverage of news actors or events is concerned (what is selected, what makes the news), Bell argues that this can be explained by considering if they meet news values criteria, have news value, or are newsworthy (e.g. Bell 1991: 180, 194, 320). This suggests that for Bell, news values are also a *quality* of news actors/events, at the same time as being *criteria* that journalists are trained to operate. Thus, Bell's writing sometimes appears to imply that news values exist independently of journalists, either as somewhat reified driving forces of news story production or in the 'nature' of events/actors. On the other hand, Bell (1995: 313, 320) also relates news values to the judgments or perceptions of journalists.

Bell's approach becomes more complex by including different phenomena under the term *news values*. Building on but also modifying Galtung and Ruge (1965), he categorizes them into three groups. The first group relates to news content and includes values such as Recency, Unexpectedness, and Superlativeness. The second group concerns news gathering and processing and includes values such as Continuity, Competition, and Prefabrication. The third group concerns three values that have to do with 'the quality or style of the news text' (160)—Clarity, Brevity, and Colour. We will discuss this categorization in more detail in section 2.3.

As far as the relationship between news values and news discourse is concerned, Bell proposes that news values can be identified through analysis of journalistic textbooks or by 'deduction from what actually happens in the media' (Bell 1991: 155) and appears to favour the latter approach. He makes the important observation that news values can be 'enhanced' through language by journalists, as they edit input material to produce final copy (Bell 1991: 65). Bell further argues that 'maximizing news value is the primary function' (Bell 1991: 76) of copy editing and provides several examples when discussing individual news stories. We will review these examples in chapter 4.

In many ways, Cotter's approach to news values is similar to that of Bell. News values are seen as journalists' '*internalized assumptions* about what is important to transmit' (Cotter 2010: 56, italics in original). Where Bell talks about news values as criteria that journalists are trained to use, Cotter (2010: 53) assumes that journalists are inculcated with news values through a socialization process. Like Bell, Cotter (2010) also assumes a key role for news values in that they influence (1) or govern (73) journalistic decisions and news practice by functioning as guidelines or parameters, establishing selection criteria and a 'hierarchy of importance' (73–74). In this sense, they 'are **used** to decide what is news' (Cotter 2010: 87, bold in original). Indeed, she sees the influence of news values as all-encompassing:

> News values are not only invoked to answer questions at the *conceptualization stage* about **what** to cover or what counts as news, but also to answer other relevant journalistic questions related to the story and

story construction: **how** to cover it, **what** to emphasize or start off with (the 'lede' [*sic*]), **who** to talk to, **when** to proceed or hold back. They are also relevant to the story's placement or *position* in the paper or on the broadcast: **where** to position it physically in time (radio and television) or space (print) and **how** to play it, incorporating non-textual demands pertaining to space and time on any one day. (Cotter 2010: 75, bold and italics in original)

Like Bell, Cotter (2010) also refers to news values as 'elements of content' (94), qualities of news actors (69), or stories (95). Here it seems again as if news values exist independently of journalists, although Cotter (2010: 87) also talks about them as 'group-agreed qualities', which implies journalists as agents. Indeed, for the most part, Cotter clearly sees news values as something that inheres in journalists.

The main contrast with Bell (1991) is that Cotter (2010) does not take as broad a view as Bell on news values and some of Bell's news values—for instance, Composition (to do with the mix of news content)—are therefore seen as outside newsworthiness (e.g. Cotter 2010: 80). The other key difference is that Cotter's (2010) main focus is on what goes on in the newsroom rather than in published news stories. For example, she shows how news values are explicitly invoked in story meetings through what she calls 'news-value-instantiated proposition' (e.g. a statement by an editor that *It'll be a little old* [Recency]).[7] Cotter (2010: 71–72, 76) also notes that news values are cited in discussions, reflections, and evaluations of news practice in newsroom meetings, memos, trade publications, columns, and opinion pieces—both to justify why something was and why it was not covered (e.g. a columnist describing someone as '*a woman nobody has ever heard of*' [Prominence]).

With respect to the relationship between news values and news discourse, Cotter suggests that news values 'shape' or 'become embedded in text' (Cotter 2010: 67). However, she also recognizes that such discourse reinforces and reproduces news values (Cotter 1999: 175, Cotter 2010: 94).

2.2.2 COGNITIVE

The cognitive approach is represented by Teun van Dijk and Roger Fowler, who both apply critical discourse analysis. While they do not discuss news values to the extent that Bell and Cotter do, they do offer their own conceptualizations. Van Dijk (1988a) distinguishes different types of news values: those having to do with the economic conditions of news production (including constraints such as budgets and sales/subscriptions); those associated with the newsgathering production process (deadlines, sections, and accessibility of sources), and a range of 'more specific cognitive constraints that define news values' (Novelty, Recency, Presupposition, Consonance, Relevance, Deviance and Negativity, and Proximity). He interprets news values as constraints that 'have a cognitive representation' (121) and underlie the production of news, including selection and formulation: 'the interpretation of events as potential news events is determined by the potential news discourse such an interpretation (model) may be used for, and conversely. News production seems circular: Events and text mutually influence each other' (113). Similarly, Fowler (1991) starts off by explaining Galtung and Ruge's (1965) original news values, but comes up with his own cognitive conceptualization. In this definition, news values are seen as socially constructed 'intersubjective mental categories' (17), although Fowler also argues that they are 'qualities of (potential) reports' and 'features of representation' (19). In other words, both Fowler and van Dijk conceptualize news values as cognitive but also recognize their social and discursive dimensions.

To offer a brief conclusion of practice-based and cognitive research here, some of the criticism that can be levelled at journalism/communications scholars also applies to linguists, partially because they are heavily influenced by such work, especially Galtung and Ruge (1965). This includes the problem of talking about an event's news value or its newsworthy qualities, the application of the label *news values* to very different aspects of the news process and a blurring or conflation of the different dimensions of news values (e.g. social, material, cognitive, and discursive). At the same time, these linguists, especially Bell (1991), provide us with an important impetus for our own 'discursive' approach (Bednarek and Caple 2012a, b; 2014)— namely, the idea that news discourse can be systematically examined for its construction of newsworthiness.

2.3 A new approach to news values

This section introduces our own 'discursive' approach to news values: discursive news values analysis (DNVA). We start by explaining how we use the term *news values* (section 2.3.1) and then revisit the idea that news values have different dimensions (section 2.3.2). We conclude by delimiting the scope of DNVA (section 2.3.3). As a reminder, chapters 3, 4, and 5 will explain DNVA in more detail, providing comprehensive frameworks for applying DNVA to verbal and visual text.

2.3.1 DELIMITING THE SCOPE OF THE TERM *NEWS VALUES*

In the previous sections, we noted that the label *news values* has been applied to very different aspects, including apparent properties of events or stories, aspects of journalistic practice, elements of content mix, fit with news agenda, and factors relating to business models or economic conditions. We concluded that there is a need to distinguish more clearly between the different aspects that the term is applied to. As we have also seen, one researcher who has attempted to do this is Bell (1991), who distinguishes between three different kinds of values (table 2.2). We will revisit his classification briefly here as a springboard for more in-depth discussion.

Table 2.2 **Bell's threefold categorization**

Bell's (1991) classification of news values	
Values in the news text	brevity
	clarity
	colour
Values in the news process	continuity (once a story appears as news it continues as news)
	competition (the competition among news institutions for scoops, the competition among stories for coverage)
	co-option (associating one story with a more newsworthy one)
	composition (the mix of different kinds of stories in the overall news bulletin or newspaper)
	predictability (the scheduling of events, such as press conferences to fit the news cycle)
	prefabrication (the existence of prefabricated input sources)
Values in news actors and events	Recency: 'the best news is something which has only just happened' (156)
	Consonance: 'the compatibility with preconceptions about the social group or nation from which the news actors come' (157)
	Negativity: 'the basic news value'; 'news is bad' (156) [includes damage, injury, death, disasters, accidents, conflict, war reporting, deviance]
	Relevance: 'the effect on the audience's own lives or closeness to their experience' (157)
	Proximity: 'geographical closeness can enhance news value'; 'related is . . . the cultural familiarity and similarity of one country with another' (157)
	Unexpectedness: 'the unpredictable or the rare is more newsworthy than the routine. Closely related is NOVELTY [in the sense of "newness"]'. (157)
	Superlativeness: 'the biggest building, the most violent crime, the most destructive fire gets covered' (157)

Table 2.2 **Continued**

	Personalization: 'indicates that something which can be pictured in personal terms is more newsworthy than a concept, a process, the generalized or the mass' (158)
	Eliteness: 'reference to elite persons such as politicians or film stars'; 'the elite nations of the First World are judged more newsworthy than the non-elite nations of the South' (158)
	Attribution: 'the eliteness of a story's sources', 'elite on some dimension, particularly socially validated authority' (158)
	Unambiguity: 'the more clearcut a story is, the more it is favoured' (157)
	Facticity: 'the degree to which a story contains the kinds of facts and figures on which hard news thrives: locations, names, sums of money, numbers of all kind' (158)

While Bell's classification is useful, it is also somewhat problematic in that the term *news values* encompasses a variety of quite different elements in the news process. For instance, the *values in the news text*—clarity, brevity, and colour—are similar to the values that Cameron finds in style books (correctness, consistency, clarity, and concision) and explains as defining 'good writing' (Cameron 1996: 319). Similarly, Cotter (1999: 174) mentions brevity and clarity alongside other values as examples of 'rhetorical goals in newswriting'. In fact Bell also talks about these as 'goals' or 'aims' of news writing and editing (Bell 1991: 160; 1995: 306, 319). Clarity, brevity, and colour are hence general linguistic characteristics expected of a news story and do not concern the newsworthiness of reported events. Further, the *values in the news process*—continuity, competition, co-option, composition, predictability, and prefabrication—may clearly influence whether or not something 'becomes' published news, but we agree with Cotter (2010: 80) that factors such as space, content mix, deadlines, and others are best treated as 'factors other than newsworthiness'. To these, we can add other factors that influence news selection and production, such as the availability of a reporter, material and sources, news cycles, or information gleaned from audience analytics (e.g. perceived shareability).[8]

In this book we therefore build on previous research (Bednarek and Caple 2012a; Caple and Bednarek 2013, 2016) to distinguish between:

- *News writing objectives* (general goals associated with news writing, such as clarity of expression, brevity, colour, accuracy, etc.);
- *News selection factors* (*any* factor impacting on whether or not an event gets covered or a story becomes published, e.g. commercial pressures, availability of reporters, deadlines, audience analytics, etc.);

- *News values* (concerning the newsworthiness of events—their potential newsworthiness in a given community, their newsworthiness as evaluated and determined by news workers in news practice, or their newsworthiness as constructed through discourse).

As a reminder, we also treat moral-ethical values (e.g. truth, fairness) and commercial values (e.g. speed, access via multiple platforms) as falling outside the scope of news values (see chapter 1). In relation to the third point, that news values concern the newsworthiness of events, we should note that when we talk about an event's potential news value, we mean a value that is socioculturally assigned, rather than 'natural' or 'inherent' in the event (see chapter 3). Our definition also highlights the need to further tease apart the different dimensions of news values—this is the aim of the following section.

2.3.2 DIMENSIONS OF NEWS VALUES

Van Dijk (1998) argues that values have cognitive, social, and discursive aspects. In his words, values are culturally 'shared mental objects of social cognition' (74); values are 'applied by social members in a large variety of practices and contexts' (74), and discursive strategies may establish values (262) or select/emphasize specific values (286). While van Dijk talks about values in general, we may also consider news values to have these three dimensions (cognitive, social, and discursive) and we can add a fourth (material). We already briefly mentioned these dimensions in relation to our review of the literature in journalism/communications studies. That is, we assume that an event in its material reality holds potential news value for a given community (material); that news workers and audience members have beliefs about news values and newsworthiness (cognitive); that news values are applied as selection criteria in journalistic practice (social), and that news values can be communicated through discourse (discursive). Table 2.3 shows that each dimension corresponds to a different research perspective on news values (Bednarek 2016a).[9]

These different aspects interact in various ways: For instance, events with potential news value happen (material); news workers use their beliefs about news values and their target audience as selection criteria for inclusion, ordering, and presentation as news (cognitive, social); news workers use language and other semiotic modes to discuss and communicate news values to each other and to their audience (discursive). News values are also constructed in input material that news workers work with—such as press releases—and in published news stories, whose newsworthiness may in turn be discussed by audience members (discursive). Recognizing these four different dimensions is thus important because it allows us to explore such connections and interactions, which becomes more difficult when material, cognitive, social, and discursive aspects are conflated.

Table 2.3 **Dimensions of news values**

Material: an event in its material reality holds potential news value in a given community	*What are an event's potential news values?*
Cognitive: news workers and audience members have beliefs about news values and newsworthiness	*What beliefs do news workers and/or audience members hold about news values?*
Social: news values are applied as selection criteria in journalistic routines and practices	*How do news workers apply news values as criteria in selecting what events to cover, publish and in how to produce them?*
Discursive: news values can be communicated through discourse	*How are news values communicated through discourse, pre-, during, and post-news production and in news products?*

To avoid such conflation and for reasons of scope we solely take a discursive perspective to news values in this book—what we call discursive news values analysis (DNVA). Before we can systematically explore connections and interactions between the four different perspectives it is necessary to develop a framework for systematically analysing **how** news values are communicated through discourse. As indicated above, there is a lack of linguistic and multimodal research in this area, and as multimodal discourse analysts with an interdisciplinary focus, we aim to fill this gap through this book. We should emphasize here that our discursive approach is to be regarded as complementary to other approaches. Thus, our aim is not to reduce values to discourse or to assume that they are only constructed through discourse. We simply argue that the study of news values should incorporate a more systematic analysis of how they are established in discourse. Results from such analyses could then be tied to ethnographic and other research on social, cognitive, and material dimensions of news values, through multidisciplinary collaborations with other researchers (Bednarek and Caple 2014: 139).

In theory, a discursive perspective could be applied to the various phases of the news process as distinguished by Cotter (2010: 73): from story conceptualization, story construction, and story position to evaluation of the reporting. For each of these phases, we could analyse how newsworthiness is communicated and negotiated through discourse. In practice, we have started by systematically investigating the semiotic resources used to construct news values in published news stories and this book continues this focus. Our aim is to introduce a framework that can be used to analyse how specific events are constructed as newsworthy in any published news story. The question is not how an event is selected as news, but how it is **constructed** as news. The focus is on presentation or treatment rather than selection, or more precisely, on what we might call the discourse of news values.

2.3.3 THE SCOPE OF DISCURSIVE NEWS VALUES ANALYSIS

As has already become apparent, there are various questions that we do not pretend to answer in this book. First, we do not assume that DNVA of published news discourse can tell us why a particular story came to be selected for a news outlet; why this story and not another; why this photograph and not another, and so on. The identification of news values in stories offers insights into the how of the reporting rather than the why. As we argued earlier, there are many factors that impact on whether or not an event gets covered or a story becomes published (e.g. commercial pressures, availability of reporters, deadlines, etc.). There are also different reasons for why a particular image or linguistic device might be chosen. For instance, being in possession of a photo that no other news organization has (an exclusive) can mean that this photo is selected for publication, while a particular linguistic device may be chosen because news workers follow an in-house style guide (Cameron 1996)[10] or other writing advice (Cotter 1999).[11] DNVA of published texts alone cannot provide insight into the influence of style guides and other advice, nor can it tell the researcher about the influence of editors and who was responsible for choosing a particular semiotic resource (e.g. journalist, subeditor, etc.) and more generally, why an event was covered, or why a story, photo, or video was selected. For such insights, we would need to undertake ethnographic research, go into newsrooms and observe or interview journalists, which is beyond the scope of this book.

Second, we do not assume that DNVA of published news discourse can tell us if a specific semiotic device was used consciously or intentionally with the strategic aim of providing news value. The semiotic devices that construct newsworthiness are conventionalized and the result of journalistic practice over time. Some of them may even be recognized as journalistic clichés (for lists, see Bender et al. 2009: 101 or Lozada 2014). Since news reporting exhibits a 'high degree of conventionalisation' (Catenaccio et al. 2011: 1848), the use of semiotic devices could be semi-automatic, with news workers following routines and conventions and using their tacit knowledge and practice-based experience.[12] In sum, we do not claim that DNVA of published news texts provides insight into speaker intention. When we use phrases such as 'DEVICE constructs/establishes the news value of Y' this is not meant to imply intentionality, but relates to the meaning potential constructed in the discourse. We do nevertheless make a general assumption about news discourse, namely that it 'is intended to attract an audience through presenting a story to them that is newsworthy' (Bednarek and Caple 2012a: 46). As Sissons (2012: 278) puts it, 'the functional goal of a news report is to publish "newsworthy" information, which will attract the target audience'.

Third, we do not assume that DNVA of published news stories can tell us how audiences read or react to the meaning potential of these texts, since audiences can decode meanings from different positions (Hall 1994). Thus, we aim to avoid the 'effects fallacy' (Boyd-Barrett 1994: 38): the assumption that discourse analysis provides insights into how discourse is read. We may argue that if particular news values (say, Negativity and Superlativeness) are consistently foregrounded in the reporting about an issue or actors (say, immigrants), then there is the potential for audiences to see events/actors in these terms (say, as big threats). But a DNVA of the texts alone cannot tell us if this is indeed the case. To investigate the understanding of actual audience members necessitates audience research (Coffin and O'Halloran 2005: 159). The study of effects on audiences is a potential application of DNVA but not one that we explore in this book. Thus, we agree with the assumption that how texts are read is an

> entirely separate investigation that may require observation and questioning of readers. . . . But if for lack of time or resource we have to disregard how readers actually interpret texts, there still remains more than an academic interest in establishing the range of texts that mainstream media provide: the spread of opportunities of exposure to different kinds of text. (Boyd-Barrett 1994: 29)

In sum, this book makes a contribution to research that investigates how news stories ' "work" in practice' (Boyd-Barrett 1994: 38) and deals with news as discourse, as semiotic practice. As we have put it elsewhere, 'examining how events are endowed with newsworthiness by the news media shows which aspects of the event are emphasized, and reveals the shape in which events are packaged for news consumption by audiences' (Bednarek 2016a: 31). Moreover, the analysis of news values can be an additional tool for critical discourse analysis (Bednarek and Caple 2014), since many researchers have argued that new values are themselves an ideological system (e.g. Hall 1973; van Dijk 1988a; Bell 1991; Cotter 2010) or that they can 'work to reinforce *other* ideologies' (Bednarek and Caple 2014: 137, italics in original). While we may not always comment on the ideological aspects of news values in this book, it is worth keeping them in mind even as we primarily examine journalism as professional practice.

In this chapter we have provided a critical, cross-disciplinary review of news values research and introduced our own discursive approach: DNVA. Our contribution to news values analysis lies not only in introducing a new approach that focuses on semiotic resources but also in offering an overview of the vast and complex area that is news values research and in teasing apart the different aspects of news values, proposing four dimensions and research perspectives (material, cognitive, social, and discursive). Our own approach focuses on analysing how semiotic resources discursively construct newsworthiness in published news stories. In chapters 4 and 5 we will discuss these semiotic resources in detail. However, we will first explain in the next chapter what exactly we mean by 'discursively constructed', which news values we investigate, and how we conceptualize these.

Notes

1. For alternative overviews, see Brighton and Foy (2007: 8–14) or O'Neill and Harcup (2008). This chapter does not take into consideration research on news frames, agenda setting, gatekeeping, etc., which have been identified as overlapping to some extent with news values analysis (see e.g. Allan 1999; Johnson-Cartee 2005). It also does not consider moral-ethical and commercial values (see chapter 1).
2. Not all researchers treat news value as inherent in events; many scholars regard news values as **perceived**.
3. In this review, we have not explored the methods used in the analysis of news values. Alongside content analysis, journalism research into news values also sometimes employs ethnographic approaches, such as interviewing (e.g. Masterton 2005) and newsroom observations (e.g. Lester 1980). Indeed, methodology in news values research is a topic that would deserve a critical review on its own. For instance, identifying news values in stories through content analysis to determine why these stories were chosen is highly problematic, as it tells us more about the **how** than the **why** of coverage (Hartley 1982: 79; Harcup and O'Neill 2001: 276).
4. This point is also made by Cotter (2010: 70) with respect to journalism **textbooks**.
5. For reasons of scope, we focus primarily on news photography here, rather than broadcast news imagery. Some of the latter research conceptualizes 'value' in moving images in relation to production and economic values (see e.g. Cummins and Chambers 2011), which falls outside of the definition we are using here. But see Maier and Ruhrmann (2008) for an approach that builds on Schulz (1982).
6. The two researchers come from somewhat different linguistic subdisciplines: Bell is a sociolinguist, whereas Cotter is an ethnographic researcher. Cotter's approach could also be subsumed under the 'cognitive' approach, because she clearly sees news values as inhering in journalists. However, her conceptualization is only implicitly cognitive and her research clearly focuses on newsroom **practice**.
7. This point is similar to Lester's (1980: 991) argument that newsroom talk 'generates' newsworthiness, for example, by framing stories through 'accounts which assemble the overall newsworthy character of particular occurrences' (e.g. *Commencements are so boring*).
8. In the twenty-first-century newsroom, audience metrics (information about what is most shared, liked, read . . .) influence both **what** stories get covered and **how** those stories are packaged (Olmstead et al. 2011: 1; Nguyen 2013: 150; Martin and Dwyer 2015; Welbers et al. 2015).
9. We started out by only distinguishing the discursive from the cognitive (Bednarek and Caple 2012a); the material perspective was inspired by a comment from John Richardson and introduced in Bednarek and Caple (2012b); the 'social' perspective was added by Bednarek (2016a).
10. To give an example, at the time of writing the BBC News Style guide (2014) included sections on grammar, spelling and punctuation, military, names, numbers, and religion, as well as an alphabetically ordered section. To provide a flavour of this style guide, the entry on 'race' is reproduced below:

    Race
    Use the term **black people** rather than 'blacks' and **white people** rather than 'whites'. But the colour of someone's skin should be mentioned only when it is relevant. The term 'black' should not normally be used to include Asians. Refer to **black and Asian people** or **Asian, African and Caribbean people**. Avoid 'non-whites'. The word 'coloured' is inappropriate in a racial context, except with reference to apartheid South Africa, where the term **Coloured** (ie initial cap) meant 'mixed race'.

Take care, too, with the word 'immigrant', which is often wrongly used to describe people who were born in the UK.
(http://www.bbc.co.uk/academy/journalism/article/art20130716151834065, accessed 6 November 2014, bold in original)

As can be seen, advice is provided on the use of particular contested words like *elderly, handicap,* and *race* (Cotter 1999: 176). For certain areas—such as the Palestinian–Israeli conflict—news organizations provide glossaries with guidelines for usage (Barkho 2008: 281–282).

11. Such guidelines are targeted towards *news writing objectives,* such as clarity of expression, brevity, or accuracy: Cotter (1999) gives examples of advice from stylebooks, grammar guides, newsroom writing coaches and industry periodicals, which include: *write clearly and lively; use intensifiers and passive voice sparingly; avoid redundancies and wordiness; correctly use grammatical rules.* A textbook for journalism students (Bender et al. 2009: 95–108) provides advice such as:

1. Be precise
2. Use strong verbs and vivid nouns
3. Avoid adjectives, adverbs, clichés, slang, euphemisms, loaded words, gush, exaggeration
4. Avoid self-mention and first person pronouns, except in quotations
5. Use specific time expressions
6. Avoid excessive punctuation
7. Avoid repetition and stating the obvious
8. Avoid the present tense in print (but not web/broadcast)
9. Avoid negated sentences

Although specific news values are not mentioned, some of this advice may result in the use of resources that construct newsworthiness: For instance, the advice to use 'strong verbs' (*rip, shatter,* or *unleash*) can be associated with Superlativeness (see chapter 4).

12. Barkho (2008) suggests that news workers are more conscious of the role of choices in lexis than syntax.

3

Discursive news values analysis

In this chapter, we consolidate what we mean by the *discursive construction* of news values, before introducing our own list of news values and their conceptualization. In order to analyse how news values are constructed through semiotic resources, we need an analytical framework that can be applied to news discourse. The following chapters will provide such frameworks for language (chapter 4) and news photographs (chapter 5). However, to avoid too much overlap we provide our conceptualization of each news value in this chapter. We also discuss the concepts of preferred reading and target audience, and conclude the chapter with an example analysis.

3.1 The discursive construction of news values

In discursive news values analysis (DNVA), we focus on how news values are constructed through discourse (i.e. semiotic resources in use). Since we have already discussed what we mean by *discourse* in chapter 1, we focus here on clarifying what we mean by *constructed*. We discuss the concept of *construction* in relation to language in the first instance, but we also bring in discussion of news photographs.

As starting point, it is useful to consider some of the verbs that linguists have used when referring to the relationship between language and news values, as summarized in chronological order in table 3.1.[1]

The most commonly used verbs centre on notions of enhancing or highlighting news value. Although in principle we concur that 'the language of a news story is . . . adapted to *highlight* its newsworthiness (in this way, it justifies or maximizes the attention it will be given)' (Durant and Lambrou 2009: 89, italics in original), we prefer to use the verbs *construct, establish,* or *construe*. In so doing, we aim to emphasize that texts have a constitutive dimension in what Fairclough (1995) regards as the dialectical relationship between texts and culture. In his words, 'texts are socio-culturally shaped but they also constitute society and culture, in ways which may be transformative as well as reproductive' (Fairclough 1995: 34). Similarly, van

Table 3.1 **Key verbs used by linguists**

Linguist(s)	Key verbs used to refer to the relationship between language and news values
Bell (1991: 2, 76, 81)	reflect and express, maximize, enhance
Ledin (1996: 56)	contribute to, create
Cotter (1999: 173, 175)	enhance, reinforce, reproduce
Vestergaard (2000: 155)	underscore
Goatly (2002: 18)	conform to, stress
Jaworski et al. (2004: 184, 195)	increase, reinforce
ben-Aaron (2005: 715)	increase, encode
Bednarek (2006a: 71, 75, 76, 149)	contribute to, relate to, express, enhance
Montgomery (2007: 93)	driven by
Stenvall (2008a: 230, 241)	construe, accentuate
Durant and Lambrou (2009: 89); Mahlberg (2009: 285)	highlight
Cotter (2010: 67)	embed
Lams (2011: 1861)	enhance
Smith and Higgins (2013: 23, 25)	articulate, emphasize

Dijk (1998: 228) assumes that cognitive representations are '(re)produced as well as (re)constructed by social practices', including discourse. There is a 'top-down' aspect of social reproduction, but there is also a 'bottom-up' aspect of social reproduction, where social practices sustain, continue, and change the system (van Dijk 1998: 229). In relation to news cultures, Luginbühl (2009: 139) proposes that:

> Accepting that cultures are semiotic practices, this means that cultures are established in and expressed by the forms and patterns of language use. The forms of news not only reflect journalistic ideals and values; new cultural practices and with them new ideals can get conventionalized before this change is conscious. . . . On the other hand, this model emphasizes that culture not only reflects existing values but that it can also establish new ones.

Our choice of the verbs *construct*, *construe*, or *establish* highlights the power of discourse in producing, transforming, establishing, and constituting society, culture, and cognition. This choice of words also aligns us with many media researchers who regard news as a construct.² However, we do not deny that there is also a 'top-down' aspect of social reproduction. At the same time, we feel that many linguists have long used verbs that focus solely on this aspect when talking about how news values *influence, drive, govern, control, mould,* or *shape* news production and presentation (see chapter 2), and that it is time to shift this emphasis.

Further, we are most comfortable with an approach that adopts a middle ground between constructionism and realism. On the one hand, we share with a constructionist perspective an interest in how reality is given meaning by the media. In the context of DNVA, we assume that material events are endowed with newsworthiness by the media, for example, by emphasizing or de-emphasizing certain news values in texts (Bednarek and Caple 2014: 139). We also assume that the potential news value of events depends on a given sociocultural system that assigns them value. Thus, Prince William is an 'elite' news actor because of the continuing cultural importance of royalty in the United Kingdom and elsewhere, and the killing of Osama bin Laden is assigned 'positive' or 'negative' value dependent on a given community. Events have potential news value in this sense—this news value is culturally assigned and can be shared by many (such as a negative evaluation of child abuse) or be limited to a particular community (such as the evaluation of particular individuals as elite). When we talk about an event's potential news value, we thus always mean a value that is socioculturally assigned, rather than 'natural' or 'inherent'.

On the other hand, we do not align solely with radical constructionism but share with a realist perspective the assumption that the media 'may represent reality [material events] more or less accurately' (Milestone and Meyer 2012: 19). In other words, events are not denied their 'ontological reality' (Cameron 2009: 190): there is a material reality beyond semiosis. For example, David Cameron became the British prime minister in 2010, and it would have been inaccurate to label him as prime minister in news stories before then. There are thus constraints and opportunities that arise from the material reality of events, in terms of how they can be represented through discourse: if there are around 200 protestors at an event, they can be referred to as *hundreds of protestors* in news stories; if there are 2,000 protestors, they can be referred to as *thousands of protestors*.

In relation to news photography rather than language, images have been described as truth-telling, objective, or authoritative, as mirrors of the events they depict—what Zelizer (2005: 171) refers to as 'photographic verisimilitude'.³ This is encapsulated in Barthes's description of the photograph as record:

> In the photograph—at least at the level of the literal message—the relationship of signifieds to signifiers is not one of 'transformation' but of 'recording', and the absence of a code clearly reinforces the myth of photographic 'naturalness': the scene is *there*, captured mechanically, not humanly (the mechanical is here a guarantee of objectivity). (Barthes 1977: 44, italics in original)

However, images do not simply record an objective truth—rather, they offer **one** visual representation of an event through the ways in which elements, contexts, and participants are framed, cropped (in or out), or angled within the image frame. There are numerous examples of images that have acquired one meaning through one kind of visual representation, but have subsequently taken on quite different meanings once more of the context or other angles were revealed. An instance of this can be seen in table 3.2. Image A shows a very young boy being assisted by UNHCR staff, surrounded by a completely empty desert landscape. The photograph was initially published in a tweet by UNHCR representative Andrew Harper on 16 February 2014 (https://twitter.com/And_Harper/status/435078098867208192/photo/1, accessed 22 March 2016).

Table 3.2 **The lost boy of Syria, 16 February 2014**

Image A

Image B

Source: Photos: UNHCR/Jared Kohler.

The meaning suggested by image A is that the little boy crossed the vast desert alone. Indeed, this is the meaning that was conveyed by the (social) media storm, following its publication on Twitter (Pollard 2014). Andrew Harper then issued another image in which the boy's situation became clearer (image B in table 3.2), simply by showing more of the context: 'He is separated—he is not alone', Harper clarified.[4]

Given the assumption that events can be represented more and less accurately through semiotic resources, it would be possible to use DNVA as a tool to analyse inaccuracies, sensationalism, and media panics (see further chapter 10). The focus of such critical linguistic analysis would be on the 'match' between the potential news value of an event and its discursive construction: Has it been made more newsworthy than it 'deserves'? However, in this book we will focus on other applications of DNVA, including a critical analysis of how a particular topic (cycling/cyclists) is constructed as newsworthy (chapter 6) as well as an examination of news values in stories that news organizations post to Facebook feeds (chapter 7) and those that are widely shared by Facebook users (chapter 8).

3.2 Our list and labels

We noted in chapter 2 that there has been a proliferation of new lists and labels for news values. We do not want to reinvent the wheel here, but rather recognize that we are standing on the shoulders of many that have come before us, starting with Galtung and Ruge (1965). In this book we only include those news values where there is some overlap in news values research overall.[5] As our review in Caple and Bednarek (2013) shows, the news values that have been recognized by many, albeit using various terms, definitions, and conceptualizations include: Negativity (and conflict), Impact (consequence, significance, relevance), Superlativeness (size, scale, scope), Proximity (geographical, cultural nearness), Timeliness (recency, currency), Unexpectedness (and unusuality), Eliteness (prominence, elite status), Personalization, Consonance (expectedness, typicality), and Aesthetics (visuals only).

Human interest/entertainment has also been proposed by several researchers, but this category is too difficult to define, operationalize, and delineate from Personalization. The term *human interest* is also sometimes used as a genre or text type label. For instance, researchers have talked about human interest narratives as a news category (Piazza and Haarman 2011). Here human interest is not conceptualized as a news value but as a type of news, usually equated with 'soft news' (Ljung 2000: 137). Instead of including a news value called human interest we therefore cover the human face of news through the news value of Personalization.

We will also consider Positivity, although this has only been proposed as a news value by some researchers and may only apply to certain types of news (e.g. soft news, sports news). Negativity has been called 'the basic news value' (Bell 1991: 156), but Feez et al. (2008: 72) argue that newsworthiness is in essence about reporting both 'destabilizing' (negative) and 'stabilizing' (positive) events. Conboy (2002: 174) mentions the 'feel-good' stories of the popular press, ben-Aaron (2003) argues that stories about national holidays are neutral or positive, and Caple (2013b: 285) finds more positive than negative emotivity in sports news. Some observers have also noticed a shift towards 'positive news' among mainstream news providers (Bech Sillesen 2014). Van Dijk (1988a: 124) claims that negative news without any positivity 'is probably hard to digest', providing the example of attention to the police in crime news and rescue operations in disaster news. At the same time, we can see that Negativity may even be emphasized in 'good news' stories, as in the beginning of the item in example (1) about a journalist's release from prison, with Negativity underlined here:

(1)

Peter Greste's family 'ecstatic' at journalist's release from Egyptian prison

Andrew Greste said his brother's delight at his release was 'tempered and constrained' by the continued imprisonment of his al-Jazeera colleagues

The family of Australian journalist Peter Greste have spoken of their elation at his sudden release from an Egyptian prison, as well as their ongoing concern for his al-Jazeera colleagues, who remain in captivity.

They also acknowledged the personal toll that his ordeal—and their campaign to end it—has taken on them all. (*The Guardian* [App], 2 February 2015)

More empirical research is thus needed into where and how positive content occurs in news discourse, and this is one reason for including it in this book.

Table 3.3 provides our own definition for each of the news values we include (in alphabetic order), in line with our discursive perspective. Before explaining these definitions further, we should note that we do not make an a priori assumption that these news values are universal (i.e. are equally relevant around the world). This is a question for empirical research to determine; in this book we mainly focus on English-language news published in Australia, the United Kingdom, and the United States. Remember that we use the term *event* as a cover term for events, issues, and happenings, including elements or aspects of these (location, news actors). To give two examples, it is frequently news actors who are constructed as

Table 3.3 **News values and their definitions in DNVA**

News value	Definition
Aesthetic Appeal	The event is discursively constructed as beautiful (visuals only)
Consonance	The event is discursively constructed as (stereo)typical (limited here to news actors, social groups, organizations, or countries/nations)
Eliteness	The event is discursively constructed as of high status or fame (including but not limited to the people, countries, or institutions involved)
Impact	The event is discursively constructed as having significant effects or consequences (not necessarily limited to impact on the target audience)
Negativity	The event is discursively constructed as negative, for example, as a disaster, conflict, controversy, criminal act
Personalization	The event is discursively constructed as having a personal or 'human' face (involving non-elite actors, including eyewitnesses)
Positivity	The event is discursively constructed as positive, for example, as a scientific breakthrough or heroic act
Proximity	The event is discursively constructed as geographically or culturally near (in relation to the publication location/target audience)
Superlativeness	The event is discursively constructed as being of high intensity or large scope/scale
Timeliness	The event is discursively constructed as timely in relation to the publication date: as new, recent, ongoing, about to happen, or otherwise relevant to the immediate situation/time (current or seasonal)
Unexpectedness	The event is discursively constructed as unexpected, for example, as unusual, strange, rare

of high status (Eliteness) and the location that is established as near the audience (Proximity).

As we will provide further detail on the conceptualization of each of these news values, we only briefly comment on this list here (following Bednarek 2016a). In naming and defining these news values, we have tried to use names for news values that are the most transparent and least ambiguous, and to follow Ockham's razor, which states that we should use no more explanatory concepts than are absolutely necessary. This means that we include related concepts under the same news value rather than establishing a separate news value for each related concept. For example, the news value of Timeliness includes the related concepts of newness, recency, currency, immediacy, and so on, since they are all concerned with establishing the relevance of the event in relation to the time of publication. Similarly, Bell's (1991) news value of Attribution is covered by Eliteness, as it concerns the elite status of sources, and Montgomery's (2007) Conflict is included in Negativity. Subcategories could be established by researchers if required for more delicate analysis, for instance, for Proximity (geographical vs. cultural) or Timeliness (newness, recency, immediacy, imminence, currency, seasonality—see figure 3.1).

Figure 3.1 Possible subcategories for Timeliness.

3.3 Conceptualizing news values

We now provide our conceptualization for each news value in alphabetical order—except for Aesthetic Appeal which only applies to the semiotic mode of image and will be discussed at the end. Our conceptualizations here are in line with our discursive approach, but when we cite other researchers we talk about the newsworthiness of events or news actors if these researchers do so (see chapter 2). In providing our own conceptualizations, we also bring to light some thorny issues that analysis of news values must consider and make some brief suggestions for how to deal with them. However, this chapter is not the place for in-depth discussion of our own analytical decisions and we advise readers to refer to chapters 6 to 8 and our coding manuals for further information (Bednarek 2016b; Caple 2016, available for download from http://www.news-valuesanalysis.com).

3.3.1 CONSONANCE

The news value of Consonance has been approached in three different ways:

1. in relation to the expectedness or predictability of events;
2. in relation to expectations about how events proceed and how they are reported;
3. in relation to the stereotypes that exist around people, organizations, and countries.

Taking the first approach, Galtung and Ruge (1965: 67) define Consonance as corresponding to what we expect to happen and what we want to happen. Schulz (1982: 152) similarly defines Consonance: Predictability as: 'The event was expected in advance, its occurrence was known before.' The second approach conceptualizes Consonance in relation to how events typically proceed and how they are reported in terms of scripts or schemas, thus assuming 'familiar contours' in their coverage (Montgomery 2007: 8). In the third approach, Consonance relates to 'compatibility with preconceptions about the social group or nation from which the news actors come' (Bell 1991: 157).[6] In our own discursive conceptualization, Consonance is defined as the construction of an event's news actors, social groups, organizations, or countries/nations in a way that conforms to stereotypes that members of the target audience hold about them. We do not include the issues covered in the first two approaches to Consonance, as these are concerned with journalistic conventions, including genre structure, the news agenda/cycle, and conformity to expectations of processes or types of reporting. Hence, they fall outside the scope of what we mean by news values (see chapter 2).

In order to analyse if an event is constructed as stereotypical (establishing Consonance), the analyst first needs to identify existing stereotypes. This challenge is also faced by analyses of stereotypes more generally, for example, those undertaken in critical discourse analysis (CDA). One approach adopted in this line of research is to consult previous research on relevant stereotypes and then identify their linguistic construction (e.g. Lazar and Lazar 2004; Mautner 2007). In their corpus linguistic CDA of the representation of Muslims in the British press, Baker et al. (2013a) identify existing stereotypes either by consulting research or intuitively. The latter approach works best in our view if the analyst is highly familiar with the target audience (see section 3.4) and/or the respective stereotypes are widely known and enduring. For instance, it would be difficult for us to analyse Consonance constructed in news texts published in Iran, as we do not know what stereotypes Iranian audience members may hold. In contrast, we can make educated guesses about the stereotypes likely to be held by British or Australian audience members. A different approach would be to undertake audience research, using surveys, interviews, databases, or other documents to gauge the stereotypes that audience members may have about particular news actors, countries, or organizations. A final possibility is to only analyse explicit constructions of Consonance (see chapter 4).

3.3.2 ELITENESS

Labels used by other researchers for the news value of Eliteness include *status, attribution, the power elite, celebrity, prominence, worth, power,* and *eliteness*. We use *Eliteness* because the adjective *elite* can be applied to different entities, including nations, events, people, and so on. *Eliteness* is also less ambiguous than *prominence*, which in cognitive linguistics can refer to perceptual prominence (e.g. in terms of figure/ground). In Harcup and O'Neill's (2001: 279) list of news values, 'the power elite' (powerful individuals, institutions, organizations) is a separate news value to 'celebrity' (famous people), and in Bell's (1991) list Eliteness (of news actors) is distinguished from Attribution (eliteness of sources). We prefer to include these under one news value because of Ockham's razor, but subcategories could be established by researchers for more delicate analysis (e.g. celebrities, politicians, athletes, academics, officials).

Further, we conceptualize Eliteness broadly, as relating to human and non-human entities and incorporating various types of 'eliteness' that can be discursively construed: status, expertise, authority, celebrity, fame, or stardom. An incomplete list of entities that may be constructed as elite includes:

- countries or nations (e.g. United States, Germany);
- various kinds of institutions/organizations: cultural (e.g. museums, libraries), political (e.g. UN, governments), academic (e.g. research institutions, universities), sporting (e.g. FIFA), business (e.g. multinational corporations), authorities (e.g. police, military, secret service, court, emergency services);
- various kinds of events/happenings: cultural (e.g. Oscars), political (e.g. presidential elections), academic (e.g. Nobel Prize), sporting (e.g. Olympics, World Cup);
- various kinds of people, including: stars/celebrities, royals, the wealthy 'jet set', politicians, religious leaders, athletes, authority figures, academics, other high-status professionals (e.g. lawyers, CEOs, managers, business groups).

Eliteness is scalar and dependent on the target audience: for example, name recognition can be local (e.g. a local MP would have status and recognition in her community, but not beyond), national (e.g. Gina Reinhart or the CSIRO are well-known in Australia but not internationally), or international (e.g. Rupert Murdoch, Barack Obama, University of Oxford are internationally known and recognized as high status or powerful). While an image of a particular person or a proper noun or role label may thus construct Eliteness, the extent to which this Eliteness is recognized depends on the audience and may vary. For instance, a label such as *beloved Norwegian comedian, musical hall artist and actor Rolf Wesenlund* (published in *The*

Norway Post) has more of a potential to construct Eliteness for a Norwegian audience than any other nationalities.

Eliteness can arise from the cultural status of professions (e.g. lawyers vs. garbage collector) but also from one's position within a professional hierarchy (seniority, e.g. police chief vs. ordinary police officers, political leaders vs. ordinary MPs). Because Eliteness is scalar, it may be difficult to decide how to classify references. For example, should generic references to the police or military and images of 'ordinary' police or military personnel be categorized as constructing Eliteness? On the one hand, the latter are members of a recognized authority with societal power; on the other hand, they are located at a relatively low level in the hierarchy. Thus, in the context of classifying speaker roles in TV war news Haarman and Lombardo (2009: 11) differentiate between legitimated (high-status) person, vox populi (ordinary member of public), and military personnel (ordinary soldier). In this book, we classify references to ordinary soldiers/vets and other debatable cases as 'weak' Eliteness (see further Bednarek 2016b).

Importantly, Eliteness does not imply positive evaluation—elites can be judged negatively or positively. In example (2) Eliteness is combined with Negativity—Berlusconi is clearly introduced as an elite news actor at the beginning (*Italian Premier Silvio Berlusconi*), but is then constructed negatively, as someone who makes inappropriate statements and jokes and 'was embroiled in a sex scandal':

(2)

Italian Premier Silvio Berlusconi says young women should follow the money when looking for a partner, noting that women seem to like him and 'I'm loaded'.

Mr. Berlusconi, who was embroiled in a sex scandal last year and is known for his gaffes, also raised eyebrows with a joke about Hitler's followers urging him to return to power.
(*The Globe and Mail* [Print], 14 September 2010)

The reliance of the press on elite news actors and sources is often criticized. For example, in her analysis of speech representation in the reporting of the Greek national elections in *The Guardian/The Observer*, Lampropoulou states:

Overall, these numbers confirm previous findings in that newspapers tend to favour official or 'legitimised sources'—in this case, through the speaking space they allocate to them—whereas ordinary people's views are mostly presented as reactions to news and are less preferred, as if they are entitled to their experiences but not their opinions. (Lampropoulou 2014: 473)

Fairclough (1988: 131) argues that what he calls 'extensive membershipping' works to 'implicitly ascribe massive legitimacy' to reported discourse. Similarly, van

Leeuwen (2008: 106-107) notes that social practices may be 'legitimated' through discourse by reference to people with institutional status/role, expertise and role models, including media celebrities (i.e. what we discuss as 'elites' here).

3.3.3 IMPACT

Labels used by other researchers for the news value of Impact include *importance, relevance, interest, social significance, (social) impact,* and *consequence*. These are used to refer to two closely related concepts:

- Relevance, in the sense of significance or appeal to the audience, for example, 'the effect on the audience's own lives or closeness to their experience' (Bell 1991: 157)
- Consequence, in the sense of impact or effects.

In our own conceptualization, Impact is defined as relating to the construction of an event as having significant effects or consequences, without restricting these effects/consequences to the lives or experiences of the target audience. This conceptualization is based on the fact that closeness to the audience is already captured in Proximity. This also allows us to analyse as Impact descriptions of an earthquake which is said to have claimed hundreds of thousands of lives in a country that is not near the target audience. Not all references to effects or consequences establish newsworthiness (i.e. Impact is not identical to agency or causality).[7] Rather, the news value of Impact is established when the actual or potential effects/consequences of a reported event are constructed as significant—either as major or as affecting the target audience directly. This means that constructions of Impact may co-occur with constructions of Superlativeness and Proximity. The constructed impact can be positive, negative, or neutral, though most often it appears to be negative (combining Impact with Negativity), exceptions being reports of medical breakthroughs, and so on. Since Superlativeness, Proximity, and Negativity can relate to aspects other than effects/consequences, these news values must be conceptualized as separate from each other even if they are frequently combined.

3.3.4 NEGATIVITY (AND POSITIVITY)

Negativity is considered 'the basic news value' (Bell 1991: 156), and a common adage by news workers is 'if it bleeds, it leads'. Labels used by other researchers for this news value include *valence, conflict, negativity,* and *deviance*; we have chosen *Negativity* because it is more general and encompassing than the other labels. Following Ockham's razor, this news value includes conflict, opposition, controversy, deviance, and related concepts. Negativity is about the construction of events as negative, and if desired, researchers could distinguish what type of negativity is constructed. An incomplete list—in no particular order—might include descriptions of environmental disasters; accidents; damage and detriments; crime and terrorism; injury, disease, and death; chaos and confusion; political and other crises; opposition and division; war and conflict; and other human suffering.

Like other news values, Negativity is dependent on the target audience. Thus, certain target audiences might perceive a particular reported event as negative, while others would not. Immigration or asylum-seeking is a prime example—while there are certainly many in support of immigration, Bignell (2002: 93) argues that there is 'widespread prejudice against immigrants as people taking advantage of supposed British goodwill and generosity'. The evaluation of certain issues (e.g. marriage equality, deregulation of university fees) as positive, neutral, or negative depends on religious and political stance. Other events would probably be evaluated as negative by many (death, famine). In analysing texts, researchers could focus on clear cases—where either the 'preferred' meaning is obvious (cf. section 3.4) or where the target audience is unlikely to be divided in their attitudinal point of view (see Bednarek 2016b).

Importantly, the news value of Negativity is **not** identical to the expression of negative bias on the part of a news organization. For instance, protests can be evaluated as worthy or unworthy (White 2006: 245), but regardless of this evaluation, the news value of Negativity would be constructed through lexis that points to conflict. An example comes from the pro-democracy protests in Hong Kong in September 2014, where 'Western' newspapers sided with protestors but stories included expressions such as *the fight for a genuine free election, in a **tense stand-off** with police, **violent clashes** with police*. Similar lexis occurs in protest stories where newspapers side with the authorities (Hart 2014a, b) and the event is constructed as negative, conflict-laden in both cases. Analysis of the news value of Negativity is not per se concerned with negative assessment or bias by a news outlet; it is concerned with how events are constructed as newsworthy in relation to negative aspects. Hence, it is different from, but can be combined with, a study of news bias.

The opposite of the news value of Negativity is that of Positivity, concerning the construction of events as positive. Like Negativity, a broad range of related dimensions can be included here, ranging from success, victory, peace, heroic or selfless acts to lack of crime, injuries, or damage, and so on.

3.3.5 PERSONALIZATION

Personalization is about giving a 'human' face to the news through references to 'ordinary' people, their emotions, views, and experiences—rather than focusing on abstract issues and processes. For example, a report of a medical discovery may establish Personalization by representing an affected news actor who tells his or her story. News stories that are personalized attract audiences more than the portrayal of generalized concepts or processes (Bell 1991: 158).

Labels used by other researchers for this news value include *personification, personalities, familiarity,* and *personalization,* alongside the related *human interest.* For reasons already provided, we do not include human interest as a news value. Further, we prefer *Personalization* as a label, since 'ordinary' news actors are not necessarily familiar to audience members nor do the latter automatically identify with them.

Personalization is sometimes conceptualized in rather broad terms, simply as involving the acts of people or individuals, rather than processes or concepts (Bell 1991: 158; Montgomery 2007: 7). It has also been approached as a general concept, rather than as a news value (e.g. Thornborrow and Montgomery 2010; Landert 2014). In contrast, we use the term *Personalization* to refer to a particular news value, which concerns references to 'ordinary' people (eyewitnesses, survivors, or other private citizens), that is, references to non-elite individuals not acting or speaking in an official capacity.[8] This explicitly excludes references to *elite* news actors, unless they are represented as **not** acting in their elite capacity or as speaking on behalf of ordinary people. It also excludes references to criminals, militants, or terrorists.

The 'opposite' of Personalization—Eliteness—has been criticized, but so has Personalization: 'The sensationalism and personalisation of the popular press have long been the subject of discussion and complaint on a national basis, particularly in advanced capitalist democracies' (Conboy 2006: 208).

3.3.6 PROXIMITY

Like Personalization, Proximity has been conceptualized in many different ways, not necessarily in relation to the newsworthiness of reported events (e.g. Cap 2008 on 'proximization'). Ahva and Pantti (2014) provide an overview of the various ways in which the term *proximity* has been used in relation to journalism, both with regards to the relationships concerned (journalists—events; audiences—events; news organizations—audiences) and dimensions of 'closeness' (geographical, cultural, social, emotional, moral, virtual). Ungerer (1997) and Luginbühl (2009) are examples of linguistic research that takes a wide view of proximity, including geographical, cultural, emotional, and temporal aspects. To clarify, we conceptualize the news value of Proximity as concerning the construction of an event as happening geographically or culturally near the target audience. It is not about any and all types of 'closeness' (e.g. temporal, emotional, moral), and it is not about the closeness of news workers to events (e.g. being live and on location) or the closeness between news organizations and audiences, for example, through direct audience address (e.g. use of imperatives, *you,* or looking directly into the camera).

Labels used by other researchers for this news value include *identification, meaningfulness,* and *cultural relevance.* We have chosen *Proximity* because this label is more general and can hence incorporate both geographical and 'cultural' nearness—what Galtung and Ruge (1965: 67) call meaningfulness (see chapter 2).

Cotter (1999: 168) argues that Proximity is one of the two 'most important defining characteristics of news. . . . The language not only reports the news, but positions its impact in relation to the community.'

Proximity needs to be conceptualized on a cline, as locations can be more or less 'near' the target audience. For instance, for the target audience of the Brisbane newspaper *The Courier Mail*, references to specific Brisbane locations construct more Proximity than references to the Asia-Pacific region (figure 3.2). News workers can thus localize stories by introducing references to the target audience's city or state (Zorger 1992: 779). Conversely, national newspapers may construct a local happening as of national relevance, since references to the country/nation construct Proximity for a wider audience (all Australians). Thus, different constructions of place are found in local versus regional reporting on the same issue (Johnstone and Mando 2015).

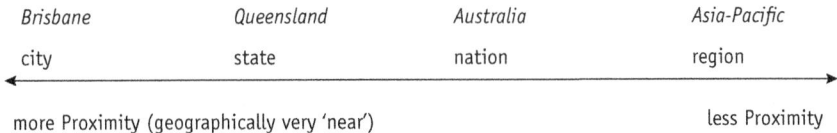

Figure 3.2 Geographical Proximity with respect to a Brisbane target audience.

In addition, cultural and geographical Proximity interact—for example, New Zealand is both geographically and culturally near Australia, whereas Papua New Guinea is also geographically near Australia but culturally more distant (different). Britain, in contrast, may be geographically far from Australia, but is culturally quite near, and so on. It might thus be possible to create a topology for Proximity (figure 3.3). Thus, a reference to Britain in an Australian newspaper would be situated in the top right of the topology; a reference to New Zealand in the same newspaper would be situated in the top left; a reference to Papua New Guinea would be situated in the bottom left, and a reference to Afghanistan in the bottom right segment of the topology.

References to the target audience's own country (state, city) and culture clearly construct Proximity, but references to neighbouring or culturally close countries do

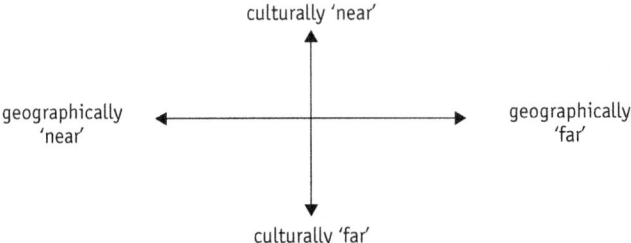

Figure 3.3 Geographical and cultural Proximity—a topology.

not do so to the same extent (think of a reference to Germany in a UK newspaper, or a reference to the United States in an Australian newspaper). In analysing texts for their construction of Proximity, it might well be worth taking this into account (for an attempt, see Bednarek 2016b).

3.3.7 SUPERLATIVENESS

Labels used by other researchers for the news value of Superlativeness include *threshold, size, superlativeness, magnitude, scale/scope,* and *intensity*. We have chosen Bell's (1991) label *Superlativeness* because, like the other news values labels we use, it is more general and encompassing than the other terms. *Superlativeness* indicates that this value is about the construction of 'more-ness' in relation to a range of aspects, including but not limited to intensity, magnitude, and scale: the bigger, the faster, the higher, the more X, the more newsworthy. Thus, Superlativeness concerns the construction of events as of high intensity or large scope/scale and can relate to the extent of a news event, the number of people involved, the impact of an event, the size of entities, the force of actions or behaviour, and many other aspects.

Since scope and intensity are scalar, a cut-off point may need to be specified (see Bednarek 2016b). For instance, should an aftermath image showing two dead people or a headline like *Two dead, one injured in US mall shooting* be analysed as establishing Superlativeness? At what point are we saying that the event is constructed as of large scope/scale? Superlativeness also depends on the target audience and interacts with Proximity. For instance, for an Australian target audience Rau (2010: 13) suggests that 'one person dead in Australia equates to fifty in Britain and 500 in a developing country'. As Montgomery (2007: 6) puts it, 'the notion of scale is situationally sensitive'; thus a reference to floods with 10 victims in St Louis would construct more newsworthiness for an American target audience than a reference to floods with 10 victims in Tehran, whereas the opposite would be the case for an Iranian audience.

3.3.8 TIMELINESS

Labels used by other researchers for the news value of Timeliness include *recency, currency, topicality,* and *timeliness*; we use *Timeliness* because we include here a range of ways in which events are made 'timely' in relation to the publication or transmission date. Recency may be at the core of newsworthiness—but Timeliness is much broader. It is about how an event is established as temporally relevant to the reader at the time of publication/broadcast: the event can be construed as having recently happened (recency), as new (newness), as still ongoing (immediacy), as happening in the near future (imminence). The event can also be constructed as relating to current trends or fads (currency) or seasonal occurrences, that is, repeated happenings such as Christmas (seasonality). As with other news values, it is possible for researchers to report which of these concepts (nearness, recency, and so on) can be identified in a given case, without creating a new news value for each of these time-related concepts (cf. figure 3.1 on page 56.).

Of these different subcategories of Timeliness, 'newness' is the most problematic. In previous incarnations of our framework, we included both 'newness' and unexpectedness under the news value of Novelty—now reconceptualized as Unexpectedness.[9] But while 'newness' does share some similarities with Unexpectedness, it is not necessarily the case that what is constructed as new is also constructed as unexpected, and 'newness' has clear temporal aspects: 'newness' implies recency, not having happened before. Indeed, many researchers align 'newness' with recency, currency, or immediacy, and contrast it with 'old' news (van Dijk 1988a: 121; Brighton and Foy 2007: 26; Montgomery 2007: 5-6; Catenaccio et al. 2011: 1844).

Like other news values, Timeliness needs to be conceptualized on a cline: The closer the temporal reference point is to the time of publication, the more timely, and thus the more newsworthy is the construction of the event (figure 3.4).

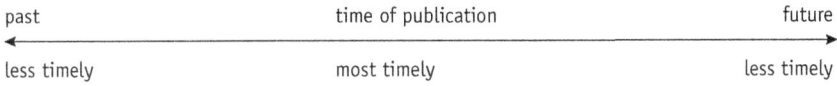

Figure 3.4 Timeliness as a cline.

A crucial question, then, is at what point Timeliness ceases to be established—for instance, some argue that recency involves one to several days (van Dijk 1988a: 121), whereas others argue that yesterday's news is not newsworthy (Montgomery 2007: 5-6). Bell talks about recency in the sense of 'reported in the past 24 hours' (Bell 1995: 320) and Chovanec (2014: 164) in the sense of 'the time between two consecutive issues of the newspaper'. Timeliness is also dependent on technological advances. News workers today have the technology to produce a news item half an hour before broadcast (Lukin 2010: 96), a significant change from the past:

> While the concept of recency was an important news value in the early seventeenth-century, it was much more widely interpreted than is the case nowadays. Whereas in the early twenty-first century 'recent' news is what has occurred in the last twenty-four hours, or, given the Internet, perhaps even the last hour, in early seventeenth-century European society the notion of 'recency' was sufficiently dilated to include dispatches telling of events taking place more than a month before their reading. (Brownlees 2012: 40)

Depending on the type of data analysed and their particular news cycle, a cut-off point may thus need to be specified, beyond which Timeliness is no longer established (see Bednarek 2016b).

3.3.9 UNEXPECTEDNESS

Labels used by other researchers for the news value of Unexpectedness include *novelty, deviance, surprise, rarity, oddity,* and *unusualness*. We prefer the term *Unexpectedness* because *deviance* clearly has negative connotations, *surprise* refers to the mental reaction that is the result of unexpectedness, and *novelty* can mean both 'unusuality' and 'newness'. As already explained, 'newness' is a subcategory of Timeliness, which makes the ambiguous *novelty* too problematic to use as a label here. Like other news values labels, *Unexpectedness* is also more general and encompassing than terms such as *oddity* and *unusualness*. The label *Unexpectedness* indicates that this value is about establishing contrast with the expected. Such contrast can arise because aspects of an event are construed as atypical, unusual, rare, different, that is, out of the ordinary in some way because they conflict with what audiences have come to expect based on their experience of the world. The event might be construed as not conforming to stereotypes, statistical norms, the laws of biology or physics, or behaviour that audience members would expect of a particular news actor. As Masterton (2005: 47) puts it, 'this is the old man-bites-dog syndrome which needs little more explanation'.

Like other news values, Unexpectedness is to some degree dependent on the target audience, as expectations may vary. Hence, it is important that we know what might be unexpected for the target audience, especially with less obvious examples. For instance, when analysing the headline *Record low number of radio-active sheep* on an English-language Norwegian news site, we would need to find out whether radioactive sheep are unexpected for Norwegian readers or if they are a familiar post-Chernobyl occurrence. It is also possible to restrict analysis to obvious assumptions and expectations (see Bednarek 2016b).

3.3.10 AESTHETIC APPEAL

The news value of Aesthetic Appeal stems from Caple's (2013a) research on news photography, where she argues that images construct Aesthetic Appeal through both composition and technical qualities and that visually challenging compositions are highly valued in photography as aesthetically pleasing (Altengarten 2004; Präkel 2006). Further, certain people and places in the natural and built environment that are depicted in the news may in themselves be considered 'beautiful' by certain cultural groups. The news value of Aesthetic Appeal thus relates to the 'beauty' of news visuals—and how these construct a news event as 'beautiful' or aesthetically appealing. An example would be the depiction of a serious oil spill through a beautiful, multicoloured news photograph (Bednarek and Caple 2010).

For several reasons, the news value of Aesthetic Appeal is only postulated for visuals, but not for language. Aesthetic devices as they occur in poetry and literature do not conform to the style of the hard news story, as 'the repertoire of journalistic creativity is rather more familiar and restricted' (Renouf 2007: 70). We may thus argue that the use of such aesthetic devices is in fact **not** valued. In his analysis of how Vietnamese journalistic writing is translated into English, van Leeuwen (2006b: 224) notes that 'overly "florid" and "rhetorical" language' is changed by foreign subeditors, as it does not conform to the Anglo-Australian conception of journalism.[10]

A larger amount of aesthetic (literary) devices may be found in narrative news or soft news, where there is more flexibility regarding linguistic style (Bell 1991: 14). The language of headlines—'headlinese'—is also an exception and rhetorical devices such as word play, sound play, idioms, proverbs, and so on often occur, especially in the UK popular press. Where such rhetorical devices are an established convention we would regard their use as a general *news writing objective* rather than as a news value (see chapter 2). Thus, it is a general objective to write a headline that will attract audiences through devices such as word play or allusion. We argue that the function of such rhetorical devices is usually not to construct the reported news **event** as beautiful/newsworthy, but rather to attract audiences and to foreground the linguistic skill of the journalist and news organization. As Renouf (2007: 70) notes in relation to lexical creativity in journalism, this is 'used to convey to the reader a sense of authorial learnedness, sophistication, distancing and so on'.

3.4 Context-dependency, preferred meaning, and the target audience

In the discussion of how we conceptualize each news value, it has become very clear that news values are context-sensitive (especially time/place of publication) and depend on the audience, as also noted by others before us (e.g. Palmer 2000: 31-33; Montgomery 2007: 6; Richardson 2007: 91; Guo 2012: 30).

There are two relevant concepts that need to be briefly considered here: the notion of preferred reading and that of target audience. The concept of *preferred reading* concerns how readers are positioned and is closely tied to ideology: As Hartley (1982: 63) puts it: 'In order to effect ideological closure, the event is put together with signs that indicate how it should be understood—what it "means".' This is what Hall (1977: 344) refers to as the 'preferred reading'. It is assumed that texts address an 'ideal reader' (Fairclough 1989: 45) who will go along with this preferred reading.[11] For instance, headlines such as *Got him! Vengeance at last! US nails the bastard* which were used in the reporting on Osama bin Laden's death (Bednarek and Caple 2012a: 48) construct an ideal reader who agrees with the preferred meaning that the killing of Osama is positive and to be celebrated. Martin and White (2005: 63, bold in original) argue that a text that 'naturalizes' a reading position is 'fairly directive in the kinds of **attitude** it wants readers to share'. In terms of DNVA, we aim to analyse the meaning potential of texts in terms of their preferred or naturalized readings where possible.

68   THE DISCOURSE OF NEWS VALUES

Coffin and O'Halloran point out that any understanding of how readers are positioned needs to 'connect the linguistic analysis to the context of the target readership' (2005: 145). The target readership or target audience can be discussed in relation to audience roles: 'the target audience who is addressed, the auditors who are expected but not targeted, the overhearers who are not expected to be present in the audience, and the eavesdroppers who are expected to be absent from the audience' (Bell 1991: 92). For news organizations, the target audience may be calculated using market research or they may base the way they address their target audience on assumptions about the 'imaginary' reader (Bell 1991: 90; Bednarek 2006a: 14–15). In the age of the digital, news organizations also use analytical statistics such as 'most read', 'most viewed', or 'most shared' that inform them about their audience. What is newsworthy to one target audience is not automatically newsworthy to another. In terms of DNVA, it is often necessary to make an educated guess about how news organizations address target audiences, especially when no preferred meaning can be identified. Consider two sentences from the *New York Post* that contain similar lexis:

> A truck driver was shot dead early Thursday.
> Al Qaeda leader Osama bin Laden is dead.

We would only analyse the first sentence as constructing the news value of Negativity, as the American target audience would be unlikely to view the information in the second sentence as negative. The surrounding text, or 'the overall trajectory of the meanings in a text' (Martin and White 2005: 25) may also need to be taken into account in the analysis, as it can indicate how factual statements such as these two sentences are intended to be read.

A final point that needs to be made concerns the scalar nature of news values. Not only is it the case that events and news actors in their 'material' reality vary in their news value potential (e.g. A, B, C celebrities), which in turn influences the news value potential of discursive representations of such events/actors (e.g. an image of Hillary Clinton versus an image of a reality TV contestant establish different degrees of Eliteness). In addition, semiotic resources can be skilfully manipulated to vary in the extent to which they construct a particular news value (e.g. *bears one of the most famous surnames in the country* vs. *bears a famous surname*). Both aspects make the annotation and quantification of texts for news values construction highly complex, as the empirical studies in this book will illustrate.

3.5 Example analysis and concluding remarks

To consolidate and clarify the discussion thus far, we offer a brief example of DNVA. Figure 3.5 displays the front page of the print newspaper the *New York Post* on Sunday, 2 November 2014 (accessed via the archive at http://www.nypost.com, 6 September 2015). As its name suggests, the *New York Post* is a newspaper

Discursive news values analysis 69

Figure 3.5 Front page of the *New York Post*, 2 November 2014.

targeted at a New York audience. On its website, it claims: 'We set the agenda for New York City' (http://nypost.com/advertising/, accessed 29 January 2015), and cites its audience as: 60% college + educated, 65% adults aged 25–54, 50% household income 75k + and average household income $125,412 (http://nypost.com/advertising/print/, accessed 29 January 2015). While it claims that its 'print product caters to the most affluent and influential people in the most affluent and influential city on earth' (http://nypost.com/advertising/, accessed 29 January 2015), we can compare some of these figures to *The New York Times*: median household income of $173,807; 82.2% college + educated, with around 30% household income of $250k + and around 25% in top management positions (http://nytmediakit.com/newspaper, accessed 29 January 2015). Bender et al. (2009: 133) note that 'The New York Post traditionally emphasizes crime, sex, sports and photographs.

The New York Times, which appeals to a wealthier, better educated audience than the Post, places a greater emphasis on political, business and foreign news.' In contrast to *The New York Times*, then, we may characterize the *New York Post* as a more 'popular' newspaper, which is also reflected in its layout and design (figure 3.5).

For ease of reading, the verbal story text is represented again as example (3).

(3)

War at the NYPD [Strapline]
'I TOLD YOU WE CAN'T TRUST HIM'! [pull quote as lead headline]
Wife Chirlane's rant to mayor about Bratton [sub-headline]
After the NYPD's highest-ranking African-American, Philip Banks III, resigned on Friday, Chirlane McCray complained to her husband, Mayor de Blasio, that they 'couldn't trust' Police Commissioner Bill Bratton (left). Tensions between Bratton and City Hall have reached a breaking point, sources told The Post. [Lead]

In example (3), the verbal text mainly constructs the news values of Eliteness and Negativity: it includes the names of people that would be recognized as high status by the New York target audience (*Chirlane McCray, Bratton*), while also clearly labelling these as elites with titles and descriptions (*mayor, Mayor de Blasio, Police Commissioner Bill Bratton, the NYPD's highest-ranking African-American, Philip Banks III*). Chirlane McCray is constructed as elite via reference to her husband (*Wife Chirlane . . . to mayor; her husband, Mayor de Blasio*), arguably establishing her as member of a political 'power couple'. There are also references to elite New York institutions (*NYPD, City Hall*). Negativity is constructed by reference to Banks's resignation (*resigned*), as well as the conflict and its associated mental states and actions (*can't trust, complained, 'couldn't trust', tensions*), while expressions such as *war* (negative metaphor), *rant* (intensified negative lexis), and *have reached a breaking point* construct the negativity as high in intensity (Negativity + Superlativeness). The events are constructed as recent in relation to the time of publication, Sunday, with the explicit time reference *on Friday*, while the present perfect aspect (*have reached*) also suggests that the event has recently finished. Finally, the references to the *NYPD* also construct Proximity for the New Yorker target audience.[12]

Considering the visuals, the photographs also construct Eliteness in showing public figures that would be recognizable by the *New York Post* target audience (but are also identified as elites through the accompanying verbal text) and Negativity (their facial expressions are serious or negative). The NYPD badge establishes both Eliteness and Proximity for New Yorkers in reproducing the label for a local authority. Finally, the black background arguably reinforces Negativity while the very large font size, and use of all capital letters seems to intensify the happenings (Superlativeness—but compare the discussion of typography in chapter 5). Table 3.4 illustrates the resulting packaging of news values.

Table 3.4 **News values construction in example (3)**

Semiotic resources	News values
Verbal	Eliteness, Negativity, Superlativeness, Timeliness, Proximity
Visual	
In the photographs	Eliteness, Negativity
In graphics (badge)	Eliteness, Proximity
Through framing/colour	Negativity
Through typography	Superlativeness

To sum up this brief analysis of example (3), DNVA allows us to identify that specific news values are emphasized (Eliteness, Negativity, Superlativeness, Proximity), while others are absent. In this case, the reported event is constructed as maximally negative and involving local elites. DNVA can also provide insights into the packaging of news—how news values are integrated and structured in the form of consumable news products and the role that different components play. In example (3), the verbal and visual text reinforce each other and construct the same news values, with the exception of Timeliness which is difficult to establish via visuals (see chapter 5). In so doing, the semiotic resources construe the reported event as newsworthy, both to attract a particular target audience (which we described earlier) and to justify to that audience how this event constitutes news. In analysing news as semiotic practice in this way, we can see how skilfully the 'discourse of news values' is used by news workers to 'sell' events to their audiences **as news** through verbal and visual resources.

In this chapter we clarified what we mean by *discursive construction* and explained why verbs such as *construct, establish*, or *construe* might be preferable to alternatives such as *highlight, enhance*, or *reflect*. Our main argument here is that we want to avoid the assumption that news values are simply 'inherent' in events or simply reflected or embedded in discourse. Rather, we emphasize that discourse has an important role to play in constituting and reinforcing news values. We then continued with a brief discussion of how we conceptualize each news value in this book. This is necessary, since—as the discussion has brought out—news values can be defined in radically different ways by researchers, even if similar labels are used. Before we can consider how semiotic resources may construct news values (in chapters 4 and 5), we must therefore first introduce our approach to these values. Since there has also been a proliferation of terms that researchers have invented for news values (at times without any justification), we have taken care here not to introduce any new labels and to justify why we selected a particular label. Finally, this chapter discussed the relevant concepts of preferred reading and target audience and illustrated DNVA with a brief example analysis. As has become apparent, DNVA focuses on the meaning potential in the semiotic resources used in texts and on how these construct newsworthiness with respect to different news values. Our example analysis has already indicated some of the linguistic and visual resources that have the potential to establish news values (such as names, titles, visual representation of recognizable public figures), but in order to undertake systematic empirical studies of English-language news (chapters 6 to 8), it is necessary to fully describe the inventory of these semiotic resources. This is the purpose of the next two chapters, which introduce an analytical framework for linguistic analysis (chapter 4) and visual analysis (chapter 5).

Notes

1. Non-linguistic research does not usually discuss the relationship between language and news values, with only some exceptions. Conboy (2006), who is interested in critical linguistic approaches to journalism studies, notes that tabloid news values are 'expressed' (15) in language, and that particular linguistic strategies are 'an essential part of' (15) or 'suit' (16) their news values. A particular word such as *Brits/Britons* can also be regarded as 'a strong indicator of newsworthiness' (Conboy 2006: 49) or 'act as a distillation of the news value of the actor to the newspaper in question' (Conboy 2007: 15). Language in the news 'fits into these existing frameworks [news values]' (Conboy 2007: 30) but also functions to 'emphasize and give value' (Conboy 2007: 35) to news stories; words can 'highlight' (Conboy 2007: 37) news value. In contrast, Hartley (1982: 79) talks about how reporting 'exploits' news values.
2. Media coverage can be seen as a socially determined construction of reality in which the 'objectivity of news is based on a social consensus among journalists' (Staab 1990: 428; see also Hartley 1982; Price and Tewksbury 1997; Bignell 2002).
3. In fact, journalists have historically put a lot of effort into denying the interpretative role of images as well as denying any form of agency in image capture. As Zelizer (1995: 146) notes in relation to journalists of the 1930s and 1940s:

    > One way of deflating the authority of the image was by constructing a vision of photography as primarily a medium of record. In appealing to the denotative function of the photograph, bypassing its potentially threatening connotative role, journalists were able to fasten photography within its position as an adjunct, rather than primary, tool of documentation.

4. An interesting outcome of the media storm surrounding this image is that as soon as the boy's situation was clarified (he was not lost, alone, or far from his family), the media lost interest in his plight. As Karl Schembri, regional manager for Save the Children in Jordan stated: 'the moment poor little Marwan no longer fits our media narrative he becomes just one of thousands again' (cited in Pollard 2014).
5. Bednarek (2016a) provides an in-depth comparison, focusing only on linguists. We exclude aspects that we conceptualize as news writing objectives or news selection factors.
6. Bell's definition of Consonance also incorporates the second approach, namely, adherence to the typical patterns in which events proceed—conformity to people's mental scripts.
7. 'Cause' is not generally recognized as a news value. As we will see in chapters 4 and 5, the representation of cause–effect relations through semiotic devices may at times construct Impact (e.g. in image sequences or sentences such as *Cyclone causes extensive damage*), but this is not necessarily the case. In fact, the absence of causality in the news is often lamented,

for example, environmental news lacking scientific descriptions of what might have caused an event or war reporting lacking background on the causes of the war. As Bender et al. (2009: 133) note, journalists have difficulty 'reporting complex phenomena, such as the causes and consequences of crime, poverty, inflation, unemployment and racial discrimination'. Causality is also very complex, despite its relevance: 'Although—or perhaps because—the relation between cause and effect is fundamental in the human experience, it is extremely difficult to establish a standard description or classification of types of cause–effect relations' (Marshman et al. 2008: 145). In our view, a general analysis of causality goes beyond the analysis of newsworthiness per se, but it is clearly a worthwhile endeavour to analyse how causality is realized semiotically and how/when/with what functions it occurs in the news.

8. At times, 'ordinary' persons become famous by virtue of being in the news again and again, which may pose a problem for classification of references to such news actors (see Bednarek 2016b).

9. In fact, there are at least four options on how to deal with newness. The first choice is to create newness as a distinct news value, different to both Timeliness and Unexpectedness. This choice is dispreferred because of added complexity and Ockham's razor. The second choice would be to classify newness as an aspect of both Timeliness and Unexpectedness, which is not ideal because such double-classification would be messy. The third choice is to include newness under Unexpectedness—our previous conceptualization, following researchers such as Bell who state that 'closely related to unexpectedness is *novelty*' (Bell 1995: 320). The fourth choice is to include newness under Timeliness, which is our preferred conceptualization now, for reasons explained here.

10. In contrast, conventionalized or 'dead' metaphors are common in the news and may construct news values such as Negativity and Superlativeness (see chapter 4).

11. Other labels include obliging (Kitis and Milapides 1996: 585) and compliant reader (Martin and White 2005: 62).

12. The last clause (*sources told The Post*) is not analysed as constructing news value, since the vague label *sources* does not indicate status, and since self-references (*The Post*) confer value to the news organization. It is important to make a distinction between creating value in the news event (constructing it as newsworthy) and creating value for the news organization (Bednarek and Caple 2015).

Part II

ANALYTICAL FRAMEWORKS

4

Language and news values

4.1 Introduction

As has become apparent in chapters 2 and 3, our aim is to systematically analyse how semiotic resources construct newsworthiness in texts. It is therefore necessary to first identify potential resources for doing so. This chapter discusses linguistic resources, while the next chapter tackles visual resources. We need to emphasize that this chapter does not provide a general introduction to the unique linguistic characteristics of news discourse, as we have done so elsewhere (Bednarek and Caple 2012a: 84–110).

As mentioned in chapter 2, most linguistic research does not offer in-depth theories about the relationship between language and news values. Nor do linguists comprehensively catalogue or categorize the different resources that can be used to construe news values. Nevertheless, we are indebted to them for commenting on particular resources. This holds especially for Bell (1991, 1995), who ties several devices to newsworthiness: the lexicon, evaluation, superlatives, labels/titles, deixis, and time adverbials. Bell (1991) has also inspired other linguists, in particular in relation to evaluation: Bell suggests that the function of evaluation is 'to make the contents of the story sound *as X as possible*, where X is big, recent, important, unusual, new; in a word—newsworthy' (Bell 1991: 152, italics in original). Ben-Aaron (2005: 714–715) proposes that evaluations of appropriateness (tradition), enthusiasm, and impressiveness 'encode' news values in anniversary stories. In her comparison of UK 'popular' and 'quality' newspapers, Bednarek (2006a) associates negative evaluations with the news value of Negativity, evaluations of importance or significance with Eliteness or Impact, evaluations of unexpectedness with the news value of Unexpectedness, and evaluations of expectedness with Consonance. Mahlberg and O'Donnell (2008), Mahlberg (2009), and O'Donnell et al. (2012) also draw on Bell (1991) in their corpus linguistic studies, identifying 'evaluative patterns' that 'interpret[ ] the subject matter of the article as newsworthy' (Mahlberg and O'Donnell 2008: 15) as well as lexical patterns that occur in the co-text of meanings that build newsworthiness (Mahlberg 2009). In sum, previous research has shown that it is clearly possible to identify linguistic resources that establish news values in news stories, including but not limited to evaluation. In section 4.2, we outline these resources systematically.

4.2 Towards an inventory of linguistic resources

In developing an inventory of linguistic resources, we followed three basic procedures: First, linguistic research on news discourse was surveyed, in particular studies that mention news values. Second, linguistic research and reference books were consulted for linguistic devices that might have the potential to construct a certain news value. For instance, research into evaluation aids in identifying how values may be expressed linguistically. Third, linguistic resources were identified inductively through analysing news stories. While some of these date from 2010 to 2011 and were originally analysed for our 2012 book, we examined additional stories in 2014 and 2015. Most of these stories are either print, online, or mobile news stories published in the 'News' or 'World News' sections or in news bulletins/podcasts. One subset of newly analysed data consists of 99 headlines and opening paragraphs from online news items (see chapter 8). Consequently, the inventory applies to prototypical news stories rather than say, business or sports news or letters to the editor, obituaries, current affairs programs, and so on. Because of time constraints, relatively few broadcast news bulletins could be examined, and further resources may thus need to be added in relation to video and audio. In particular, we have not explored sound features such as stress/emphasis, intonation, prosody, and so on (see van Leeuwen 1984, 1992, 1999).[1] Since there are clear linguistic differences between different types of news and between different semiotic modes, further research will need to be undertaken into such areas.

Resources were allocated to a specific news value according to their meaning potential, typical usage, and function. For instance, devices which function to intensify are categorized under Superlativeness; lexis that carries negative meaning is categorized under Negativity; and the present progressive and present perfect are categorized under Timeliness, as they can be used to indicate that an activity is ongoing or has recently been completed.

Two caveats before we continue: First, there is no closed list of resources— news values can be constructed by an open-ended range of lexical or grammatical resources (word forms, lemmas, phrases, whole clauses, or sentences). Although we can include some typical examples in our inventory, it is not possible to list all possible devices that analysts may encounter. Second, this framework should not be taken as an automatic checklist. Close attention needs to be paid to the meaning potential of the linguistic resource as used in the news story, as well as to the target audience and time/place of publication.

Table 4.1 **Linguistic resources for establishing news values**

News value	Linguistic resources and examples
Consonance ([stereo]typical)	References to stereotypical attributes or preconceptions; assessments of expectedness/typicality (*typical, famed for*); similarity with past (*yet another, once again*); explicit references to general knowledge/traditions, and so on (*well-known*)
Eliteness (of high status or fame)	Various status markers, including role labels (*Professor Roger Stone, experts*); status-indicating adjectives (*the prestigious Man Booker prize, top diplomats*); recognized names (*Hillary Clinton*); descriptions of achievement/fame (*were selling millions of records a year*); use by news actors/sources of specialized/technical terminology, high-status accent or sociolect (esp. in broadcast news)
Impact (having significant effects or consequences)	Assessments of significance (*momentous, historic, crucial*); representation of actual or non-actual significant/relevant consequences, including abstract, material or mental effects (*note that will stun the world, Australia could be left with no policy, leaving scenes of destruction*)
Negativity/Positivity (negative/positive)	References to negative/positive emotion and attitude (*distraught, condemn, joy, celebrate*); negative/positive evaluative language (*terrible, brilliant*); negative/positive lexis (*conflict, damage, death, success, win, help*); descriptions of negative (e.g. norm-breaking) or positive behaviour (*has broken his promise, unveiled a cabinet with an equal number of men and women*)
Personalization (having a personal/human face)	References to 'ordinary' people, their emotions, experiences (*Charissa Benjamin and her Serbian husband, 'It was pretty bloody scary', But one of his victims sobbed, Deborah said afterwards: 'My sentence has only just begun'*); use by news actors/sources of 'everyday' spoken language, accent, sociolect (esp. in broadcast news)
Proximity (geographically or culturally near)	Explicit references to place or nationality near the target community (*Australia, Canberra woman*); references to the nation/community via deictics, generic place references, adjectives (*here, the nation's capital, home-grown*); inclusive first person plural pronouns (*our nation's leaders*); use by news actors/sources of (geographical) accent/dialect (esp. in broadcast news); cultural references (*haka, prom*)

(*continued*)

Table 4.1 **Continued**

News value	Linguistic resources and examples
Superlativeness (of high intensity/ large scope)	Intensifiers (*severe, dramatically*); quantifiers (*thousands, huge*); intensified lexis (*panic, smash*); metaphor and simile (*a tsunami of crime, like a World War II battle*); comparison (*the largest drug ring in Detroit history*); repetition (*building after building flattened*); lexis of growth (*a growing list of, scaling up efforts*); only/just/alone/already + time/distance or related lexis (*only hours after*)
Timeliness (recent, ongoing, about to happen, new, current, seasonal)	Temporal references (*today, yesterday's, within days, now*); present and present perfect (*it is testing our emergency resources*); implicit time references through lexis (*continues, ongoing, have begun to*); reference to current trends, seasonality, change/newness (*its 'word of the year' for 2015, keep their homes well heated this winter, change from GLBT to LGTB, after fresh revelations, for the first time, a new role as*)
Unexpectedness (unexpected)	Evaluations of unexpectedness (*different, astonishing, strange*), references to surprise/expectations (*shock at North Cottesloe quiz night, people just really can't believe it*); comparisons that indicate unusuality (*the first time since 1958*); references to unusual happenings (*British man survives 15-storey plummet*)

Keeping this in mind, table 4.1 and table A4.1 (appendix) summarize the linguistic resources, building on our previous research, while additional examples are provided at the discursive news values analysis (DNVA) website (http://www.newsvaluesanalysis.com). Some linguists may be interested in Bednarek's (2014) outline which uses systemic functional linguistic terms. In the following sections, we discuss these news values in alphabetical order without implied priority, including multiple examples from authentic English-language news stories. For ease of reading, shorter examples are not attributed, and we mostly focus on one news value per example, even if other news values are present. Where examples *are* attributed, the following abbreviations are used to identify their origin: O (online/website), P (print/newspaper), A (app [Ipad]), PO (podcast).

4.2.1 CONSONANCE

> The event is discursively constructed as (stereo)typical (limited here to news actors, social groups, organizations, or countries/nations)

There is a wide range of potential resources for constructing stereotypes, and it is not possible to give an exhaustive list here.[2] We are looking for any reference to stereotypical attributes, typically negative or positive (Baker et al. 2008: 282). For instance, it has been argued that a phrase such as *asylum run as criminal racket* 'confirm[s] the widespread prejudice against immigrants as people taking advantage of supposed British goodwill and generosity' (Bignell 2002: 93). Collocation analysis can be helpful: Goatly (2002: 15) notes how the collocates of *cholera—outbreak, epidemic, Latin America*—provide stereotyping. Bednarek and Caple (2012a) mention the potential association of countries or nationalities with widely held stereotypes through word combinations (e.g. *Britain + rain, stiff upper lip*).

These and similar constructions of stereotypes do not explicitly say 'this behaviour is (stereo)typical of these people/nations'. Explicit representations can, however, occur through:

- Lexis that expresses an assessment that a news actor's behaviour is in line with past behaviour (i.e. typical or to be expected): *a man* [former Italian Prime Minister Berlusconi] *whose love of luxury and lavish parties is **legendary**, his **notorious** wandering gaze, . . . as dire Diaz* [Australian political candidate] *campaign ends in **typical** style*;
- Comparisons with the past that establish the current happening as expected: *as the US came to terms with **yet another** mass shooting . . . , America is **once again** torn apart by race and police power, it's **not the first time that** FIFA has been accused of bribery*;
- Explicit references to general knowledge, assumptions, customs, traditions, expectations, or stereotypes: *In keeping with the Germans' **well-known** love of beer, Tokyo is a city **well-known for** its work ethic*.

While such resources do occur in the news, more commonly events are assessed as **un**expected or **a**typical (Bednarek 2006a: 98), constructing Unexpectedness rather than Consonance. Further, where these explicit references do occur, they often construct Negativity as well as Consonance (e.g. *yet another mass shooting*). In example (1), it might be argued that typical expectations (in the context of multiple past discoveries of paedophilia) are constructed about Britain through the phrases in **bold** font. This construction of Consonance is contrasted with constructions of difference in terms of extent, arguably construing Unexpectedness and Superlativeness (underlined). Negativity is established throughout.

(1)

When the full extent of child abuse in the South Yorkshire town of Rotherham was revealed this week, **a sigh of recognition** was quickly followed by a sharp gasp of horror.

There was **an element of 'not again', of yet another chapter of** Britain's still-unfolding paedophile nightmare. <u>But this was something else. It had sheer scale, scope, the length and the breadth of the evil unfolded, the malice of the perpetrators and the close-eyed, back-turned, passive immorality of those who let it continue.</u> (*The Sydney Morning Herald* [P], 30–31 August 2014)

4.2.2 ELITENESS

> The event (including the people, countries, or institutions involved) is discursively constructed as of high status or fame

Several linguists have noted that descriptions, titles, or labels can claim status for named and unnamed news actors and sources (Bell 1991; Jucker 1996; Ungerer 1997; Bednarek 2006a; Stenvall 2008a). Jucker (1996: 376) suggests that 'the journalist faces the twin tasks of naming the news actors . . . and of justifying their newsworthiness by describing or labeling them'.

We have used the term 'role label' to refer to such descriptions (Bednarek and Caple 2012a: 52) and continue to do so here. Only *high-status* role labels construct Eliteness. Frequently, this is achieved through either titles or quasi-titles (descriptive noun phrases in apposition), and includes a proper noun identifying the news actor: *U.S. District Court Judge Scott Skavdahl, Professor Roger Stone, Snohomish county fire district 21 chief, celebrity chef Jamie Oliver, Abba legend Björn Ulvaeus*. Bell (2011) argues that appositional noun phrases where determiners are deleted (*Finance Minister Bill English*) '[elevate] the name to equal status with the description. It treats the description as a pseudo-title on a par with 'President' or 'professor'. . . . It thus embodies a person's entitlement to be newsworthy' (Bell 2011: 181). A more complex example for a role label, without determiner deletion, is: *the foreign office minister responsible for the Middle East Baroness Symon* (from Montgomery 2007: 149, who calls such labels *identifiers*). Role labels may also occur in predications: *Matthew Atha is the director of the Independent Drug Monitoring Unit* (from Montgomery 2007: 171). They are not always accompanied by a name, either when sources remain anonymous (Stenvall 2008a) or when they are named elsewhere in the text: *community leaders, experts, business groups, the supermarket giants, US researchers, authorities, officials, the US military, the Scandinavian superstars*.

Eliteness may further be constructed through status-indicating premodifiers and may be boosted through superlative adjectives: *the city's **top** cop, a **key** federal government minister, **long-term** industry observers, **well-placed** government sources, the **prestigious** Man Booker prize, a **high-profile** arrest, the **VIP** event, **celebrity** bad boy, the **famed** Japanese author Yukio Mishima, Swedish **super** group Abba, **the most senior** black officer*, . . . *bears **one of the most famous** surnames in the country, **one of the best known** artists, **some of the biggest** names in U.S. television, the country's **highest** office*.

The use of proper nouns alone may also construe Eliteness, when the named entity is recognizable to the target audience and of high status: *Abba, Barack Obama, the Olympics, the Oscars, Harvard University, the World Health Organisation*. Thus, certain names carry authority, fame, or prestige for particular communities.[3] In addition, the status, authority, or expertise of news actors can simply be described, for example, in relation to fame, achievements, or expertise: *Ronnie Barker **of the Two Ronnies fame**, a Roman Catholic nun in the US **who founded a global media empire**, two people who **were selling millions of records a year**,* [source] **knows Iraq well**, *The Norwegian entertainer was also **very popular in neighbouring countries**, **dominated** the 1970s disco scene*.

Finally, the status of sources can be established through what they say—for example, the use of specialized or technical terms may indicate status as expert. This goes beyond just using particular terminology, however. Eliteness may be constructed through high-status accent and sociolect, constructing the speaker as a voice of the 'elite'. Fairclough (1998: 159) provides an example from a British news and current affairs program, where, he argues, 'authoritativeness . . . has another basis . . .: his marked upper-middle-class accent and the easy authority of his delivery'. This resource, then, is particularly relevant for broadcast news.

Different resources for Eliteness may be combined. In example (2), labels (*world leaders*), a proper noun (*Nelson Mandela*), and premodifying adjective (*powerful*) co-occur to establish the Eliteness of news actors participating in the reported event:

(2)

World leaders were last night making preparations to converge in unprecedented numbers on South Africa for **Nelson Mandela**'s funeral, likely to be one of the biggest global gatherings of **powerful people** in modern history. (*The Guardian* [P], 7 December 2013)

4.2.3 IMPACT

> The event is discursively constructed as having significant effects or consequences (not limited to impact on the target audience)

The news value of Impact can be established through linguistic resources that assess the significance of the happening (Bednarek 2006a: 104), such as *milestone, momentous, historic,* or *crucial*. Such evaluations construct the event as high in impact (e.g. setting precedence). Such lexis constitutes typical journalese (van Dijk 1988a: 81). Thus, the 2014 referendum in Scotland was referred to in news reports as *the historic referendum* or *historic opportunity*.

Constructions of causality also have the potential to construct Impact, but only if they construct the news event as having significant effects or consequences. Kemmer and Verhagen (2002: 451) note that 'the grammar of causative constructions has inspired what is probably one of the most extensive literatures in modern

Linguistics'. We therefore cannot provide a comprehensive overview of resources here, but they include causal connectives, causal verbs, and causal coherence relations. Lexis can mark cause–effect relations through verbs such as *produce, give rise to, result in, lead to, increase, turn, render, remove, destroy* (Haupt 2014: 252) or *cause, affect, trigger* (Goatly 2002: 17). Other parts of speech may also signal cause–effect relations (e.g. *outcome, impact, effect*). Cotter (1999: 173) notes that a phrase such as *a determinant of future telecommunications jobs* enhances news value and 'situates the news for maximum importance'.

Finally, grammatical structure can be a resource for establishing Impact. Indeed, many researchers have shown that different grammatical structures work to construct the impact of an event in different ways, although the focus of such research has typically been on agency and responsibility (e.g. Lukin et al. 2004; Hart 2011, 2014a, b). One exception is Goatly (2002) who associates transitivity with newsworthiness in terms of impact.

Importantly, the represented consequences can be non-actual/hypothetical.[4] Jaworski et al. (2004: 184) note that 'prediction, speculation and discussion of future implications of past and current events' increase news value. In example (3), the non-actual (*proposed*) price rises by an Australian telecommunications company (Telstra) are constructed as potentially having a big impact on the national community. In example (4), a non-actual military event (*threatening to*) is established as having significant consequences for the 'West', whereas in example (5), a non-actual military event (*if*) is seen to result in major human suffering in the region.

(3)

Millions of Australian homes and businesses could be hit with bigger phone and internet bills under proposed price rises that Telstra says are being pushed on it by the national broadband network. (*The Sydney Morning Herald* [P], 11–12 October 2014)

(4)

Islamic State militants are threatening to overrun a key province in western Iraq in what **would be a major victory for the jihadists and an embarrassing setback for the United States-led coalition targeting the group**. (*The Sydney Morning Herald* [P], 11–12 October 2014)

(5)

A U.N. envoy has said **thousands of people may be massacred** if Kobani falls to the Islamist terror group. (*NBC News* [A], 18 October 2014)

These examples also illustrate the combination of Impact with Negativity, which is a general tendency in the news. For example, the representation of nature frequently features descriptions of negative effects (Goatly 2002; Bednarek and Caple 2010), which has ideological implications, as it characterizes nature as hostile to humanity (Goatly 2002: 19). Example (6) shows how flooding in Mozambique is constructed as newsworthy in terms of its direct negative impact on people and infrastructure:

(6)

Rita Almeida, spokeswoman for the Disaster Management Office, said Wednesday **nearly 20,000 people have been displaced by flooding.** . . . **Flooding has also damaged one of main roads connecting the north and south of the country**. (*Fox News* [O] /AP, 14 January 2015)

However, Impact—whether actual or non-actual—can also be positive, as in example (7):

(7)

It's a cross between LinkedIn and Tinder and **it's set to make business travel a little less lonely**. (*The Sydney Morning Herald* [P], 11–12 October 2014)

Finally, Impact can be relatively neutral, for instance, in references to significant uptake by news and social media (*Alabama cop buys shoplifting grandmother a dozen eggs and video* ***goes viral***).

There are additional means by which Impact might be constructed on occasion, such as causal connectives and rhetorical structure, but we will not provide further illustration here. Rather, we suggest analysts work with a general category of REPRESENTATION OF ACTUAL OR NON-ACTUAL SIGNIFICANT/RELEVANT CONSEQUENCES, INCLUDING ABSTRACT, MATERIAL, OR MENTAL EFFECTS. When coding text, researchers will need to decide if both implicit and explicit constructions are coded as Impact and at what point consequences are classified as 'significant' (see further Bednarek 2016b).

4.2.4 NEGATIVITY (AND POSITIVITY)

The event is discursively constructed as negative (positive)

A news event is constructed as negative through reference to emotions that are culturally considered as negative (Bednarek 2006a: 179: Bednarek 2008: 194). Examples include: ***concerns*** *about even remote chances of Ebola exposure,* ***fury*** *as primary head takes week off in term to fly to Caribbean, a move that has* ***outraged*** *local politicians, amid signs of* ***panic***. Closely associated are references to negative attitude (e.g. *condemn, criticise*). While there are many ways of referring to news actors' emotions (Ungerer 1997; Martin and White 2005; Bednarek 2006a, 2008; Stenvall 2008b), two key devices include the labelling of emotions and the description of what is clearly emotional behaviour:

- Labelling emotions, including via fixed figurative expressions: *distraught, worried, shock, disappointment, anger, fear, hatred, upset, alienate, antagonize, offend, breaking our hearts*;
- Describing emotional behaviour: *'There are others inside' she **screamed**, Deborah **sobbed** to the jury.*

In broadcast news, non-verbal negative affect can be expressed rather than described, in instances when we hear news actors shouting, crying, sniffing, or see them distraught (Pounds 2012).

Negativity can further be constructed through negative evaluative language. We define this here as language that expresses the writer's negative opinion,[5] for instance, *the **malice** of the perpetrators and the **close-eyed, back-turned, passive immorality** of those who let it continue*. Negative category labels for news actors—what Davis and Walton (1983: 40) call 'heavily value-laden labels'—also fall under this category (*the nut, the loon, the radical animal rights group Sea Shepherd, extremist group Boko Haram*). The negative opinion may come directly from the institutional voice (the news organization) or from a quoted source, although the latter tends to be the norm in news stories from the 'quality' press (White 1997: 107):

- News organization: [UK Labour leader] *Corbyn's **shambolic** reshuffle . . .* (*The Daily Mail* [O], 6 January 2016).
- Source: *Robin Clarke adds: 'Only this week,* [Australian Prime Minister] *Tony Abbott was saying how wonderful coal is for humanity. **Dickhead***'. (*The Sydney Morning Herald* [P], 18–19 October 2014)

Negativity can also be construed by what we call negative lexis. This encompasses what others have labelled 'disaster' (Ungerer 1997: 315), 'crime' (Davis and Walton 1983: 40), or 'conflict' vocabulary (Bell 1991: 177; Baker et al. 2013b: 261). We prefer the more general *negative lexis* as a cover term for expressions that describe negative events or news actors, but that do not explicitly inform the audience that the writer disapproves of them. This includes the use of labels for socially defined negative behaviour, for instance, *offence* or *crime*, which can be regarded as originating in 'the institutionalised legal process' (White 1998: 131). To give some examples, we would include any reference to the different dimensions or types of Negativity that we introduced in chapter 3, ranging from lexis referring to environmental disasters (*floods, bushfires*), accidents (*a fatal drunken-driving accident*), damage and detriments (*deluged the town, linked with brain abnormalities*), crime and terrorism (*incest and child abuse, terrorist attack*), injury, disease, and death (*bodies, taken to hospital with injuries*) to references to chaos and confusion (*turmoil, chaos*), political crises (*corruption inquiry*), opposition and division (*pro-/anti-, controversial*),[6] war and conflict (*the Ukraine conflict, violent clashes*), and other human suffering (*malnutrition, ordeal*). The use of verbs like *threaten* and *warn* to establish conflict or danger is also common in the news (Bednarek 2006a: 137).

In addition, we can include descriptions of a negative state-of-affairs or action, such as the breaking of promises (8), ill-treatment of bodies (9), or delayed admissions of uncomfortable truths (10). The use of 'overt' or 'covert' negation (Hermerén 1986: 66) may indicate lack or failure (11–13).

(8)

[Australian] Treasurer Joe Hockey **has broken his promise** to balance the budget by 2019 (*The Sydney Morning Herald* [P], 13–14 December 2014)

(9)

Paramedics **dumped a dead body next to rubbish bins** because they wanted to finish work on time. (*The Daily Mail* [O], 18 October 2014)

(10)

Burger King **has tonight admitted** that it has been selling burgers and Whoppers containing horsemeat **despite two weeks of denials**. (*The Daily Mail* [O], 1 February 2013]

(11)

Some journalists arriving in Sochi [host of 2014 Winter Olympics] are describing appalling conditions in the housing there, where **only** six of nine media hotels are ready for guests. (*The Washington Post* [O], 4 February 2014)

(12)

Sea Shepherd activists held, **fail to** halt dolphin slaughter (*The Australian* [O]/AFP, 1 September 2014)

(13)

Hospitals **don't** have enough beds, and there **aren't** enough ambulances (*USA Today* [O], 3 September 2014)

There is no clear dividing line between negative evaluative language and negative lexis, and sometimes the same word can be used in different constructions where one is more evaluative and the other less so. Examples include the words *fail* and *failure* (Bednarek 2006b: 142) and compounds with *terror*, whose meaning varies significantly (Montgomery 2009), alongside contested words such as *chaos, crisis, scandal, challenge, problem, catastrophe, disaster, danger, tragedy*. Many researchers discuss 'the degrees of neutrality or bias which are inscribed in the choice of words which reporters make' (Carter 1988: 8), but evaluative meaning is a very complex linguistic category which involves various clines (Bednarek 2006a: 46–48). Different names, criteria, and tests for distinguishing between evaluative and non-evaluative language, or more explicit and more implicit evaluative language have been suggested (e.g. Gruber 1993; White 2004; Martin and White 2005; Bednarek 2006a, 2009; Hunston 2011). It is beyond the scope of this section to review these, but whichever criteria are adopted it is good practice to specify them and to apply them consistently. Example (14) shows the construction of a non-actual (future) event as newsworthy in terms of Negativity, with manifold references to controversy and clashes of opinion (*front, face, controversial, row, critics*) and negative emotion (*disquiet*), but no evaluative language (following our own conceptualization).

(14)

British Speaker to **front** MPs over **controversial** recommendation of Australian Carol Mills as clerk of the House

British parliamentary Speaker John Bercow will **face** MPs on Monday for the first time since a **row** erupted over his recommended candidate for the post of clerk of the House amid growing **disquiet** among **critics** of the choice of Australian Carol Mills. (*The Age* [O], 1 September 2014)

The counterpart of Negativity is Positivity, which can arguably be constructed with similar linguistic devices, with opposite valence: reference to positive emotion/attitude (e.g. *joy, celebrate*), positive evaluative language and labels (e.g. *the brilliant astrophysicist, natural intellectuals*), positive lexis (e.g. *success, win, help*), and descriptions of positive behaviour (e.g. *unveiled a cabinet with an equal number of men and women*). In certain contexts 'negative' events such as a death can be constructed as positive, as happened in some newspapers in the reporting on Osama bin Laden's killing (Bednarek and Caple 2012a: 48–49). The negativity of words such as KILL can also be co-textually reversed, for instance, in research news: *Researchers might have found the Holy Grail in the war against cancer, a miracle drug that has* **killed** *every kind of cancer tumor it has come in contact with.*

4.2.5 PERSONALIZATION

> The event is discursively constructed as having a personal or 'human' face (involving non-elite actors, including eyewitnesses)

Fowler (1991: 92) and Bignell (2002: 91) suggest that personalization strategies include the use of names, ages, job descriptions, residence, personal appearance, and gender roles, which heighten the 'concreteness of individual reference'

(Fowler 1991: 92). Others propose that first names and anaphoric pronouns (Ledin 1996) and vox populi quotes (ben-Aaron 2005: 715) create Personalization. Building on such research, we distinguish the following key resources.[7]

References to 'ordinary' people, either by name (e.g. *Jean Baxter*) or non-elite role label (e.g. *a mother of five*): Identifying a person by name is arguably more personalizing than referring to individuals only by a category label. Similarly, references to one individual (e.g. *a 31-year-old plumber*) are more personalizing than references to groups of individuals (e.g. *relatives, fans*). We would in fact consider generic or group references, functionalization and genericization (van Leeuwen 2008) as constructing only weak Personalization (if at all).

Descriptions of emotional experience—negative and positive—can also establish Personalization, when it is attributed to ordinary news actors. This includes labels and descriptions, as already described above:

- Labelling emotions: *Gilles Boulanger . . . told French TV channel Itele: '. . . It was really **upsetting**. . . .'*, *Mike's **devastated** owner*;
- Describing emotional behaviour: *Reeva Steenkamp's cousin **sobbed** while testifying . . .*, *she **screamed** at him to stop.*

As these examples show, emotional reference can occur in the voice of the institution or in the voice of the ordinary person (i.e. as reported speech). The use of reported speech and thought also constructs Personalization more generally, if it represents the views, experiences, or thoughts of ordinary news actors. We include both direct and indirect speech/thought, although we consider direct quotes as more personalizing, since audience members access the voice of the individual directly. However, news discourse often intertwines direct and indirect speech/thought when reporting contributions by individuals, as in example (15) (indirect speech underlined).

(15)
Another man, who lives near the offices, first mistook the sounds of gunshots for celebrations of Chinese new year. However, he said he soon realised the gravity of the situation when he saw 'police officers playing hide-and-seek with the criminals'. (*BBC* [O], 7 January 2015)

Both direct and indirect representations can thus render an issue personal in incorporating the thoughts, emotions, or experiences of non-elite news actors. In broadcast news, audience members can **hear** people speaking. Features such as accent and sociolect may then contribute to Personalization, when these features are associated with non-eliteness. Lexico-grammatical features associated with 'everyday' spoken language may further increase Personalization, reinforcing the notion that audiences are hearing from 'ordinary', non-elite people.

We noted in chapter 3 that we exclude elite news actors from Personalization. However, at times such news actors do speak on behalf of or talk about ordinary citizens' experience. An example of this is New Zealand Prime Minister John Key's comment on the 2011 Christchurch earthquake: *'People are just sitting on the side of the road, their heads in their hands. This is a community that is absolutely in agony.'* Here Key's quote arguably construes some degree of Personalization by referring to the community's emotional reactions. Further, elite news actors and journalists may at times speak as eyewitnesses rather than in their professional capacity, as in example (16).

(16)

Wandrille Lanos, a TV reporter who works across the road, was one of the first people to enter the Charlie Hebdo office after the attack. 'As we progressed into the office, we saw that the number of casualties was very high. There was a lot of people dead on the floor, and there was blood everywhere', he told the BBC. **Another journalist** from the same office described seeing 'bodies on the ground, rivers of blood and people seriously injured', in an interview with Itele. (*BBC* [O], 7 January 2015)

As with all DNVA, context is important to determine the construction of Personalization through reported speech and thought. It is not advisable to simply count any and all occurrences of reported speech/thought as constructing Personalization.

Different types of Personalization include instances where the whole story is about one individual's experience. Example (17), a widely shared news story in 2014, is about one specific couple, rather than using Personalization to concretize an abstract issue.

(17)

Woman, married 72 years, dies 6 hours after husband

Harry and Anna Norman were not outwardly romantic during their 72 years of marriage but held hands on their last night together.

Anna Norman, 97, a strong, independent woman who never complained and was not considered seriously ill, died six hours after her husband Oct. 2, according to officials at Arlington Care Centre nursing home here. (*The Advocate/USA Today* [A], 17 October 2014)

But often an abstract issue or process may be personalized through reference to ordinary individuals, as in example (18), the first paragraph of a UK news story about the bedroom tax.

(18)

Memories—happy and sad—suffuse the modest, neatly decorated three-bedroom house that Jean Baxter has lived in for 35 years. Treasured pictures of her children and grandchildren smile down from the walls. From her bedroom window, she can see the gravestone of her baby daughter, who died soon after being after being [*sic*] born, not long after they moved in. (*The Guardian* [P], 21 September 2013)

This is a strategy to make 'the story of relevance to the reader by characterizing a larger issue in terms of a single individual' (Cotter 2011: 1894). Other types of Personalization include instances where the experiences, thoughts, and opinions of affected individuals are represented via 'vox pop' quotes.

4.2.6 PROXIMITY

> The event is discursively constructed as geographically or culturally near (in relation to the publication location/target audience

The most obvious way in which Proximity is established is through references to places which are near the target audience, for example, *a* **Baltimore county** *democrat* constructs Proximity for an audience in Baltimore or in the state of Maryland (United States). Grammatically, such spatial references are constructed through nominal groups/phrases (*Queensland's residents, Wellington researchers, Australia*) or prepositional phrases (*at Arlington National Cemetery*).

We also include references to people from the community or nationality of the target audience and to communities/nationalities that are (culturally) near them. It is well-known that in reporting on negative events in 'distant' countries reference will be made to casualties from one's own country or other 'western' countries—'us' not 'them'. Such reference does not construct the event as geographically near the audience, but rather establishes that someone from the audience's community is involved. Montgomery (2007: 9) mentions the example of reporting on the Indian Ocean Tsunami where UK news reporting focused first on the suffering of Westerners before shifting to the local population. This is an example of the ideological nature of news values. Here are four more recent examples:

- **Australian** nurse in Ebola scare (*The Sydney Morning Herald* [A], 9 October 2014)
- A 33-year-old **American** working in Liberia as a freelance cameraman for NCB News has been infected with Ebola ... (*The Sydney Morning Herald* [A], 3 October 2014)
- An avalanche and blizzard in Nepal's mountainous north have killed at least 12 people, including eight **foreign** trekkers, officials said Wednesday. (*Fox News* [O]/AP, 15 October 2014)

- He is the fifth **Western** victim to be beheaded on video by IS. (*The Mirror* [O], 17 November 2014)

While references to the target audience's own nationality establish the most Proximity (*Australian* in an Australian publication), references to other 'Western' nationalities (*American* in an Australian publication), and use of general labels (*foreign trekkers, Western victim*) may establish Proximity for a 'Western' audience in contrast to references to culturally and geographically distant communities.

Proximity may also be constructed via deictics (Bell 1991: 219; Ungerer 1997: 315), generic place references such as *the county/region* (Bednarek and Caple 2012a: 52; Johnstone and Mando 2015), and adjectives such as *local* or *home-grown* where it is clear that they concern the target audience: *the Ebola cases* **here**, *a potential attack on* **the nation's** *capital and* **the country's** *highest office,* **local** *veterans tell us their story,* **home-grown** *terror threat*.

Ungerer (1997: 315) notes that Proximity is expressed by personal pronouns/determiners, giving the example of *Our boys have won*. More precisely, we argue that **inclusive** first person plural pronouns/determiners establish Proximity, when the referent includes the target audience's community. In contrast, the use of **exclusive** first person plural pronouns does not establish Proximity: '**We**'*ve been told her prognosis is not good . . .*', *Mr Ansalone told the newspaper* (*Daily Mail* [O], 19 November 2014). It is either the news outlet itself who uses inclusive reference or a source—frequently a politician:

- *Red alert over the plot to attack* **our** *nation's leaders* (*The Daily Telegraph* [O], Australia, 19 September 2014)
- *President Barack Obama turned his focus Wednesday to the pocketbook issues that Americans consistently rank as a top concern, arguing that . . . the growing income gap is a 'defining challenge of* **our** *time'.* (*Huffington Post* [O]/AP, updated 12 May 2013)

In broadcast news, another resource for Proximity is a news actor's use of an accent or dialect that is similar to that of the target audience (geographically close). This is because audience members can hear people speaking in broadcast news, when direct quotes are used in news bulletins.

As Proximity encompasses cultural nearness, cultural references may also be seen as constructing this news value. This includes references to cultural heritage and to people, institutions/organizations, products, events, and so on that are famous in or tied to a particular culture (e.g. *D-day, prom, haka, Obamacare, gun carry rights, Calpol*). These establish cultural familiarity for readers but may be difficult to code (see Bednarek 2016b). In example (19), a British news report about French academics speaking at a French conference is established as newsworthy in terms of Proximity via national reference (*English*) and reference to historical figures and events that are culturally important to the British (*Shakespeare, the Battle of Agincourt, King Henry V*):

(19)

English heroes of Agincourt? They are just war criminals (say the French)

To **Shakespeare**, it was the moment a feckless youth turned into a great king, leading his army to victory against seemingly impossible odds.

But French academics have a very different view of **the Battle of Agincourt**—claiming that **English** soldiers acted like 'war criminals'.

They also accuse **King Henry V** of giving his permission for captives to be burnt to death and ordering his bodyguards to execute a noble who had surrendered. (*The Daily Mail* [O], 25 October 2008)

A specific strategy for creating Proximity is to transfer a distant event to a closer location, for instance, by outlining the potential danger for the target audience (Ungerer 1997: 321). This strategy is illustrated by example (20), where three different devices construe Proximity for an Australian target audience: the adjective *homegrown*, the deictic *here*, and the nationality reference *Australians*.

(20)

Homegrown terrorist Mohamed Elomar pledges to bring the horror **here**: **Australians** should be worried, he says (*The Daily Telegraph* [O], Australia, 31 July 2014)

As already noted, the above-mentioned linguistic devices do not automatically establish Proximity whenever they are used. For instance, it is common in TV news reports for deixis and demonstrative reference to refer to what is visible in the visuals or a news worker's in-field location (Montgomery 2005; Luginbühl 2009; Lukin 2010), both of which may be far away from the target audience. Place references can also be used in ways that are unrelated to Proximity (Potts et al. 2015).

4.2.7 SUPERLATIVENESS

> The event is discursively constructed as being of high intensity or large scope/scale

The large scope/scale or high intensity of an event can be established through the linguistic resources of intensification and quantification. Expressions of number, amount, quantity, size, degree, and intensity have been linked to both hyperbole (McCarthy and Carter 2004) and gradability (Martin and White 2005).[8] Researchers of news discourse have discussed the rhetorical functions of intensification/quantification, for example, in relation to drama or exaggeration (e.g. van Dijk 1988b: 278–280; Duguid 2010), but not always explicitly with reference to news values. In relation to newsworthiness, Bell (1991: 169) associates what he calls 'forceful words' such as *pressure, rebel, seize* with the 'push for the superlative'. White (1997: 128) states that intensification in the form of lexis or comparison is a distinctive feature of hard news stories where it occurs with high frequency in headlines/leads and represents 'the incident or statement selected for the reader's attention as inherently newsworthy'. Finally, Cotter (1999: 173) notes that a phrase such as *biggest strike since the historic Bell-system breakup* enhances news value and 'situates the news for maximum importance'.

4.2.7.1 Grammatical or lexical intensifiers

Intensifiers, whose function is to scale upwards and which focus on the high degree, force, or intensity of actions, attributes, events, and so on, tend to construct Superlativeness. We include degree adjectives and adverbs here (*full fury, complete destruction*) as well as journalese such as *sensational* and *dramatic*—the latter seem to simply ramp up the intensity of the event:

- A **sensational** corruption inquiry has concluded . . .
- [Russian] *President Vladimir Putin has **dramatically** raised the stakes in the Ukraine conflict*

Other intensifying adjectives and adverbs used in news stories include: *stark, ferocious, extreme, fierce, severe, completely, badly, dramatically, severely, deeply,* and *just*.[9]

We classify a linguistic resource as an intensifier, rather than quantifier, if it relates to force, degree, or intensity, rather than amount or size, although some instances may be borderline. Thus, we classify *extreme effects* as intensification, since it concerns the degree of the effects rather than their amount or size. In contrast, we classify phrases such as *a super precinct* as quantification, since *super* relates to the size of the entity. We also include instances where the force of phenomena is expressed through reference to time (*rapidly rising, continuous rain*), but note here that Martin and White (2005) classify the latter as quantification.

4.2.7.2 Quantifiers

Ungerer (1997: 315) links numerals and other quantity expressions to the news value of 'volume'. We include under the general heading of *quantifiers* various parts of speech which function to emphasize amount (e.g. **thousands of** *kilometres apart,* **many** *Iraqis, at* **all** *levels*) or size (e.g. **huge** *waves, a* **giant** *ash cloud, a tragedy of* **epic** *proportions*). We also include numerals here, whether precise (*a* *shock $356 million loss*) or vague (**hundreds** *who flew with an infected nurse*). Vague numbers are often premodified with phrases like *at least, up to, more than, as many as*, which may indicate lack of knowledge but also seem to construct the ensuing number as high: . . . **more than 200** *kidnapped schoolgirls*. It is worth noting that the label *quantifier* does not just relate to grammatical quantifiers; we also include lexicalized expressions that indicate or imply a large amount or size. For example, saying that malnutrition is *very common here* emphasizes the amount of people that are affected by malnutrition and referring to a *nationwide manhunt* emphasizes how large it was. Such 'quantification' may even happen on a morphological level, via suffixes such as *-fest* and *-athon*, which 'designate or allude to large-scale public events, and are thus ideal for use in news reporting' (Renouf 2007: 65).

4.2.7.3 Intensified lexis
Another way of expressing intensification is through high intensity lexis. This corresponds to what Martin and White (2005) call 'non-core' vocabulary items. Here, 'the scaling is conveyed as but one aspect of the meaning of a single term' (Martin and White 2005: 143), and the item contrasts with other semantically related items in intensity (e.g. *disquiet—startle—frighten—terrify*, 144). It is somewhat unclear if this derives from Carter's (1988) distinction between 'unmarked' (9) core and 'non-core evaluative vocabulary' (13), as Carter is not cited. Carter and McCarthy (2006: 443) label adjectives that 'express an extreme or maximum degree of a property' as *implicit superlatives*. Duguid (2010) provides some examples from journalistic discourse. Building on this research, we do regard 'implicit superlative' adjectives as intensified lexis but also include verbs (*stun, wreck, smash, sweep, hammer, ravage, devour, vandalize*), nouns (*panic, epidemic, dash, terror, blaze, rampage*), and adverbs (*desperately*), in addition to adjectives (*petrified, desperate*). Some of these implicit superlatives additionally construct non-literal meanings and could also be classified as metaphor. Thus, in *flames* **devoured** *much of their arid land*, *devour* is an intensified verb in both figurative and non-figurative usage, but is used metaphorically.

4.2.7.4 Metaphor and simile
Metaphors have attracted the attention of many researchers examining news discourse, often with a focus on 'flow', 'water', or 'disaster' metaphors used in the reporting on immigration or refugees (van Dijk 1988b; Charteris-Black 2006; Baker et al. 2008) or on 'war' metaphors used in the reporting on terrorism (Montgomery 2009) or protests (Hart 2014a, b). While these and other researchers do not necessarily tie metaphor to newsworthiness, they do associate metaphor with meanings of intensification (Ungerer 1997: 318) or dramatization (Semino 2008: 100). Bednarek has argued that metaphors are 'particularly important for establishing construals of "newsworthy" events' (Bednarek 2005: 24). Metaphors do not

incorporate explicit comparative devices such as *like, as if*, whereas similes do, but both are instances of figurative language that may construct Superlativeness:

- *a bruising four-year airline price **war*** [metaphor]
- *... country towns in northern NSW are **battling** a **tsunami** of crime* [metaphor]
- *New ice epidemic **swallowing** Sydney* [metaphor]
- *it was **like a World War II battle*** [simile]
- *a June wildfire that ... ripped through **as if the land had been doused with gasoline***. [simile]

4.2.7.5 Comparison

Bell (1995) talks about the 'common superlatives of the news' (1995: 306) with reference to superlative adjectives such as *biggest*. In fact, English news discourse has many resources for establishing that aspects of events were 'more intense', more 'dramatic', or of a larger scope than other events. This includes grammatical resources such as comparative (*worse*) and superlative (*most shocking*) adjectives, comparative clauses that upscale (e.g. *so strong that*), and the comparative item *more*. Frequently, the comparison is made stronger by the specific yardstick that is used for comparison, for instance, in relation to time (e.g. *higher than any time since ... , ... in living memory*) and space (*the country's most ...*). Comparison with other events may also be established through vocabulary such as *surpass, max out, unparalleled*. Some examples for these different comparative constructions are:

- *Foxtons' stock price was rising **faster than** the cost of a Mayfair penthouse*;
- *Brad Pitt and Angelina Jolie's wedding was **so secret** Jolie's father Jon Voight did not know it had taken place*;
- *... around 5,000 **more** suicides in Europe and North America*;
- *... **the largest** drug ring **in Detroit history***;
- *... one of the **world's most prolific** serial killers*;
- *... 2014 **surpassed** 2010 as the warmest year.*

4.2.7.6 Repetition and additional resources

Repetition of words can be used to intensify and may construct Superlativeness when it relates to the reported event. This resource does *not* appear to be common in news stories, but does occasionally occur, as in the following examples:

- *They were **petrified. Absolutely petrified***;
- *... with **building after building** flattened or punctured by shells.*

Two further resources can be identified which construct Superlativeness in news stories. The first is what we might term the lexis of growth: certain lexical items simply reference growth or a rise in intensity, scale, or scope:

- *The volume of email cloaked in encryption technology is **rising***;
- *. . . adding to a **growing** list of healthcare workers in West Africa hit by the epidemic;*
- *. . . after Britain's official threat level was **raised** to 'severe';*
- *President Vladimir Putin has dramatically **raised the stakes** in the Ukraine conflict;*
- *It had sheer **scale, scope, the length and the breadth** of the evil unfolded;*
- *. . . dramatically **scaling up** efforts;*
- *. . . the **mounting** effects of climate change.*

The second is the use of *only, just, alone,* or *already* with expressions relating to time or distance and related lexis, which seem to function to dramatize happenings, increasing their intensity and hence establishing Superlativeness (Bednarek 2006a: 94).[10]

- ***only** hours after;*
- ***just** 10 miles from;*
- *almost a hundred foreigners . . . were arrested **in one raid alone**;*
- ***Already this year** 64 clandestine ice labs have been busted and dismantled.*

Example (21) illustrates how the different resources can be combined in the construction of Superlativeness:

> (21)
> The Ebola outbreak **sweeping** through West Africa will get **significantly worse** before it subsides, infecting **as many as 20,000** people, the World Health Organisation said, even as US researchers announced plans to begin human safety trials next week **in a race** to develop an effective vaccine. (*The Sydney Morning Herald* [P]/*The Washington Post*, 29 August 2014)

This story contains intensified lexis (*sweeping*), an intensifier (*significantly*), a comparative adjective (*worse*), a vague high numeral (*as many as 20,000 people*), and metaphors (*sweeping, race*). Instances such as these, where it is the negative effects that are maximized, appear frequently in the news, combining Superlativeness with Negativity and Impact.

4.2.8 TIMELINESS

> The event is discursively constructed as timely in relation to the publication date: as new, recent, ongoing, about to happen, current, or seasonal

Since Timeliness is concerned with temporality, important resources for constructing this news value include temporal references (e.g. time adverbials) and tense and aspect, as noted by previous researchers on news discourse: Bell summarizes the different ways in which print and broadcast news stories can incorporate time (Bell 1995) and mentions different means by which 'temporal news value' (Bell 1995: 322) can be enhanced. Thus, he notes that news workers try 'to make events sound as immediate [more recent/imminent] as possible' (Bell 1995: 320), for example, through the use of time deictics such as (*later*) *today*, and the omission of time frames to make future occurrences seen imminent (Bell 1995: 321). When time is not specified, Bell says, recency is assumed (Bell 1995: 320). Other researchers have also argued that the present tense (Montgomery 2005; Lams 2011; Chovanec 2014), references to the recent past (Facchinetti 2012), references to future events and temporal organization (Jaworski et al. 2003, 2004) can convey timeliness in different types of news discourse (print, online, radio, television). While not mentioning newsworthiness, Luginbühl's (2009: 129) analysis of the American CBS evening news illustrates that 'the temporal importance of the reported event is stressed' by correspondents via simple present, present progressive, and time deixis (*now, today*).

Temporal references and tense/aspect are hence fairly uncontested means of construing Timeliness, but they only do so when they locate an event close to the time of publication (e.g. *today, currently, this week, last night, recent, yesterday's*). However, when they refer to events in the distant past or remote future, such temporality fulfils functions other than constructing Timeliness. Attention therefore needs to be paid to temporal reference, and a cut-off point must be set (see Bednarek 2016b). It is also clear that conventions govern the choice of tense; for instance, the unmarked choice for headlines is to use the present tense even when referring to past or future events. It could be argued that this convention has arisen precisely to construct newsworthiness, making the reported event seem 'timely' (immediate)—as one of several devices that headlines use to attract readers.

We further suggest that the simple present, the present progressive, and the present perfect may establish Timeliness even when their temporal reference is unclear. In relation to the present tense, Montgomery (2005: 242) distinguishes three different uses, but argues that the common use of the present tense works to:

> project the news as right up to date and dealing with 'the now'; it also helps to create a sense of referring to a present reality. The frequent selection of the present tense helps to collapse the distance between the event and its telling in such a way that it undermines chronology. (Montgomery 2005: 243)

The present progressive implies that events are occurring at the moment of speaking (*it **is testing** our emergency resources*), while Bell (1995: 320) talks about the 'immediacy of present perfect tense'. While this has a range of different uses (Ritz and Engel 2008), it often establishes that a past event is 'particularly relevant to the present state of affairs' (Ritz 2010: 3414) and one of its usages is to express 'the perfect of recent past or "hot news"' (Ritz 2010: 3402).

In addition, Timeliness can be constructed through lexis such as *have begun to, latest, ongoing,* or *still unfolding*.[11] Whatever the resource used, the closer the reference is to the time of publication, the more timely the constructed event (see chapter 3). Thus, adverbials such as *today* construct Timeliness to a higher degree than adverbials such as *earlier this week*. It is also important to emphasize that time references may not construct newsworthiness but rather clarify the temporal flow between happenings.

So far, we have only discussed Timeliness in terms of locating an event close to the time of publication (recency, immediacy, imminence), and this is where most linguistic research has taken place. But Timeliness also includes currency, seasonality, and newness. These three aspects can be constructed, respectively, by reference to current trends, seasonal happenings, and newness.

- References to current trends: . . . *'selfie'—the smartphone self-portrait—has been declared word of the year for 2013.*
- References to seasonal happenings: . . . *as Public Health England urged people to keep their homes well heated this winter* (published at the start of the cold season), *Crowds flocked to the beach* (published in summer), *The new owner of a Blue Mountain butchery is determined to avoid the pignominy [sic] of being hit by a second pre-Christmas ham heist* (published mid-December).
- References to newness, including changes, discoveries: *In an unexpected **development**, Bowser says **change** from GLBT to LGTB is 'in keeping with the mainstream vocabulary', Mint 1969 Shelby GT500 **found** under 40 years of dust, EU leaders pick **new** top diplomats.*

Regarding the last category, there may be an argument to be made that verbs such as *unveil, release, discover, uncover, expose* also construe newness, as they imply that the reported information is somehow new (Bednarek 2006a: 149). However, lexis relating to change, discovery, or findings can be used in many ways which differ in the extent to which they express 'newness' and establish Timeliness (see Bednarek 2016b). The adjectives *new* and *fresh* and the ordinal number *first* are also commonly used to convey different aspects of 'newness', such as the latest in a series of happenings (e.g. *after **fresh** revelations*), shifts/replacements (e.g. *EU leaders pick **new** top diplomats*), change in responsibilities (e.g. *will take up a **new** role as*) or 'being the first' (**For the first time**, *scientists have* . . . , *the **first** conclusive evidence*). 'Firstness' is sometimes connected to Impact, since one can 'make history' by being the first to do something. In the reporting on the 2014 US midterm elections, a number of publications emphasized newsworthiness in this way. For example, *USA Today* [A] ran a story with the headline *Political **firsts**: Who **made history** last night*, with the lead paragraph: *The midterm elections on Nov. 4 were **groundbreaking** for several reasons. Here are five **history-making firsts**.* This constructs the event as both high in impact (historic, setting new precedence) and as new (never having happened before). As we will see in section 4.2.9, 'firstness' is associated with the news value of Unexpectedness rather than Timeliness, when it constructs an event as rare—as not having happened in a long time (e.g. *the first time since 1958*). Again, it is important not to automate the analysis in a mechanical way, for example, searching for *first* and counting all instances as constructing newness without looking at meaning and usage.

4.2.9 UNEXPECTEDNESS

> The event is discursively constructed as unexpected, for example, as unusual, strange, rare

Unexpectedness can be constructed linguistically by evaluations of unexpectedness (Bednarek 2006a: 79), for example, as premodifiers: *a **shock** $356 million loss, one of the **strangest** scandals*. Other examples include adjectives such as *astonishing, unprecedented, different, rare, curious*, and adverbs such as *unusually, unexpectedly*, or *extraordinarily*. We are here dealing with language that expresses an assessment that aspects of the event are unexpected, strange, or unusual.

Example (22) demonstrates the use of adjectives in constructing an event as unexpected in the lead paragraph of a news story about police violence:

(22)

Two New York police officers have been charged with assaulting a teen-aged boy during his arrest in Brooklyn, prosecutors said on Wednesday, an **unusual** case in a city where prosecutions of police for excessive [sic] are **rare**. (*Huffington Post* [A]/Reuters, 11 May 2014)

Here, the attributive and predicative adjectives *unusual* and *rare* establish that the news event is newsworthy because it only rarely happens in New York.

In addition, it is possible to refer to people's expectations or surprise (example 23), which also implies that the event was unexpected: ***no one was expecting** it, people just really **can't believe it, shocking** footage*:[12]

(23)

Shock at North Cottesloe quiz night when the MC, a WA barrister, launched into 'sexist, racist, homophobic utterances' (*WA Today* [O], Australia, 1 September 2014)

Further, Unexpectedness may be construed through comparison with other events, usually in the past, when that comparison establishes the current happening as unusual in some way, for example, because it has not happened in a long time. These comparisons can be constructed via superlative adjectives or *first* with a historical yardstick (*Sydney's **wettest August in 16 years**, the **first time since 1958***) or other comparative constructions (*I've lived in Toowoomba for 20 years and I've never seen anything like that*). Such comparison may simultaneously up-scale the event, constructing Superlativeness. The ordinal number *first* only constructs Unexpectedness if it establishes the event as rare; in other usages it more likely establishes Timeliness (newness), as we have seen in section 4.2.8.

In addition to these rather explicit resources that construct Unexpectedness, we can find factual references to happenings that would be considered unusual by most, for example, because they fall outside established societal expectations, physical laws, statistical probability, or biological tendencies (see chapter 3). Authentic examples include:

- *a homeless man who returned a diamond engagement ring to a woman after it fell into his cup;*
- *Woman secretly filmed dancing at bus stop wins theatre role;*
- *German MPs considering a return to typewriters to combat spy activity;*
- *Queensland woman fights off kangaroo with backpack;*
- *Dead state legislator headed for re-election;*
- *Police in southern Sweden have filed a police report against themselves.*

Descriptions of situational irony can be included here, too (e.g. *A Kentucky pastor who starred in a reality show about snake-handling . . . has died—of a snakebite*). Finally, contrast, concession, and negation can be linked to unexpectedness (Bednarek 2006a: 48–49; White 2006: 235). Thus, the negation in example (24) works in connection with an evaluative adjective to construct the non-discovery of bodies as unexpected.

(24)

In an **unexpected** development **no** bodies have been found inside Christchurch's quake-ravaged cathedral (*Radio New Zealand* [PO], 5 March 2011)

However, while it is worth paying attention to lexical, grammatical, and pragmatic negation, contrast, and opposition (Jeffries 2010; M. Davies 2013), the co-text needs to be considered in determining whether such linguistic devices construct an event as unexpected. While the contrast expressed through *even though* in example (25) works to construct the main news event as unexpected, it does not do so in example (26).

(25)

An incumbent Democratic state representative in Washington was headed for a decisive re-election victory on Wednesday **even though** he died last week, results indicate. (*NBC News* [A]/*Reuters*, 6 November 2014)

(26)

The developments underscore growing tensions between the U.S. and Russia, **even though** Obama met briefly with Putin during the Asian summit this week in Beijing. (*Fox News* [O], 13 November 2014)

Ironically, by using contrast and negation (in **bold**) to construct a news actor as not conforming to expectation, news stories simultaneously invoke stereotypes (underlined), as in examples (27)-(29).

(27)

He bears <u>one of the most famous surnames in the country</u>, **but there are no** <u>super-models, glittering casinos, Hollywood party pals, superyachts or private jets</u> to give his family lineage away. Indeed, the only tell-tale sign of 52-year-old Francis Packer's privileged upbringing ...
(*The Sydney Morning Herald* [A], 29 August 2014)

(28)

Correspondent: <u>Tokyo is a city well-known for its work ethic</u> **but** for another day company owners told some employees to stay home to conserve electricity. (*NPR* [PO], 18 March 2011)

(29)

Nate Duivenvoorden looks like any other rugby-playing carpenter. The scruffy 30-year-old is built like a stocky half-back. On the pitch he goose-steps, tackles and passes like any other player. <u>But Mr Duivenvoorden isn't any other rugby-laying carpenter. Until the early 2000s, he was a female.</u>
(*The Sydney Morning Herald* [P], 30–31 August 2014)

Here, stereotypical expectations about the rich and famous and the well-known Australian family of the Packers (27), about the work ethic of Tokyo residents (28), and about rugby-players (29) are cited only to negate them, thereby constructing Unexpectedness. But by the very act of invoking these stereotypical expectations, such instances reinforce stereotypes and establish an ideology of what counts as 'normal' or 'typical'.

4.3 Combining news values and example analysis

In illustrating linguistic resources in section 4.2, we have mostly discussed one news value per example, for the sake of clarity ignoring other news values where present. However, it is generally the case that more than one news value is constructed in a news item:

(30)

The people of Scotland are to be offered a historic opportunity to devise a federal future for their country before next year's general election, it emerged on Saturday night, as a shock new poll gave the campaign for independence a narrow lead for the first time.

Amid signs of panic and recrimination among unionist ranks about the prospects of a yes vote on 18 September, the Observer has learned that a devolution announcement designed to halt the nationalist bandwagon is due to be made within days by the anti-independence camp.

(*The Guardian* [A], 7 September 2014)

In example (30), the event is constructed as newsworthy for a British audience by reference to Proximity (*Scotland, their country*), Timeliness (e.g. *on Saturday night, new poll, for the first time, within days*), Impact (*historic*), Unexpectedness (*shock*), Negativity (*panic, recrimination, anti-independence camp*), Superlativeness (*panic*), and Eliteness (*unionist ranks*). This is not an exception; rather news values are frequently combined in news items (see chapter 8).

News organizations may emphasize similar or different news values in reporting on the same event and they may employ similar or different linguistic resources in so doing. This will also be influenced by shared input material (e.g. from wire agencies). By way of illustration, table 4.2 offers a brief comparison of the lead paragraphs on the same event from Australian, UK, and US online news sites published on 19 November 2014.

Both the Australian and the US news site construct this event primarily in terms of it being high in negative impact (Negativity, Impact, Superlativeness) and both

Table 4.2 **Example analysis of three lead paragraphs**

Australia	United Kingdom	United States
In a city already deeply riven with sectarian tensions, the brutal slaughter of four rabbis in an ultra-Orthodox synagogue has pushed Jerusalem to the edge of what many fear could escalate into another Palestinian uprising. An Israeli police officer also died. (*The Sydney Morning Herald*)	Three Americans and one Briton were among four Jewish worshippers killed in an attack on a Jerusalem synagogue on Tuesday morning. (*The Guardian*)	The gruesome slaying of five Israelis at a synagogue early Tuesday left many residents of this city fearing that the worst is still to come, as Jerusalem descends deeper into a cycle of terror attacks and violent protest over its religious sites. (*The Washington Post*)

use not only negative lexis (*tensions, terror attacks, violent protests*) but also reference to negative emotions experienced by many (*what many fear, many . . . fearing*) and intensified evaluative language (*brutal slaughter, gruesome slaying, worst*). Both also emphasize the potentially high negative impact of the event (*has pushed to the edge, could escalate into another Palestinian uprising, the worst is still to come, left many . . . fearing, as Jerusalem descends deeper into a cycle of . . .*). The main difference between these two sites is that *The Sydney Morning Herald* also constructs 'weak' Eliteness (*police officer*) and that Timeliness is construed more explicitly in *The Washington Post* (*early Tuesday*), while it is implied in the *Herald*, for example, through use of the present perfect (*has pushed*). Both leads construct the event as highly newsworthy. In contrast, *The Guardian* emphasizes Proximity (*three Americans and one Briton*) and Timeliness (*on Tuesday morning*) and only uses negative lexis (*killed, attack*) to construct Negativity. It is much more restrained in its linguistic construal of newsworthiness. While a full discussion is beyond the scope of this chapter, this example illustrates that the framework for linguistic analysis introduced in this chapter can be used to investigate how an event is packaged as news at the micro level of linguistic construction, what news values are emphasized, rare, or absent, how news values are combined (see also example 30), and how this may be similar or different among news organizations. It can thus offer valuable insights into news as linguistic practice.

4.4 Summary

Cotter's suggestion that 'in order to fulfil their function (and ensure their survival), the media must maintain the interest and attention of their readers' (Cotter 1999: 167) remains true more than ever. The rhetoric of newsworthiness that we have outlined is *one* way of doing so but not the only one. Further, resources that construct newsworthiness may also have other functions, for instance, to establish a reported event's '"five W's and an H": who, when, where, what, how, why' (Bell 1991: 175) or to enhance truthfulness, credibility, and objectivity (van Dijk 1988a: 84–85, 93; 1988b: 114, 243).

Importantly, there is no one-to-one relationship between language and news value. On the one hand, the same linguistic device can be used to construe different news values. Thus, quasi-titles can either construct Eliteness (*Top scientist Christoph Gabor*) or Personalization (*Mother-of-two Ms Adkins*). On the other hand, the same linguistic device can simultaneously construct several news values, as when negative intensified lexis represents an event's effects (*towns **ravaged** by the Black Saturday bushfires*).

Nevertheless, the aim of this chapter was to introduce an inventory of linguistic resources which can be used as an analytical framework for the systematic analysis of news discourse. Chapters 6 and 8 will illustrate its application through empirical case studies. Adaptation and selective use is also possible—for instance, a researcher may be particularly interested in how Consonance is established in a range of news stories, focusing on just one news value. However, it is worth repeating the importance of context and co-text: the inventory of resources introduced in this chapter should not be mechanically and unreflectively applied in DNVA. It is not appropriate, for example, to count every single time reference as constructing Timeliness or every first person plural pronoun and every place reference as constructing Proximity or every reference to agency or causality as constructing Impact. Language is multifunctional and words vary their meaning according to co-text and context. Minimally, we need to at least take into account the target audience of the news outlet and its time and place of publication. Maximally, we need to carefully consider the likely meaning potential of each resource as used in the text (e.g. its preferred meaning). For example, does it construct the event as negative, unexpected, recent, near? This is not an exact science and there will be different interpretations of texts. To make analyses more accountable, it may be necessary to research the news outlet and its target audience. Some degree of familiarity with the target audience's culture is preferable. Replicability may be increased when analyses focus on explicit meanings or uncontested and obvious constructions of news values, such as conformity to widely known stereotypes (Consonance) or descriptions of events such as disaster, crime, and so on, which are likely to be perceived as negative by most of the social mainstream (Negativity).

Despite the care that is thus needed when applying DNVA, the distinctiveness and advantage of this approach lie in the systematic and explicit link that it establishes between semiotic resources and news values. This makes it possible to analyse news discourse in a manner that is justifiable and based on a linguistic framework rather than an intuitive response to text. It also makes it possible to tease out **how** news values are construed, allowing a focus on the micro-level of linguistic construction rather than the macro-lens provided by content or textual analysis. This chapter has introduced an inventory that can be used for such a linguistic analysis, which can be applied or adapted by other researchers in their own subsequent explorations. If semiotic devices other than language are to be included, DNVA also provides a framework for visual resources, which will be introduced in the next chapter.

Notes

1. Van Leeuwen (1984, 1992) ties intonation features in radio newsreader's announcements to factuality, impartiality, credibility, and authority—which are not news values in the sense in which we define them here. But van Leeuwen (1984, 1992) also notes that accented content words in newsreader's announcements tend to create a sense of importance, and van Leeuwen (1999: 64) ties newsreader speech to urgency, recency, and drama, in terms of rapid rhythm and dramatic staccato. Van Leeuwen (1984: 95) suggests that 'this great phonological hurry of the news serves ... to signify its immediacy and recency'. Bednarek (2016a) suggests that marked emphasis on words is used to stress news values which are established by grammatical and lexical resources.

2. Previously, we included conventionalized metaphors and story structure as resources for Consonance—the reason we no longer include these here is because our conceptualization of Consonance has since changed (see chapter 3).
3. References to news organizations are not regarded as establishing Eliteness because we do not generally treat them as news actors. In instances of 'second-hand hearsay' (Geis 1987: 86) or 'nested speech' (Garretson and Ädel 2008: 178) such as the following:

> **The Department of Homeland Security's Federal Protective Service** confirmed that the vehicles belong to them, reports <u>Fox News.</u> (*The Daily Mail* [O], 19 November 2014),

we only consider the role label in **bold** as construction of Eliteness, but not the name of the news institution (<u>underlined</u>). Such attributions have functions other than establishing newsworthiness.
4. Almeida (1992: 249) defines hypothetical situations as 'situations that are not claimed to be actualities', including future situations and non-actual present or past situations.
5. This definition differs from one that conceptualizes evaluative items as expressions that carry explicit negative or positive meaning regardless of context (White 2004: 231). Thus, there is no doubt that *crisis* carries a negative sense even if removed from context, and White (2004) therefore classifies it as 'attitudinal item'. But its use in phrases such as *Georgia coalition in crisis* does not necessarily signal whether the speaker/writer approves or disapproves of, celebrates or laments, this crisis. In this book, we prefer to treat such and similar occurrences as negative lexis, rather than evaluative language.
6. We restrict this to opposition between news actors, thus excluding interview styles which may construct adversarial relationships between news worker/interviewer and news actor/interviewee (Clayman 1990; Greatbatch 1998; Garces-Conejos Blitvitch 2009; Clayman 2010).
7. In line with our conceptualization of Personalization, strategies such as direct audience address are not included.
8. Martin and White (2005: 140–152) propose that relevant linguistic resources for what they call GRADUATION include grammatical or lexical intensifiers, grammatical or, rarer, lexical modifiers of number, mass, extent, infused intensification via lexis, metaphor and simile, comparatives and superlatives, and repetition. Although we do not adopt this framework here, we use this categorization as a springboard for our discussion of linguistic resources for Superlativeness in sections 4.2.7.1 and following, cautioning that not all devices and instances of GRADUATION construct Superlativeness. The system of Graduation only includes interpersonal meaning (e.g. excluding precise numbers) and it also includes hedges (such as *sort of*) and resources that down-scale (e.g. *slightly, somewhat*), which are not usually used to construct Superlativeness.
9. In examples like *the water was just roaring*. However, *just* can express a range of meanings, and not all of its usages are used to intensify (cf. the invented example: *he's just a child*).
10. Martin and White (2005: 151) do not discuss these specific expressions, but incorporate extent of time as a Graduation resource. However, this includes expressions such as *recent arrival*, which construct Timeliness rather than Superlativeness.
11. News organizations explicitly label particular news stories as 'breaking news' or use captions and other devices to indicate 'live-ness'—these are meta-comments on the news story or the time/location of news reporters. They package the 'story' as new and the reporters as being present. While these may ultimately contribute to the audience's perception that the **event** is new, we exclude such meta-comments from analysis because of their different scope.
12. Whether or not the use of *shock/shocking, surprise/surprising*, and so on in constructions such as *shock loss, came as a shock*, or *shocking footage* is classified as assessment of unexpectedness or a reference to surprise is a matter of debate (Bednarek 2009: 119–124).

5

Visuals and news values

5.1 Introduction

While the previous chapter introduced an inventory of linguistic resources that construct news values, this chapter focuses on visual resources. In developing our inventory of visual resources, we borrow concepts from seminal works in social semiotics (van Leeuwen 2005, 2006a, 2008, 2011; Kress and van Leeuwen 2006), as well as work by Caple (2013a) on compositional balance. There are also certain similarities between language and image that we are able to draw on. The repetition of words in a sentence (e.g. *car upon car*) and the repetition of depicted elements in an image frame (e.g. cars piled on top of each other), for example, work in similar ways to construct the news value of Superlativeness. Thus, we draw on parallels between verbal and visual resources where they exist. In principal, though, visual resources have been identified inductively through the analysis of news stories.

Although visuals in the news include more than just images (e.g. cartoons, interactives, graphics), the main focus of this chapter is on news photographs. These play a very important role in news storytelling; they are full partners in news relay, and deserve to be recognized as such (Caple 2013a, in press). Images have long been thought of as visual verification of an event (Dondis 1973; Zelizer 1998; Barnhurst and Nerone 2001; Bignell 2002). They can also be used to attract readers to a particular story, encourage readers to engage more deeply with an issue or they can even be the story themselves (Bednarek and Caple 2012a). They are also capable of constructing news values. News images usually co-occur with verbal text (captions, headlines, paragraphs) and readers (and researchers) engage with both the verbal and visual elements of a story together. However, since our key aim in this chapter is to introduce the visual resources that contribute to the construction of news values, we restrict our analysis to examining the image only, without relying on any attendant verbal text to clarify the meaning of an image. We deal with relationship between words and image in our multimodal analysis in chapter 8. For reasons of scope, we are unable to fully account for the role that other semiotic resources such as typography, layout, framing, and colour play in the construction of news values. We shall briefly introduce such resources, but we do not provide a complete inventory.

5.2 The relationship between images and news values

As discussed in chapter 2, there is little research that accounts for the relationship between images and news values. Images are most often discussed in terms of their availability and quality (Harcup and O'Neill 2001: 274)—although without explanation of what constitutes a 'good' photograph—and these criteria determine their selection as news. But such arguments lose impact when we consider broadcast news, which 'nearly always relies on pictures' (Montgomery 2005: 251), or when we consider the fact that the visual has taken centre stage in most forms of news packaging online and in apps. In other words, the mere availability/ubiquity of 'good' imagery tells us nothing of its contribution to the construction of newsworthiness.

Thus, we must look for other ways to assess the contribution of visuals to the construction of news values. We mentioned in chapter 2 that Hall (1973) argues that a newsworthy image should depict an elite person involved in an unexpected, dramatic, and recent event. The idea of looking to the image content, what it depicts—and to this we would add how it depicts that content—is one that aligns with our discursive perspective. We therefore suggest that the visual resources that constitute the news photograph clearly have the potential to contribute to the construction of news values.

We have already introduced the concepts and techniques we use for identifying these visual resources in chapter 1. To recap briefly here, in relation to the analysis of images, we have developed two strands of analysis: of the actual image **content** (what is depicted in the image frame); and of the **capture** of the image (how the information is arranged in the image frame [composition] and how camera settings impact on image content [technical affordances]). As also mentioned, some of the terms we introduced in chapter 1 are borrowed from Kress and van Leeuwen (2006), although we use them somewhat differently and always with a focus on news values. We re-emphasize here that we are not applying Kress and van Leeuwen's (2006) framework in terms of a metafunctional analysis of images, using the systems of choices that they propose.[1] We explain this further using the concept of camera angle as an example.

If we were applying Kress and van Leeuwen (2006: 140), the meaning relation between vertical camera angle and the viewer of an image would be one of 'power'. A high camera angle means that 'the represented participant [the person photographed] is seen from the point of view of power' (140), that is, the viewer is in the more powerful position. A low camera angle shifts the power to the image participants and gives them 'symbolic power over us [the viewer]' (140). These are what Kress and van Leeuwen (2006) would call interactive meanings. In discursive news values analysis (DNVA), we examine the potential role played by the camera angle in the construction of news values rather than interactive meanings between represented participant and viewer. Camera angle is therefore examined in terms of its role in contributing to the reinforcement of news values constructed in image content. For example, an image of the current US President Barack Obama taken from a low camera angle will **reinforce** his elite status. In contrast, an image of an ordinary citizen taken from a low angle will not construct Eliteness—the citizen is not turned into an 'elite news actor' (i.e. a news actor with high societal status) simply by showing her in a position of symbolic power over the viewer. In other words, the news value of Eliteness is not the same as the symbolic 'power' granted to either represented participants or viewers of an image.

This example also reminds us of the importance of being sensitive to the ways in which image content and image capture interact. To give another example in relation to moving images: camera shake/movement will result in poor quality, jerky, and mainly blurred images and would suggest that footage was captured under extreme conditions. These extreme conditions, however, could be caused by a number of factors: The image content could show the cameraperson surrounded by revellers at a party (e.g. New Year's Eve celebrations). By immersing herself with the camera among the people, she may be attempting to capture the sense of the celebrations, the party atmosphere, thus allowing herself and the camera to be jostled. In a different context, such extreme conditions could involve explosions, gunfire, or clashes between authorities and protesters, where the camera movement may be caused by the cameraperson needing to take cover or back out of a dangerous situation. This means that we cannot assume that blurred images (caused by camera shake) automatically construct Negativity. Equally, we cannot say that the camera shake/blurred images construct Positivity or Negativity in these respective scenarios; rather, the camera shake **reinforces** the Positivity and Negativity already constructed in the content. However, when such movement is extreme or prolonged, resulting in excessive blurring of the image (especially in moving images), it is also likely to construct Superlativeness.

Likewise, the noise (graininess) in a still photograph can have multiple effects. It can add a painterly quality and may therefore enhance the Aesthetic Appeal of an image, or it could dramatize the content of the image, by reducing the brightness, contrast, and colour differentiation in the image, and thus would work to reinforce any Negativity already constructed in the image. The example front-page analysis given in section 5.5 at the end of this chapter further discusses the effect of noise in reinforcing the construction of newsworthiness.

In sum, we do not expect researchers to treat each of these analytical strands (content, composition, and technical affordances) as separate entities, as it may be difficult at times to separate them out and they clearly influence each other. Our discussion in this section also reinforces a point that we have made in chapter 4: namely that this framework should not be taken as an automatic checklist or rule book, but should be sensitive to the context. It is also not a closed list of resources.

The remainder of this chapter will systematically introduce visual resources for the construal of news values, building on previous research (Bednarek and Caple 2012a; Caple 2013a). As in chapter 4, we present the news values in alphabetical order without implied priority and mostly focus on one news value per example, even if additional news values are present. Table A5.1 (appendix) provides a summary of all resources.

5.3 Visual resources in images

5.3.1 AESTHETIC APPEAL

> The event is discursively constructed as beautiful

Potential resources for constructing Aesthetic Appeal can be found in both image content and capture. In relation to image content, people, places, and environmental phenomena that are culturally recognized for their natural beauty construct Aesthetic Appeal merely by being photographed in ways that show off their 'natural assets'. This is, however, a somewhat contentious claim, and researchers would need to argue on a case-by-case basis what makes for a beautiful person, place, or environmental phenomenon.

To give an example: arguments confirming the Aurora Borealis as an environmental phenomenon of outstanding beauty can be found in a number of sources. The travel media describe it as something that we 'marvel at' (*The Guardian*, UK), and travelling north to see and experience it is described as 'a trip of a lifetime' (*The Telegraph*, UK).[2] Further evidence can be found in the number of tourism companies that profit from encouraging people to see it. An image of the Aurora Borealis has been used in the story in figure 5.1. We would argue that this image constructs Aesthetic Appeal by photographing an environmental phenomenon that is culturally recognized as being beautiful. However, in this image, there are other factors that further contribute to the event's Aesthetic Appeal: in particular, the composition of the image. The dark, solid object (hut) in the bottom right-hand corner of the image is counterbalanced by the vast, open skies and coloured light fanning out from this point along the diagonal axis towards the upper left-hand side of the image. Such composition creates tension and stimulates the eye to resolve the potential imbalance between these differently weighted elements in the frame and it is in the resulting dynamic asymmetry that Aesthetic Appeal is constructed.[3]

Other technical aspects of image capture can also be used to enhance the Aesthetic Appeal of an image (see Caple 2013a: 115). These include manipulation of speed, ISO, and aperture for controlling light, contrast, sharpness, and noise. As noted in section 5.2, increased noise in an image can add a painterly quality to an image, which could, depending on the context, enhance the Aesthetic Appeal of an image.

Figure 5.1 The construction of Aesthetic Appeal in news imagery. (*CBC News* photo: Greg Johnson).

5.3.2 CONSONANCE

> The event is discursively constructed as (stereo)typical (limited here to news actors, social groups, organizations, or countries/nations)

Enduring stereotypes may be visually represented in the typical costumes, actions, and attributes that are widely considered to represent a particular nationality or group. Examples include the depiction of beer, breasts, and traditional costumes in reporting on Munich's *Oktoberfest* (Bednarek and Caple 2012a: 69) and visual representations of military parades in North Korea or China (Caple and Bednarek 2016: 446). To give a different example here, major sporting events attract fans who make their allegiance known through the clothes they wear and the regalia they carry. That they are 'fans' (i.e. passionate and committed to their team and not just supporters) may be further typified through their behaviour/actions: the joyful singing of team songs or well-known chants, and even through more permanent body art (image C in figure 5.2). Therefore, the enduring stereotype of the football *fan* is visually represented in the three images in figure 5.2, and as such these visual representations construct the news value of Consonance for the respective news audiences.

Figure 5.2 The typical behaviour, clothing, and regalia associated with 'football' (Example A: *The Australian* photo: Getty Images; Example B: *ABC News* photo: Scott Barbour/Getty Images; Example C: *The Telegraph* photo: Getty Images).

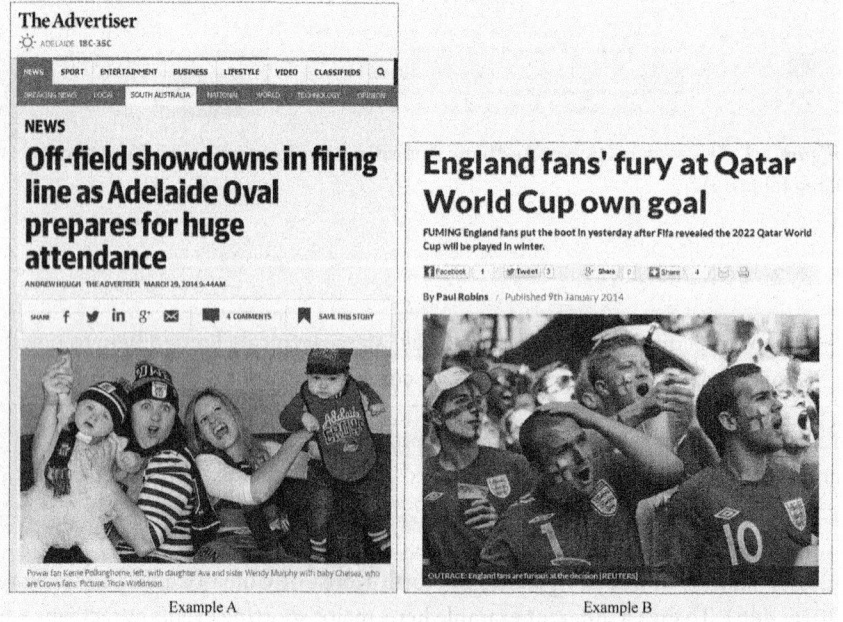

Figure 5.3 (Stereo)typical portrayals of Australian and British football fans (Example A: *The Advertiser* photo: Tricia Watkinson; Example B: *The Daily Star* photo: Reuters).

Further stereotypes that are particularly associated with football fans in Australia and the United Kingdom are also implied in the images in figure 5.2: those of integration (A and B) and separation (C). Australian Rules Football fans in Australia are widely known to mix with rival supporters at matches, they are gender-balanced, and are family-oriented. Indeed members of the same family will often support different teams. Thus, in figure 5.3, for the target Adelaide audience (*The Advertiser* is Adelaide's main newspaper) the rivalry depicted in the image in example A may be considered as typical, and thus constructing Consonance. An enduring stereotype concerning British football (soccer) fans, on the other hand, is that they are mostly male and known for their drinking culture, aggression, and sometimes violence towards rival fans. Thus, the image in example B in figure 5.3 might be considered to depict a more globally known stereotype, even though the target audience for this story is a British one.

5.3.3 ELITENESS

> The event (including but not limited to the people, countries, or institutions involved) is discursively constructed as of high status or fame

There are a number of ways in which visual resources contribute to the construction of Eliteness through both content and capture. As noted in chapter 3, we view Eliteness as scalar, and in terms of visual depictions of elite persons and places, some will be more universally known than others. Therefore, an image showing a widely known and easily recognizable key figure (e.g. a political leader like Angela Merkel) would construct Eliteness for a wide range of audiences (example A in figure 5.4). Images of other elites who are not as widely known—for example, individuals of high status in a particular community or with expertise in a particular field—would not necessarily construct Eliteness merely through depicting them. Other attributes or aspects of the setting might be included in the shot to place the person in an elite context (e.g. in a lab). Thus, the recognizability, the attributes, official regalia, activity sequence, and context in which the image participant is located may all contribute to the construction of a person's status.

Figure 5.4 Constructions of Eliteness (Example A: *CBC News* photo: Kai Pfaffenbach/ Reuters; Example B: *Huffington Post* photo: Wikimedia Commons; Example C: *The Sydney Morning Herald* photo: AP).

Example B in figure 5.4, for instance, is a photograph of a woman taken from an oblique angle where she is gazing at a point outside the image frame. There is nothing in this shot to suggest that this is a person of high status: her clothing, a woollen cardigan/jacket, looks like that which could be worn by anyone on any ordinary occasion and is not representative of the business attire that is culturally associated with elite professionals. Thus, the image content per se would not construct Eliteness for most audience members, unless they were familiar with bioethics research or Nobel Prize winners, since this is an image of the 2009 Nobel Laureate in Physiology or Medicine, Professor Elizabeth Blackburn. In example C in figure 5.4, however, Professor Blackburn is depicted in an elite setting, a medical laboratory, both using and surrounded by highly technical gadgetry. Here we could argue that even though most readers may still not recognize Professor Blackburn as a person of high status, the attributes, activity sequence, and the setting in which she is photographed all assist in constructing her as an elite professional.

To be clear, the wearing of a suit does not automatically construct an individual as being of high status. Ordinary citizens might also wear a suit when attending a court hearing, for example. Thus, we again caution that analysis should remain sensitive to context. However, there are some visual attributes such as elaborate costumes and associated regalia that quite clearly construct the high status of a person. Such attributes might be seen as the visual equivalent of the verbal 'role label'. These include gowns (and hood and cap)—as in figure 5.5—and certain

Figure 5.5 The construal of Eliteness through attributes associated with the represented participants (*BBC News* photo: Tarek Chowdhury).

Figure 5.6 The construction of Eliteness in relation to man-made structures (Example A: *Russia Today* photo: Stan Honda/AFP; Example B: *New York Times* photo: Guia Besana).

uniforms, as well as adornments on such clothing (e.g. medals, decorations, or stars/stripes) that may indicate official rank. Other regalia that may accompany a person (podium/signage, flag) or that may be carried by a person can also indicate high status. For example, the image in figure 5.5 also shows a mace and its bearer, the role of which is to indicate (in British and Australian societies) that the person following is of high office.

In certain contexts, the media scrum, when reporters and camera people crowd around a person with microphones and cameras, constructs Eliteness, as does the depiction of a person being flanked by officials (military, police, or bodyguards), through association with the need to be protected, perhaps from adoring fans. We can also look for other visual markers that may equate to verbal role labels, although these may also be rendered verbally in the image, for example, in signage: 'Police Headquarters' or the seal of the President of the United States.

The idea of a cline of recognizability may also be applied to the construction of Eliteness in man-made structures. A building like the UN headquarters in New York may be widely recognized by the target audience of many publications, and not just those in New York. It may be argued that English-speaking audiences of *RT* (*Russia Today*, launched in 2005), a relative newcomer to the international news scene with broadcasting studios in the United States and United Kingdom, would be familiar with the iconic UN buildings in New York, as depicted in example A in figure 5.6. For audience members not familiar with this building, its status would instead be established through the caption and headline texts that label it as the UN 'headquarters'. In the image in example B in figure 5.6, the number of people congregating outside the building as well as queuing to get into the building assists in constructing this place as important/of high status.

Finally, aspects of image capture, in particular composition/angle, may contribute to the construction of Eliteness. As stated in section 5.2, camera angle can be regarded as contributing to the reinforcement of news values constructed in image content, while the use of a low angle does not in and of itself construct Eliteness. Referring back to figure 5.6, the use of the low angle in photographing the UN headquarters in example A reinforces the Eliteness already constructed through the recognizability (renown/status) of the building. The danger in automatically associating low camera angle with the construction of Eliteness can be seen in the image in figure 5.7. This image is taken from a low angle, showing three female participants holding signs at a public gathering relating to the Chibok schoolgirls that were kidnapped by Boko Haram in northern Nigeria. The women are 'ordinary actors' (the use of 'our' in the signs they are holding suggest they could be the relatives of some of the missing girls), and we can analyse the construction of news values in this image as Personalization and Negativity. The women in the image are not turned into elite, high-status news actors by virtue of the fact that the image is composed from a low angle. Rather, the low angle reinforces the Negativity already

Figure 5.7 Low camera angle reinforcing Negativity (*USA Today* photo: Tony Karumba/AFP/Getty Images).

constructed in the image by making the verbal text on the posters (*bring back our girls*) the centre of the viewer's attention.

5.3.4 IMPACT

> The event is discursively constructed as having significant effects or consequences (not necessarily limited to impact on the target audience)

The default hard news imagery used by the news media has for centuries been the aftermath image, showing the serious negative effects of an event, such as scenes of destruction, images of victims and their caused emotions. The depiction of such content in images constructs the news value of Impact. The causes of an event were traditionally never captured by photographers and camera people, unless they were, by coincidence, caught up in the unfolding of an event or able to predict it (especially natural disasters like cyclones) and were willing to risk their own safety to capture it from start to finish. The digital revolution, however, has completely changed this. Most people now carry smartphones with inbuilt cameras and there has been a significant shift in the types of imagery now available, often via social media in the first instance and then repurposed by the news media in the second. Eyewitnesses or even victims themselves are beginning to capture and publish the unfolding of major disasters (e.g. the 2004 South Asian tsunami, the London bombings of 2005: see Liu et al. 2009; Allan 2013).[4]

One of the consequences of such changes in the production and availability of imagery is that constructions of causality are becoming increasingly possible. This means that an image showing the causes of a happening may now be shown alongside an image showing the effects. Relations of causality can be constructed through sequences of images in a TV news bulletin or in a picture gallery at a news website, or just by putting two images side by side. Such image sequences, however, have the potential to make the analysis of the news value Impact more difficult.

To give an example, the reporting of a cyclone event could make use of images depicting any of the following: the cyclone itself, which causes huge waves and storm surges, which in turn may cause major flooding, damage to property, and erosion of the coastline, which in turn may lead to the loss of habitat for flora and fauna, and even the loss of human and animal lives. A cause–effect chain of this nature depicted in images, especially when there are gaps in the image sequence, may lead the researcher to make claims for the construction of Impact beyond what is depicted in the image. We would argue that the satellite image of a cyclone approaching the Australian coast does not construct the news value of Impact (example A in figure 5.8). Rather, it constructs Negativity and Superlativeness, given the size (in relation to the map of Australia) and density of the depicted cyclone. In contrast, the second image (example B in figure 5.8) does construct Impact. Here we can see

Example A   Example B

Figure 5.8 Reporting of a tropical cyclone in the Australian news media (Example A: *Daily Telegraph* photo: Japan Meteorological Agency; Example B: *ABC News* photo: Lisa Clarke/ABC Open Capricornia).

fallen trees, blocked roads, and damage to power lines. Such content constitutes the typical depiction of the aftermath of a natural disaster.

5.3.5 NEGATIVITY (AND POSITIVITY)

> The event is discursively constructed as negative (positive)

Negativity is constructed through image content and may be reinforced through various camera techniques. Aftermath imagery which depicts the negative effects of an event establishes Negativity in addition to Impact. Images showing events or happenings that are negatively evaluated within a society also construct Negativity, for instance, activity sequences depicting norm-breaking behaviour or conflict, such as representations of violent clashes between groups of people—be they ordinary citizens or authority figures. Images showing people experiencing negative emotions construe Negativity (as in example A in figure 5.10), as do images showing people being arrested or handcuffed and behind bars (i.e. the visual depiction of suspected criminal activity). As already noted in section 4.2.4, moving images can show non-verbal negative emotions when we see news actors screaming, crying, or distraught.

We noted in section 5.3.3 that the depiction of a person being flanked by officials (military, police, or bodyguards) or facing a media scrum constructs the news value of Eliteness. However, we also suggest that in some situations, such depictions may rather construe Negativity. A well-known actor or sporting star may require bodyguards when out in public to protect them from being overwhelmed by adoring fans and the media. Such imagery would generally show the celebrity smiling, engaging in direct eye-contact with fans or with the cameras, and possibly reaching out to shake hands with fans or to sign autographs. In such an instance, the news value of Eliteness would be constructed through the combination of such elements. The positive facial expression (smiling, cheerful) would also construct Positivity.

Stars, however, sometimes fall or are brought down through crime, scandal, gossip, or innuendo. A public appearance by a high status individual in such circumstances would still see them surrounded by bodyguards or police or lawyers and a media scrum, but they would be more likely to avoid eye-contact with anyone, especially the cameras, and would be displaying serious or negative emotions or trying to hide or obscure their faces. In such images, the news value of Negativity would be construed (see Caple and Bednarek 2016: 450–451).

The two images in figure 5.9 illustrate how *setting* can also impact on the construction of news values. Both stories concern Oscar Pistorius, an elite athlete who has been both courted and haunted by the media. In the first image (example A), Pistorius fronts the media with a smile and direct eye-contact. He is dressed in the formal attire of academia and is standing on the steps of a very large entrance to a sandstone building, which resembles the type of buildings found at a prestigious university. The key news values constructed in this image would be Eliteness and Positivity. In the second image (example B), the elite athlete Oscar Pistorius fronts the media with a bowed head, and a serious expression. He is dressed in a suit and is standing in the dock of a courtroom. The key news values constructed in this image would be Negativity and Eliteness.

As noted above, camera technique may also be used to reinforce the construction of Negativity. Camera movement and blurring, especially in moving images, as well as poor image quality, both in terms of focus and noise, suggest that an image has been captured in difficult or unstable circumstances, and as such may reinforce the Negativity already constructed in the image content.

Figure 5.9 The media scrum and the construction of Eliteness, Positivity, and Negativity (Example A: *The Guardian* photo: Jeff J. Mitchell/Getty Images; Example B: *Daily Herald* photo: AP).

The counterpart of Negativity is Positivity. Whereas the negative experiences of news actors may be represented through negative facial expressions and negative gestures or postures, their positive experiences can be depicted visually in positive facial expressions, and gestures or postures that represent positive actions, feelings, or reactions, and would construct Positivity (as in example A in figure 5.9). The depiction of the positive effects of an event, or images showing events that are positively evaluated within a society (e.g. award ceremonies) would construct Positivity. In certain contexts, the Positivity constructed in an image may be counterbalanced by the Negativity constructed in the verbal text. The case studies in chapters 7 and 8 both exemplify this point in relation to the reporting of the death of news actors. It is common practice in journalism for a news report to include images of a person 'in life' (often smiling), while the verbal text reports their death.

5.3.6 PERSONALIZATION

> The event is discursively constructed as having a personal or 'human' face (involving non-elite actors, including eyewitnesses)

If the news value of Personalization is about giving a 'human' face to the news, then some might argue that any image depicting a human being constructs the news value of Personalization. However, as stated in chapter 3, we limit this news value to involving 'ordinary' people (e.g. eyewitnesses, survivors, or other private citizens), rather than elite news actors. We also exclude the generic depiction of people that is common in stock photography (see chapter 7 for further discussion of generic imagery).

In news photography, the depiction of large groups is less likely to construct Personalization than the singling out of an individual to represent that larger group. Like the news value of Eliteness, aspects of dress, attributes (non-elites are often photographed holding a bag), activity sequence, and setting can be used to assess whether the person depicted is an 'ordinary' actor. Ordinary people are usually photographed in the news media because something has happened to them. Therefore, Personalization is also constructed in their reactions, especially emotional responses (as shown in example A in figure 5.10).[5] In moving images/broadcast news stories, the inclusion of a series of vox pop images showing ordinary individuals speaking into a microphone can construct Personalization. The setting in which an individual is photographed or filmed may also point to their 'ordinariness'. In example B in figure 5.10, for example, the woman in the photograph is photographed standing in front of a bus stop on the street.

Aspects of image capture may also enhance the construction of Personalization in a photograph. In terms of composition, a close-up shot may help to focus on a person's emotional response (examples A and B in figure 5.10). Positioning an individual in a more salient position in relation to others in the image frame

Figure 5.10 The construction of Personalization in news imagery (Example A: *The Sydney Morning Herald* photo: not attributed; Example B: *The Sydney Morning Herald* photo: Maarten Holl/Fairfax, NZ; Example C: *Daily Telegraph* photo: Lyndon Mechelson).

(e.g. through foregrounding) may enhance the construction of Personalization, as that person comes to represent others in the same situation. This is true of example C in figure 5.10. In this photograph, a mother and her child are heavily foregrounded in the frame, making them much more salient than the hundreds of people in the background. They both gaze directly into the camera. By singling these two out from the many, through composition, Personalization is constructed.

5.3.7 PROXIMITY

> The event is discursively constructed as geographically or culturally near (in relation to the publication location/target audience)

The news value of Proximity can be constructed in image content by including landmarks, natural features, or cultural symbols that are widely recognized or known by the target audience. Thus, depictions of recognizable locations may establish that the event is taking place near the target audience. Flags are an example of cultural symbols that construct Proximity. Example A in figure 5.11 shows Pope Francis waving to crowds of people and while many different nations are represented by the many flags in the image, there is one flag that dominates the image: the Australian flag. Published on an Australian news website (*news.com.au*), the inclusion of the Australian flag in this image constructs cultural Proximity for an Australian reader.

Example B in figure 5.11 was also published in an Australian newspaper, *The Daily Telegraph*, and shows a lot of debris covering the footpath outside a building, and as such constructs Negativity and Impact. While the exact location of this shot is not clear, the image does construct Proximity for an Australian audience through the inclusion of the phone box and the Telstra signage on the phone box, which shows that the place depicted is somewhere in Australia. Verbal references to place included in the image (e.g. in signage) also construct Proximity.

Example A   Example B

Figure 5.11 The construction of Proximity in news imagery (Example A: *News.com.au* photo: Reuters; Example B: *Daily Telegraph* photo: Rick Rycroft/AP).

Example A   Example B

Figure 5.12 The construction of Superlativeness in news imagery (Example A: *BBC News* photo: AP; Example B: *The Sydney Morning Herald* photo: Nick Moir).

5.3.8 SUPERLATIVENESS

> The event is discursively constructed as being of high intensity or large scope/scale

The large scope/scale or high intensity of an event can be established through a number of visual resources, many of which have already been introduced in this chapter. These include the depiction of extreme emotions, like those expressed by the female participant in example A, figure 5.10; and the depiction of comparisons that emphasize scale/size, as in the size of the cyclone compared to the size of the Australian continent it is heading towards in example A, figure 5.8. Repetition of elements within the image frame also has the ability to construct Superlativeness: example A in figure 5.12 shows not just one or two flooded houses, but an entire suburb underwater, following Hurricane Katrina. The second example, B, in figure 5.12, not only shows 10 mosquitoes gathered together on the skin at the same time (thus also constructing Unexpectedness), but also magnifies them to a size and detail we do not usually see (much larger than life).

In terms of camera technique, camera movement, especially when excessive (and in moving images for a prolonged time period), is likely to construct Superlativeness, for example, by emphasizing the scale of danger or the intensity of celebrations (cf. the discussion in section 5.2). The use of a wide angle lens, or a macro-lens in the case in example B in figure 5.12, can also construct Superlativeness by exaggerating the size or scope of the elements depicted.

5.3.9 TIMELINESS

> The event is discursively constructed as timely in relation to the publication date: as new, recent, ongoing, about to happen, current, or seasonal

Like Proximity, it is very difficult for images to construe Timeliness, except when recognizable cultural and environmental conditions are depicted—for example, Christmas trees indicate Christmas, hot cross buns indicate Easter, cherry or Jacaranda blossom indicates springtime—or when there is verbal text in the images that indicates time in relation to the publication date. Example A in figure 5.13 is a good example of the latter, in that a signboard for the local newspaper, with a banner headline, has been included in the image. Not only does the signboard state the date, it also suggests that a cyclone event is imminent (through the use of the present tense in the headline). The inclusion of the sandbags in front of the shop windows further suggests preparation for an event that is about to happen.

Figure 5.13 The construction of Timeliness in news imagery (Example A: *Daily Telegraph* photo: Ian Hitchcock/Getty Images; Example B: *Motoring Research* photo: not attributed; Example C: *The Guardian* photo: Justin Sullivan/Getty Images).

Newness—when relating to an event experienced for the first time—can be depicted in images through the action of revealing. At the launch of a new car or technological gadget one might expect curtains to be drawn back, or a screen to be lifted, or a sheet to be lifted (e.g. in example B in figure 5.13), or a box to be opened.

124 THE DISCOURSE OF NEWS VALUES

At a launch event, the new item might be projected onto screens with the creators on hand to explain the new technology to an amassed audience of journalists and camera crews (example C, figure 5.13).

5.3.10 UNEXPECTEDNESS

> The event is discursively constructed as unexpected, for example, as unusual, strange, rare

If the construction of Unexpectedness involves the unusual, odd, rare, or weird, then images depicting unusual, odd, or weird happenings clearly construct the news value of Unexpectedness. Whole galleries of images claiming to show odd happenings can be found on most news websites. The front page of a gallery entitled 'Oddest photos of the year' from *The Washington Post* depicting a dog paragliding (example A in figure 5.14) exemplifies such construction of Unexpectedness. Images showing people with a shocked/surprised expression also construct Unexpectedness. Example B in figure 5.14 shows Australian hurdler Sally Pearson (then McLellan) clearly in shock as she realized that she had won a silver medal at the Beijing Olympics. Unexpectedness can also be constructed through comparison, especially when the elements depicted are vastly different to each other, as shown in example C in figure 5.14, in which the world's smallest dog, Chip, is photographed with his somewhat taller owner.

Figure 5.14 The construction of Unexpectedness in news imagery (Example A: *Washington Post* photo: Jim Urquhart/Reuters; Example B: *The Age* photo: not attributed; Example C: *Daily Mirror* photo: SWNS).

5.4 Other semiotic resources constructing news value

As already noted, it is beyond the scope of this book to give a full and just account of the ways in which other semiotic resources contribute to the construction of news values. We would encourage other researchers to investigate this area (adding a cross-cultural dimension might reveal some interesting differences—see chapter 9). We will only briefly discuss typography, framing, colour, and layout.

5.4.1 TYPOGRAPHY

There are a number of techniques concerning the typographic representation of words that have the potential to reinforce newsworthiness. Capitalization, for example, has the effect of drawing attention, especially when included in a string of words that are otherwise lower case, as in the following headlines from the *Daily Mail* (UK):

(1) *British man becomes first person to visit all 201 countries . . . WITHOUT using a plane*
(2) *Tears of a mother who lost her FOUR children to Chicago's gun crime epidemic*

In the first example, the use of capital letters reinforces the construction of Unexpectedness that is established through the lexico-grammar. The use of ellipsis (. . .) before the capitalized word also draws attention to what follows and thus reinforces the unusualness of this event. In the second example, the capitalized word FOUR emphasizes Superlativeness and Unexpectedness in the description of a mother whose four children died as a result of gun crime. Generally, it appears that typographic choices draw attention to and therefore reinforce the newsworthiness constructed through the words.

The use of screamer headlines (all capital letters) on the front pages of the popular press is highly conventionalized, as can be seen in the front pages of newspapers announcing the death of Osama bin Laden in 2011 (figure 5.15). It could be argued that the convention of using such headlines has arisen precisely to dramatize and intensify the happenings. Together with size on the page, underlining, and the use of the exclamation mark they may reinforce the construction of Superlativeness (see also Bednarek and Caple 2014).

Figure 5.15 The use of all caps in front-page headlines in the popular press.

5.4.2 FRAMING, COLOUR, AND LAYOUT

We have noted in previous research (Bednarek and Caple 2014) that the use of a black background framing a story, often placed behind words and/or photographs, may reinforce or intensify the construction of newsworthiness. In figure 5.16, the cover of the *New York Post* (US) on 14 November 2014 makes use of a completely black background, which seems to reinforce and intensify the Negativity constructed in the words on the page. Colours have particular cultural associations and 'symbolic qualities'—for black this includes negative associations with death, grieving, fear, and evil (van Leeuwen 2011: 2).

Again, we advise caution in assessing the role of frames and colour in the construction of newsworthiness. In online news galleries compiled by many news organizations, the default template is often a black frame. In such instances, the frame does not necessarily contribute to the construction of newsworthiness. It is in the breaks with routine, in marked choices, where typography, colour, and layout draw attention to themselves that we see a higher potential for constructing newsworthiness.

Other layout choices that have the potential to reinforce the construction of news values include when one photograph covers the entire front page of a newspaper,

Figure 5.16 Front-page news: 'PARIS TERROR', *New York Post*, 14 November 2014, p. 1.

often with the masthead, headline, and other text superimposed onto the image. When one story dominates the front page in this way, it suggests that the newspaper is giving the reported event its (and the reader's) undivided attention and may thereby imply that it is a highly negative event. This is the case in the front page in figure 5.17 in section 5.5. The layout here maximizes the construction of Negativity and Superlativeness established in the words and image through the intensified negative noun *terror* and visual depiction of extreme negative emotion. Once again, there is a need to be sensitive to context and convention/markedness when making assessments about layout. The popular press often only has one story on its front page to the extent that this, like the use of screamer headlines, may be highly conventionalized. It is rarer for the quality press (especially those that still publish in the broadsheet format) to reserve the whole of the front page for one story.

There is much work to be done in fleshing out the contribution of typography, framing, colour, and layout to the construction of newsworthiness, especially in the digital news environment where the most significant innovation in the packaging of news is taking place. It is also important to look at how visual and verbal resources are used together in a multimodal news story. For the purposes of illustration, we provide a brief example analysis of a front-page news story in the next section. Our case study in chapter 8 provides a more detailed exemplification of multimodal analysis with a focus on the semiotic modes of language and image.

5.5 Front-page news: An example analysis

This chapter has introduced various ways in which visual resources contribute to the construction of news values, while chapter 4 introduced verbal resources. The insights provided by DNVA of both visual and verbal semiotic resources and how they combine are probably best explained through a brief example analysis, although the three empirical case studies that follow this chapter will provide fuller demonstration. An examination of front-page news is a good way to demonstrate the range of resources that may be deployed in the construction of news values.

The newspaper front page has been referred to as 'a preferential media space where the journalistic selection and hierarchy are explicitly reflected' (López-Rabadán and Casero-Ripollés 2012: 470) or as it is referred to among industry professionals, 'the most valuable real estate in journalism' (Mnookin 2004: 101). Throughout the twentieth century, the front page has been the battlefield for newspaper sales and has thus found itself at the centre of redesign upon redesign (Utt and Pasternack 2006). Some news organizations even employ a 'front-page impact team' charged with finding ways to 'promote their news and analyze trends in single-copy sales' (Shaw 2006: 27). Key design shifts include the use of banner headlines, larger images (usually in colour), illustrations, varying column widths, and overlines (banners across the top of the page) and promotions pointing to stories inside the paper (Shaw 2006; Utt and

Pasternack 2006). Newspapers have also reduced the number of stories covered on the front page (Tiffen 2010), and with many newspapers moving from broadsheet to compact/tabloid size, this may at times result in one story dominating the whole of the front page—as discussed in section 5.4.2. Research examining the mix of front-page news items suggests that local news still dominates (Shaw 2006), while Bridges and Bridges (1997: 828) found that Timeliness, Prominence, and Proximity were the dominant news values in front pages in American newspapers in both 1986 and 1993.

The newspaper front page that we will examine here is shown in figure 5.17, and comes from *The West Australian*, a right-leaning daily tabloid newspaper that serves the metropolitan area of Perth in Western Australia. It is the only metropolitan newspaper in Australia that is not owned by either News Corp or Fairfax (Tiffen 2010), the two organizations that dominate Australian newspaper publishing. In 2011 *The West Australian* acquired Seven Media Group (a television company), becoming Seven West Media and Australia's largest diversified media business, with publishing interests in broadcast television, radio, newspapers, magazines, and online (Yahoo!7). *The West* (as it is known locally) claims a cross-platform readership of 1.8 million per month, with a 52% to 48% split between male and female readers, respectively. Average household income is $105,000 with 80% or more defined as 'professionals', 'big discretionary spenders', and 'people in top A social grade'.[6]

The front page in figure 5.17 was published on 16 December 2014 and concerns an attack that took place in Sydney, Australia, on 15 December 2014. To give a little context, a lone gunman entered a café in Sydney's central business district at approximately 9:45 a.m. on 15 December and took café employees and customers hostage. The stand-off between the gunman and authorities lasted for approximately 16 hours and ended at 2 a.m. on 16 December in a gun battle that resulted in the deaths of the gunman and two of the hostages. The moment captured in the image in figure 5.17 happened 7 hours into the incident at 5 p.m., when two hostages managed to escape from the café and run to safety. As can be seen in figure 5.17, this event received extensive coverage in *The West Australian* (a 'special edition' with 14 pages).

If we consider the layout of the front page first, the page is dominated by a single photograph, with the verbal text (headline, sub-headline, and image caption) superimposed onto the image. The merging of visual and verbal semiotic modes through such weak framing maximizes their connection (Kress and van Leeuwen 2006: 203–204), thus creating a single unit of information and suggesting that they be read together. The verbal text constructs Negativity through use of *terror hits our heart, hostage drama, gunman takes over*. Arguably, *terror* and *drama* are instances of intensified lexis and thus also establish Superlativeness. Proximity is construed through reference to an Australian location (*Central Sydney*) as well as through use of the inclusive first person plural possessive determiner *our*. It could further be argued that the phrase *terror hits our heart* construes this event as having an emotional impact not just on the Sydney population but the whole of Australia,

Figure 5.17 Front-page news: 'TERROR HITS OUR HEART', *The West Australian*, 16 December 2014, p. 1 (*The West Australian* photo: Rob Griffith/AP).

including *The West Australian* target audience who may be reading this headline over 3,000 kilometres away in Perth. That is, the event is constructed as having consequences for all Australians (news value of Impact).

Typographically, both headlines are capitalized with the main headline using a very large font size. Further, the image is of exceptionally large size and this one story dominates the front page, with a black frame at the bottom. This appears to be a marked choice—the average number of stories on the front page of *The West* in 2006 was 2.2 (Tiffen 2010: 355). Together, these configurations of visual resources seem to reinforce the Superlativeness, Negativity, and Impact that is established through the linguistic resources.

Turning to analysis of the image and looking first at the image content, we see two participants: an adult female and a uniformed person. We can be more precise in the labelling of these two image participants based on other attributes in the image. The woman works in hospitality, identifiable by the brown apron she is wearing (readers familiar with the Lindt Café in Australia would further identify her as a Lindt Café employee, given their distinctive black and brown uniforms). The authority figure in the image is a specialist police officer, identifiable as police by the badge on the sleeve of the uniform, and as a specialist by the full riot gear, helmet, and bulletproof vest, also visible in the image. The activity sequence (what they are doing in the moment captured in the image frame) could be described as running into the arms of safety (and away from danger): the position of the female participant's hair and right leg indicate that she is running and the grasping gestures of both participants in relation to each other suggest protection rather than aggression. The setting of this activity is unknown, since the two participants fill the frame, thus eliminating any identifiable background that could fix the participants to a particular location. We can also say something about the emotional state of the woman, since she is positioned in the image frame from a frontal angle and we engage directly with her and her extreme emotional response. This is further enhanced by the fact that the police officer is unidentifiable, since his back is turned to the camera and his face is completely obscured both by the woman and by the helmet he is wearing. From the facial expression, her furrowed brow, tightly closed eyes, downward turning mouth, we can say that the woman is experiencing extremely negative emotions. The configurations of visual resources in the image content thus far construct the following news values:

- Personalization: the image depicts a central protagonist (facing the camera) who is an ordinary individual;
- Eliteness: the image depicts a specialist police officer being called on to protect an individual;
- Negativity: the image depicts a dangerous situation (running to safety; presence of police wearing riot gear);
- Negativity and Superlativeness: the image depicts extreme negative emotion on the face of the woman facing the camera.

We can add to this analysis of the image content a further layer of analysis of the image capture (i.e. how the image has been constructed through both composition and technical affordances). We have already indicated the compositional features of this image, in that the image is composed from a frontal and eye-level angle to the female participant, as a mid-shot and filling the frame.[7] These compositional configurations make her and her emotional response the centre of attention and as such reinforce the construction of Personalization. The frontal angle also reinforces the audiences' direct engagement with the negative emotions of the female participant and as such emphasizes the construction of Negativity. Technically, the image has been captured using a high shutter speed, through a telephoto lens and in lower than average lighting conditions. The high shutter speed freezes the action, the telephoto lens condenses the action and eliminates the background (through blurring/minimizing the depth of field), and in so doing keeps the focus on the participants. The high shutter speed and high ISO result in a very grainy effect on the image, further dramatizing the action in the frame. The compositional and technical aspects of image captured in this example work to reinforce the construction of Personalization, Negativity, and Superlativeness.

In combination (table 5.1), the resources deployed on the front page of *The West Australian* construct this event as maximally negative for an individual ordinary citizen and by extension, the Australian nation—including the local West Australian target audience. The verbal text establishes Negativity, Superlativeness, Proximity, and Impact. Negativity, Superlativeness, and Impact are also reinforced in the layout, framing, and typography. The image additionally constructs Eliteness and Personalization, which combines with Superlativeness and Negativity, establishing this event as maximally negative for the woman photographed. Together, visual and verbal resources therefore complement each in other in construing this event as maximally negative both on an individual and a national level. It is noteworthy that Negativity and Superlativeness are established or reinforced through all resources, while it is the image that engages audiences emotionally by showing the plight of an ordinary individual (Personalization). This example analysis illustrates

Table 5.1 **News values in figure 5.17**

Semiotic resources	News values
Verbal	Negativity, Superlativeness, Proximity, Impact
Visual	
Through typography, layout, framing	Negativity, Superlativeness, Impact
In the news photograph	Personalization, Negativity, Superlativeness, Eliteness

that the frameworks introduced in this chapter and the previous can be applied to investigate how an event is multimodally packaged as news, what news values are emphasized, and how news values are combined. The role that different (verbal/visual) components play can also be examined, whether or not they reinforce, complement, or contradict each other, offering valuable insights into news as multimodal, rather than purely linguistic, practice. We provide further discussion of the contributions of different semiotic modes in chapter 8 and return to reporting on this incident in chapter 9.

5.6 Concluding remarks

In this chapter we have introduced an inventory of visual resources that can be used to construct or reinforce news values. We have repeatedly emphasized that this does not provide a checklist or rules for analysis. Rather, we see this as a framework that can guide the analysis of visual resources in news discourse, for example, with the help of table A5.1 in the appendix. As a reminder, we argue that close attention needs to be paid to the meaning potential of the semiotic resource as used in a news story, as well as to the target audience and time/place of publication.

The chapter focused primarily on news images, rather than on layout, typography, and so on, which are a subject for future research. Both this chapter and chapter 4 provided frameworks for subsequent discursive news values analysis—that is, they can be used as analytical tools in future research on news discourse. In the remainder of this book, we will provide empirical case studies that exemplify the application of these frameworks and further illustrate the insights that DNVA can provide into contemporary news discourse.

Notes

1. As a reminder, a metafunctional approach assumes that semiotic modes fulfil three major functions: an 'ideational' or 'representational' function (representing the world around and inside us); an 'interpersonal' or 'interactive' function (enacting social relations); and a 'textual' or 'presentational' function (presenting a coherent whole).
2. http://www.theguardian.com/travel/2015/oct/31/northern-lights-guide-aurora-borealis, accessed 28 January 2016; http://www.telegraph.co.uk/travel/activityandadventure/9496404/The-northern-lights-Trip-of-a-Lifetime.html, accessed 28 January 2016.
3. The case for Aesthetic Appeal as constructed through technical aspects of image composition and capture is based in the research that Caple (2013a) conducted on 1,000 news images published in a particular news story genre in the Australian metropolitan newspaper, *The Sydney Morning Herald*. In this study, Caple examined the images for their compositional configurations, using the Balance System (Caple 2013a: 97), and found that virtually all of the 1,000 news photographs were compositionally well-balanced. While the Balance System was created inductively out of the compositional analysis of these photographs, it closely reflects the discussion of the relation between the compositional configurations of

symmetry and dynamic asymmetry and aesthetic pleasure among professional photographers. For example, the use of the diagonal axis in composing an image is seen as a more challenging and dynamic way to arrange information in the image frame (Altengarten 2004; Präkel 2006), in that it creates tension and stimulates the eye to resolve the potential imbalance. The resulting asymmetry is highly valued in photography as an aesthetically pleasing form of composition (Altengarten 2004; Präkel 2006). Symmetry in an image is also seen to produce well-balanced images and patterns in images are also said to be aesthetically pleasing (Romano 2015). However, the aesthetic pleasure in viewing symmetrical images can be enhanced by interrupting the symmetry (Caple 2013a; Romano 2015). Again, the extra stimulation for the eye/brain to resolve any potential imbalance is what enhances the aesthetic value in the image (Caple 2013a: 116; see also figure 4.8 in Caple 2013a:177 for further example images).
4. While such imagery is able to offer a more complete picture of events as they unfold, they come with major ethical and moral issues, for example, in relation to their graphic content and potential invasion of privacy. Such issues are subject to intense academic scrutiny and key studies on the ethics of news images can be found in Chouliaraki and Blaagaard (2013) and associated articles in the 2013 special issue of *Visual Communication* 12(3).
5. Ordinary people are also more likely to be depicted as 'patient' (the done to) in an image, although this would need to be confirmed through large-scale analysis.
6. http://ratecard.thewest.com.au/circulation-a-readership, accessed 6 October 2015.
7. The terms 'compositional features/configurations' and 'composed' are here meant in a technical photographic sense and not in the metafunctional sense used by Kress and van Leeuwen (2006).

Part III

EMPIRICAL ANALYSIS

6

What is newsworthy about cyclists?

6.1 Introduction

This chapter presents the first of three empirical case studies where discursive news values analysis (DNVA) is applied. It focuses on language and applies corpus linguistic techniques and tools (as introduced in chapter 1). It aims to illustrate that DNVA can be used to examine whether particular topics or news actors are associated with specific news values, which may have ideological implications. The topic for this case study is cycling, in particular cyclists. We analyse news items about cycling in US, UK, and Australian news outlets in the decade from 2004 to 2014. In terms of the topology that we introduced in chapter 1 (reproduced here as figure 6.1), this study is located in zone 2. It is mono-modal (analysing language) and focuses primarily on patterns that occur across texts.

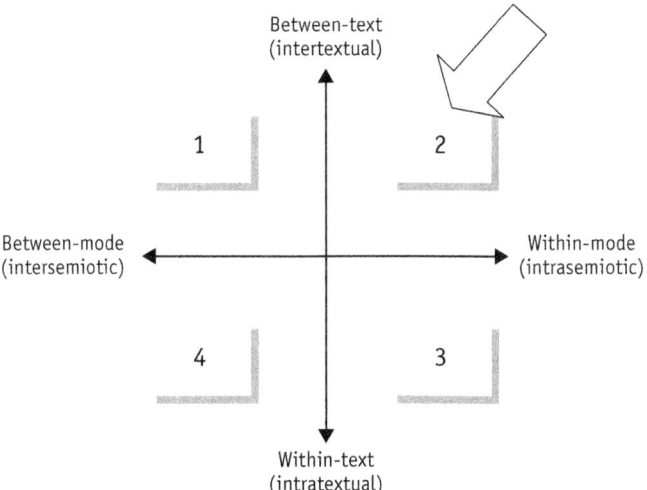

Figure 6.1 Situating the case study.

The topic of cycling was chosen for several reasons: On the one hand, the inspiration comes from personal experience: we both commute to and from work on bicycles and having lived (and cycled) in different locations it is clear that attitudes towards cycling vary considerably across both countries and cities. Further, cycling is a divisive issue and cyclists often clash with other road users, experiencing physical and verbal violence and attacks (e.g. Walker 2015).

On the other hand, discourse about cycling and cyclists, who are 'a minority user group' (Davies 2015) in the countries examined here, deserves much more attention. Corpus studies of news discourse have understandably tended to focus on more obvious vulnerable groups such as asylum seekers/refugees (e.g. Baker et al. 2008; Khosravinik 2009), the LGBTQI community (e.g. Baker 2005), or Muslims (e.g. Baker et al. 2013a). In relation to environmental matters, there are linguistic studies of news discourse on climate change (e.g. Grundmann and Krishnamurthy 2010), sustainability (e.g. Mahlberg 2007), and environmental reporting (e.g. Bednarek and Caple 2010, 2012b), but barely any on cycling. Davies's (2013, 2015) studies are recent exceptions, focusing on the British Highway Code and examining debates around rules relating to the use of cycle facilities as well as representations of different road users.

In non-linguistic research the same neglect can be observed, as Rissel et al. (2010: 2) point out. Hence, the need for more research on news coverage of cycling/cyclists is a major motivation for this case study. We require a better understanding of such coverage, since this 'is likely to be shaping public understandings of cyclists and cycling and is of importance to the uptake of cycling and to public policy support for cycling' (Rissel et al. 2010: 2). Our analyses proceed from two key assumptions:

1. That cycling has economic, environmental, and health benefits;[1]
2. That we should therefore support cycling and encourage its uptake.

Our key research question for this chapter is to identify the typical news values that are associated with cyclists/cycling, while we will also touch upon other issues, such as the assignation of blame.

6.2 The corpus

6.2.1 CORPUS DESIGN AND BUILDING

Following established protocol in corpus studies of news discourse on a given topic (e.g. Baker et al. 2013a), we used a database (Factiva) to compile a corpus of articles comprising words relating to cycling in selected US, UK, and Australian publications in the years 2004, 2005, 2009, 2013, 2014. The decision to use five years to stand for a decade with one data point in the middle was adopted from Rissel et al (2010).

Our aim was to include a mix of publications from less bike-friendly and more bike-friendly cities, as well as a mix of more 'popular' (POP) and more 'quality' (Q) publications, but we were also limited by what was available in the database (Factiva).

Table 6.1 lists the publications/cities included in the corpus. These cities have different cultural environments for cycling, including different uptake of cycling. For instance, Bristol has high levels of cycling (Davies 2015), and cycling in Melbourne has increased much more than in Sydney between 2001 and 2006 (Rissel et al. 2010: 6). The categorization of a city as more or less bike-friendly was undertaken on the basis of various online lists of bike-friendly or dangerous metropolitan areas (e.g. bicycling.com, news coverage, blogs) and is open to debate, as cycling cultures can also change over time. For instance, New York was ranked most cycling-friendly city by bicycling.com in 2014 (No. 1), but was at rank No. 7 in 2012, and while Memphis was ranked very low in 2008 and 2010, it was named as 'most improved city' in 2012.[2] Further, even if a city is dangerous for cycling, it may be governed by politicians who are adamant campaigners for cycling, which was the case with London mayor Boris Johnson. Each newspaper may also be classified as more or less in favour of cyclists. For example, the *London Evening Standard* campaigned for safer cycling, while *The Daily Telegraph* has been criticized for being anti-cycling.[3] In other words, each city and each newspaper may be seen as representing different cultural environments for cyclists. However, table 6.1 only provides categorization for *cities* because it is difficult to measure the cycling cultures of *newspapers* reliably. The included newspapers are a mix of 'popular' and 'quality', but it is worth noting

Table 6.1 **Newspapers included in the corpus**

Country	Cycling culture	City	Publication
Australia	Less bike-friendly	Sydney	*The Sydney Morning Herald* (Q); *The Daily Telegraph* (POP)
	More bike-friendly	Melbourne	*The Age* (Q); *Herald Sun* (POP)
United Kingdom	Less bike-friendly	London	*London Evening Standard* (POP)
		Bradford	*Bradford Telegraph and Argus* (POP)
		Glasgow	*The Herald* (Q)
	More bike-friendly	Oxford	*The Oxford Times* (Q)
		Bristol	*Bristol Post* (POP)
United States	Less bike-friendly	Memphis	*The Commercial Appeal* (Q)
	More bike-friendly	New York	*The New York Times* (Q); *New York Post* (POP)

that what counts as 'popular' in one country is not equivalent to what counts as 'popular' in another, and that it is difficult to categorize local/regional newspapers and freesheets.

The search syntax used to query the database to retrieve articles from these 12 newspapers was:

> cycling OR cycled OR cyclist* OR bicycl* OR biking* OR bike* OR "to cycle" OR cycleway OR cycle path* OR cycle rac* OR cycle rack* OR cycle route* OR cycle shop* OR cycle lane* OR cycle helmet* OR cycle horn* OR cycle batter* OR cycle clip* OR cycle shorts OR cycle track* OR racing cycle* OR cycle highway* OR cycle superhighway* OR cycle super highway*
>
> (* stands for any number of characters and " " stands for an exact phrase; see table A6.1 of the appendix for frequencies of each term)

This combination includes more terms than Rissel et al.'s (2010) study and was developed through trial and error. For instance, because the newspapers come from different English varieties, it was necessary to include both the verbs BIKE and CYCLE, but we could not search for *cycle* by itself as this would have resulted in too many unrelated instances (e.g. *cycle of violence, vicious cycle*). Because we did not want to exclude CYCLE altogether, we searched instead for *cycling, cycled,* and *"to cycle"* as well as common compounds with *cycle* identified with the help of the *Oxford English Dictionary*. In order to maximize the relevance of results, the search was restricted to the headline and lead paragraph, whereas recurring pricing and market data, obituaries, sports, calendars as well as identical duplicates were automatically excluded using Factiva's search options.

Even though the search was automatically restricted, we wanted to make sure that only news about cycling was included in the corpus. Hence, the research assistant who compiled the data was asked to view each result and exclude items unrelated to cycling or where bikes or cycling are only mentioned in passing, sports news (about sporting events/competitions),[4] items about other types of bikes (motorbikes, exercise bikes), opinion pieces, editorials, letters to the editor, 'photo-only' items, and any other non-news items. In addition, one of us speed-read each of the texts provided to us by the research assistant and excluded further texts.[5] The decision to exclude certain articles aligns our approach with that of Rissel et al. (2010), but distinguishes it from other corpus studies of news discourse where little manual checking of texts is undertaken, and which include opinion as well as news.

During the speed-reading process, files were also roughly edited for obvious typos or errors—for instance, containing unrelated stories after a first cycling story. All photo captions were also deleted, since not all files included them. Since this involved speed-reading over 2,000 items, there is no guarantee that all errors were identified. Minor differences between corpus files may remain, such that some files may contain an integrated by-line (... *writes* Journalist), location (*Memphis—*), a pointer to related content (*editorial comment, page* 21), an evaluative meta-comment (*EXCLUSIVE*); or a section heading (*MY SMALL BUSINESS*), while others do not. A very small minority of texts were found to be incomplete—for example, missing a headline or the end of a sentence—but were retained in the corpus. These are minor issues which are unlikely to affect the findings significantly.

6.2.2 CORPUS COMPOSITION

The final corpus can be divided into three sub-corpora, as it contains 386 articles from Australian, 906 articles from British, and 395 articles from American newspapers—a total of 1,687 articles and 506,324 words ('tokens in text' according to Wordsmith). This corpus will from now on be referred to as Cycling Corpus, or CyCo. Tables 6.2, 6.3, and 6.4, provide more detailed information on its composition. These tables show that although the Australian sub-corpus is the smallest, it is the most balanced with similar proportions from the different newspapers. In contrast, the UK sub-corpus is the biggest, but contains very few texts from *The Oxford Times* and is somewhat dominated by the *Bristol Post* and the *London Evening Standard*. It can also be seen that there are no texts from 2004 and 2005 for *The Oxford Times* or the *Bradford Telegraph and Argus*. Finally, the US sub-corpus contains more texts from New York than Memphis because no suitable 'popular' newspaper from Memphis or another 'less bike-friendly' US city could be sourced through Factiva. It is also necessary to stress that the three sub-corpora do not represent *all* news about cycling/cyclists in each country. Clearly, three newspapers from the United States are not representative of news reporting in the United States, and local/regional newspapers are only a subset of all news reporting in the United Kingdom.

To provide a first flavour of the corpus contents, figure 6.2 on page 144 presents the most frequent word forms in CyCo visualized through a word cloud.[6] Items in the cloud reflect both general features of news discourse (Bednarek and Caple 2012a)—for example, the use of the neutral reporting expression *said*—the topic and search terms (*cyclists, bike*, etc.), and the different countries/cities represented (*London, Brooklyn, Australia*, etc.). They give a first impression of some of the news values that we may expect to be established in the corpus (e.g. *killed, suffered, dangerous*: Negativity; *millions*: Superlativeness; *London, Brooklyn*: Proximity; *spokesman, government*: Eliteness). However, since we have applied frequency analysis in much of our previous corpus linguistic DNVA research, we will apply different techniques in this chapter. As in previous studies we will not distinguish reported speech/thought from other speech, since both contribute to establishing newsworthiness.

Table 6.2 UK sub-corpus

United Kingdom	Oxford Times		The Herald		Bradford Telegraph and Argus		Bristol Post		London Evening Standard		Total	
	Articles	Words	Articles	Words	Articles	Words	Articles	Words	Articles	Words	Articles	Words
2004	0	0	6	752	0	0	51	12,208	13	3,857	70	16,817
2005	0	0	10	1,364	0	0	49	11,164	13	3,012	72	15,540
2009	22	4,558	18	4,381	28	5,326	77	21,847	50	16,422	195	52,534
2013	0	0	59	13,556	58	10,868	78	25,489	109	35,708	304	85,621
2014	0	0	47	9,294	67	13,481	67	16,845	84	25,513	265	65,133
Total	22	4,558	140	29,347	153	29,675	322	87,553	269	84,512	906	235,645

Table 6.3 Australian sub-corpus

Australia	Daily Telegraph		Sydney Morning Herald		Herald Sun		The Age		Total	
	Articles	Words	Articles	Words	Articles	Words	Articles	Words	Articles	Words
2004	26	5,388	7	3,494	18	3,497	11	3,394	62	15,773
2005	21	3,424	8	4,574	21	4,600	10	3,563	60	16,161
2009	17	2,912	16	7,876	14	3,371	21	9,030	68	23,189
2013	25	7,735	18	7,640	30	6,296	29	9,804	102	31,475
2014	28	6,983	19	6,403	30	7,139	17	6,569	94	27,094
Total	117	26,442	68	29,987	113	24,903	88	32,360	386	113,692

Table 6.4 **US sub-corpus**

United States	New York Post		New York Times		Commercial Appeal		Total	
	Articles	Words	Articles	Words	Articles	Words	Articles	Words
2004	26	4,771	21	8,777	22	8,151	69	21,699
2005	27	5,248	24	11,952	9	3,319	60	20,519
2009	18	4,384	22	13,724	18	7,844	58	25,952
2013	70	18,973	24	19,865	26	10,719	120	49,557
2014	48	15,615	24	16,688	16	6,957	88	39,260
Total	189	48,991	115	71,006	91	36,990	**395**	**156,987**

144 THE DISCOURSE OF NEWS VALUES

Figure 6.2 Wordsmith word cloud (default settings, with stoplist).

6.3 Analysis of 'typical' news values

As a first step, we used ProtAnt (Anthony and Baker 2015a) to identify the 'typical' construction of newsworthiness in CyCo. Since the corpus contains different varieties (British/American/Australian English), each sub-corpus must be contrasted with a different suitable reference corpus. As British and American reference corpora we used the one-million-word BE06 and AmE06 corpora (Baker 2009; Potts and Baker 2012). These corpora consist of 500 files of 2,000 word samples of 15 written genres from 2006—British and American English, respectively. The design of these corpora matches the well-known Brown and LOB corpora from the 1960s and 1990s. As Australian reference corpus, we used an untagged version of the Australian Corpus of English, as it has the same design, although it dates from 1986 (https://www.ausnc.org.au/corpora/ace, last accessed 22 March 2016).[7]

The ProtAnt ranking of the top most prototypical corpus files (in table 6.5) seems to suggest (i) that Negativity is the most typical news value constructed and (ii) that this news value is established in relation to accidents. In the headlines of such items, Negativity is primarily construed through what we call *negative lexis* (chapter 4), in particular descriptions of injury and death through verbs such as INJURE, DIE, KILL, CRUSH, HIT, HURT and nouns such as COLLISION, CRASH, ACCIDENT, HIT-(AND-) RUN, DEATH, TOLL. The person(s) injured or killed are referred to in these headlines as (*bi*)*cyclist(s), man, bicycle gal, girls on bicycle*, establishing a low degree of Personalization. The headline provides the ultimate summary or abstract of a news story (Bell 1991: 186), but the remainder of the text may establish additional news values, which would require analysis of all complete texts. To give just one example here, *The Oxford Times* news story 'Cyclist injured in Oxford collision'—presented below as (1)—also constructs Proximity (*in Oxford, in West Oxford, at the junction of Henry Road and Botley Road*), Timeliness (*is being treated, today*), Eliteness (*a spokesman for South Central Ambulance*) and includes some Positivity at the end (*not thought to have suffered any serious injuries*).

(1)

Cyclist injured in Oxford collision

A cyclist is being treated by paramedics following a collision with a car in West Oxford today.

The accident happened at 8.20am at the junction of Henry Road and Botley Road.

A spokesman for South Central Ambulance said: 'Our staff attended following the collision between a cyclist and a car.

The female cyclist is still being treated at the scene but she is not thought to have suffered any serious injuries.' (*The Oxford Times*, 3 December 2009)

But other news items are also ranked high because they contain many keywords. In the US sub-corpus this includes a short item about the expansion of a bike business ('Bikes Plus expanding Germantown store'), which contains keywords such as *bikes, bike, Memphis, ride, lanes*. Similarly, an item in the US sub-corpus about an officer being injured by a bicyclist ('Officer struck by cyclist') contains many words

Table 6.5 Most 'prototypical' news items about cycling (ProtAnt)

	United Kingdom	United States	Australia
Top 25 keywords (ranked according to keyness)	bike, cyclists, cycle, cycling, cyclist, bikes, road, Bristol, I, said, ride, police, London, charity, Bradford, collision, you, lorry, roads, route, Mr, driver, that, accident, city …	bike, bikes, said, bicycle, city, cyclists, ride, lanes, citi, riders, bicycles, police, street, Memphis, park, riding, transportation, traffic, cycling, lane, bicyclists, avenue, share, Mr, Brooklyn …	bike, cyclists, bicycle, said, cycling, cyclist, bikes, road, ride, city, lanes, riders, riding, h [occurs as part of the phrase $N° km/h$], Melbourne, note, path, traffic, roads, street, lane, council, transport, cycleway …
Headline [and further information if headline is not transparent about content of news item]	Cyclist injured in Oxford collision (*Oxford Times*, 2009)	Bicyclist Killed in Crash (*New York Times*, 2004)	Cyclists to ride high (*Herald Sun*, 2014) [THE Napthine Government will consider a plan to build a bike skyway through the CBD.]
	Cyclist dies in hospital after Bristol road crash (*Bristol Post*, 2009)	MAN BUSTED IN FATAL 'HIT-RUN' (*New York Post*, 2004)	Riding into town (*Sydney Morning Herald*, 2014) [Daily bicycle trips in the Sydney local government area have risen]
	Sixth cyclist dies on London's roads (*The Herald*, 2013)	Man Critically Injured in Hit-and-Run (*New York Times*, 2014)	Bike path future (*Sydney Morning Herald*, 2013)
	City cyclist killed (*London Evening Standard*, 2013)	Cyclist Killed in Hit-and-Run Accident (*New York Times*, 2004)	Helmets on the go (*Herald Sun*, 2013) [FREE helmets will be trialled as part of the Melbourne Bike Share scheme.]

Cyclist is killed (*London Evening Standard*, 2013)	Bikes Plus expanding Germantown store (*The Commercial Appeal*, 2013)	Cyclist death brings Easter toll to three (*The Age*, 2013)
Cyclist still in a critical state (*Bristol Post*, 2014)	Officer struck by cyclist (*New York Post*, 2014)	Bicycle expressway proposed for East West Link (*The Age*, 2014)
Cyclist killed and two others hurt (*London Evening Standard*, 2013)	Bus crushes bicycle gal (*New York Post*, 2014)	More city lanes (*The Age*, 2013)
Cyclist injured in lorry accident (*London Evening Standard*, 2013)	Girls on Bicycle Hit by Car (*New York Times*, 2005)	Cyclist dies after crash (*Herald Sun*, 2005)
Cyclist killed by HGV an 'accident' (*London Evening Standard*, 2014)	Driver 'cycle' of violence (*New York Post*, 2013) [A hotheaded city worker was arrested yesterday after he hit a biker with his car, then punched him in the face]	Three cyclists hit by cars (*Daily Telegraph*, 2004)
Cyclist badly injured in accident with lorry (*Bradford Telegraph and Argus*, 2014)	Cyclist Killed in Truck Accident (*New York Times*, 2005)	Brakes on city cyclists (*Herald Sun*, 2014) [POLICE and the city council are seeking to slam the brakes on speeding cyclists in a $220,000 campaign]

also expected to occur in items about cyclists being injured (*cyclist, struck, injured, hit, pain, hospital, injury, police*), showing that our ProtAnt analysis will not necessarily distinguish between who is hit by whom. Hence, we should not deduce that items about cyclists injuring others are in any way 'typical'. Indeed, our hypothesis is that it is more typically cyclists who are described as injured.

In the Australian sub-corpus, items ranked high include an item about a trial of free helmets in Melbourne's Bike Share scheme,[8] an item about a police campaign targeting speeding cyclists, an item about the rise in trips by bicycle in Sydney, and several items about cycling infrastructure.[9] To identify which news values are constructed in these stories would necessitate a closer look, but they are likely to include Proximity (*Melbourne Bike Share scheme, in the Sydney local government area, East West Link, through the CBD*); Negativity/Positivity (bike lanes can be evaluated as positive or negative; *speeding cyclists* is negative), Superlativeness (*daily bicycle trips have risen, a $220,000 campaign*), and Unexpectedness (*a bike skyway*). The presence of several items about cycling infrastructure may indicate that a subcategory of prototypical news about cycling in Australia concerns cycling facilities. It also suggests a rise in such items in recent years, since Rissel et al.'s (2010) study of the same newspapers between 1998 and 2008 quantified the news angle 'bike facilities improved' as making up less than 5%. Indeed, if we compare occurrences of *cycleway/cycleways, track/tracks, path/paths, lane/lanes, trail/trails*, and *route/routes* in 2004/2005/2009 with 2013/2014, we find statistically significant 'underuse' (LL = 65.58; $p < 0.0001$) and a lower range (about 45% vs. 61%) in the older news texts—although we do not know if all occurrences refer to bike paths. Nevertheless, this appears to reflect a larger investment in such infrastructure in more recent years and shows the constraints and opportunities that arise for news reporting from the material reality of events (see chapter 3).

If we consider the items ranked as least typical in table 6.6, these include health, fashion, and business news; items about new ways of learning to cycle; items about inventions and e-bikes; portraits of cycling advocates/politicians; and items about unusual bike trips such as cycling to Timbuktu. Table 6.6 also contains one item each about gangs on bikes, a sports person cycling to practice, a cyclist suing a radio station, a motorist filming cyclists, a man cycling in Australia 100 years ago, a bicycle show, ministers on bikes, and an advertising campaign. Several of these are clearly less 'newsy' in content and style than traditional hard news stories and some researchers might have excluded these from a corpus of news about cycling (see section 6.2.1). With most of these files, it does look like their classification as atypical by ProtAnt is credible.

Perhaps more surprisingly, there are also two texts in table 6.6 that appear similar to items ranked 'most typical', namely two items about cyclists' deaths in the Australian sub-corpus ('Riders pause for a lost comrade'; 'Cyclist's death: 13 years' jail for drunken driver').[10] However, the first item is written in a very peculiar style, at times quite poetic (*An ill wind, though, took her—a sudden, unrepeatable gust timed to cruel perfection, a face in the crowd in the sea of tents that mushroom where the ride beds down*), at times almost like a travel item (*about halfway between Cohuna and Echuca, the Murray Valley highway*

Table 6.6 Least 'prototypical' news items about cycling (ProtAnt)

	United Kingdom	United States	Australia
Headline [and further information if headline is not transparent about content of news item]	Wheels turning Bike store chain starts here (*Bristol Post*, 2014)	A Girl Gets Mothers to Start Biking Again (*The New York Times*, 2014)	On your bike? One student fights back ... with a design for rail commuters (*The Age*, 2009)
	WHY ROBBEN PLANS TO GET ON HIS BIKE AGAIN (*London Evening Standard*, 2004)	A Bicycle Evangelist with the Wind Now at His Back (*The New York Times*, 2009)	Riders pause for a lost comrade (*Herald Sun*, 2005)
	Halfords to wheel out cycling stores (*Bradford Telegraph and Argus*, 2014)	SHIFT could take fear out of learning to ride (*The Commercial Appeal*, 2005)	Cyclist's death: 13 years' jail for drunken driver (*The Age*, 2009)
	GETTING THE BALANCE RIGHT; The days of stabilisers are over and now kids learn to ride on pedal-less bikes (*Bristol Post*, 2013)	Two-Wheeled Turf Battles [gang violence] (*The New York Times*, 2005)	Cyclist sues comedy radio (*The Daily Telegraph*, 2005)
	Angered driver films bad cyclists (*Bristol Post*, 2014)	Cyclists Go Glam into the Night (*The New York Times*, 2014)	One woman's epic bike trek to Timbuktu and beyond (*The Age*, 2014)
	Keen cyclist Mike takes county's transportation agenda to heart (*Bristol Post*, 2009)	These cyclists are delivering God's message (*The Commercial Appeal*, 2013)	The life cycle: a man takes to the road less travelled (*The Age*, 2004) [John Lloyd is cycling around Australia five times, spurred on by a girl's spirit]

(*continued*)

Table 6.6 Continued

Headline [and further information if headline is not transparent about content of news item]	United Kingdom	United States	Australia
	BIKES OF BEAUTY; Pick of the week Bespoked Bristol, Handmade Bicycle Show (*Bristol Post*, 2013)	THE CLAIM—Bicycle seats can cause impotence for male riders. (*The New York Times*, 2004)	For these two riders, the cycle of life keeps turning (*The Age*, 2009) [AFTER 4 years and 31,000 kilometres, the end is almost in sight for Lina and Andreas Killat. They have travelled overland from Germany to Melbourne]
	Duo aim to put female cyclists into top gear; Fashion (*Bristol Post*, 2013)	Power to the Pedal [e-bikes] (*The New York Times*, 2014)	Sales dream takes off on the internet (*The Age*, 2013) [Two years ago entrepreneurs James van Rooyen and Jonathon Allara were making a modest income from their bike hire company.]
	BRING ON THE STYLE REVOLUTION (*London Evening Standard*, 2009)	Seeing the Light, and Finding Their Balance [glow-in-the-light bikes] (*The New York Times*, 2014)	Coffee company blends jobs with a social flavor (*The Age*, 2009) [a specially adapted bicycle for delivering wholesale coffee packs to customers]
	Bike of future goes on show (*The Herald*, 2013) [bike with ultrasonic sensors]	Serious Riders, Your Bicycle Seat May Affect Your Love Life (*The New York Times*, 2005)	Not the easiest rider (*The Sydney Morning Herald*, 2005) [Francis Birtles cycled across Australia seven times before there was a road to follow] [100 years ago]

is straight and visibility excellent. You can see across almost bare paddocks to far-off stands of gums along the Murray), and the item does not focus on the accident, but rather on the remembrance ceremony. The second item is an instance of court reporting, which—in addition to briefly describing the original accident a year prior and its effects—describes the background of the people involved, in particular the perpetrator. These characteristics may explain why these two items are ranked as atypical by ProtAnt.

Since ProtAnt is a new software tool, it has not yet been fully tested for all conditions, although it has performed very well in a range of experiments (Anthony and Baker 2015b). The developers conclude that ProtAnt 'does a useful job generally, but we should note that it does not perform perfectly' (288). Since the corpus contains 1,687 files, it is not easily possible to identify its most typical/atypical files independently, in order to test whether ProtAnt has produced reliable results. However, from speed-reading all texts we are fairly sure, for instance, that it is *not* the case that business news items are prototypical of the US sub-corpus, although ProtAnt's top ten includes one such story. One issue that might possibly affect the ProtAnt findings here is that the corpus files are very dissimilar in size. It could also be the case that the topic (cycling) is too broad and hence too lexically diverse. Thus, news about cycling can be about the injury or death of cyclists, support or objections to cycling/cycling facilities, celebrities who cycle, cycle tourism and cycle events, cyclists committing misdemeanours or injuring/killing pedestrians, bike theft, cycling facilities (Rissel et al. 2010), and so on. However, ProtAnt was apparently able to correctly rank texts with other fairly general topics such as Islam (Anthony and Baker 2015b).[11]

In sum, the findings derived from ProtAnt do appear credible, but we need further evidence that they are. In addition to ranking a few items high that may not in fact be typical of the corpus, we have also seen that the ranking is not concerned with the grammatical structure that the words partake in (e.g. whether cyclists are hit or whether they hit someone else). Finally, our analysis here was limited to examining the 'extreme' ends of the ranks (ten most/least typical), and we mainly considered the headlines of the ranked texts. It is thus useful to undertake further analyses of CyCo to corroborate whether Negativity is the most typical news value constructed and how this value is typically construed. In the remainder of this chapter, we will do so through collocation analysis and concordancing. We will also illustrate how one can combine analysis of one general news value (Negativity) with more delicate analysis of different ways or categories in which this is established (see chapter 3).

6.4 Analysis of news values around cyclists

6.4.1 INTRODUCTION TO COLLOCATION ANALYSIS

Collocation analysis can provide useful insights into the news values constructed around a particular topic or entity (Potts et al. 2015). In this case, we undertook collocation analysis of the word forms *cyclist* and *cyclists* because we wanted to focus on the main news actors involved in items about cycling, namely the people using a bicycle. The query term *cyclist** is one of the top four most frequent in all three sub-corpora (table A6.1 in the appendix) and all but two instances (*cyclista/cyclistist*) of the query term are usages of the noun CYCLIST. According to Wordsmith, *cyclist* has a raw frequency of 1,300 in 599 CyCo texts (35.5%), while *cyclists* has a raw frequency of 2,307 in 759 CyCo texts (45%). Together, they occur in 1,063 files, or 63% of CyCo.[12] Figure 6.3 shows the Wordsmith dispersion plot for *cyclist/cyclists*, where the left-hand side stands for the beginning and the right-hand side for the end of a text file, with vertical lines showing occurrences of the search term. Figure 6.4 shows the frequency distribution of the lemma CYCLIST over concordance positions (default software settings applied). Here, the x-axis shows the concordance positions, as calculated by Sketch Engine (100 columns for 100 corpus slices), and the y-axis shows the relative frequency of the search term within a concordance part. Both figures, along with the dispersion value (0.751), suggest some variation in frequency and distribution, without this being extremely high or problematic.

According to Wordsmith, *cyclist* has 306 collocates and *cyclists* has 534 collocates with an MI3 score of at least 9. Figure 6.5 visualizes the large amount of collocates for *cyclist* in CyCo using GraphColl.[13] It will thus be necessary to narrow down the results. In order to do so, we examine collocates that are (1) in the top 50 for three collocation measures—MI3, T-score, and log likelihood—*and* (2) in the top 50 when ranked by range (tables A6.2 and A6.3 in the appendix). This means that we focus on collocates that have high association scores and have a reasonable distribution. We will first discuss *cyclist*, before moving on to the plural form, *cyclists*.

Figure 6.3 Wordsmith plot for *cyclist/cyclists* (dispersion: 0.751).

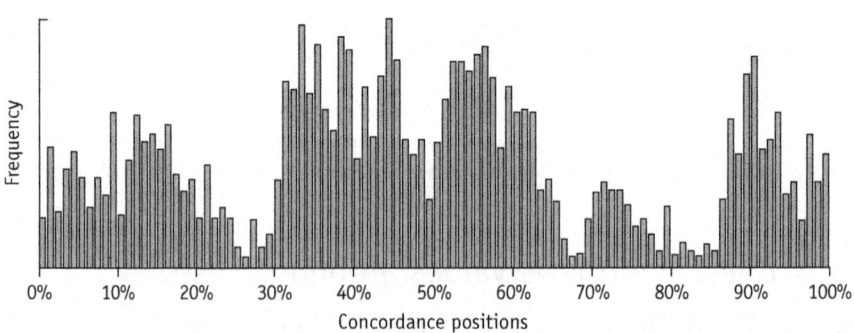

Figure 6.4 Sketch Engine frequency distribution over concordance positions (granularity 100).

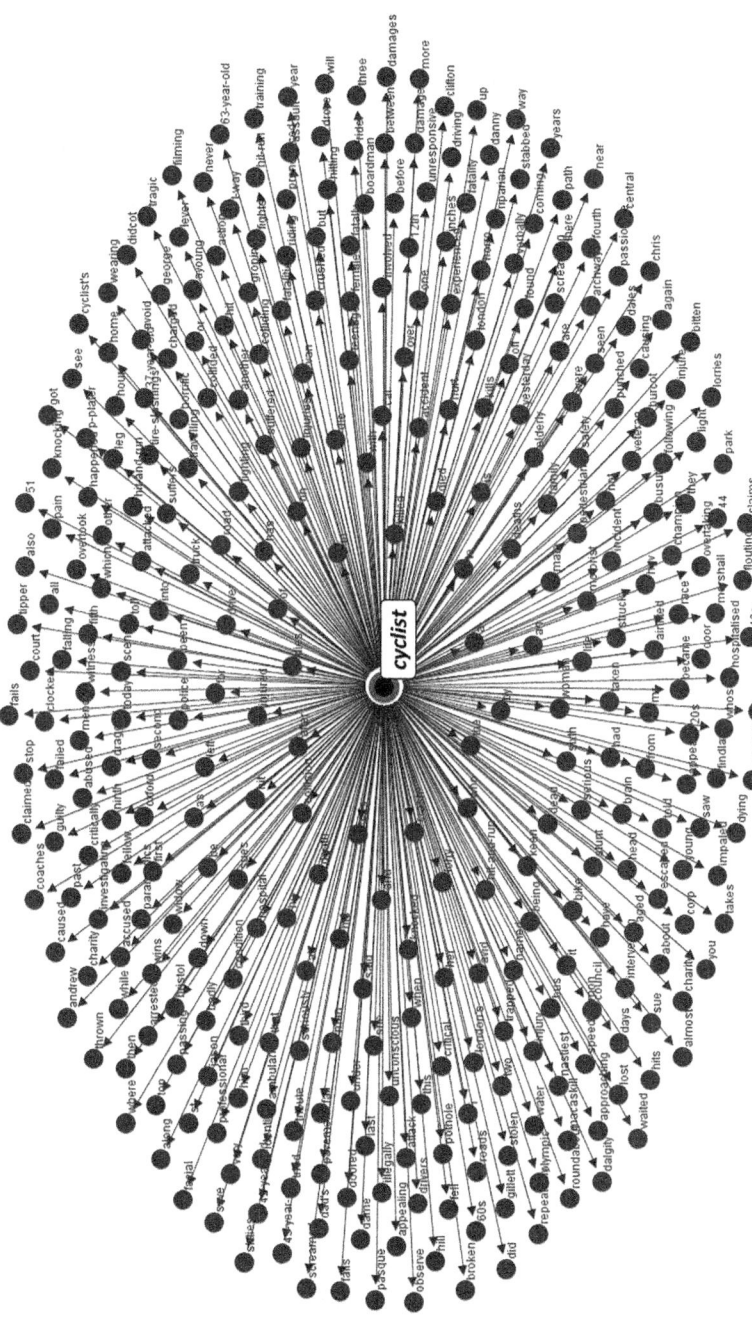

Figure 6.5 5L–5R collocates of *cyclist* (MI3 ≥ 9, min. frequency = 2).

6.4.2 CYCLIST

Table 6.7 lists the collocates that are representative of the words with which *cyclist* is regularly and consistently associated in CyCo. In relation to newsworthiness, the grammatical collocates in this table do not clearly point to a specific news value: Although conjunctions and prepositions like *after, at, in* can situate an event in time and space, pronouns and determiners like *he, her, his* can refer to ordinary or elite news actors, and verb forms like *has* point to the use of present tense or present perfect, without further investigation it is not possible to hypothesize that these are used in CyCo to construct particular news values. These word forms are simply too multifunctional, and we will therefore have to set them aside.

Table 6.7 **Collocates for *cyclist* in top 50 (MI3, T-score, LL, and range)**

	Collocates for *cyclist*
Grammatical words and forms of DO, BE, HAVE	*a, after, an, and, at, for, has, he, her, his, in, is, of, on, the, to, was, who, with*
Lexical words	*accident, car, collision, crash, death, died, dies, driver, hit, injured, injuries, killed, knocked, left, lorry, old, road*

In contrast, the vast majority of the lexical collocates are likely to refer to accidents involving cyclists (*accident, collision, crash, death, died, dies, hit, injured, injuries, killed, knocked*), hence construing Negativity.[14] Since these are all in the top 50 when collocates are sorted according to range, we know that they do not just occur in a few CyCo texts but are distributed across the corpus. However, we do not yet know if these occur in *all* of the publications in CyCo regardless of their cycling culture. To discover if this is the case, we checked if these eleven collocates are collocates for *cyclist* in each newspaper, by treating each newspaper as an individual corpus. For US newspapers we also included collocates for *bicyclist*, since this is a fairly common variant of *cyclist* in this sub-corpus (see table A6.4 in the appendix). Table 6.8 shows that there is indeed a considerable spread of these collocates across newspapers. Namely, *killed* is a collocate in all 12 CyCo newspapers; *hit, crash* are collocates in ten, *death* in eight, *injured* and *accident* in seven, and *died* and *collision* in six (50% of CyCo). The remaining word forms are collocates in five (*injuries*) and four (*dies, knocked*) newspapers. This finding corroborates the ProtAnt results and confirms that Negativity is constructed in relation to accidents across the corpus, regardless of publication.

Since we examined collocates for the singular form (*cyclist*) we can further argue that Negativity is combined with Personalization. As noted in chapter 4, identification of these individuals as *cyclist* (by a category label) is less personalizing than if they are identified by name or with further social information (e.g. age, gender, kinship relations). However, such personalizing information may be provided in the immediate or wider co-text—the former can be discovered through examining the collocate

Table 6.8 The spread of collocates across CyCo publications (MI3)

	London Evening Standard	Oxford Times	The Herald	Bradford Telegraph and Argus	Bristol Post	Daily Telegraph	Sydney Morning Herald	Herald Sun	The Age	New York Post	New York Times	The Commercial Appeal
KILLED	X	X	X	X	X	X	X	X	X	X	X	X
HIT	X	X	X		X	X		X	X	X	X	X
DIED	X		X	X	X	X		X				
CRASH	X	X	X	X	X	X		X		X	X	X
COLLISION	X	X	X	X	X	X						
INJURED	X	X	X	X	X	X					X	
DEATH	X		X	X	X	X	X	X	x			
DIES	X		X		X			X				
ACCIDENT	X	X	X	X	X	X	X					
INJURIES	X		X	X	X			X				
KNOCKED	X		X		X	X						

Table 6.9 **Nominal phrases containing *old***

a/the	number-year-old	Optional gender or location specification	cyclist
a	15-year-old		cyclist
the	35-year-old	female	cyclist
a	92-year-old	Brooklyn	cyclist

old (table 6.7). Wordsmith's advanced search function retrieves 32 instances where *old* occurs within five words of *cyclist* (L5:R5) and in the same sentence. In the clear majority of cases, *old* occurs as part of a nominal phrase and modifies *cyclist*, as shown in table 6.9. There are 27 instances of this structure, mainly without the optional gender/location specification. An additional two instances from two UK newspapers specify age, location, and gender through an appositive phrase (e.g. *The cyclist, a 44-year-old Bristol man*). In other words, the word *cyclist* is only regularly accompanied by age specification in the immediate co-text, while further personalizing information is not present in the immediate co-text—though it might be present in the larger textual environment (i.e. beyond the 5:5 span investigated here).

In addition, most of the 32 concordances concern a cyclist injured or killed in an accident (n = 26). Considering the remaining six occurrences, the news value of Negativity can also be construed without reference to accidents where a cyclist is the victim, for example, in relation to crime (bike theft), accidents where pedestrians are victims (*elderly jogger Irving Schachter was fatally struck . . . by a 17-year-old cyclist*) or in relation to cyclists committing traffic or other offenses (e.g. *a 37-year-old cyclist . . . was stopped . . . for running a light, a 37-year-old cyclist . . . who slashed almost 2,000 car and truck tires over 10 days*). Conversely, the news value of Positivity can also be construed, as seen in example (2):

(2)

AN 80-year-old cyclist is dedicating a 17,800km trip around Australia to his late wife of 60 years, while raising money for mental health research. (*The Daily Telegraph*, 20 March 2009)

Interestingly, table 6.7 also identified *driver* as a collocate of *cyclist*. In most of the 42 instances where this noun occurs within five words of *cyclist*, the driver is referred to without any further modification (*driver, a/the driver*) or with reference to the vehicle that was driven (*a lorry driver, the Peugeot driver, van driver, the driver of a silver Ford Fiesta, a white van driver*), very rarely with further specification of location (*Bradford van driver*), name (*lorry driver John Stewart*), age (*a bus driver, 64*) or experience (e.g. *rookie driver*). There are occasional instances that directly refer to the driver's involvement in an accident (*hit-and-run driver, bus lane crash driver*), sometimes implying blame (*a speeding lorry driver*). In two instances the drivers are categorized with negative emotions (*An incensed pickup driver, An enraged driver*). Thus, noun phrases with *driver* that are collocates of *cyclist* rarely construct a high degree of Personalization and rarely construct other news values such as Negativity (*hit-and-run driver, enraged driver*) or Proximity (*Bradford van driver*).

Many instances (n = 23) again relate to accidents where drivers killed or injured cyclists, including drivers being questioned, charged, sentenced, or cleared. However, there is also a recurring practice of construing Negativity in relation to altercations between drivers and cyclists. Specifically, there are eight instances in five newspapers from six news stories (including one follow-up story) where cyclists are aggressors (e.g. punching driver). Conversely, there are only three instances from two news stories (in two newspapers) where the driver is the aggressor. The news value of Negativity, then, can also be established through 'road rage' items. While we could undertake further qualitative analysis of the three remaining lexical collocates of *cyclist* (*car, lorry, road*), for reasons of scope we will now move on to the collocation analysis of the plural form *cyclists*.

6.4.3 CYCLISTS

Table 6.10 lists the collocates of *cyclists* that are in the top 50 for all three measures *and* in the top 50 when sorted according to range.

Table 6.10 **Collocates for *cyclists* in top 50 (MI3, T-score, LL, and range)**

	Collocates for cyclists
Grammatical words and forms of DO, BE, HAVE	a, about, and, are, as, at, be, been, being, by, for, from, have, in, is, it, more, not, of, on, than, that, the, their, they, to, two, were, who, will, with
Lexical words and proper nouns	cyclist, drivers, killed, London, motorists, number, pedestrians, ride, road, roads, use

What we have already observed for the grammatical collocates for *cyclist* is also true for those of *cyclists*: Many are simply too multifunctional to allow hypothesis as to their use. Potential exceptions are *more* and *than*, since *more than* constructs an ensuing number as high, establishing Superlativeness (chapter 4). Figure 6.6 provides a visualization of a collocational network, showing that *than* is indeed a collocate for *more*.

There are 31 instances where *more than* occurs in a 5L:5R span of *cyclists* and in the same sentence. In most occurrences (n = 24), *more than* modifies a number (ranging from 15 to 40,000) which quantifies cyclists, in the structure

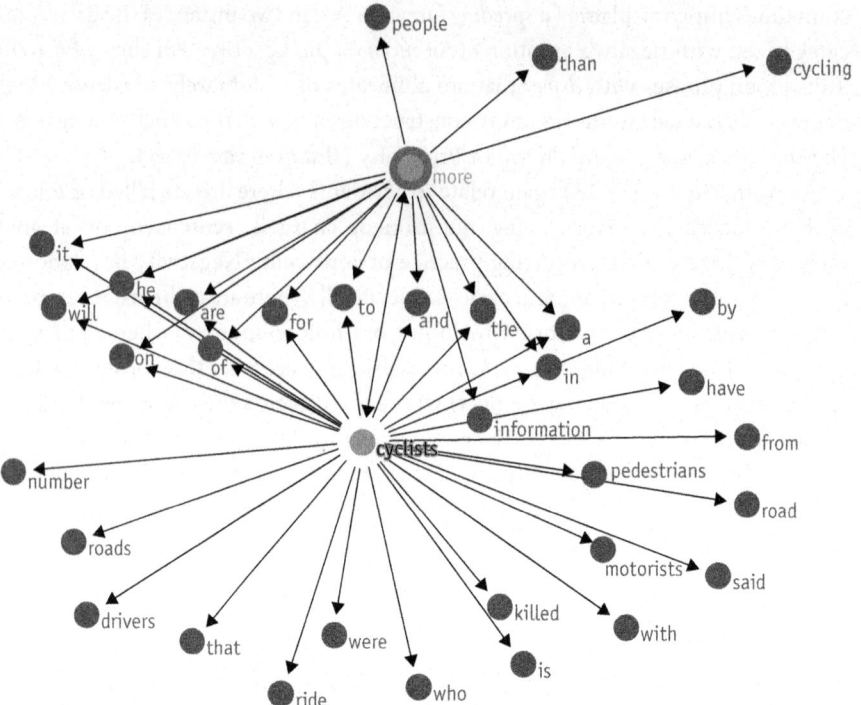

Figure 6.6 GraphColl network (*cyclists, more*; MI3 ≥ 17, min. frequency = 2).

more than + NUMBER + *cyclists*.[15] The concordances in figure 6.7 show that Superlativeness is constructed around different aspects, including cyclists' injury and death (e.g. 1, 3, 6, 22, 23), cyclists committing offenses (e.g. 2, 4, 5, 13, 18), and participation in cycling, bike hire schemes, charity rides, or other cycling events (e.g. 7, 8, 10, 14).

Not is another potentially interesting grammatical collocate of *cyclists*, as negation can construe Negativity when it indicates lack or failure (chapter 4). While space does not permit a full investigation, a visualization of a collocational network (figure 6.8) shows that both *helmet* and *wearing* are collocates of *not*.

In turn, a search for *helmet** within a 5L:5R span of *not wear** retrieves 34 instances (excluding one about a motorcycle helmet) across 26 texts and 9 newspapers. About half occur in relation to offenses, warnings, fines, or surveys (n = 16), while the other half (n = 18) occur in relation to accidents (i.e. reporting that cyclists were not wearing a helmet when they had an accident). The latter can be in relation to an individual (n = 10) or groups (n = 8), as illustrated in examples (3) and (4):

(3)

The woman, **who was not wearing a helmet**, was hit by a Citywide Demolition & Rubbish Removal truck pulling out into traffic in the same direction, witnesses said. (*New York Post*, 5 January 2013)

```
1   the right to get where they need to be safely," she said. There have been more than 100       cyclists  admitted to hospital after crashes in Melbourne in the past 12 months and four
2   hours a day and have to take a 45-minute break every four and a half hours. More than 100     cyclists  were also stopped in today's operation and given advice or warnings for issues
3   2000 and June this year, there were nine fatalities and 164 serious injuries. More than 1000  cyclists  suffered minor injuries. The first week of the campaign will focus on education
4   night and wearing the right safety gear - especially helmets. "The fact that more than 11,000 cyclists  have received an infringement notice or penalty in 2008 serves as a timely rem
5   being taken." PCSO Adam Needs said: "It was a great success. "We spoke to more than 15        cyclists  who were travelling at excessive speeds. One cyclist was going so fast that h
6   and pedestrians. Latest figures available from the Scottish Government show more than 15     cyclists  a week were injured in road accidents last year, up 6% from 2010, while the
7                                    Bikes 'revived' during health check! MORE than 150           cyclists  took the opportunity to give their bikes a well-deserved health-check at a work
8   for bladder health. Neville Parnell, 43, a garage owner from Hanham, joined more than 16,000  cyclists  taking part in the 100-mile race from London to Surrey and back on Sunday. A
9   first 12 days, a figure that has since risen to over 3000. Latest figures show more than 1600 cyclists  have registered to use the bikes. The longest journey so far was to Loch Lo
10  the number of commuters who use public transport has gone just slightly up. More than 2,300   cyclists  use Gloucester Road each day, slightly more than the cycleway. The high numb
11  Council, which has put $1.36,000 into the pilot project, because it is used by more than 2,300 cyclists a day - more than use the Bristol Bath Cycle Path. Assistant mayor for transp
12  last night. Police and CityLink were forced to close the Bolte Bridge while more than 200     cyclists  from the Critical Mass activist group took over the freeway. An accident on th
13  a handful of arrests. But during the Republican National Convention in August, more than 200  cyclists  were busted for blocking traffic. NYPD spokesman Paul Browne said the cyclists
14  of just two cycling routes between the inner west and CBD, is crossed by more than 2000       cyclists  a day. Making it safer for cyclists is VicRoads' top cycling project for Melbourn
15  the trial, which ran from January to June this year, the system detected more than 40,000     cyclists, pedestrians and motorcyclists. Its alarm alerted the lorry driver on 15 occasion
16  Square. Swanston Street is now Melbourne's busiest bike route, used by more than 4900         cyclists  a day, Bicycle Network Victoria says. Melbourne City councillor Cathy Oke said
17  staff from Eastville-based Ikea. Last year's Cyclists' Breakfast event attracted more than 500 cyclists and it is hoped that this year's event will match this and possibly better it. S
18  red lights. But despite the heightened police presence, The Post observed more than 60        cyclists  whizzing out of the bike lanes at the scene of the tragic collision on West Dri
19  medical use of ultrasound in pregnancy. This year, the charity aims to recruit more than 650  cyclists  and raise more than $1.60,000 in funds. To register for the Action 100 Bike Rid
20  of off-road cyclists refuse to wear them. The figures were obtained from more than 800        cyclists  at five A&E departments across the Lothian and Borders area who were injured
21                                    900 cyclists join bike ride MORE than 900                   cyclists  turned out for a charity bike ride in Chipping Sodbury. The Saddleback Sodbury
22  of a motorist who has never been traced. In a year which has seen more than a dozen          cyclists  killed on London's roads alone, the father-of-three has called for better safety
23  in bid to reduce bike casualties A HOSPITAL that has saved more than 660 critically injured   cyclists  in a decade is asking riders to send it details of crashes and near-misses on
```

Figure 6.7 The construction of Superlativeness around cyclists.

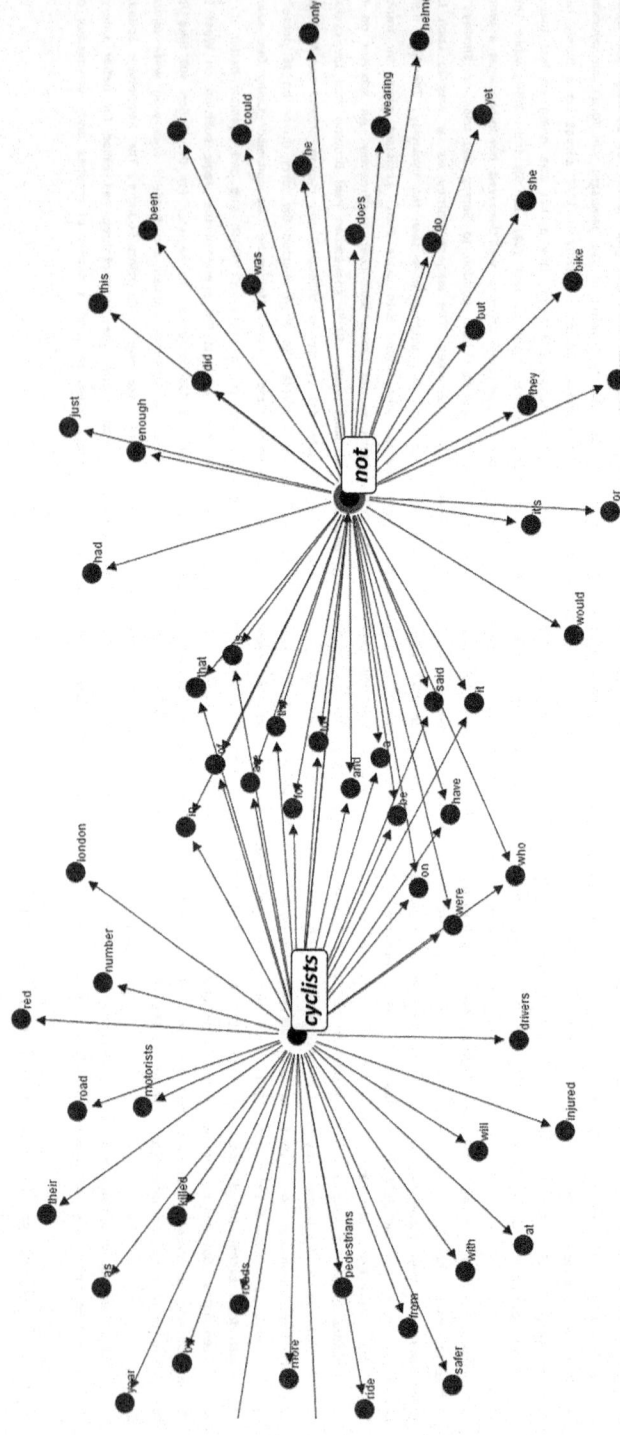

Figure 6.8 GraphColl visualization (*cyclists, not*; MI3 ≥ 16, min. frequency = 2).

(4)

In several cases [of accidents] adult cyclists **were not wearing helmets** or were wearing helmets that were incorrectly secured. (*The Daily Telegraph*, 6 July 2014)

Piper et al. (2011) identify a frame supportive of helmets which assumes that cyclists who do not wear helmets are to blame if they are injured. From a critical perspective, Davies (2015) identifies requests to use helmets as an example of 'entrenched and largely invisible' incidents of 'victim-blaming against vulnerable road users'. Such constructions may hence establish newsworthiness while simultaneously implying blame.

Moving on to the lexical collocates of *cyclists*, we can identify pointers to Negativity (*killed*), Superlativeness (*number*), and Proximity (*London*). *Killed* is an instance of negative lexis that we have already encountered in relation to the singular form *cyclist*, and will discuss further below. *Number* construes Superlativeness in more than 70% of instances where *it* occurs with *cyclists* in the same sentence within a 5L:5R span. More specifically, *number* primarily occurs in references to large numbers (e.g. *a large/an alarming number*) or increases in number (e.g. *the number . . . is growing, has more than doubled, has increased drastically, has jumped to, soared, the increased/rising number of*). A high number is also implied by using the verbs REDUCE, CUT, or HALT in the co-text of *the number of*. In relation to the only proper noun collocate, the vast majority of the 69 instances of *London* occurring within five words of *cyclists* are from the *London Evening Standard* (65 instances in 54 articles), hence clearly construing Proximity for the target audience of Londoners.

The remaining lexical collocates of *cyclists* likely refer to road users and road use, vehicles, and infrastructure (*cyclist, drivers, motorists, pedestrians, ride, road, roads, use*). To understand their role in establishing newsworthiness requires further comprehensive analysis, which is beyond the scope of this chapter. However, we will briefly consider the co-occurrence of *cyclists* with *pedestrians* and *drivers/motorists*. Table 6.11 shows that *cyclists* are more often grouped with *pedestrians* using *and*

Table 6.11 **Grouping cyclists with other road users**

	Pedestrians	*Drivers*	*Motorists*
X *and cyclists*	30 (*pedestrians and cyclists*)	14 (*drivers and cyclists*)	18 (*motorists and cyclists*)
cyclists and X	49 (*cyclists and pedestrians*)	4 (*cyclists and drivers*)	18 (*cyclists and motorists*)
Total	**79**		**54**
Total instances within 5L:5R span of *cyclists* (no limits)	129	62	86

than with *drivers* or *motorists*, even when frequencies of the latter are combined.[16] This might reflect a discourse where car drivers are seen to differ from non-car users (Davies 2015).

Analysis of all 54 instances where *cyclists* is conjoined with *drivers/motorists*, and analysis of the four most frequent Wordsmith clusters (cf. chapter 1) for *cyclists and pedestrians/pedestrians and cyclists* (default settings) allows the identification of major themes. In addition to 'danger/safety' and 'infrastructure' (see tables A6.5 and A6.6 in the appendix), there is a theme around 'collisions and conflict'. This is particularly strong in relation to conflict between cyclists and motorists/drivers which is construed with a 'battle' or 'war' metaphor, whereas conflict between cyclists and pedestrians primarily involves actual collisions. Examples of metaphorical expressions include *the ongoing battle between, are at war, the war between, hostile encounters between, enmity between, fight for space*, while other expressions also occur (e.g. *love blaming each other, called for more respect between*). Interestingly, in surveys cyclists themselves construct their experience of cycling metaphorically as a battle (Davies 2015), which makes this a prevailing cultural metaphor that is not limited to news discourse.

6.4.4 COMMON COLLOCATES

So far we have discussed collocates for the singular and plural form separately, but tables 6.7 and 6.10 include one identical lexical collocate, namely *killed*. A comparison of *cyclist* and *cyclists* using Sketch Engine's word sketch differences (default settings) suggests that this commonality extends to other negative lexis, since shared collocates include the lemmas DIE, FALL, KILL, HIT, INJURE, INJURED. This provides further evidence for the assumption that Negativity is most typically constructed in relation to accidents. However, we have not yet explored who is involved in these accidents and in what role. Word sketches can again be useful here. Thus, a word sketch for CYCLIST (def. settings) shows that *injured* occurs ten times as modifier, with the concordances provided in figure 6.9. Conversely, a word sketch for INJURED (def.

```
will be completed by summer 2015. Injured  cyclist  urges police to prosecute bus lane crash
             Wakefield Road, Brighouse. The injured  cyclist , believed to be a man in his 50s, has been
       stopped and ran to the aid of the injured  cyclists , it is alleged the driver of the Nissan
            yesterday and offered to visit the injured  cyclists  to offer their condolences and apology
 dedicated bike lane on the promenade. Injured  cyclist  wins his damages action A SCOTS cyclist
          injuries, and stole his wallet. The injured  cyclist  was taken to Edinburgh Royal Infirmary
          "tactic" of putting pressure on injured  cyclists  to accept partial liability for accidents
            said it was "not good enough" for injured  cyclists  to be left lying in the street for up to
        driver stopped briefly to give the injured  cyclists , what one witness described as, a "smart
             charge their lithium batteries. Injured  cyclist  's pity for driver One of the cyclists badly
```

Figure 6.9 Concordances for *injured* as modifier of CYCLIST.

settings) shows that the second most frequent noun after CYCLIST that is modified is *man* (*injured man*)—who is always co-textually identified as cyclist.

Moving on to the verb collocates, the word sketch automatically identifies whether or not the noun CYCLIST occurs as object (e.g. *a motorist who fatally injured a cyclist*) or subject (e.g. *the 35-year-old female cyclist died at the scene*) of verb collocates, including whether or not the node is connected to the collocate through use of a prepositional phrase with *by* (e.g. *she was hit by a cyclist*). In theory, this would allow automatic analysis of the role of cyclists in reported accidents. However, since the word sketch contains several errors, its results were examined manually by reading each concordance.

Unsurprisingly, in all 92 instances of the collocate DIE it is cyclists who die, with the majority of lemma occurrences in the singular form (n = 73). The plural occurrences (figure 6.10) often construct Negativity alongside Proximity (e.g. *in London, on London/Australian/NSW roads*) and possibly Superlativeness (e.g. *28 cyclists died in accidents with HGVs in London*), depending on whether the respective number of reported deaths is considered high.

```
              want all HGVs fitted with sensors after 28 cyclists died in accidents with HGVs in London since
                on London's roads this year. Last year 14 cyclists died in London. Lorries make up five per
                      are doing the right thing." Last year, 43 cyclists died on Australian roads, compared with
     collisions in the 12 months to October, while 13 cyclists died in crashes with heavy vehicles between
                 continuing public health issue. Already 13 cyclists have died on NSW roads in the first eight
   Australian Transport Safety Bureau said. About 35 cyclists die on Australian roads each year, but
                       alone. So far this calendar year, eight cyclists have died on NSW roads. Fourteen were killed
                        had just launched his own business. Five cyclists have died in nine days and Mayor Boris
                        seven months of this year alone. Fourteen cyclists died on London's roads in 2013. So far
                                killed in the capital this year. Fourteen cyclists died last year. His family released the
                     roads in the first half of this year. Nine cyclists have died on NSW roads since the start
                  rush hour traffic at around 7pm. Nineteen cyclists died last year on London's roads - only
                        n't done soon then so will the number of cyclists dying on our roads. The last few weeks
                protest demanding safety improvements. Six cyclists have died this year. Meyer learned of the
                 whether the Mayor was suggesting any of the cyclists who died had jumped red lights, said it
                        we definitely need decent lights." Three cyclists have died and 126 seriously injured in
                      rapid changes to a junction where three cyclists have died in the past decade. Mary Hassell
                      Graeme Obree alongside relatives of two cyclists who died . Audrey Fyfe, 75, was killed
               alleged hit-and-run accident in which two cyclists died . Police have appealed for witnesses
```

Figure 6.10 The verb collocate DIE + *cyclists*.

In contrast, the singular occurrences are mainly connected to reports about an ordinary individual dying, combining Negativity with Personalization—as already suggested in section 6.4.2. As figure 6.11 illustrates, the cause of death is often specified in a phrase or clause following *after* or *in*. In a few cases, further personalizing information occurs in the co-text (*an elderly cyclist, young cyclist*), we hear from relatives (*the daughter/family/mother of a cyclist*), or the individual death is connected

Crimestoppers anonymously on 0800 555 111.	Cyclist	*dies* <u>after</u> collision with car A CYCLIST
her for sponsorship by calling 301 2600.	Cyclist	*died* <u>after</u> ambulance delay. Ambulance bosses
the incident were carried out by police.	Cyclist	*dies* <u>after</u> being hit by lorry A 42-YEAR-OLD
Cyclist dies after collision with car A	CYCLIST	has *died* <u>after</u> colliding with a car while
cyclist is slap on the wrist' THE family of a	cyclist	who *died* <u>after</u> being knocked off his bike
curbs THIS is the "vibrant and stylish"	cyclist	who *died* <u>in</u> an accident with a lorry on
said. Tributes paid to dead cyclist, 51 A	cyclist	who *died* <u>in</u> a crash on his way to work
Three held after cyclist dies in crash A	CYCLIST	has *died* <u>in</u> an apparent hit-and-run in
his bike collided with bus THE mother of a	cyclist	who *died* 48 hours after his 21st birthday
to cyclist killed in accident <u>AN elderly</u>	cyclist	who *died* after being hit by a lorry was
including motorists and cyclists. <u>Young</u>	cyclist	*died* after crash on dangerous bend; Inquest
year and the first involving an HGV. <u>Second</u>	cyclist	*dies* in Crossrail lorry collision A CROSSRAIL
surge of interest in the activity. <u>Sixth</u>	cyclist	*dies* <u>on London's roads</u> A man in his early
being sought. Hit-and-run kills cyclist A	CYCLIST	*died* instantly <u>last night</u> in a hit-and-run
4000 jobs. Help needed in cyclist death A	CYCLIST	*died* in hospital <u>yesterday</u> after colliding

Figure 6.11 Selected concordances for DIE as collocate of *cyclist*.

to wider trends, construing Superlativeness (*sixth cyclist dies on London's roads*). Timeliness is occasionally established through tense/aspect (*dies, has died*) or time references (*died instantly last night, died in hospital yesterday*), while Proximity can also be construed co-textually (e.g. *on London's roads*).

In relation to the verb collocates that can take an object (KILL, HIT, INJURE), we analysed each of the 314 concordances that the word sketch produced for the role of the cyclist. Table 6.12 illustrates that in most cases, the cyclists are the patient rather than the agent.[17] The 11 instances where a cyclist is the agent occur in 6 newspapers: *London Evening Standard* (3), *New York Post* (2), *The New York Times* (1), *Bristol Post* (1), *The Daily Telegraph* (3), and *Herald Sun* (1), most using the phrase *hit by a cyclist/cyclists*. In some cases, negative evaluative language or negative lexis occurs in the co-text (*careless cyclists, A cyclist peddling a $4,000 racing bike at high speed, mowed down, cyclists riding illegally the wrong way*). However, since such instances are rare, these results confirm our hypothesis above that the news value of Negativity is prototypically constructed in relation to cyclists who are injured or die in accidents. In their analysis of news frames in the Australian media, Rissel et al. (2010) likewise identify injury to cyclist(s) and death of cyclist(s) as the most common news angles.

6.5 Summary and conclusion

Before summarizing the key findings from our study, it is worth pointing out some of its limitations. In addition to the general limitations of a corpus linguistic analysis of news values (Potts et al. 2015), a limitation is that we primarily focused on ProtAnt analysis and collocation analysis of CYCLIST, which only occurs in 63% of CyCo (cf. section 6.4.3). Analysis of variants for referring to people on bikes would

Table 6.12 **The role of cyclists**

Collocate	Agent ('cyclist kills/ hits/injures others')	Patient ('cyclist is killed/hit/injured')	Other
kill	2	198	—
hit	9	44	6 unrelated (*cyclists have hit back; stunt cyclist hits new heights; the cyclist has hit the side of my car;* [website] *crashed as it was hit by angry cyclists, about a thousand cyclists hit the streets; cyclists occasionally hit potholes*); 3 instances of cyclists hitting other cyclists; 1 instance of an attack (*the two cyclists hit him in the head with bricks*)
injure	0	48	2 instances with negation (*the cyclist was not injured*) 1 instance of cyclist injuring other cyclist

provide additional valuable insights, especially in the US sub-corpus. A different node (e.g. BIKE, CYCLE, HELMET, LANE, PATH) or different starting point such as a frequency or keywords list would have led us in other directions—see Marchi and Taylor (2009), Baker (2015) on variation in corpus linguistic research. We might then have focused on how newsworthiness is constructed around bike share schemes, or cycling infrastructure. We might have examined whether those quoted through use of the frequent neutral reporting expression *said* (see figure 6.2) are constructed as ordinary or elite or we might have examined the frequent lemmas *new, today, now, yesterday* (figure 6.2), homing in on Timeliness. Starting with linguistic resources that are known to construct particular news values (e.g. *controversial, first*) would have provided further insights.

Further, a focus on prototypicality and range may background variety to some extent. Not all CyCo stories construct Negativity in relation to accidents, and it may be interesting to focus on alternative ways of constructing newsworthiness (e.g. in relation to charity rides, 'elites' who cycle, etc.). A focus on consistency also backgrounds variety between newspapers such as particular themes, differences in frequency (of accident stories), or unique collocates. For instance, *demon* is only a collocate of *cyclist* in the *New York Post* (MI3 = 9.283), which ran a series of articles in September 2014 about a cyclist killing a pedestrian and named and shamed the cyclist with the label *speed-demon (racing) cyclist Jason Marshall*. In the same way in which a focus on differences (which is generally more common in corpus linguistics) may 'create a "blind spot"' (Taylor 2013: 83) a focus on similarities may do so, too.

We were also unable to fully explore the correlation of frequency with social events, in that spikes and falls (Gabrielatos and Baker 2008) or peaks and troughs (Gabrielatos et al. 2012) are influenced by such. In relation to CyCo an obvious example is the introduction of bike hire schemes. We did, however, briefly note in section 6.3 that the potential increase in Australian news reporting about cycling facilities may reflect a larger investment in such infrastructure. There is clearly an interaction between the material world and its newspaper coverage, whether the media initiate change or respond to it (Rissel et al. 2010: 6).

Notwithstanding these limitations, the various corpus linguistic analyses suggest that Negativity is the most typical news value constructed in CyCo and that this news value is established through negative lexis in reports of accidents where cyclists suffer. Such constructions occur in all newspapers, regardless of their cycling culture. In corpus linguistic terms, *cyclist* has a negative semantic prosody (cf. chapter 1). Less common ways of establishing Negativity that we were also able to identify include reports of crime (bike theft), altercations between drivers and cyclists (road rage), accidents where pedestrians are the victims of cyclists, cyclists' traffic and other offenses as well as the metaphorical 'battle' between cyclists and car users. In some cases, we found instances of negative evaluations of cyclists, but we also found an example where a cyclist is constructed as hero.

In addition, there is some evidence for the establishment of Personalization (with *cyclist*) and Superlativeness (with *cyclists*), as well as Timeliness and Proximity. However, noun phrases with both *cyclist* and *driver* rarely construct a high degree of Personalization. Both are rather general category labels that moreover assume that the world of those who cycle differs from those who do not (Rissel et al. 2010: 7). Such labels may sustain attitudes by both cyclists and car users about positive in-groups and negative out-groups (Rissel et al. 2010; Davies 2015)—they construct monolithic and simplified categories of road users. This is also the case with the 'battle' metaphor, which may fan the tensions between those road users who happen to be on a bike and those who happen to be in a car. Finally, the initial word cloud (figure 6.2) pointed to the construction of Eliteness in news items about cycling, but for reason of scope we could not explore this further.

Our results here can be compared to Rissel et al.'s (2010) findings based on a manual framing analysis of 326 Australian articles, where it was found that 'almost half of all articles include the frame of cycling as a risk to cyclists and that death, injury and danger were the main ways in which cycling attracted news media attention' (Rissel et al. 2010: 7). Our findings suggest that this is a journalistic practice which extends to other countries and is the most typical way in which the news value of Negativity is construed in English-language news media. In other words, target readers of these newspapers are routinely exposed to contexts where cycling is constructed as dangerous, which could mean that these readers absorb such negative connotations, as argued by corpus-based critical discourse analysis such as Coffin and O'Halloran (2005).

On the one hand, then, this practice can be criticized, since it construes cycling as risky and cyclists as vulnerable victims. This may reduce the uptake of cycling. Safety fears are cited by questionnaire respondents as a major factor in rejecting cycling, while larger numbers of cyclists on roads increase their safety (Davies 2015). Rissel et al. (2010: 6) also argue that 'negative newspaper stories about cycling may deter people from considering cycling as a transport option'. This type of reporting could thus indirectly result in a reduction of the potential economic, environmental, and health benefits that a country may gain from high rates of cycling as well as in an increase of collisions on account of lower numbers of cyclists.

At the same time, there is a valid argument that such reporting can put the lack of adequate infrastructure on the political agenda and result in the improvement of cycling facilities. It could perhaps also raise awareness about the need for care. Better infrastructure could in turn lead to increased uptake of cycling and fewer collisions. For this second reason, we do not view such reporting as highly problematic. But our analyses have also uncovered more problematic cases where victim-blaming occurs alongside constructions of newsworthiness and cases where cyclists are presented negatively (e.g. as aggressors, perpetrators). The former is an example of cultural emphasis being placed on the responsibility of those cycling which implicitly reduces the need of care by other road users (Davies 2015), while the latter might be instantiations of the negative framing of cyclists as irresponsible and dangerous lawbreakers (Rissel et al. 2010: 6).

It would now be interesting to compare reports about accidents that involve **bikes** and cars, with those involving **cars** and cars, and to consider news reporting in countries with high cycling use such as the Netherlands. A Dutch report cited in Piper et al. (2011: 145) suggests that in such countries it is not bicycling and cyclists that are seen as causing danger, but cars and car drivers. Such analysis remains important, since it 'can shed light on the climate of beliefs and values in which policies that support or hinder cycling are made' (Rissel et al. 2010: 1).

To conclude, this chapter has illustrated one application of DNVA: the critical analysis of the construction of news values around a particular topic or news actors, including identification of any common linguistic practices and ideological implications. It also provides illustration of how the framework for linguistic analysis introduced in chapter 4 can be drawn upon in corpus linguistic research (see further Bednarek and Caple 2014, Potts et al. 2015, Bednarek 2016c). The analyses further demonstrated how one can combine analysis of one general news value (Negativity) with more delicate analysis of how this is discursively constructed. Through its analysis of agency and its identification of victim-blaming the chapter further showed that DNVA can be combined with other tools used in Critical Discourse Analysis (CDA), as explored more fully elsewhere (Bednarek and Caple 2014).

Notes

1. See Rissel et al. (2010), Davies (2015) for relevant research.
2. http://www.bicycling.com/culture/advocacy/2014-top-50-bike-friendly-cities, accessed 25 August 2015.
3. http://www.abc.net.au/mediawatch/transcripts/s4045873.htm, accessed 28 October 2015. Rissel et al.'s (2010: 3) study indeed found that this newspaper had the least amount of positive stories about cycling when compared to three other Australian newspapers.
4. Items about charity rides were included in the corpus, however.
5. In this 'second' round of exclusions we mainly excluded opinion (e.g. reader comments and editorials) but also advice, expert views/analysis, interviews, first person narratives, most tourism/travel pieces, and reviews (about books, exhibitions, gadgets, etc.). But note that the corpus is not restricted to just 'hard news' and includes soft news, longer feature stories, business news, third person portraits of cyclists, announcements, and so on. Thus, announcements of upcoming cycling-related exhibitions were included, but reviews of such were not. Similarly, fashion or tech news stories were included, while advert-like descriptions of a fashion item or tech gadget were excluded. There is undoubtedly some subjectivity in deciding what counts as news and what does not, and what counts as 'cycling' news and what does not (e.g. stories about combined bike/hike rails; stories about a car-free life; stories about traffic safety). However, we tried to be consistent in our decisions and the analysis will focus on recurring patterns as well as identify 'atypical' items. The disadvantage with our approach lies in introducing researcher decisions at the stage of data construction. The disadvantage of the alternative is that the corpus would contain every item that references cyclists/cycling, regardless of whether it is news or opinion.
6. # represents a number. The letters *m, p, e* occur in words with punctuation like *p.m., e-mail, e-bike, A&E*.
7. The ProtAnt settings are the same for all comparisons: the default statistic LL, the default *p*-value (0.01), the default normalized frequency (per 1,000 words), and the default sorting (by normalized key types). The minimum frequency was set to '2' to focus on repeated occurrences. Changing the cut-off *p*-value and ordering the files by number of key tokens apparently has little effect on the ranking of texts (Anthony and Baker 2015b: 284–285).
8. It is mandatory in Australia to wear a helmet when cycling.
9. As with keywords analysis, the reference corpus is important and influences which texts are ranked as prototypical (Anthony and Baker 2015b: 286). Since the ACE dates from 1986, while the node corpus dates from 2004 to 2014, the BE06 was also used as a reference corpus for the Australian data, although it represents a different variety of English. Seven of these ten files also rank among the top ten when the BE06 is used for comparison.
10. Five of these files rank among the ten least typical when BE06 is used as reference corpus.
11. ProtAnt also disregards the range of keywords. For instance, *note* is among the top 25 keywords in the Australian sub-corpus (table 6.5), but occurs only in two files. While it is possible to specify a minimum frequency (which to some extent correlates with range, in that higher frequency items tend to have a higher range), ProtAnt does not currently allow the setting of a minimum range or the sorting by range. Together with the related fact that log likelihood seemingly foregrounds corpus differences at the expense of within-corpus variation (Brezina and Meyerhoff (2014), this might affect the ranking of texts. The usual caveats

for frequency lists also apply, as there are other issues that affect any analysis based simply on form (e.g. homographs).
12. Frequencies for the plural form of the lemma CYCLIST are the highest, followed by frequencies for the singular form and the possessive. Because the possessive is rare we have not included it in our analysis.
13. As a reminder, each circle represents a word and the length of lines between words represents collocational strength (the shorter the stronger). Hyphens do not separate words here. Thus, the GraphColl visualization identifies 343 collocates and shows collocates such as *45-year-old* and *37-year-old*, while Wordsmith identifies *old* as a collocate (Table 6.7).
14. Concordancing also shows that *left* is usually associated with reports of injuries, e.g. *left with life threatening injuries/ brain damaged/ to die/ fighting for his life/ in a critical condition*. If we relax the criteria for collocates, further collocating word forms can be identified that likely relate to accidents, e.g. *hospital, deaths, die, suffered, hurt, dead, serious, struck, seriously, crushed, collided, injury, fall, badly, ambulance, toll, fatalities, colliding, paramedics*.
15. This includes one instance with an intervening adjectival phrase (*critically injured*) and one with *cyclists* elided (*An average of 35 cyclists are killed and **more than 2500** are seriously injured*).
16. Word sketches for the lemmas CYCLIST, BICYCLIST, BIKER, RIDER, PEDESTRIAN, DRIVER, and MOTORIST confirm the strong association between people who cycle and those who walk.
17. Numbers include attributed, modalized, and irrealis cases such as *claim their dogs could be killed by, a cyclist who was almost killed*.

7

Images, news values, and Facebook

7.1 Introduction

This chapter presents the second of our empirical case studies where discursive news values analysis (DNVA) is applied. It focuses on the construction of news values in visuals using the concepts and frameworks introduced in chapters 1 and 5. It aims to illustrate that DNVA can be used to examine journalism as social and semiotic practice, and how DNVA can be combined with the analysis of other aspects of news practice. Since this chapter acts as a case study of how news values are discursively constructed in images, the research presented in this chapter is situated in zone 2 of the topology presented in chapter 1 (reproduced here as figure 7.1). It is mono-modal (analysing images) and focuses primarily on patterns that occur across texts, in this case across Facebook news feeds used by established news media organizations in Australia, Canada, Ireland, United Kingdom, and United States.

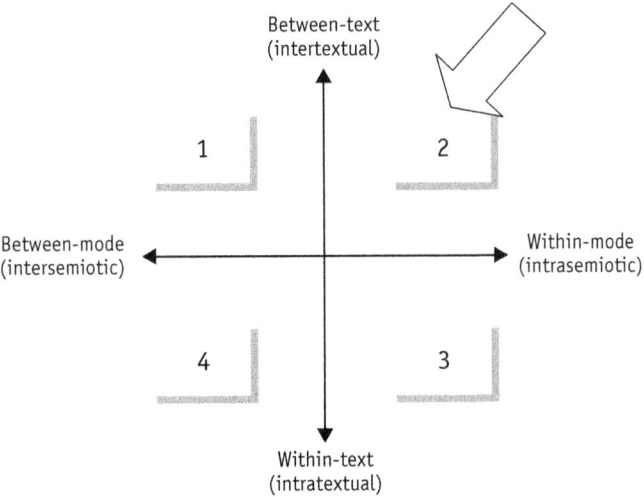

Figure 7.1 Situating the case study.

More specifically, we investigate the push/pull tactics used by news organizations to send stories out via social media news feeds (at Facebook and Twitter), which have the potential to bring readers back into the domain of the news website as people click on the links, arrive at the website story page, and read on. These are known as 'social referrals' and are becoming a vital source of incoming traffic for news websites (Ingram 2015). Two important factors drive our research focus on the social media organization Facebook and on visuals in this case study: (i) Facebook has recently taken over from Google in directing readers to news websites (Ingram 2015); and (ii) virtually all Facebook posts uploaded by news organizations include an image or video (Reid 2014). We have already established that news images have the potential to do more than illustrate a story, as they can and do construct news values, and thus establish the newsworthy aspects of an event for social media audiences—whether they choose to click on the link or not. Therefore, the key question we ask in this chapter is: What news values, if any, do the images used in these social media newsbites construct?

7.2 Social media and news feeds

Research carried out by the Pew Research Center (2015) has found that 63% of both Twitter and Facebook users say that these social media platforms serve 'as a source for news about events and issues outside the realm of friends and family' (Pew Research Centre 2015: 2). How social media users receive such news varies in a number of ways, from actively searching for and subscribing to the news feeds of major news organizations to consuming posts and tweets that others (e.g. friends or family) have 'shared', 'liked', or 'retweeted'.

In this study, we are not so much interested in how users access, search, or subscribe to news (a task for ethnographers). As discourse analysts, we are interested in the stories that news organizations choose to post on social media via their own Facebook pages or their own Twitter accounts. What news values do such stories construct? Is there a tendency to favour particular types of stories that will generate certain configurations of news values? For example, Maria Breslin, digital editor of the *Liverpool Echo* in the United Kingdom, has found that 'People and community stories, on Facebook particularly, tend to do very, very well' (Reid 2014). This would suggest that the news values of Personalization and Proximity would most likely be constructed in news posted on Facebook. Is this indeed the case?

Before we begin answering this and other questions, we need to know what news posted by news organizations on Facebook and Twitter looks like. Simply put, images dominate these spaces. While the posts and tweets that news organizations publish via social media are constrained by the template conventions of these platforms, the space reserved for the images in such templates is large. Figure 7.2 exemplifies the layout of a post and tweet of a story from the Facebook and Twitter accounts of the news organization *Al Jazeera English* alongside how it appears on the website of that news organization.

As can be seen in figure 7.2, the Facebook posts and tweets are verbally minimal, and combine words, images, share options, and hyperlinks. The use of images across platforms is quite varied: images may differ across platforms (as is the case in figure 7.2); the same image may be used on all three platforms (more commonly the case); images may appear in full; or they may be cropped sections of the image used on the story page of the website.[1] The aim of this case study is to examine the discursive construction of news values in the images used in the social media posts published by news media organizations, thus demonstrating the newsworthy aspects of events that are constructed in the news imagery on social media.

7.3 Data and methodology

For this case study, we sampled a range of English-language news organizations that have an established digital presence in the form of a Facebook page, a Twitter account, and a website, and that are regularly updated. These are 22 news organizations covering Australia, Canada, Ireland, United Kingdom, and United States, and include public broadcasters (*ABC, BBC, CBC, NPR, RTE*), 'quality' (*The New York Times, The Guardian*), and 'popular' (*Daily Mail, New York Post*) legacy news media, and digital natives (*Crikey, BuzzFeed, Huffington Post*). News organizations from South Africa (*Mail & Guardian*), India (*The Times of India*), and the Middle East (*Al Jazeera English*) have been included as an unrepresentative sample of reporting from other nations that have English-language news websites.[2] Table 7.1 offers a full list of the news organizations and their social media sites sampled in this study.[3]

For data sampling, we followed the constructed week method, which is a type of stratified random sampling in which the complete sample represents all days of the week to account for cyclical variation of news content (Luke et al. 2011: 78). We collected ten days' worth of data over ten weeks between January and March 2015 (counting weekdays only),[4] thus yielding two constructed weeks, which is in line with the minimum recommended by Hester and Dougall (2007: 820) for the content analysis of online news. Figure 7.3 shows the constructed week sampling for this case study (the first column being Sunday).

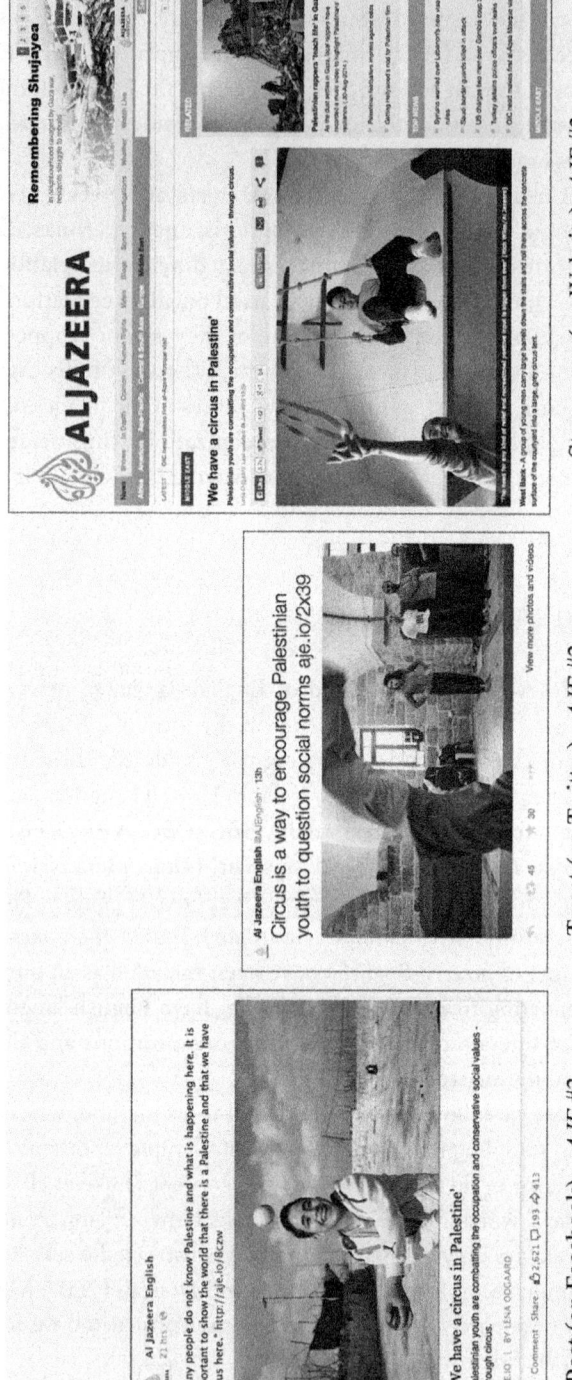

Post (on Facebook) *AJE #3*   Tweet (on Twitter) *AJE #3*   Story page (on Website) *AJE #3*

Figure 7.2 Layout of story posts and tweets on Facebook and Twitter and the corresponding website (*Al Jazeera English* photos: Rich Wiles/Al Jazeera English).

Table 7.1 **News media organizations sampled for the social media case study**

		Facebook page	Twitter page	Abbreviations used for data collection
Australia (5)				
		The Sydney Morning Herald	@smh	SMH
		The Australian	@australian	AUS
		News.com.au	@newscomauHQ	News
		Crikey.com.au	@crikey_news	Crikey
		ABC News	@abcnews	ABC
United Kingdom/Ireland (6)				
United Kingdom		The Guardian	@guardiannews	GUA
		The Times and The Sunday Times	@thetimes	Times
		Daily Mail	@MailOnline	DM
		BBC News	@BBCBreaking	BBC
Ireland		The Irish Times	@irishtimes	IT
		RTE News	@rtenews	RTE
North America (8)				
United States		The New York Times	@nytimes	NYT
		USA Today	@USATODAY	USA
		New York Post	@nypost	NYP
		NPR	@nprnews	NPR
		BuzzFeed News	@BuzzFeedNews	Buzz
		Huffington Post	@HuffingtonPost	Huff
Canada		The Globe and Mail	@globeandmail	GM
		CBC News	@CBCNews	CBC
Other regions (3)				
South Africa		Mail & Guardian	@mailandguardian	MG
India		The Times of India	@timesofindia	TOI
Middle East		Al Jazeera English	@AJEnglish	AJE
TOTAL: 22 news organizations				

Figure 7.3 The constructed week sampling method.

A research assistant (RA) collected the data on the assigned date, as per the calendar in figure 7.3. The RA collected five stories per publication per day (110 stories per day) according to the guidelines outlined below, and in three forms: a screen capture of the Facebook post, the related tweet at Twitter, and the story page at the news organization's website. This resulted in a total of 50 stories per publication over the whole period. Across 22 publications, this meant that a total of 1,100 stories were captured in these three forms—we will call this data set the Facebook Corpus, since Facebook was the departure point for the data collection. As noted above, this platform leads social media platforms in directing traffic to the websites of news organizations.

Since we are interested in Facebook posts that direct audiences **from** Facebook **to** the news organization's website, we only collected social media posts that contained links to the online story page (not, e.g., shared photos or posts from other social media users). To ensure that we only collected news stories (not opinion), the RA first checked that the link from Facebook directed readers to stories appearing in the 'News' section of the website, that is, they were labelled as generalist news (News, Political News, Breaking News, Local News, Regional News, National News, World News, etc.). Once this connection was established, the RA screen captured the Facebook post, any associated tweet (not all items included one), and the story page on the news organization's website (see figure 7.4). Screen captures ensured that the integrity of the original page layout was maintained, including any images used in the stories (as per figure 7.2).

The RA also collected basic information about each item in an MS Office Excel spreadsheet. This included the date of publication, URL to the original story (for quick access if there is a query on the data), and the story's section on the news website (e.g. Political News, World News). He also noted whether a tweet relating to the item was posted at Twitter, and if yes, if the tweet included a photograph and whether the same image was used across all platforms. Additionally, we collected information on image attribution and the caption, if any, that was used with the image on the story page at the news organization's website. We discuss the insights arising from this data collection in section 7.4.1 in relation to the emerging social media and online practices of news organizations.

Having completed the initial data collection, the subsequent news values analysis of the images was carried out by Caple, using a relational database (MS Access),

Images, news values, and Facebook 177

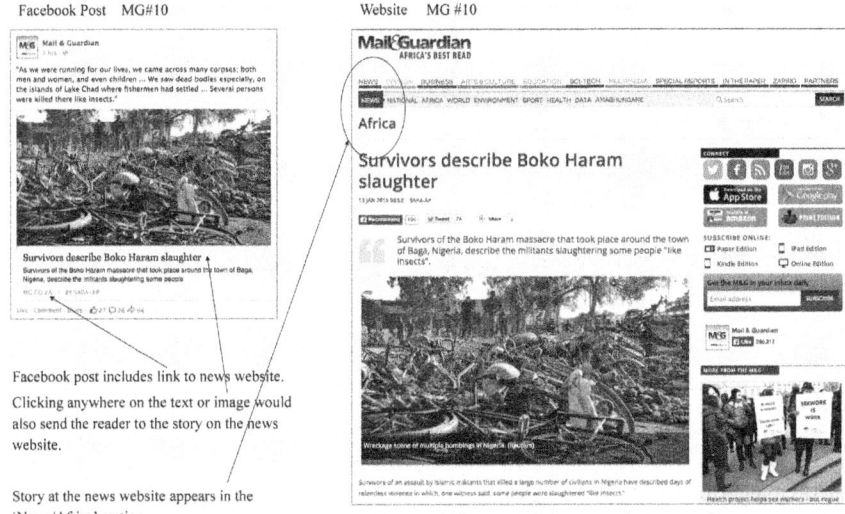

Figure 7.4 Cues used to determine eligibility for inclusion in the data collection (*Mail & Guardian* photos: Reuters).

and applying the framework for visual DNVA introduced in chapter 5. A coding manual was created for the analysis of the images in this chapter and in chapter 8 (available at the DNVA website: http://www.newsvaluesanalysis.com). Since the main difference in the use of imagery in Facebook posts and tweets on Twitter was absence (related tweets, in general, were much less likely to include an image), we proceeded by only analysing the images used in the Facebook posts. Thus, the analysed visuals comprise the 1,100 images captured from Facebook posts from 22 news organizations.

The most time-efficient method of collating the analysis of these images was to use a relational database (introduced in chapter 1), designed specifically for this case study. The 'form' interface of this database is shown in figure 7.5. The database allows the analyst to design fields to capture the required form of analysis, in this case whether a particular news value is ('Yes') or is not ('No') constructed in the image. An additional option of 'Possible' was used for all news values except for the category Valence, which offered three choices of Negative, Positive, and Unclear/None (the most efficient means of coding the news values of Negativity and Positivity). The choice of 'Possible' was added to the coding scheme to be able to account for problematic or more subjective cases, where it was difficult both to account for target audience preferences and to eliminate coder bias. Such cases are explained and exemplified in the coding manual. Since we were dealing with a large data set requiring manual analysis of

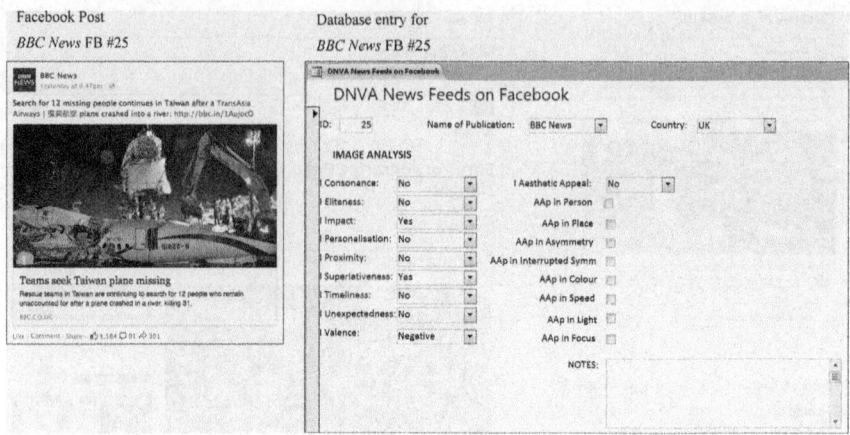

Figure 7.5 The relational database user interface alongside the analysed image (*BBC News* photo: not attributed).

each image in turn, we did not include details of **how** each news value was constructed in this database (with the exception of Aesthetic Appeal, as outlined in section 7.4.2.2).

To demonstrate how the database works, figure 7.5 shows the DNVA analysis of an image from the *BBC News* data set. The Facebook post of story #25 *BBC News* includes an image showing the wreckage of an aeroplane, a section of which is suspended in the air behind the main body of the wreckage. This image constructs the news values of Negativity, Impact (the aftermath of the disaster), and Superlativeness (the large scale of the destruction of the plane). The database record shown on the right reflects this analysis, with Impact and Superlativeness selecting 'Yes', Valence selecting 'Negative', and all other news values selecting 'No', as none of the remaining news values are constructed.

For the analysis of Aesthetic Appeal, fields have been included in the database that demonstrate how this news value has been constructed in the image. For reasons outlined in chapter 5, this news value can be constructed through compositional means (asymmetry, interrupted symmetry), through the technical aspects of image capture (movement, focus, noise), or through content that appeals to the cultural/social conventions of what makes for a beautiful place or person. Since assessments of Aesthetic Appeal are subjective, we wanted to clarify in our analysis how this particular news value was constructed in the images.[5]

The database query function was used to assess how often each news value was constructed and in what kinds of combinations, as explained in chapter 1. The results of the visual DNVA are presented and discussed in section 7.4.2, but we first discuss the results from the data collection in section 7.4.1.

7.4 Results

7.4.1 EMERGING NEWS PRACTICES

Table 7.2 collates the information that the RA collected about each item in the data collection. The information collated in table 7.2 shows some interesting trends regarding the social media habits of these 22 news organizations and the use of images at their websites. South Africa's *Mail & Guardian* newspaper, for example, is the only news organization in this data set that consistently posts and tweets the same news items on both Facebook and Twitter (all 50 stories). It also consistently uses the same photograph for both Facebook posts and within the story page at the news website. *The Guardian* (UK), on the other hand, has the lowest correlation between items posted on Facebook and items posted on Twitter (12 tweets relating to the 50 Facebook posts we collected), which suggests that *The Guardian* uses these two social media platforms for quite different purposes. The *ABC* (Australia), the *Daily Mail* (UK), and *USA Today* (US) post items only from their main 'News' section on Facebook, while *NPR* and *Huffington Post* (US) both post news items from a wide variety of news subsections (e.g. Black Voices, Latino Voices, Weird News, Good News).[6]

It is interesting to note that a number of institutions do not include images with the story on their websites, even though their post to Facebook does include an image. *Huffington Post* (US) has 19 stories without images on their website, likewise *The Australian* (14) and *The Times of India* (13). Australia's *Crikey.com.au* tends not to tweet images (44 verbal tweets related to their Facebook posts and only one tweet with an image), while Canada's *CBC News* does the opposite (45 related tweets with images). *Al Jazeera English*, *BBC News*, and the *Daily Mail* show the greatest variation in image use across Facebook, Twitter, and their websites, as they are more likely to use different images on each platform from the same event. Figure 7.2 demonstrates this variety in image selection at *Al Jazeera English*, where three different aspects of the same event (Circus in Palestine) are depicted in the three images that appear on the Facebook post, the tweet, and the story page at the website.

Such findings suggest that the use of social media by news organizations has yet to settle on a model of best practice—hence the level of variation and experimentation that appears to be evident in these results. In other words, these are clearly variable and emerging rather than stable and conventionalized news practices, which makes them an important object of study. Each of these organizations also has different target audiences, which may account for variation in how different social media platforms are used.

The attribution of images to a photographer, contributor, or publishing news agency (e.g. Reuters) also varies widely across this data set. Only four of the 22

Table 7.2 General information regarding the makeup of the Facebook Corpus

Country/Region	Name of publication	Facebook Posts	Related tweets						News website			
			Related Tweet (no image)	Related Tweet with image	Repetition within Tweets	Total unique tweets	Number of sections stories taken from	Same images used across platforms	Stories without images	Images with NO attribution	Images with NO Captions
Australia	ABC	50	28	12	1	39	1	31	6	3	0
	The Australian	50	32	26	10	48	2	28	14	1	1
	Crikey.com.au	50	44	1	1	43	1	45	3	47	43
	news.com.au	50	10	23	4	29	2	23	1	1	0
	The Sydney Morning Herald	50	40	10	2	48	4	29	5	2	0
Canada	CBC News	50	5	45	4	46	4	29	4	1	0
	Globe & Mail	50	37	17	7	47	5	43	0	0	0
Ireland	The Irish Times	50	6	33	2	37	7	41	0	12	2
	RTE	50	14	39	5	48	3	22	0	42	0
Other regions	Al Jazeera English	50	12	14	2	24	12	13	11	2	2
	Mail & Guardian	50	50	1	1	50	5	50	0	2	0
	The Times of India	50	44	4	0	48	5	21	13	24	6

Country	Source										
United Kingdom	BBC News	50	11	8	3	16	6	18	5	19	5
	Daily Mail	50	8	10	1	17	1	15	0	8	0
	The Guardian	50	13	1	1	12	3	39	4	1	0
	The Times of London	50	7	38	2	43	12	40	0	6	0
United States	BuzzFeed	50	11	42	5	48	5	31	7	0	30
	Huffington Post	50	21	4	0	25	14	25	19	4	10
	NPR	50	23	3	1	25	15	38	2	2	1
	New York Post	50	24	22	4	42	2	38	5	4	11
	The New York Times	50	39	10	2	47	8	32	2	0	0
	USA Today	50	22	7	1	28	1	45	0	0	0

news organizations sampled are consistent in their attribution of images to an author (*BuzzFeed, The Globe and Mail, The New York Times,* and *USA Today*), while the Australian online news organization *Crikey.com.au* never attributes any of the images it publishes to either the author of the image or to the publisher who owns the rights to those images.[7] Twelve of 22 news websites consistently use captions on the images on their story pages, while *Crikey* again does not use captions on its website images. Thirty out of 43 images used on the *BuzzFeed* website also do not have a caption. While the accuracy and informative function of caption writing is remarkably inconsistent across all forms of news storytelling (see Caple and Knox 2012, 2015), captions could serve an important function in the storytelling process in both anchoring the meaning of the activity sequence in the image per se, and anchoring the image to the news context in which it is situated (Caple 2013a). The fact that several news organizations either omit captions completely from the images used or provide limited and uninformative captions suggests that the images are considered as self-explanatory.

7.4.2 NEWS VALUES ANALYSIS

7.4.2.1 *Dominant news values and their clusterings*

The most general question that we could ask of the Facebook Corpus is: Which news values are constructed in the images in this corpus? The answer is that all news values, except Timeliness, are constructed in the images that news organizations post with their Facebook newsbites. The three dominant news values are Eliteness (33%), Personalization, and Proximity (both 29%), as outlined in table 7.3. These are followed by Negativity (at 26%) and Positivity (19%). As noted in chapter 5, Timeliness is only rarely constructed in news images, either by depicting culturally or seasonally relevant events or by including verbal text that references current time. Thus, it is not surprising that these images do not clearly construct this news value. Generally, then, the images used in the social media posts by news organizations construct events as involving people, both well-known and ordinary actors. These events are also generally constructed as geographically close to the target audiences of these publications.[8]

Other interesting results for this data set arise from an exploration of the ways in which news values co-occur. Since Eliteness, Personalization, and Proximity are most commonly construed in this data set, do these news values cluster together in any way? They do indeed, and they also co-occur with Positivity. Table 7.4 shows the most common clusterings of these news values across the whole data set. Combinations of these news values with Negativity are also included in table 7.4 as a point of comparison.

The most common clustering of news values is Eliteness with {Positivity or no valence}, meaning that the images do not construct the event as overtly negative. This is closely followed by the same clustering with the addition of Proximity. By

Table 7.3 **News values constructed in the Facebook Corpus**

News value	Yes	% of Total (1,100) Images
Aesthetic Appeal	23	2
Consonance	6	1
Eliteness	**362**	**33**
Impact	92	8
Negativity	**287**	**26**
Personalization	**320**	**29**
Positivity	206	19
Proximity	**319**	**29**
Superlativeness	113	10
Timeliness	0	0
Unexpectedness	131	12

Table 7.4 **The most common clusterings involving Eliteness, Personalization, and Proximity**

News value clusters	% of Total (1,100) images
Eliteness + {Positivity or No valence}	28.3
Eliteness + Proximity + {Positivity or No valence}	24.0
Personalization + {Positivity or No valence}	21.0
Personalization + Proximity + {Positivity or No valence}	4.4
Personalization + Negativity	3.6
Eliteness + Proximity + Negativity	1.8

and large then, the images published in the Facebook posts of these news organizations construct (aspects of) reported events as positive, as involving widely known elite news actors, and of relevance to the target audiences of these publications.

Personalization also co-occurs with {Positivity and no valence}. Interestingly, the combination of Proximity with Personalization is very low, occurring in 4.4% of images—which contrasts with the combination of Proximity with Eliteness in 24% of the images. This may be explained by the fact that elite news actors tend to be photographed in widely known (potentially also elite) settings or that such images may also include regalia (flags, insignia) that clearly place the event in a particular geographical setting (cf. example A in figure 7.6). With images of ordinary news actors, the setting may be difficult to place or may simply be eliminated—hence the very low clustering of Personalization with Proximity. This may also indicate that ordinary news actors do not carry the same cultural capital that may be attached to elite news actors. The images in figure 7.6 exemplify these most common clusterings of news values in images from the Facebook Corpus.

The image in example A in figure 7.6 depicts an elite news actor, former Senator Edward Brooke, who one could reasonably assume would be known to readers of *USA Today*, where this story originated from (he was the first African American to be elected to the Senate by popular vote). The setting (which is depicted behind the senator) also confirms that events are taking place in America (with the statue of Lincoln, and the large painting depicting the surrender of Lord Cornwallis placing the events in the image specifically in the Capitol Rotunda, also widely known as an

A: Eliteness + Proximity + Positivity (USA #4)

B: Eliteness + Positivity (AUS #20)

C: Personalisation + Proximity + Positivity

D: Personalisation + Positivity (BBC #29)

Figure 7.6 The clusterings of Eliteness and Personalization with Proximity (A: *USA Today* photo: Alex Brandon/AP; B: *The Australian* photo: AP; C: *NPR* photo: Emily Jan/NPR; D: *BBC News* photo: not attributed).

elite setting). Thus, the news values of Eliteness and Proximity are constructed in this image. Brooke is also enthusiastically laughing and waving in the image, establishing Positivity. The image in example B in figure 7.6 also depicts widely known elites in US President Obama, First Lady Michelle Obama, and Saudi King Salman bin Abdul Aziz. These are elites that one could reasonably expect readers of *The Australian* newspaper to recognize, and as such the image constructs Eliteness. These three elite news actors are also smiling (Positivity). This image, however, does not show any of the wider context in which this event is taking place (it is completely whited out). The fact that they are surrounded by only Saudi officials/bodyguards suggests that events may be taking place in Saudi Arabia, and as such does not construct geographical Proximity for the Australian target audience.

The images in examples C and D in figure 7.6 both construct the news values of Personalization and Positivity. The young women depicted in these images are not easily recognizable as elites or famous news actors. They are all wearing the less formal attire we associate with depictions of ordinary people, and the young women in the image in example C are participating in activities associated with the young. The presence of the photographer does not appear to be interfering with these activities (intensive use of mobile phones).[9] Both of the images in examples C and D also include verbal text. In example C, one of the young women is wearing a cap with 'The Washington Times' embroidered on it. Such verbal text helps to locate the image in an American setting, and as such establishes Proximity for the target audience of *NPR*, where this story comes from. In the image in example D, the young woman is holding up a poster. However, none of the words that are legible on the poster place the location of events in a specific context, apart from suggesting that the person in the image could be from an English-speaking background. The setting depicted in the image in example D is also sufficiently vague and limited to not be able to discern a specific or known setting for the events happening in this image. Therefore Proximity is not constructed in this image.

While all four images in figure 7.6 construct the news value of Positivity, this does not mean that the news stories as a whole concern positive events. It appears to be a conventionalized journalistic practice to make use of images of smiling news actors in stories about their deaths, as is the case in examples A and D in figure 7.6 (see chapter 8 for further examples), or when stories concern a matter of controversy, as is the case in example B in figure 7.6. Thus, while the images may construct Positivity, the verbal text may construct Negativity. We discuss this issue further in the next chapter where we move to multimodal/intersemiotic analysis (zone 1 of our topology).

Returning to the results listed in table 7.4, the clustering of Eliteness or Personalization with Negativity occurs in very few stories in this data set. In other words, images posted on the news feeds at Facebook rarely construct events as negative for the people involved in them. When they do, they are more likely to be constructed as negative for ordinary news actors (3.6%) rather than for elites (1.8%). Such findings may be explainable through the constraints and interests of journalism.

The public appearances of elite news actors are often highly orchestrated, and press access to these elites is often limited to those public engagements where the person is shown in a positive light. One can assume that the imagery produced out of such engagements would overwhelmingly construct Positivity. Ordinary citizens are more likely to be of interest to news organizations when something negative has happened to them. Such representations could also be commented on critically, since it appears to result in politicians and other people with elite status being only represented in positive contexts—a representation that is more similar to public relations than news.

The news value of Negativity is more likely to co-occur with the news value of Impact (in 7.7% of all stories). This is a common clustering of news values, which also tends to co-occur with Superlativeness, especially in hard news reporting. The images used in the *BBC News* Facebook post in figure 7.5 and in the *Mail & Guardian* post in figure 7.4 are good examples of the clustering of Negativity, Impact, and Superlativeness. In both of these cases, human participants are not the main focus in the image; rather the damage to machinery and the built environment is depicted.

Only about 2% of the images in the Facebook Corpus also construct Personalization alongside Negativity and Impact. The image in figure 7.7 is an example of this

Figure 7.7 The construction of Negativity, Impact, Personalization (and Superlativeness) (*The Times* photo: Vantagenews.co.uk).

combination of news values. The image shows a man and child being escorted by a police officer. Like in the example concerning the Sydney siege in chapter 5, the actions and gestures of the police officer appear to be protective towards the man, escorting him away from danger, towards safety. This action, combined with the extreme negative emotion shown in the man's face (caused by the event) also construct this event as maximally negative for the man and the child.

7.4.2.2 The construction of Aesthetic Appeal

While Aesthetic Appeal is constructed in only 2% (23 images) of the Facebook Corpus, it is interesting to note how this news value is constructed in this corpus. As noted in chapter 5, we suggest that there are a number of ways in which Aesthetic Appeal can be established in images: through compositional means (asymmetry or interrupted symmetry), through the technical aspects of image capture (speed, focus), or through content that conforms to the cultural/social conventions of what makes for a beautiful place or person. Since these often combine with each other, table 7.5 summarizes the total number of instances of each technique, while figure 7.8 exemplifies how these techniques combine with each other in examples taken from the Facebook Corpus.

Interestingly, the images in all of the examples in figure 7.8 accompany principally negative news stories. The stories report, for example, on the death of an actor, the potential negative health consequences of wind farms, an act of vandalism, and an accident involving a newborn baby being flushed onto the tracks of a railway from a moving train. As we have argued elsewhere (Bednarek and Caple 2010; Caple 2013a), the construction of Aesthetic Appeal in the image has the potential to create an evaluative clash with the construction of Negativity in the verbal text. We have not investigated the impact that such clashes have on audiences, but since this is a practice that we have now seen occurring across different forms of and platforms for news storytelling, such audience research would be worthy of further study.

Table 7.5 **The construction of Aesthetic Appeal in the Facebook Corpus**

Constructed in	Total number of instances
Composition	15
Technical affordances	15
Content (person/place)	9

7.4.2.3 Variation across countries

Since we collected information regarding publication and country of origin for our study, we are able to assess the extent to which publications or countries/regions

188 THE DISCOURSE OF NEWS VALUES

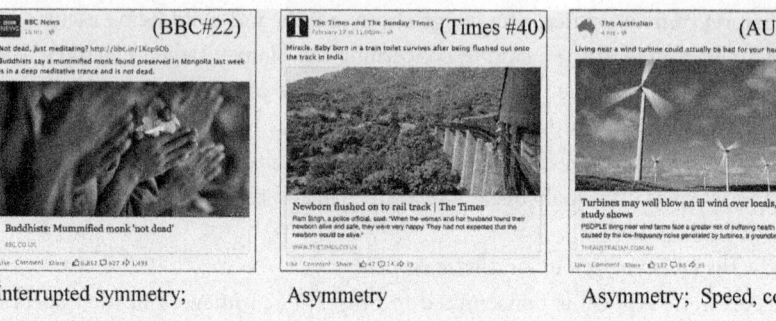

| Interrupted symmetry; Colour, light, focus | Asymmetry | Asymmetry; Speed, colour |

| Person; Light | Architecture; Light, colour | Nature; Asymmetry; Colour, light, speed |

Figure 7.8 The construction of the news value Aesthetic Appeal in the Facebook Corpus (BBC #22: *BBC News* photo: AFP; Times #40: *The Times* photo: Amar Grover/Corbis; AUS #13: *The Australian* photo: not attributed; BBC #33: *BBC News* photo: AFP; GM #48: *Globe and Mail* photo: Tony Gentile/Reuters; GUA #15: *The Guardian* photo: David Clapp/Getty Images).

give preference to particular constructions of news values. Table 7.6 summarizes the total number of times that each news value is constructed in the images in the Facebook Corpus, according to the country/region the publications come from.

Table 7.6 suggests that the United Kingdom is somewhat different to the other regions included in this study. By comparison, publications from the United Kingdom carry a lot more images that construct the news values of Aesthetic Appeal and Unexpectedness, and considerably fewer images that construct Proximity. Publications from the United States score highest on images that construct Personalization and Positivity, while Irish publications publish more images constructing Negativity and Impact that any other region, also scoring highly on the construction of Superlativeness. The group of publications that sample reporting from other regions score highest on the construction of Eliteness and Superlativeness in the imagery they published on their Facebook posts. Australian publications score highly on images that construct Proximity, Positivity, and Eliteness. Canadian publications occupy the middle ground in virtually all

Table 7.6 **Total number of news values constructed according to country/region**

Country/region	News values (as % of total number of publications/stories surveyed per region)										
	Aesthetic Appeal	Consonance	Eliteness	Impact	Negativity	Personalization	Positivity	Proximity	Superlativeness	Timeliness	Unexpectedness
Australia	2.4	1.2	37.6	4.8	26.0	28.4	19.6	41.2	8.0	0.0	7.6
Canada	3.0	0.0	33.0	7.0	21.0	32.0	18.0	26.0	5.0	0.0	8.0
Ireland	0.0	1.0	32.0	13.0	31.0	23.0	14.0	31.0	13.0	0.0	8.0
Other	0.7	0.0	40.7	12.0	28.7	16.0	18.0	39.3	14.0	0.0	9.3
United Kingdom	4.5	0.5	21.0	10.0	29.5	33.0	19.0	8.5	12.5	0.0	19.5
United States	1.3	0.3	33.3	7.3	22.7	34.7	20.0	27.7	9.7	0.0	14.3

categories of news value construction, except for the construct of Negativity, which is least likely to be constructed in images.

Since research on the sharing practices of news organizations is still somewhat in its infancy and since we have discovered much variation between individual newspapers (section 7.4.1), it is difficult to state whether these findings indicate established practices among publications from these different regions of the world. One could also query whether the results are skewed by the inclusion of more or less 'popular' or 'quality' publications within each region. In relation to the findings for the United States, for example, this data set includes two digital native publications (*BuzzFeed* and *Huffington Post*), and a 'popular' newspaper (*New York Post*). One could hypothesize that these publications particularly favour the sharing of images that construct Personalization and Positivity. In fact *BuzzFeed* published the least number of images that construct Personalization (13 images), while *The New York Times* and *Huffington Post* published 15 images constructing Personalization. With regards to the construction of Positivity, all six US publications published a similar number of stories (all within two to three of each other) that construct Positivity.

The opposite is true for the range of publications surveyed from the British news media. In this data set, the *Daily Mail* published a lot more images constructing Unexpectedness than any of the other UK publications surveyed: 19 images compared to 9 from *The Times*, 7 from *The Guardian*, and 4 from *BBC News*. Similarly, *The Guardian* published the most images constructing Aesthetic Appeal (5), while the *Daily Mail* published none. While it might be possible to conclude that US publications tend to focus on the more personal and positive newsworthy aspects of events in their Facebook posts, one could not generalize about the focus of newsworthiness in the UK news media. As we briefly noted in chapter 1, DNVA can be used to compare particular news outlets or outputs, including differences across cultures/countries. What the results in this section clearly point to is the value of comparing not just countries but also types of news publications ('popular', 'quality', 'heritage', 'digital native') and even individual newspapers. However, for this purpose new and representative data sets would need to be collected, which is beyond the scope of this chapter.

7.4.2.4 *Why do some images not construct any news values?*

Finally, we turn our attention to another notable finding from the Facebook Corpus in that 8.3% (or 91) of the images arguably do not construct any news values at all. Closer inspection of these 91 images shows that they are likely to be images of landscapes, buildings, or animals and without human participants, or they are stock photographs, generally of objects (a piece of fruit, machinery, a bottle), and usually sourced from agencies like Alamy or Getty Images. The image in figure 7.9 is an example of a hard news story that has used a stock photograph from Getty Images on its Facebook post. The corresponding story page at *ABC News* does not use a photograph at all.

Images, news values, and Facebook 191

Figure 7.9 The use of stock photography in the Facebook Corpus (*ABC News* photo: Getty Images).

Since we only collected Facebook posts that linked to **news** stories on the websites of news organizations, the question this leads us to is: What is the function of images that do not construct any news values in such posts? Images that show us objects, food items, animals, or landscapes/buildings could be classified as conceptual images (Kress and van Leeuwen 2006), giving audiences examples of types of things (as a taxonomy would), and as such would contribute little to the narrative or news storytelling potential of the story beyond offering illustration of a concept or thing. This seems to be particularly pertinent when there is a form or template to be filled. Stock photography can easily be used to fill a space, no matter how tenuous the link between image and story (as in figure 7.9), thus simply making the news more 'visible' and 'visual'. The use of stock photography in news contexts, however, may have other, possibly more significant implications.

Machin (2004: 317; Machin and van Leeuwen 2007: 151) describes the increased reliance on stock photography in news discourse as shifting the emphasis away from photography as witness and towards photography as a symbolic system. Images made available through stock photography services, like Getty, can be classified according to their genericity, timelessness, and low modality (Machin and van Leeuwen 2007: 151). This means photography that 'no longer captures specific, unrepeatable moments' (Machin and van Leeuwen 2007: 152), but rather 'denotes general class or types of people, places and things'. Such generic images 'come to represent the whole of a particular time, place and way of life' to the extent that 'we gradually come to accept that these are showing us how the world really is' (Machin and van Leeuwen 2007: 157). In the case of the image used in the *ABC News* Facebook post in figure 7.9, we can ask the question: Which 'way of life' is being represented in this image? It is certainly a heteronormative life that is being represented in this image, and it is certainly one where the female in this partnership is sexualized, given the choice of lacy/sexy, very small knickers for 'her' and the very large unglamorous y-fronts for 'him'.

Interestingly, there is no relation between this image and the actual hard news story it accompanies. The story concerns two males (no females are mentioned in the story), arrested at Brisbane Airport, after 5kg of drugs were seized from the underpants of one of the men. If the *ABC* was aiming to have a little fun with this story (e.g. that the men were 'hung out to dry' as it were and 'by their underpants'), why did they not choose an image showing two pairs of male y-fronts? A simple Google Image search for 'underpants on a washing line' gives an almost infinite number of permutations of underpants on washing lines, including the image in figure 7.9 but also including plenty of examples of two pairs of y-fronts. The latter would have at least been marginally more accurate and would have equally captured the attention of Facebook users who may simply be browsing news posts, thus also functioning as 'visual clickbait'. Instead, the dominant patriarchal and sexist position is reinforced, which, we would argue, has the potential to insult the more liberal sensibilities of *ABC* audiences.

The reasons for using stock photography are tied up in the digital disruption of recent decades, but their use has implications that extend far beyond the comical, the illustrative, or indeed the innocent. Like many other industries, the news media industry has undergone tremendous changes. Of particular relevance to the arguments made here, is the fact that many news organizations have completely eradicated their photography departments (Young 2010; Bowers 2014; Peterson 2015), instead now relying on the imagery available for purchase through news agencies like Reuters, AFP, AP, Rex, as well as from stock photography providers like Getty Images.[10] Other factors including the 24-hour news cycle, the additional responsibilities given to individuals to upload content to social media platforms, and the template format of such platforms that come with ready-made slots for images have also impacted on how images are chosen for inclusion in a publication and where such images are sourced from. Such transformations have significant implications for the news storytelling potential of the imagery used, a potential that is gradually being replaced by imagery that merely reflects or reinforces dominant ideologies.

In sum, the discursive news values analysis presented in this chapter has demonstrated the potential for studying both the construction and the absence of news values in images. The images associated with the news items posted to Facebook by international news organizations, by and large, construct the news values of Eliteness, Personalization, Proximity, and Negativity. The news value of Timeliness was absent in this study, and it proved very difficult to assess the construction of Consonance across this diverse set of publications. Aesthetic Appeal was also a somewhat marginal news value. The news values Superlativeness and Impact are equally represented in the data set, and tend to cluster around Negativity, especially when the images focus more on material or environmental negative happenings, rather than on the people involved.

7.5 Conclusion

This chapter showcased visual DNVA and the use of a relational database for analysis and querying of data in large-scale DNVA (examining 1,100 images). The case study has confirmed that the task of establishing the newsworthiness of reported news events is not the sole responsibility of words. News images also have a job to do that is beyond the purely illustrative, including the construction of news values in events. We use the term *news images* here quite deliberately to mean images that have been sourced from photojournalists attending and recording events as they unfold (i.e. photography as witness, capturing specific, unrepeatable moments). This is because—as we have also demonstrated in this chapter—the provenance of some of the imagery used in the news media is not from photojournalistic contexts. Such images are increasingly sourced from stock photography agencies, which rarely convey any newsworthiness. In this chapter, we have offered close and critical analysis of only one example of imagery taken from a stock photo supplier, but there is plenty of scope for future research projects to focus specifically on the key differences between news and stock photography and their construction of newsworthiness. In general, it appears to be useful to consider both the presence and the **absence** of news values in images and to explore the ramifications this may have.

In this case study we examined the type of Facebook posts that draw readers away from that platform and onto the website of the news organization producing the respective post. Companion audience research could examine whether the construction of news values in these posts are an important factor in compelling the reader to click on the link (i.e. to leave Facebook and engage with the full story elsewhere). Since social referrals are now such a vital contributor to the flow of traffic entering news websites, such knowledge would be very helpful for digital content editors tasked with packaging story posts for their social media platforms. Finally, the analysis of Facebook posts provided in this chapter can act as a reference point for future research tracing the developments in social media use by news organizations over time. It can also stand as a reference point for research investigating the emerging practices at Facebook and other social media platforms as they themselves become 'neo-publishers' (Bell 2015; see chapter 10).

To conclude, this chapter has illustrated one application of DNVA: the analysis of the semiotic practices of journalism in the twenty-first century, including common practices or conventions of news reporting (such as the clustering of particular news values) as well as variation between news organizations. The use of stock photographs that do not establish newsworthiness has been identified as a problematic practice for multimodal news stories. The chapter also provides illustration of how the framework for visual analysis introduced in chapter 5 can be draw upon in large-scale research. It also shows how DNVA can be combined with the analysis of other aspects of news practice (e.g. around the use of captions, image attribution, aspects of layout/templating) to provide insights into emerging news practices involving the use of images in social media and online.

Notes

1. The website story page is the page which social media users would be directed to should they click on the links provided at Facebook or Twitter.
2. Beyond having researched these organizations in previous research projects, there is no further reason for choosing these news organizations over any others, apart from the fact that they all have an established digital presence in the form of a Facebook page, a Twitter account, and a website, and are regularly updated.
3. A research assistant was employed for the data collection and was tasked with collecting the data, capturing screen grabs of all images, and with entering basic information in an excel spreadsheet regarding publication and other on-screen details. Screen grabs of each official Facebook page for all news organizations were provided for the research assistant to ensure that the correct page was analysed.
4. We restricted our data collection to week days, since staffing and editorial decision-making vary considerably across the 22 publications in relation to their weekend editions.
5. Moreover, since only 23 images construct Aesthetic Appeal, this task is a manageable addition to the analysis.
6. For the public broadcaster *NPR*, we collected news stories from more specialized news subsections (e.g. Latino Voices) because it was very difficult to find five generalist news stories on each day of the collection period. *NPR* also posts a wide variety of information, which very often comes from other organizations (i.e. not generated by *NPR* itself), which made it even more difficult to distinguish 'news' stemming from *NPR*.
7. For discussion of the effects of the lack of image attribution on the photojournalism profession, see Reich and Klein-Avraham (2014).
8. Proximity was measured in relation to the target audience of the publication only, and not in relation to potential readers from Facebook, as we cannot assess who those readers are and where they are located in the world.
9. In representing these two young women as 'smombies' (smart phone zombies) one could also argue that this image constructs a stereotype of the young as being constantly on their phones without paying any attention to their surroundings (Consonance).
10. We categorize Getty Images first and foremost as a stock image bank, as this is the way that this company promotes itself online and in its marketing literature.

8

'All the news that's fit to share'

News values in 'most shared' news

8.1 Introduction

This chapter presents the third empirical case study where discursive news values analysis (DNVA) is applied—but whereas the last two chapters focused on only one semiotic mode, this study brings together analysis of language **and** image, and illustrates how corpus-assisted multimodal discourse analysis (CAMDA) can be applied in discursive news values analysis. We start by presenting the reader with a seemingly disparate collection of news images and headlines in figure 8.1. What might these verbal and visual texts have in common?

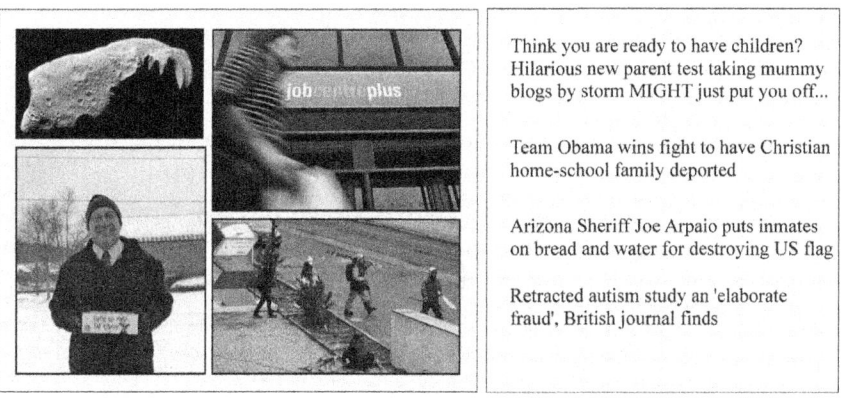

Figure 8.1 Images and headlines appearing in the most shared news on Facebook.

The answer is that they all belong to news items that have been widely shared by Facebook users. As already mentioned in the previous chapter, accessing and sharing news via social networks is now a significant part of online media use (Newman 2011; Hermida et al. 2012; Pew Research Center 2014). The Reuters Institute

Digital News Report (Newman and Levy 2014: 15) suggests that sharing news via social networks is more common among young people, which indicates that this social practice may be on the rise. As Olmstead et al. (2011: 10) put it: 'If searching for news was the most important development of the last decade, sharing news may be among the most important of the next.'

News organizations are thus aware that to capture the attention of a flighty and fickle audience, they need to produce stories that are likely to be shared. In doing so, they ensure two things: first that their news stories are viewed multiple times, and second that readers are directed back to their website by clicking on the link to read more (cf. chapter 7 on social referrals). Audience metrics (information about what is most liked, read, shared, etc.) influence both **what** stories get covered and **how** those stories are packaged (Olmstead et al. 2011: 1; Nguyen 2013: 150; Martin and Dwyer 2015; Welbers et al. 2015). For example, there are indications that news organizations are creating new sections such as 'weird' or 'positive' news in response to audience behaviour (Beckett 2015). Debates have therefore arisen about whether journalism is at risk of being dumbed down (Nguyen 2013: 154) with the rise of news that is 'popular rather than important' (Hermida et al. 2012: 822).

However, there is little linguistic research on the semiotic characteristics of viral online news (but see Blom and Hansen 2015 on 'clickbait'), especially in relation to news values. While Papacharissi and Oliveira (2012) analyse tweets around the #egypt hashtag using a combination of content and discourse analysis, their conceptualization of news values does not align with ours—they apply 'news values' analysis to all tweets, regardless of type and origin, including expressions of opinion by bloggers and activists. Some non-linguistic research has examined the content of shared news, including research on emailed (Berger and Milkman 2012) and re-tweeted (Hansen et al. 2011; Newman 2011) articles, suggesting that affect-laden and surprising/funny/weird content is likely to be shared. There is some debate about whether positive or negative articles are more viral, with different results by Berger and Milkman (2012) and Hansen et al. (2011). In addition, Crawford et al. (2015) provide an industry perspective on shareability, arguing for four qualities that make content shareable: simple, emotional, new/unexpected, and triggered (prompted by something). Because of their disciplinary origin, such studies do not focus on answering questions about language and do not incorporate comprehensive micro-level analysis of semiotic resources.

Our question, then, is what does shared news look like in terms of its semiotic characteristics? In line with the topic of this book, we focus on the construction of newsworthiness—what kinds of news values are construed in shared news and how? What societal ideologies and priorities do they reflect? Are only particular kinds of items shared widely? What semiotic patterns can be found within and across verbal-visual text?

8.2 Data and methodology

8.2.1 INTRODUCING THE DATA

For this case study, we compiled a corpus of 99 online news items whose URLs were shared many times among users via Facebook. As noted in chapter 7, this social media platform plays a major role in sharing news and other content (Olmstead et al. 2011; Pflaeging 2015). The decision to start with a small corpus was deliberate, as it allows us to combine quantitative and qualitative analysis. The corpus is limited to English-language items originating with print and broadcast 'heritage' news media organizations, both 'popular' (e.g. *Daily Mail*) and 'quality' (e.g. *The New York Times*).[1] The corpus includes mainly hard news (including reports of the death of famous people), soft news, and research news. Non-news items (e.g. advice, opinion, quizzes), visual-centric items (e.g. picture galleries, videos), and items from other media organizations were excluded ('digital natives' such as *Buzzfeed*, magazines such as *Time*, and specialist publications such as *Hollywood Reporter*). To compile the corpus, we used Share War's Likeable Engine (http://likeable.share-wars.com/) to extract the top items by total Facebook share count as at early September 2014.[2] The resulting corpus is US-centric: in total, it contains 69 items from 10 US news outlets, 24 items from 6 UK news outlets, 5 items from 3 Australian news outlets, and 1 item from a New Zealand news outlet. The three organizations represented with most items are *CNN* (23) and *FOX* (20) from the United States, and the *Daily Mail* (13) from the United Kingdom. Further detail on the Likeable Engine is provided in Martin and Dwyer (2015) and on the corpus design in Bednarek (2016c). Table A.8.1 in the appendix includes a list of all 99 URLs.

With the help of research assistants, we divided this 'shared news corpus' (SNC) into four sub-corpora:

- *Full text* (FT) corpus: contains the complete item;
- *Headlines* (H) corpus: contains the main headline (excluding sub-headlines);
- *Opening paragraph* (OP) corpus: contains the opening paragraph;[3]
- *Image* corpus: contains images associated with the 99 items.

Our analyses of these corpora are situated in various zones of analysis (figure 8.2). The first area we will focus on is zone 2, analysing patterns that hold across items, staying within-mode. First we look at linguistic patterns using the verbal sub-corpora; then we examine visual patterns using the image corpus. Finally, we move on to patterns that can be observed across the verbal and visual (zone 1). Since we want to compare results across the two semiotic modes, we do not analyse Aesthetic Appeal, a news value which is only postulated for images (see chapter 3).

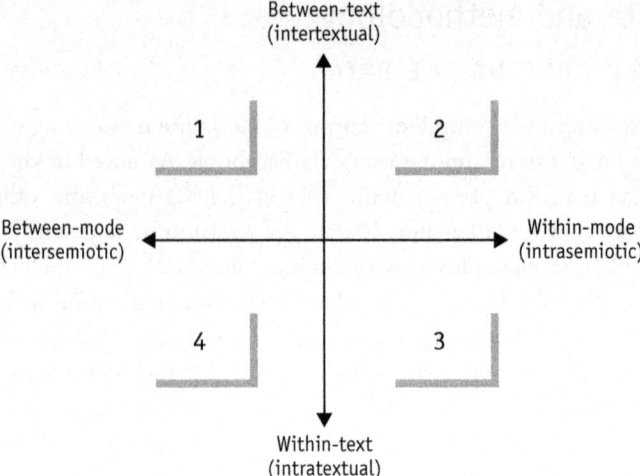

Figure 8.2 Zones of analysis.

8.2.2 ANALYSIS OF PATTERNS ACROSS VERBAL TEXT (LANGUAGE)

In relation to the verbal sub-corpora, we limit part of the analysis to headlines and opening paragraphs because in traditional news stories these act as *summary* (van Dijk 1988a), *abstract* (Bell 1991), or *nucleus* (Iedema et al. 1994), and contain language that represents the topic as newsworthy (White 1997; Mahlberg and O'Donnell 2008). Often, the OP establishes the 'news values angle', although this is not necessarily the case with all SNC items (Bednarek 2016c). We are combining two different approaches here—a positional approach where news values established in the nucleus may be seen as the most emphasized and a frequency-based approach where de/emphasis corresponds to frequency of occurrence. We will report patterns for Hs and OPs separately, although an alternative approach would be to treat them as one complex structural unit. The linguistic analysis of the SNC combines traditional corpus techniques using Wordsmith (Scott 2015) with computer-assisted manual annotation using UAM Corpus Tool (O'Donnell 2015), as introduced in chapter 1.

8.2.3 ANALYSIS OF PATTERNS ACROSS VISUAL TEXT (IMAGES)

In relation to the image corpus, we limit our analysis to the first photographic image that appears on the first screen of the online story page. Of the 99 SNC items, 27 do not include any photographic images, but of the 72 items that do, 51 lead with a single still photographic image, and 21 stories lead with an embedded image gallery.

Five stories from *The New York Times, The Washington Post,* and *USA Today* offer a rich visual-verbal experience combining both single still images and image galleries. The *Daily Mail* makes most use of single images, with between 6 and 16 images per story. In total, there are 1,010 images (including image galleries)—hence, for reasons of scope, we limit analysis to the first image in the story page. The first screen has been argued as the location where the most important information is to be found (Djonov and Knox 2014: 187), and since we are not conducting audience studies and cannot predict whether readers will engage with content further down the page, will watch a video, or will click through all of the images in a gallery, we limit our analysis to the image that appears on this first screen. For stories leading with an image gallery, we analysed the first image in the gallery, as it appears embedded in the story page (shown in figure 8.3).

As an instance of within-mode analysis, the images will be analysed without reference to meanings made in accompanying verbal text (such as the caption). There are two reasons for this: the first is that several images do not include any captions, so incorporation of caption analysis would make the image analysis inconsistent across texts. The second reason is that we want to assess the construction of news values in the images in and of themselves, before moving on to comparisons between semiotic modes. Again, an alternative approach would be to treat image and caption as 'a visual-verbal complex' (Caple 2013a: 206).

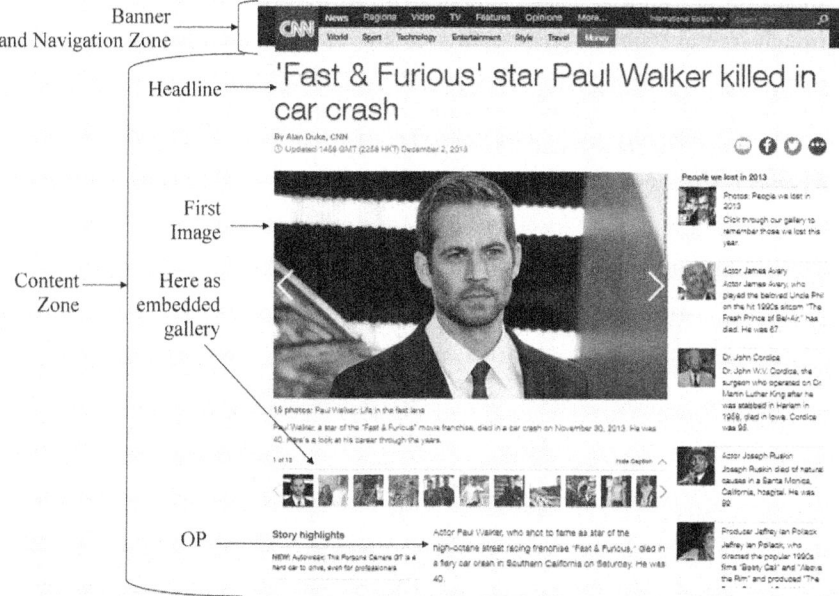

Figure 8.3 Layout of the first screen of a story page on the CNN website; labelled according to Djonov and Knox (2014: 176-178) (*CNN* photo: P. Whitby/Getty Images).

8.2.4 ANALYSIS OF PATTERNS BETWEEN SEMIOTIC MODES

As mentioned, we are also interested in examining relations between semiotic modes across texts (zone 1 of figure 8.2), answering questions such as:

> How do words and images **combine** to construct news values? Do they construct the same news values? Do they construct a wide variety of news values? Or do they appear to be at odds with each other?

Such analyses can tell us the extent to which words and image *reinforce* the same news values, the extent to which they construct *complementary* news values, and the extent to which they *clash* with each other. This analysis will be carried out using a relational database (MS Access) designed specifically to compare the construction of news values across semiotic modes. We do this by collating all of our findings from the separate verbal and visual analysis in the database and then creating queries to be able to compare the data (as shown in figure 8.4).

The database interface includes a unique ID number for each story and a hyperlink to the original story online, for quick retrieval. Each element (image, headline, and opening paragraph) lists a separate field for each news value and makes use of a drop-down menu (Yes, No, Possible) to select whether the news value being analysed is constructed or not. This ensures that any combination of queries can subsequently be created to compare the collected data. Each image/H/OP was coded only *once* for each news value, even if a particular news value was construed through several semiotic devices. The coding manuals used for this analysis are available at http://www.newsvaluesanalysis.com. Briefly here, we have used three choices for most news values: 'yes' (the news value is constructed), 'no' (the news value is not constructed), and 'possible' (for debatable, unclear, uncertain, or special cases). The news value of Proximity, for example, has been coded as 'possible'

DNVA Shared News Case Study

ID: 8 URL: http://www.cnn.com/2012/08/14/showbiz/obit-palillo/index.html

IMAGE ANALYSIS		HEADLINE ANALYSIS		OPENING PAR ANALYSIS	
I Consonance:	No	H Consonance:	No	OP Consonance:	No
I Eliteness:	Yes	H Eliteness:	Yes	OP Eliteness:	Yes
I Impact:	No	H Impact:	No	OP Impact:	No
I Personalisation:	No	H Personalisation:	No	OP Personalisation:	No
I Proximity:	Possible	H Proximity:	Possible	OP Proximity:	Possible
I Superlativeness:	No	H Superlativeness:	No	OP Superlativeness:	No
I Timeliness:	No	H Timeliness:	N/A	OP Timeliness:	Yes
I Unexpectedness:	No	H Unexpectedness:	Possible	OP Unexpectedness:	Possible
I Valence:	Positive	H Valence:	Negative	OP Valence:	Negative

Figure 8.4 A screen shot of the MS Access Database.

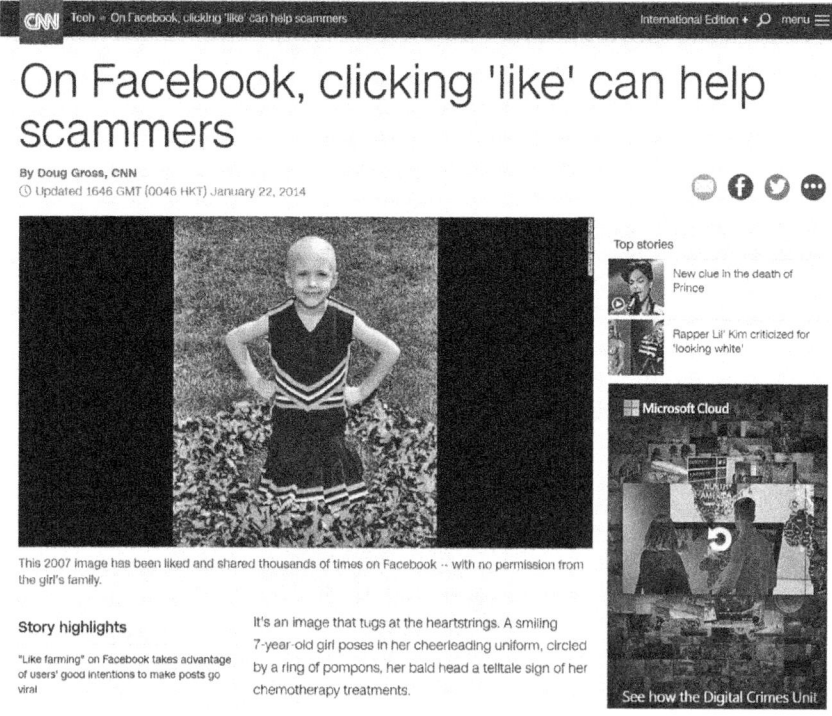

Figure 8.5 The construction of 'possible' Proximity across words and image (*CNN* photo: Courtesy Amanda Rieth).

when it concerns cultural rather than geographical nearness (references to famous people, institutions, products, events, etc.). This coding does not imply that cultural Proximity should not count as Proximity; rather it is to acknowledge that such references are difficult to code and are more 'subjective'. The first screen of a story from *CNN* (figure 8.5) will be used to illustrate these difficulties.

Here, there are some elements that are relatively straightforward constructions of cultural Proximity: The visual representation of a cheerleader and the corresponding verbal text (*in her cheerleading uniform, circled by a ring of pompons*) are likely to establish cultural nearness for American readers. However, should the reference to Facebook in the headline also count as Proximity? While it is a reference to a familiar organization and may be contrasted with a reference to *Renren* from China, should each occurrence of *Facebook* (and similar instances, e.g. each reference to a well-known politician) be coded as Proximity? It is possible to do so and thereby follow a less conservative approach—but in this case, we predict that most news items would construct Proximity in some element of the story text.

Given the scalar nature of Eliteness (discussed in chapter 3), we also took a conservative approach to the coding of this news value. Where the elite status of a news actor is relatively 'weak', we have used the coding choice 'possible' rather than 'yes'.

HOME » NEWS » UK NEWS

'Drummers are natural intellectuals'

 134K   24   62   134K   Email

By Gary Cleland
12:01AM BST 17 Apr 2008

Drummers are better known for their beats than their brain power, but research has suggested that they might actually be natural intellectuals.

Scientists who asked volunteers to keep time with a drumstick before taking intelligence tests discovered that those with the best sense of rhythm also scored highest in the mental assessments.

Born smart? The late Keith Moon, drummer with The Who, could have had natural intellect

Prof Frederic Ullen, from the Karolinska Institutet in Stockholm, concluded that there was a link between intelligence, good timing and the part of the brain used for problem-solving.

He said: "The rhythmic accuracy in brain activity that is observed when a person maintains a steady beat is also important to the problem-solving capacities measured with the intelligence tests."

Figure 8.6 The construction of 'Possible' Eliteness across words and images (*The Telegraph* photo: Getty Images).

The story in figure 8.6 exemplifies such a case. In the verbal text, the generic noun *drummers* is used to identify the news actor at the centre of the story. We take the view that the elite status of 'ordinary' artists and musicians, especially when only referred to generically, is weak, and therefore the coding choice 'possible' is appropriate for the verbal text here. The image has also been coded as 'possibly' constructing Eliteness because of the potential subjectivity in the analysis. As analysts based in Australia, we are not totally sure that the target audience of *The Telegraph* (UK) would recognize the person playing the drums as the drummer of a famous band.

The coding option 'possible' was also important for Consonance—the construction of stereotypes. We acknowledge that it is difficult for the analyst to know the stereotypes that target audiences of a particular publication hold. Therefore, we have taken a very conservative approach to the coding of this news value, in that we have **always** chosen the 'possible' option. Other coding decisions are justified in detail in the coding manuals, and the remainder of this chapter now focuses on the results. We report first on verbal patterns (section 8.3), followed by visual patterns (section 8.4). Finally, we move on to patterns that can be observed across the verbal and visual (section 8.5).

8.3 Verbal patterns

8.3.1 CORPUS LINGUISTIC ANALYSIS OF THE FULL TEXT CORPUS

An analysis of the full text (FT) corpus of lemmas, word forms, and *n*-grams that occur across at least 20 items in the SNC, and of the top 100 most frequent semantic tags is described in detail in Bednarek (2016c) and can provide first insights into news values. For instance, frequent lemmas such as UNIVERSITY, GOVERNMENT, PRESIDENT, OFFICIAL suggest that Eliteness is constructed in relation to research, political leadership, and official authority, while US, UNITED STATES, and AMERICAN reference a widely recognized elite country/nationality and simultaneously construct Proximity if occurring in an American news outlet. Such lemmas also reflect the US-centric nature of the SNC. The lemmas POLICE, KILL, and DIE point to the construal of Negativity in relation to crime and death. Semantic tags further suggest that Negativity is established in relation to areas such as disease, crime, death, warfare, violence, damage, and bad weather. The lemmas LATE [including *latest*] and NOW point to the construction of Timeliness as do the lemma FIRST and the bigram *the first*. The latter may also construct Unexpectedness when unusuality is construed (chapter 4). Numbers, quantification, intensification, and word forms/lemmas such as *at least* and WORLD also recur and establish Superlativeness.

There are two key limitations to this analysis (Bednarek 2016c). First, much further qualitative analysis is necessary because not all lemmas/word forms are good predictors for newsworthiness construction, and a semantic tagger cannot simply be used as a news values tagger. Second, news values may not necessarily be established by recurring word forms or words from the same semantic field. Thus, Unexpectedness can be construed via factual reference to happenings that would be considered unusual by most (without explicit markers), and Consonance may also be difficult to detect through frequency analysis alone (see also Potts et al. 2015: 170). Qualitative analysis is thus crucial—this could be undertaken via concordancing or through manual annotation. In this chapter we will use both techniques, starting with a corpus linguistic analysis which makes use of only the H and OP versions of the SNC, before moving to the results that derive from computer-assisted manual annotation.

8.3.2 CORPUS LINGUISTIC ANALYSIS OF THE HEADLINES AND OPENING PARAGRAPHS

First, a frequency list using Wordsmith's default settings shows that 724 types occur in the headlines (H) and 1,427 types occur in the opening paragraphs (OPs). Of all types 96% only occur across three or fewer headlines and 93% are present in three or fewer OPs (table A8.2/appendix). This is to be expected since we are dealing with very short texts. However, it does show that different kinds of news items are shared by Facebook users—for example, users do not just share items on one topic or about one person. We hence expect different news values to be construed in the SNC.

As table 8.1 shows, lexical words that occur across at least four headlines and OPs are: *years, home, found, school,* and *study*. While *new* and *died* only occur across at least four OPs but not headlines, the arguably related *first, dead,* and *killed* do occur across at least four headlines (table 8.2). Qualitative examination of all concordances for these 10 word forms suggests that *new* and *first* frequently construe Timeliness or Unexpectedness, while *killed/died/dead* usually construct Negativity. The fact that items relating to death are clearly amongst those that are widely shared signals a similarity between Facebook and Twitter, as Newman (2011: 22) proposes that

Table 8.1 **Lexical words across at least four headlines and OPs**

	Headlines		OPs	
	Frequency	*Range*	*Frequency*	*Range*
years	5	5	4	4
home	4	4	7	6
found	4	4	7	6
school	5	5	6	5
study	4	4	6	6

Table 8.2 **Other lexical words**

	Headlines		OPs	
	Frequency	*Range*	*Frequency*	*Range*
new	Range < 4		13	12
died			5	5
first	4	4	Range < 4	
dead	5	5		
killed	6	6		

items relating to disasters/deaths are amongst those that tend to do well on the latter. However, the situation with *study* and *found* is more complex (Bednarek 2016b), since *study* does not tend to co-occur with explicit role labels that construct Eliteness, and instances of *found* differ in the extent to which they express Timeliness ('newness'). Finally, *years, school, home* only construe newsworthiness on occasion, and often only as part of larger phrases (e.g. *Christian home-school family*) or when co-occurring with other resources (e.g. *years* in connection with large numbers referring to the scope of an event). The word form *home* occurs with very different meanings (*home-school family, Irish home for unwed mothers, leaving home, home loans*), and this is perhaps the reason for its range.

For a more detailed analysis, it is useful to examine the OP corpus further, which comprises more words than the H corpus. In addition to the above-mentioned *found, study, new, died*, we will focus here on some other word forms that occur across at least four OPs as summarized in table 8.3: *city, American, US*, and *state* as potential

Table 8.3 **Additional word forms**

	Frequency in OPs	Range across OPs
city	5	5
American	5	5
US [United States]	4	4
state	4	4
Monday	6	6
Saturday	5	5
Wednesday	4	4
last	5	5
night	4	4
world	9	8
officials	5	5
federal	4	4
will	8	5
could	5	5
said	6	6
according	5	5
says	4	4
told	4	4

Proximity devices; *Monday, Saturday, Wednesday, last, night* as potential Timeliness devices; *world* as potential Superlativeness device, and *officials* and *federal* as potential Eliteness devices. In addition, we will consider the modal verbs *will* and *could*, and the reporting expressions *said, according, says,* and *told* because the modal verbs might be connected to Timeliness or Impact, and analysis of reporting expressions can inform us about the constructed status of quoted sources (Eliteness/Personalization).[4]

As we will see, analysis of these 22 word forms allows insights into the construction of Eliteness, Impact, Negativity, Proximity, Superlativeness, and Timeliness. We only discuss key findings in this chapter, rather than describing all uses of these words. Although news values are often combined, we mainly focus on one news value per section (in alphabetical order) to avoid too much overlap in discussion.

8.3.2.1 Eliteness
Study, officials, and *federal* are potential Eliteness devices. *Study* is frequently used as what one might possibly (cf. Bednarek 2016b) consider an 'elite origin' for findings which are linked to the scientific study through use of the expressions *finds, has revealed,* and *according to*. In fact, *according (to)* is most often used in the OP corpus to attribute a proposition to a semiotic research product (*review, study*). Only occasionally is the assumed eliteness of academic research withdrawn, as is the case in one instance (*a now-retracted British study . . . was an 'elaborate fraud'*). The co-text of the reporting verbs *said, says,* and *told* confirms the establishment of Eliteness in the SNC, since far more sources are constructed as elites than as non-elites, most often via high-status role labels, with or without name. Table 8.4 provides examples.

The co-text of *officials* (*federal/United Nations/school/state officials*) and *federal* (*federal judge/court/officials/government*) further illustrates the construction of Eliteness. Instances of *officials* are most often used in co-texts of reporting (*saying,*

Table 8.4 **Sources constructed as Elite**

Reporting verbs	Sources constructed as Elite
said	authorities
	a senior UN diplomat
	state officials
	Police ['weak' Eliteness; cf. chapter 3]
told	the CIA chain of command
	fire department squad leader Markus Mozer
says	the producer of the movie 'Noah'
	the head of a northeast Ohio charity
	Kiss guitarist Paul Stanley
	new research ['possible' Eliteness; cf. Bednarek 2016b]

described, said, say) but may also occur as news actors rather than sources (one instance). *Federal* also labels actors or sources associated with institutions. Finally, although not initially considered an Eliteness device, *world* construes Eliteness as part of the label *world leaders* (and, possibly, World War II combat vets). Similarly, *state* constructs Eliteness when it is part of a high-status role label such as *Arizona State University* or *The South Carolina State House*.

8.3.2.2 Impact

The news value of Impact can relate to actual and non-actual significant consequences (chapter 3). Concordancing of the verbs *will* and *could* illustrates that they are at times used in co-texts where the impact of a reported event is constructed as significant, as in the following examples:

(1)

The Obama administration is engaged in a broad push to make more home loans available to people with weaker credit, <u>an effort that officials say</u> **will** <u>help power the economic recovery but that skeptics say</u> **could** <u>open the door to the risky lending that caused the housing crash in the first place.</u> (*The Washington Post*)

(2)

Doctors announced on Sunday that a baby had been cured of an HIV infection for the first time, <u>a startling development that</u> **could** <u>change how infected newborns are treated and sharply reduce the number of children living with the virus that causes AIDS.</u> (*The New York Times*)

(3)

Kiss and Def Leppard will team up this summer for a 42-city North American tour that **will** <u>'deliver good news and excitement',</u> ... (*USA Today*)

The consequences are 'non-actual' in all three examples—either a fairly certain prediction as in examples (1) and (3) (*will*) or a possibility as in examples (1) and (2) (*could*). In examples (1) and (2), a political effort and a medical discovery are evaluated in terms of potential significant impact on society, while the impact constructed in example (3) is emotional. Although neither *will* nor *could* construe Impact in and of themselves, they may act as important **co-textual cues** to the establishment of Impact in their right-hand co-text.

8.3.2.3 Negativity

As already noted, the word form *died* constructs Negativity in the OPs. It combines Negativity with Eliteness (e.g. *Actor Paul Walker, who shot to fame as star of* the high-octane street racing franchise 'Fast & Furious', died) and Personalization (e.g. *a neglected toddler died*).[5] The death or its circumstances may also be constructed as surprising, simultaneously establishing Unexpectedness:

(5)

A Kentucky pastor who starred in a reality show about snake-handling in church has **died**—of a snakebite. (*CNN*)

Situational irony of this kind seems to be a special subcategory in the SNC, as other examples from the corpus illustrate, (e.g. *Suicide Bomb Trainer in Iraq Accidentally Blows Up His Class*).

8.3.2.4 Proximity

To analyse the potential Proximity devices *city, American, US, state*, and *new* (in some location names), we examined all relevant instances of these word forms in the OPs and aligned them with the news outlet in which they occur (table 8.5).

As can be seen, these references usually construct Proximity: it is US news outlets that tend to refer to Americans, American locations, institutions, and aspects of American culture. References to San Francisco and New York occur in respective local outlets (*San Francisco Gate, The New York Times*). Interestingly, one reference to an American program occurs in an Australian outlet, but as the co-text shows, Proximity is here constructed for the Australian target audience through use of an inclusive first person plural pronoun:

(5)

Satirical **US** news program Last Week Tonight with John Oliver today aired a segment ruthlessly collating <u>our</u> embattled PM's most embarrassing moments. (*news.com.au*)

Note that analysis of the construction of Proximity for the original target audience of these publications ignores the audience of Facebook users, for which Proximity may or may not be established (our data collection does not tell us who these users are and where they are located).

8.3.2.5 Superlativeness

When it is not used as high-status role label (e.g. *world leaders*), *world* establishes Superlativeness in all but one instances in the OPs. There are several occurrences of the pattern NEWS ACTOR (*from*) *around the world* and one instance each of:

- superlative ADJ *in the world*;
- *a whole* [ADJ] *world of*;
- negative emotion noun *to the world*.

Table 8.5 **The construction of Proximity** (*city, American, US, state, New*)

Location reference	News outlet	Same city/state	Same country
the New York Post	Fox News		x
New Zealand	New Zealand Herald		x
will transform San Francisco into Gotham city	San Francisco Gate	x	x
The storm was only supposed to dust the city [Birmingham, Ala.]	Fox News		x
in the eastern Ukrainian city of Donetsk	USA Today		
New York City	New York Times	x	x
a 42-city North American tour	USA Today		x
An American exchange student	NBC News		x
living the American dream	CNN		x
their American flag T-shirts	Fox News		x
Arizona State University	New York Times		x
state officials [Kentucky]	CNN		x
The South Carolina State House	Washington Times		x
at Colorado State University	CNN		x
for desecrating US flags	Fox News		x
a former US Marine	Daily Mail (UK)		
US news program Last Week Tonight	News.com.au		
during the attack on the US consulate	Fox News		x

A search for *in the world* in the full text corpus reveals similar instances (*the strongest tropical cyclone . . . anywhere in the world, one of the most contagious in the world*) while no further instances of the other patterns can be found, indicating that these might be less conventionalized Superlativeness devices. This use of *world* conforms to a general journalistic practice where *world's* collocates with comparative and superlative adjectives and has the meaning 'of the highest measure' (Duguid 2010: 120).

8.3.2.6 Timeliness

Timeliness in the sense of nearness to the time of publication (based on dates published on websites) can be examined in relation to the word forms *Monday, Saturday, last, night* in instances where these refer to points in time.[6] As table 8.6 shows, these invariably refer to events in the near past or sometimes near future within a span of 1-6 days, but often within the very near past or future—referring to the same day, the day before, or the next day. The latter construct Timeliness the most. Again, this analysis identifies nearness in relation to the time of publication rather than the time of sharing. While we may assume that most news items are shared upon publication, some items might be shared at a later stage.

In addition, concordances for *new* indicate that 'newness' is construed in several OPs. Of ten instances of *new* that do not occur in location names, most establish an aspect of the reported event as new.[7] The vast majority of these relate to semiotic research products (as premodifier of the head nouns *study, research,* and *survey*) or to discovery:

(6)

A whole **new** world of magic animals, brave young princes and evil witches **has come to light** with the **discovery** of 500 **new** fairytales. . . . (*The Guardian*)

In the full text corpus, too, *study* and *research* are clear collocates of *new*. That newness occurs in reports of research news and discoveries is also confirmed by examination of *found*, where three of seven instances relate to research discoveries:

(7)

Researchers at Granada University in Spain have **found** that . . . (*The Washington Times*)

(8)

Researchers might have **found** the Holy Grail in the war against cancer . . . (*FOX*)

(9)

A skeleton **found** beneath a Leicester car park . . . (*BBC*)

Table 8.6 **The construction of Timeliness (*Monday, Saturday, last, night*)**

	Publication date	Very near past	Near past	Very near future	Near future
Saturday (1)	30 November 2013 (Saturday)	x			
on Saturday (4)	10 February 2013 (Sunday)				x
	27 July 2014 (Sunday)	x			
	15 July 2013 (Monday)		x		
	2 December 2013 (Monday)		x		
last week	15 October 2012 (Monday)		x		
last Wednesday night	14 July 2014 (Monday)		x		
last night	8 December 2014	x			
Thursday night	26 April 2013 (Friday)	x			
on Monday night	17 June 2013 (Monday)	x			
Monday (2)	19 November 2013 (Tuesday)	x			
	6 May 2013 (Monday)	x			
on Monday (3)	15 June 2014 (Sunday)			x	
	5 February 2013 (Tuesday)	x			
	18 April 2013 (Thursday)		x		

8.3.3 CORPUS-ASSISTED MANUAL ANNOTATION OF HS AND OPS

The qualitative examination of 22 word forms in the OPs has given us some information about the linguistic construction of six news values. However, we have not learnt much about Consonance, Personalization, Positivity, and Unexpectedness, and analysis was restricted to how these 22 words construct newsworthiness. For a more comprehensive picture, it is necessary to manually code each headline and OP.

We start with some brief comments in relation to Consonance, Personalization, Positivity, and Unexpectedness, as they arise from this manual coding. First, the manual analysis identified some potential co-textual cues to Consonance, such as place and nationality names (e.g. *Texas, Ireland, German*), proper nouns (e.g. *George Zimmerman, Aldi*) and references to professions or roles (e.g. *UKIP candidate, artist, D-day vet*) as well as explicit and implicit evaluation (e.g. *drug addict parents, wacky piano*) and characteristics attributed to a group (*many animal lovers find, most broody mothers see*). But this does not mean that such linguistic practices always construct Consonance or that others do not. For instance, co-textually the headline and OP in example (10) evoke and reinforce what one might call the stereotype of the courageous soldier:

(10)

70 years later, D-Day vet Jim 'Pee Wee' Martin jumps again

Jim 'Pee Wee' Martin acted like he'd been here before, like jumping from a plane is as easy as falling off a log. (*CNN*)

To do so the identification of Martin as a *D-day vet* is essential, but this does not mean that the noun phrase in itself establishes the stereotype.

Second, with respect to Personalization, references to ordinary news actors either occur when they are described as agents or patients of negative activities or as otherwise suffering but also in the context of positive or unexpected events/actions or significant social media impact:[8]

(11)

A Kentucky mother stepped outside of her home just for a few minutes, but it was long enough for her 5-year-old son to accidentally shoot and kill his 2-year-old sister. [Negativity] (*CNN*)

(12)

Teens chase kidnapping suspect on bikes, save 5-year-old girl [Positivity] (*CNN*)

(13)

Teenager takes his great-grandmother to prom [Unexpectedness] (*FOX*)

(14)

A touching moment between a zoo worker and one of his favorite animals has gone viral. [Impact] (*FOX*)

Third, Positivity seems to be construed in a variety of contexts, including in research news and in descriptions of positive acts of heroism, wit, tenacity, or kindness:

(15)

Two teenage boys are being hailed as heroes after they chased a car carrying a kidnapped girl—on their bicycles. [heroism] (*CNN*)

(16)

Following Tim Howard's brilliant performance against Belgium, someone briefly changed the Wikipedia entry for Secretary of Defense Chuck Hagel, and it was perfect. [wit] (*USA Today*)

(17)

What was meant to be a final gathering of heroes Tuesday instead became a final victory for dozens of World War II combat vets who refused to let the government's budget battle block a visit to their memorial in the nation's capital. [tenacity] (*FOX*)

(18)

… it's likely the ever-popular starlet [Amy Adams] just gained more fans—through a subtle act of kindness. [kindness] (*FOX*)

Finally, the manual analysis shows that Unexpectedness is frequently established simply by references to happenings that would be considered unusual by most, and that unexpected research findings are an important subcategory of shared news (examples 19–21):

(19)

Researchers at Granada University in Spain have found that beer can help the body rehydrate better after a workout than water or Gatorade. (*The Washington Times*)

(20)

Tequila shots may do more than lighten the mood at a party; the drink may be beneficial for your health as well. (*FOX*)

(21)

Logically it may be assumed that the more children a mother has, the more stressed out she will be, but a new study has revealed that this is not the case. (*Daily Mail*)

Here findings are constructed as counter-intuitive—for instance, that consumables with a reputation of being harmful are beneficial or that more children do not mean more stress.

Finally, tables 8.7 and 8.8 summarize the results for all news values. These numbers should be interpreted as tendencies/trends rather than facts, since researcher subjectivity plays a role. As these tables demonstrate, it appears that news values established in shared items are varied, although all 'traditional' news values can be found. For example, users share both items about news actors constructed as 'elite' and 'ordinary' and about news constructed as 'positive' and 'negative'. Eliteness, Superlativeness, Unexpectedness, and Negativity seem especially important, and

Table 8.7 **Tendencies in the construction of news values in headlines and opening paragraphs**

News values	'Yes'		'No'		'Possible'	
	H	OP	H	OP	H	OP
Consonance	—	—	79	72	20	27
Eliteness	44	49	35	34	20	16
Impact	12	18	86	78	1	3
Personalization	22	19	54	44	23	36
Proximity	15	31	34	40	50	28
Superlativeness	40	54	59	42	—	3
Timeliness	69	78	8 (+ 16 N/A)	17 (+ 4 N/A)	6	—
Unexpectedness	41	26	17	25	41	48

Table 8.8 **Tendencies in the construction of Negativity and Positivity**

	H	OP
Negativity	55	51
Positivity	17	21
Unclear or no valence	27	27

Proximity becomes significant if cultural references and references to neighbouring or culturally close countries are included (all coded as 'possible'). While Timeliness is also frequent, this may result from the corpus design (see Bednarek 2016c).

In relation to these quantitative trends, we must also emphasize that news values are frequently combined. On the one hand, noun phrases package several news values, for example, Proximity and Personalization (*a Kentucky mother*), Superlativeness and Eliteness (*a growing group of lawmakers*), Superlativeness and Timeliness: newness (*a whole new world of magic animals, brave young princes and evil witches*). This is in line with the noun phrase's general capacity for informational density and makes it a useful device for **encapsulating** newsworthiness. On the other hand, news values can also be combined across phrases, for example, by associating news actors with states, actions, or places, as illustrated in table 8.9.

Timeliness (newness) is often linked with Unexpectedness, for instance, in the *Daily Mail* headline *British man becomes **first** person to visit all 201 countries ... WITHOUT using a plane*, where both the 'covert negation' (Hermerén 1986: 66), that is, *without*, and the typography (capitalization) contribute to the construal of Unexpectedness. The fact that news values are frequently combined in these and other ways adds to the complexity of annotating and quantifying them. This is compounded by the scalar nature of news values and the different ways in which these can be constructed through language, as was shown in section 8.3.2.

Table 8.9 **Combining news values**

Stranded Dave Matthews hitches ride with fan to show (CNN)	
Dave Matthews	Eliteness and cultural Proximity
hitches	Timeliness
with fan	Personalization
Dave Matthews hitches ride with fan	Unexpectedness
Boy, 8, one of 3 killed in bombings at Boston Marathon; scores wounded (CNN)	
Boy, 8	Personalization
one of 3 killed in bombings	Negativity
at Boston Marathon	Proximity; possible Eliteness
scores wounded	Superlativeness, Negativity, Impact

8.4 Visual patterns

Moving on to the analysis of visual patterns, we start with a summary of trends in table 8.10. First, table 8.10 shows that Timeliness is not established in any of the images in the SNC. As discussed in chapter 5, this news value is rarely constructed in news images without the aid of verbal/numerical signage or other cultural/environmental cues. This clear contrast with verbal patterns, where Timeliness *is* frequent, thus derives from general differences between the two semiotic modes.

Second, images in the SNC are just as likely to show ordinary news actors as elite news actors, constructing Personalization in 32% of images and Eliteness in 29%. There are more images constructing Positivity than Negativity (29% to 22%), and 15% of the images construct Proximity, thus depicting people and locations that are relevant or known to the target audience. These people are likely to be elites, as 7 of the 11 images constructing Proximity also construct Eliteness (see discussion of this clustering in section 7.4.2.1).

Third, if we look more closely at the construction of Negativity and Positivity and the type of news actor depicted in the image corpus (table 8.11), there are no images of news actors that are constructed as both negative and elite. In contrast, images establishing Personalization (depicting ordinary news actors) clearly construct both Negativity and Positivity, as the images in figure 8.7 show, where these values are principally constructed through negative or positive facial expression (see discussion in chapter 7).

Table 8.10 **The construction of news values in the image corpus (72 images)**

News value	Number of images	% of total
Consonance	3	4
Eliteness	21	29
Impact	7	10
Personalization	23	32
Proximity	11	15
Superlativeness	6	8
Timeliness	0	0
Unexpectedness	5	7
Negativity	16	22
Positivity	21	29

Table 8.11 **Negativity/Positivity and the construction of Personalization and Eliteness**

News value	Negativity	Positivity	Unclear/none
Personalization (23 images)	8	12	3
Eliteness (21 images)	0	6	15

Image A: Negativity · Image B: Positivity

Figure 8.7 The construction of Personalization and Negativity/Positivity (Image A: *Daily Mail* photo: Reuters; Image B: *Fox News* photo: Courtesy: Home School Legal Defense Association).

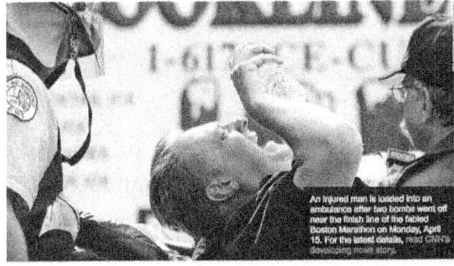

Image A · Image B

Figure 8.8 The construction of Superlativeness through the depiction of extreme emotions (Image A: *CNN* photo: Jim Rogash/Getty Images; Image B: *Washington Post* photo: Gbemiga Olamikan/AP).

Further, images constructing the news value of Impact (n = 7) also construe Negativity (n = 7) and three of these images further establish Superlativeness. In two instances, Superlativeness is constructed through the extreme emotional responses of ordinary actors, as can be seen in the images in figure 8.8.

If we compare image A in figure 8.7 with the two images in figure 8.8, we can see that all three images construct Negativity through negative facial expression. However, there is a clear difference in the **degree** of negative emotions being expressed in these images. We would argue that the negative emotions depicted in the images in figure 8.8 are much more intensified (eyes tightly closed, mouths wide open), and this is further intensified through the gestures of the represented participants (raised arms, hands on head). Such intense emotional depictions thus also construct Superlativeness. The Superlativeness constructed in image B in figure 8.8 is further reinforced through the use of a wide angle so that the gesturing of the main participant fills the image frame and intensifies the scope/scale of her grief.

Finally, there are a number of images in this corpus that construct no news values at all (9 in total—12%). These are all images either of objects (a car, a shot glass), food (a piece of cake), animals (a rhino), or of landscapes/buildings, and all exclude human participants. Most are stock photographs, sourced from image banks. As already noted in chapter 7, such conceptual images contribute little to the narrative or news storytelling potential of the story beyond offering illustration.

To sum up sections 8.3 and 8.4 (within-mode analysis), the construction of news values in the SNC is varied and differs between semiotic modes. Interestingly, Positivity occurs more than Negativity in images, while the opposite is the case in language. In the verbal text, the news values of Eliteness, Superlativeness, Unexpectedness, and Negativity seem especially important. The visuals, since they deal largely with the depiction of human actors, favour the construction of Personalization and Eliteness, while Timeliness is absent. The establishment of news values thus conforms to the strengths of each semiotic mode.

8.5 Visual-verbal patterns

Having examined patterns in language and image separately, we now bring together analysis of both semiotic modes, asking how words and images combine to construct news values. This means that our analysis shifts to zone 1 of figure 8.2, by examining relations between semiotic modes and the extent to which these are generalizable across the SNC.

Table 8.12 gives a snapshot of the overlap in the construction of news values across semiotic modes. By selecting the value 'yes' for each news value (meaning that this news value is constructed in this element) and then querying the number of instances where 'yes' is selected across words and images, we can see the extent to which the construction of news values is reinforced across semiotic modes and elements of the news story (image, headline, opening paragraph).

The right-most column in table 8.12 shows that Eliteness (n = 41), Superlativeness (n = 54), Timeliness (n = 68), and Negativity (n = 45) are construed in at least one element (image, H, OP) in more than half of the 72 SNC items, while Unexpectedness and Positivity occur in 31 (43%) and Personalization and Proximity in 26 (36%). Such figures give us an indication of the general flavour of the SNC: that reported events are established as being timely, high in intensity or of large scope, and concerning both elite and ordinary news actors. Many events

Table 8.12 **Correlation in the construction of news values across semiotic modes (out of a total of 72 stories that include both language and image)**

	Value = 'Yes' (This news value IS constructed)				
	In All Three Elements (I, H, OP)	In Image and Headline Only	In Image and OP Only	In Headline and OP Only	In Either Image, Headline, or OP
Consonance	0	0	0	0	3
Eliteness	16	3	1	5	41
Impact	2	1	0	4	23
Personalization	7	4	2	1	26
Proximity	3	0	0	3	26
Superlativeness	5	0	1	20	54
Timeliness	0	0	0	41	68
Unexpectedness	1	3	0	16	31
Negativity	10	1	0	18	45
Positivity	3	2	1	6	31

are also clearly constructed as unexpected and either positive or negative. Note that these numbers ignore results for the coding choice 'possible', explaining for example why there are zero instances of Consonance (cf. section 8.2.4).

However, the other columns show us that the construal of identical news values across image, headline, and opening paragraph is generally low, even lower between image and headline, and minimal between image and opening paragraph. In contrast, there is greater overlap within-mode between headline and opening paragraph, because of the close relationship between the two elements in traditional hard news stories, which make up part of the corpus. Additional database queries consistently pointed to cross-modal variety and showed that no two news items are alike in their configurations of constructed news values. This suggests that the construction of news values **accumulates** across semiotic modes and that both semiotic modes are important in establishing newsworthiness, since they each construe different, complementary aspects of an event as newsworthy.

Table 8.12 further suggests that when the same news value is constructed across semiotic modes, it is likely to be reinforced across all three elements of the story opening—the headline, the image, and the opening paragraph. Eliteness is the news value that is most reinforced between image, headline, and opening paragraph (in 16 items), and 10 items similarly construct Negativity across all three analysed elements. The example in figure 8.9 demonstrates the construction of Eliteness across

Figure 8.9 The construal (and reinforcement) of the news value Eliteness across headline, image, and opening paragraph (*Fox News* photo: AP).

all three elements. The headline and opening paragraph both construct this news event as concerning elite news actors through the use of noun phrases such as *Alaska senators, lawmakers, (President) Obama, Congress,* and *federal officials.* The image depicts the recognizable elite, President Obama, and the background graphic, while largely out of focus, is of the famous landmark The White House.

The results of our analysis have also highlighted a small number of cases where there is a **clash** in the construction of news values across semiotic modes. These clashes relate specifically to the construction of Negativity and Positivity. In seven stories, the images construct Positivity, while the verbal text (both headline and OP) constructs Negativity. Likewise, there are two images constructing Negativity, while the verbal text constructs Positivity. In all seven stories where the images construct Positivity, they show smiling human participants. Two stories concern the deaths of actors, and in both of these stories archive images of the actors at recent red carpet events are used to illustrate the story (text A in figure 8.10). One story concerns the death of the world's oldest horse and includes an image of the horse alive and well with his smiling handler (text B, figure 8.10). We view these examples as clashes in the construction of news values because of the

News values in 'most shared' news   221

Text A   Text B   Text C

Figure 8.10 Clash in Valence between image and verbal text (Text A: *CNN* photo: Jonathan Leibson/Getty Images; Text B: *Daily Mail* photo: Martin Rose/Eastnews. co.uk; Text C: *Daily Mail* photo: Facebook).

evaluative force of lead images. Martin (2001: 334) suggests that images evoke 'a reaction in readers of multi-modal texts—typically in positions that preview the value of following text'. This means that when readers engage with largely positive lead images that dominate the first screen of the story page (like those in figure 8.10), they are likely to be positively disposed towards the accompanying text. If the text, however, constructs the reported events as extremely negative (e.g. death), this may jar with the initial reaction of the reader. However, clashes of this nature also point to the conventionalized nature of news discourse, in that it is common practice to use images of people (and animals) when they were alive and (usually) well with news stories dealing with their deaths. Such clashes in the construction of Negativity and Positivity may also serve to emphasize the tragedy of the reported event.

Four stories with clashes in Negativity/Positivity concern ordinary actors. In these instances two images have been sourced from Facebook and one has been supplied by a private institution. Only one image comes from a news worker acting on behalf of the news organization where the story was published. The sourcing of images from social media platforms, like Facebook, is now common practice, especially when the story involves negative happenings and contacting next of kin or the person themselves for a photograph would not only take time but could also be seen as insensitive or intrusive. Such social media imagery is overwhelmingly positive; thus, it is not surprising that images sourced from social media are likely to construct Positivity in items where the verbal text constructs Negativity. Figure 8.10 (text C) shows an example. The verbal text describes the very negative happenings that have affected this teenage girl, while the image, taken from Facebook, shows a healthy young woman with a neutral if not positive facial expression. Contrasts in the construction of Positivity and Negativity between visual and verbal elements add to the evaluative effect of this story and highlight a common trope in news storytelling—that of the fall. Here we get the healthy, happy, free 'before' (established through images) contrasted with the unhealthy (or dead), unhappy, incarcerated, and so on 'after' (established through the verbiage).

The complexity of visual-verbal relations cannot be fully accounted for within the necessary limitations of the printed page. Therefore, we have provided a visualization of the findings discussed in section 8.5 at our website http://www.newsvaluesanalysis.com. This visualization consists of an animated infographic demonstrating how and when news values are co-constructed across words and images in this corpus.

In sum, the packaging of news stories in the digital news environment appears to follow a limited number of template options which favour the placement of at least headline, lead image (or video), and opening paragraph on the first screen (see figure 8.3). To briefly return to the question asked at the beginning of this chapter, what patterns and practices can be found within and across semiotic modes in this part of the online news text? As shown, both visual and verbal elements play an important role in the construction of news values, which can serve to *reinforce* each other, thus emphasizing the same news value(s). Only rarely do visual and verbal components *clash*. They are most likely to *complement* each other, thus accumulating a range of news values. To put it differently, the news stories shared by Facebook users are multimodally constructed as highly newsworthy. News values are combined through different semiotic modes, perhaps to make news stories as newsworthy as possible, which would be in line with Galtung and Ruge's (1965: 71) original assumption that news stories are more newsworthy if they register on more than one factor.

To bring our three strands of analysis together, we can briefly summarize what each has shown. The analysis of linguistic patterns using corpus linguistic techniques identified salient lemmas, word forms, *n*-grams, and semantic tags (section 8.3.1). This technique suggested that Eliteness, Proximity, Negativity, Timeliness, Unexpectedness, and Superlativeness are constructed in the full text corpus. Qualitative analysis of word forms in the headlines and opening paragraphs (section 8.3.2) confirmed that these news values are indeed established in the SNC and identified particular word forms that appear to be good predictors of news values (such as *new, first, killed, died, dead, officials, federal, world*) as well as certain co-textual cues (such as modal verbs). In general, concordancing illustrated how particular news values are established through language in the SNC. However, the corpus linguistic analyses did not provide equal insights into all news values. In particular, the computer-assisted manual annotation (section 8.3.3) allowed us to investigate how Consonance, Positivity, Personalization, and Unexpectedness are constructed, including through relatively factual descriptions. For instance, we discovered that Positivity does occur in the corpus, although it is less frequent than Negativity.

The analysis of patterns across visual text in section 8.4 suggested that the images in the SNC deal largely with the depiction of human actors and thus favour the construal of Eliteness and Personalization. Interestingly, Positivity is more frequent than Negativity in these images. We identified how news values are combined, or not. For example, we showed how depictions of emotion can construe Negativity and Superlativeness in relation to Personalization. Comparing the results from sections 8.3 and 8.4 demonstrated that the construction of news values in the SNC is varied and differs between semiotic modes, conforming to the strengths of each. This also means that an analysis of verbal patterns would result in different results than an analysis of visual patterns. It is by bringing the analyses together, as we did in section 8.5, that we could more clearly identify the patterns and practices within and across semiotic modes (reinforcing, complementing, clashing). We focused here on clear cases (coding choice = 'yes'), and future research could more fully investigate other cases (coding choice = 'possible'), which we explain in our coding manuals (Bednarek 2016b; Caple 2016, available at http://www.newsvaluesanalysis.com). In combining all three strands we nevertheless gained a much fuller picture of the construction of newsworthiness in the SNC than would have otherwise been possible.

8.6 Conclusion

To conclude, we will revisit some of the other questions that we asked at the beginning of this chapter: What kinds of news values are constructed in shared news? Are only particular kinds of items shared widely? What societal ideologies and priorities do they reflect? Briefly, our study on shared news from heritage organizations suggests that the 'traditional' news values of Eliteness, Superlativeness, Timeliness, Negativity, Unexpectedness, Personalization, and Proximity remain important, while Positivity is also constructed in a considerable amount of shared news. Our study also confirms that unexpected news is an important subcategory of viral news, including unexpected research news. This audience interest in sharing such research news might be to the detriment of other research that is equally if not more important but cannot easily be constructed as unexpected and is hence not as widely shared.

In general, we have discovered considerable variety in the news items that are widely shared, ranging from stories about elites and ordinary people to negative items about deaths, positive acts of heroism or kindness, or items with significant social media impact, to name but a few. The news values constructed in shared news thus reflect a range of different societal ideologies and priorities. One reason for this variety could be because the users that share such news are not a uniform group. This is supported by research into news-sharing communities which suggests that there are different clusters or types of online news consumers (Herdağdelen et al. 2013; Zeller et al. 2014), 'each of which behaves differently' (Olmstead et al. 2011: 1).[9] If 'users are more likely to share news stories that they like and find relevant' (Ma et al. 2014: 612), and if they differ in their likes and interests, it logically follows that the content that is shared is also varied. Ultimately, then, this case study has shown that the type of news that is deemed 'fit to share' depends at least to some extent on the user who shares it. In addition to aiming for the largest number of shares in total, news institutions might thus be able to aim for items that are likely to be shared by particular groups of consumers, who might be valuable to particular advertisers.

Summing up this case study on shared news, this chapter demonstrated how CAMDA can be applied in discursive news values analysis. It illustrated how such an approach can be used to examine the multimodal packaging of news products and to identify the role that verbal/visual components play—whether they reinforce the same news values, construct complementary news values, or even clash with each other in their construction of newsworthiness. Such research fits with research interests in intersemiotic relations (Caple 2013a) but also has potential applications in media literacy and journalism education. By deconstructing professional texts in terms of how news values are integrated in the form of multimodal news products and by carefully examining the contribution of different semiotic modes, students can gain a fuller understanding of contemporary journalism as social and semiotic practice and identify un/successful practices for multimodal news storytelling.

Notes

1. We also included News Corp Australia's site news.com.au, bringing together reporting from their print newspapers such as *The Daily Telegraph, The Courier Mail, Herald Sun*, etc.
2. The Likeable Engine collects URLs from selected news media homepages primarily based in the United States, United Kingdom, and Australia, tracking their share counts. While the Likeable Engine tries to load region-specific homepages (theguardian.com/uk, not theguardian.com/), the sample is most likely influenced by the Likeable Engine computer's location in Melbourne. Together with the fact that the set of collected homepages has varied over time, this means that the corpus does not represent the actual set of most shared articles, but rather is representative of the type of news stories that are most shared by users.
3. The term *OP* refers to the first paragraph, which may not necessarily represent the complete LEAD stage in the generic structure of the item, following the genre conceptualization by Feez et al. (2008). In contrast to Mahlberg and O'Donnell (2008), we focus on the complete first paragraph, rather than just the first sentence, although sometimes the two coincide (i.e. the first paragraph consists of one sentence). Headlines, sub-headlines, and OPs were identified non-linguistically, so that the OP is the first paragraph following the headlines and sub-headlines (which are usually identified by bold face, font size, or bullet points).
4. Other words that have a range of at least four in the OPs but are not discussed are listed in table A8.2 of the appendix. Some of these do have the potential to construct newsworthiness on occasion (cf. chapter 4), for instance, markers of negation and contrast; comparatives, intensifiers and numerals, and prepositions such as *against/over* when occurring with negative lexis (*battle/protests/war against, debate/irate over*).
5. There is also one occurrence relating to the death of the oldest known horse.
6. Examining concordances for numbers (#) shows that most date and time references do not establish Timeliness. It may be general journalistic practice to use numbers for events that are *not* near the publication date. Examining concordances for the modal verbs *will* and *could* shows that they occur only rarely with a specific time reference in the same sentence, although *will* does so more than *could*.

7. Two instances do not clearly construct news value.
8. Instances where non-elite news actors were described as engaging in criminal activity or referred to in a generic sense or as a group were coded as 'possible', as it is questionable whether Personalization is established (see chapter 3).
9. Further, surveys where respondents identify to what extent they are interested in or consume different types of news (such as science/technology, health/education, entertainment/celebrity) clearly shows variation, with some influence of age and gender (Anderson and Caumont 2014; Newman and Levy 2014). However, what respondents **say** they are interested in may not be identical to the types of news they actually view or share, and results may be different if only social media users are questioned (see Anderson and Caumont 2014 on what types of news Facebook users regularly see, and Bruns et al. 2013 on Australian news topics that receive attention from Twitter users).

Part IV

EXTENSIONS

9

Discursive news values analysis as an opportunity for diachronic and cross-cultural research

While the previous three chapters presented empirical case studies where we applied discursive news values analysis (DNVA), there are clearly many opportunities for research in areas that we have not yet explored. In this chapter we describe and illustrate two such key areas: diachronic and cross-cultural research, in the hope that it might inspire future studies by other researchers adopting DNVA.

9.1 *Salacious Fiends* and *News from the Dead*: Diachronic research

The focus of our studies in this book is synchronic, rather than diachronic, examining newsworthiness in contemporary English-language news. It would, however, be very worthwhile to study how the discourse of news values has emerged over time, investigating both stability and change. Both Tunstall (1996) and Cecconi (2009) mention some enduring themes of the British press, which we could link to news values such as Eliteness, Superlativeness, Unexpectedness, Negativity, and Personalization:

> Since the birth of the British daily press in 1702 editors and journalists have always been looking for celebrities, drama, conflict, 'human interest', and 'good stories'. Already in the eighteenth century there was a strong focus on actors, the theatre, and gossip about the king and the royal court. ... War then as now was the best news story. (Tunstall 1996: 199)
>
> As happens in modern-day news market [sic], also in Tudor and Stuart England, dramatic storms, bizarre prodigies, disastrous earthquakes and

bloody crimes were what readers commonly craved and what publishers were willing to supply for commercial interests. (Cecconi 2009: 138)

The enduring themes of photojournalism similarly focus on celebrity and the power elite. Gernsheim (1955: 344) recalls that the subjects of news photography at the turn of the twentieth century tended to be celebrities or 'news events of lasting interest', like Queen Victoria's funeral or the coronation of Edward VII.

This does not mean that news values have quantitatively and qualitatively remained the same. For instance, Bell (1991: 197) notes how the notion of 'celebrity' has changed, such that nobility and military titles which dominated the *Daily Mirror* until the 1940s are almost absent now. Hence, it would be possible to identify differences in the semiotic construction of news values over time, which also result from developments in the news industry. In relation to news photography, for example, the 1930s saw the introduction of tabloid newspapers like the *Daily Mirror* (UK), and the *Daily Graphic* (US), which fully embraced photography, using large, sensational photographs that usually revolved around the themes of violence, sex, scandal, and accidents. Barnhurst and Nerone (2001) describe such developments as a shift in tenor from personage to person. By this they infer that photography shifted from the 'posed icons of a ritual event to the active dramatic moments preferred by photojournalism' (Barnhurst and Nerone 2001: 171). Such shifts will also have clear implications for the semiotic construction of news values.

Thus, we can investigate both what news values (e.g. Eliteness) are discursively constructed in different time periods and how these are constructed (e.g. use of formal portraiture, use of military titles), as well as shifts in frequency. We can also tie findings to the socio-historical context, including technical constraints which mean, for example, that recency or 'newness' (Timeliness) 'has changed considerably during the last two centuries' (Ungerer 2000a: 183). Many other social, economic, and political factors have impacted on the development of newspaper style and language (Schudson 1978; Conboy 2010; Facchinetti et al. 2012). In relation to photojournalism, changes in the ways that both images and photographers have been perceived have had a significant impact on how and where images are reproduced (see, e.g., Barnhurst and Nerone 2001; Reich and Klein-Avraham 2014).

How might one go about such a diachronic study of news values? There are several databases and corpora available for such studies in different countries. To name some examples, *The New York Times* archive allows fee-based access to articles from 1851 onwards.[1] In the United Kingdom, *The Times* archive allows subscribers to search articles from 1785 to 1985.[2] The British Library has two collections of early English newspapers/newsbooks and a comprehensive collection of British newspapers from 1840s onwards.[3] Similarly, the National Library of Australia provides free online access to digitized Australian newspapers from 1803 onwards.[4] ProQuest Historical Newspapers is a fee-based digital archive with American and some international newspapers from the eighteenth century and beyond.[5] While these archives are fully digitized, thus maintaining the original page layout, images, and illustrations, it is not possible to search for images only, or only for stories that make use of images. This means that analysis focusing on images would have to make use of manual page-based searches or take a search for words as a starting point.

In terms of corpora for linguistic analysis, the BROWN family includes news text types from 1931, 1961, 1991, and 2006 (Baker 2011), and allows analysis of changes in newspaper language (Hundt and Mair 1999). Uppsala University hosts the Corpus of Nineteenth-century Newspaper English, with editorials and reportage from English newspapers from 1830 to 1850 and 1875 to 1895.[6] The Rostock Newspaper Corpus comprises news reports from 1700 to 2000 from six British newspapers (Bös 2012). The Zurich English Newspaper Corpus is comprised of complete English newspapers from 1661 to 1791 (Fries and Schneider 2000; Fries et al. 2004). Even earlier, the Lancaster Newsbooks corpus (McEnery and Hardie 2001-2007) covers newsbooks from 1653 to 1654 and the Florence Early English Newspapers corpus contains newsbooks from 1641 to 1661 (Brownlees 2006a: 7). Further corpora are listed on the CHINED website which is dedicated to research on historical news discourse.[7]

While this chapter cannot provide a full case study of diachronic DNVA, we will offer a few comments here on how such analysis might be approached. In terms of language, analysis of the emergence and development of the rhetoric of newsworthiness could proceed through a combination of qualitative and quantitative research, for example, moving from close reading and discovery of linguistic devices to searching for these devices. One could also search for devices that exist in contemporary English-language news discourse to trace their presence, frequency, and usage. Purely for the purpose of illustration, table 9.1 lists some examples yielded through a selective and non-comprehensive look at *The Washington Post* (1877-1907), accessed via the ProQuest database.

Palmer (1998: 177) argues that news values and other standards which spread worldwide were developed by late-nineteenth-century newsmen. Without going into detail, table 9.1 does illustrate some similarities with contemporary news discourse such as the use of large vague numbers (*thousands of*), reference to emotions (*disappointment/surprise*), the phrase *for the first time since*, and negative lexis (*rape, conflict*). On the other hand, differences also emerge. Although it is common in contemporary news discourse to use metaphor/personification with storm reporting (see Potts et al. 2015), it would be unusual to see this to the extent to which it is done in the story from *The Washington Post* from 6 August 1878. Common contemporary phrases such as *violent clashes* or *community leaders* are absent in *The Washington Post* before 1910 (search in article, front-page article, war news), while negative category labels such as *salacious fiends* do not occur in contemporary news discourse.

Table 9.1 **Selected examples from *The Washington Post* (1877–1907)**

Eliteness	**Prof. Hughes, the well-known inventor of the type-printing apparatus so largely employed on the continent**, has made the wonderful discovery that some bodies are sensitive to sound as selenium is sensitive to light. ('Another wonderful discovery', p. 2, *The Washington Post*, 15 May 1878, by-line: From Nature) Gun Play Too Rapid.: How **Wild Bill Hickok** Unwittingly Killed His Best Friend (headline, p. R6, *The Washington Post*, 6 October 1907, by-line: From Denver Field and Farm)
Impact	A **Momentous** Crisis Which **May Plunge All Europe into War** (headline, p. 1, *The Washington Post*, 11 February 1878) It was quite impossible last night to accurately estimate **the damage done throughout the city; but, in the aggregate, it cannot fall far short of $100,000**, for the pathway of the storm covered the entire District, and **marked every part of it with its destructive violence. Flower beds were demolished, trees torn up and broken down, window panes fractured, houses unroofed, cellars flooded, sewers broken to pieces, trees and houses struck by lightning, and human life was lost.** ('Drenched and Torn.: A City filled with Lightening, Wind and Rain', p. 4, *The Washington Post*, 6 August 1878)
Negativity	The **Salacious Fiends.**: High Time That Parents Should be on their Guard (headline, p. 1, *The Washington Post*, 19 April 1878) The Ohio State Journal, having reported that the General Land Office was selling maps of the United States and Territories at two cents apiece, and several hundred letters having poured into that office inclosing orders, the Commissioner yesterday forwarded a letter to the above journal, saying that its statement were unauthorized and untrue, not only the cause of loss and **disappointment** to many citizens in Ohio, but a source of **annoyance** to the Land Office, besides adding very greatly to its correspondence. ('A Two-Cent Map Business', p. 4, *The Washington Post*, 5 January 1878) The result is said to prove positively a very **violent** but unsuccessful **attempt at rape.** ('The Salacious Fiends.: High Time That Parents Should be on their Guard', p. 1, *The Washington Post*, 19 April 1878)

Table 9.1 **Continued**

	In his message to the Legislature Governor Irwin refers to the Chinese question, to the effect that the presence of the Chinese has initiated **an irresistible conflict**: that if the right of unlimited immigration is conceded to the Chinese there is **danger of their civilization overriding our own** . . . ('The Chinese "Irrepressible Conflict"', p. 1, *The Washington Post*, 7 December 1877)
Personalization	'If he would come back and act decently', she sobbed, 'I would forgive and try to forget, but it is shameful of him to leave me in such a plight, in debt as I am, in poor health and with one child to support. . . .' ('Richard Grant White.: His Wicked Perversion of "Words and their Uses."', p. 1, *The Washington Post*, 14 January 1878) The *Messager Franco-American*, of New York, on Thursday last contains a detailed account of the recent earthquake in Venezuela. . . . The particulars are given by **Mr. Guardia, a coffee planter, who was in the city when the disaster occurred. He says:** . . . ('The Yawning Earth.: The Recent Opening of Terra Firma in Venezuela', p. 1, *The Washington Post*, 1 June 1878)
Proximity	The Brazilian Government subsidizes an **American** mail line [headline] It has long been the wish of the Brazilian Government that the direct mail service between **this country** and Brazil should be restored and should be performed in **American** steamers. (p. 3, *The Washington Post*, 6 December 1877, byline: From the *New York Tribune*) The public schools of **the neighboring city of Alexandria** owe their prosperity and general success to the encouragement of the causes of education in General Washington's endowment of $5,000 to the orphan school in 1785. ('George Washington.: His Endowment of Free Schools in Alexandria', p. 4, *The Washington Post*, 29 January 1878)
Superlativeness	The **heaviest rains and floods which have occurred here for many years** prevailed between the 15th and 20th of September. The rice crops were **greatly** damaged. . . . ('Oriental News.: Burning Churches in Japan—The News from China', p. 1, *The Washington Post*, 11 October 1878)

(*continued*)

Table 9.1 **Continued**

	The corpse of the late lamented Father White is reposing in funeral state at the parsonage of St. Matthew's church, and **thousands of** persons, among whom were many Protestants, have visited it. . . . It is expected that this will be **one of the most imposing funerals ever seen in this city**. ('Father White's Funeral To-day', p. 4, *The Washington Post*, 4 April 1878) A storm, for this section, **almost unexampled in its fury**, broke over the city yesterday afternoon, commencing about a quarter to three and lasting until 5 o'clock. The thunder was something fearful to hear, the lightning **danced** in fantastic shapes **all over** the sky, the wind **swept** through the streets **with terrific force**, the rain come down **in one vast unbroken sheet**, while **huge** hail stones **slaughtered** the poor sparrows **right and left**, and **played** on window panes **the fine notes of the awful music** of the elements. ('Drenched and Torn.: A City filled with Lightening, Wind and Rain', p. 4, *The Washington Post*, 6 August 1878)
Timeliness	Father White's Funeral **To-day** [headline] The corpse of the late lamented Father White **is reposing** in funeral state at the parsonage of St. Matthew's church. . . . The funeral ceremonies **begin this morning at 10 o'clock**. . . . ('Father White's Funeral To-day', p. 4, *The Washington Post*, 4 April 1878) It is too early to review the trial of Fitz John Porter, **now in progress** at West Point, because all the evidence has not yet been presented. (Article 1—No Title, p. 2, *The Washington Post*, 23 July 1878)
Unexpectedness	The death, yesterday morning, of John M. Van Buskirk . . . , after a very brief illness, was a source of painful **surprise** and regret to a very large circle of friends. Mr. Van Buskirk was a man of robust physique and vigorous health, and consequently his demise was **the more unexpected**. (p. 1, *The Washington Post*, 28 January 1878) The cellars and basements of the houses on R street, between Seventh and Tenth streets, were filled with water **for the first time since they were built**. . . . ('Drenched and Torn.: A City filled with Lightening, Wind and Rain', p. 4, *The Washington Post*, 6 August 1878)

No doubt a systematic analysis would throw up further differences and it would also be necessary to go back further in time. Thus, it appears that in early English news discourse newsworthiness was established through comparisons with *like* and *as . . . as* (Claridge 2009: 103), and seventeenth-century broadside ballads and news pamphlets illustrate the use of evaluative adjectives (*sad, fearful, wonderful, terrible, dreadful*), numbers, metaphors, and quotations as precursors of 'the persuasive language of modern journalism' (Cecconi 2009: 155), including the construction of news values such as Negativity, Timeliness (recency), and Proximity (Cecconi 2009: 144). Newsbook titles such as *Strange and Wonderful Relation*, or *News from the Dead* show an emphasis on weird and supernatural stories (Conboy 2010: 30), constructing Unexpectedness.[8]

Analysis of the emergence and development of newsworthiness in photojournalism cannot proceed in the same way as for the discovery of linguistic resources, since digital archives do not (yet) consistently associate keywords or tags with images. One way of proceeding could be to focus on the photographic representation of key historical events in news print where known photographic coverage exists. For example, the 1850s Crimean War was photographed extensively by Roger Fenton, and Mathew B. Brady similarly photographed the American Civil War. The 1880s and 1890s saw the emergence of documentary photography, where photojournalists such as Jacob Riis photographed slum conditions in New York. Well-resourced newspapers of the time would have made use of photographs from these and other photographers. Searches could begin by using verbal keyword searches (e.g. Crimea) and identifying whether the respective articles or surrounding pages also published pictures.

Alternatively, one could focus one's research on a particular newspaper and trace the development of news values in photojournalism by manually searching the archives for use of images. Table 9.2 shows example photographs that were published in the Australian newspaper *The Sydney Morning Herald* in the first half of the twentieth century.

As with the linguistic examples already mentioned, these photographs show some similarities with contemporary news discourse in their construction of news values. The image in the example from 1917 is a portrait of the Vice-chancellor of the University of Sydney, a news actor with high-status and dressed in formal attire, thus constructing the news value of Eliteness. Likewise, in the second example from 1939, the represented participants in the first image are wearing uniforms (one looks like a senior officer, given the type of hat and lapel decorations we can see), thus also constructing Eliteness. In the two images on the right, the close-up photographs of small children concentrating on their tasks establish the news value of Personalization. Again, it would be necessary to go back further in time to identify the emergence of visual resources that construct newsworthiness, for example, to the beginnings of photographic reproduction from 1839 onwards (see Caple 2010; Bednarek and Caple 2012a: 113).

Table 9.2 **The use of photography in** *The Sydney Morning Herald* **during first half of the twentieth century**

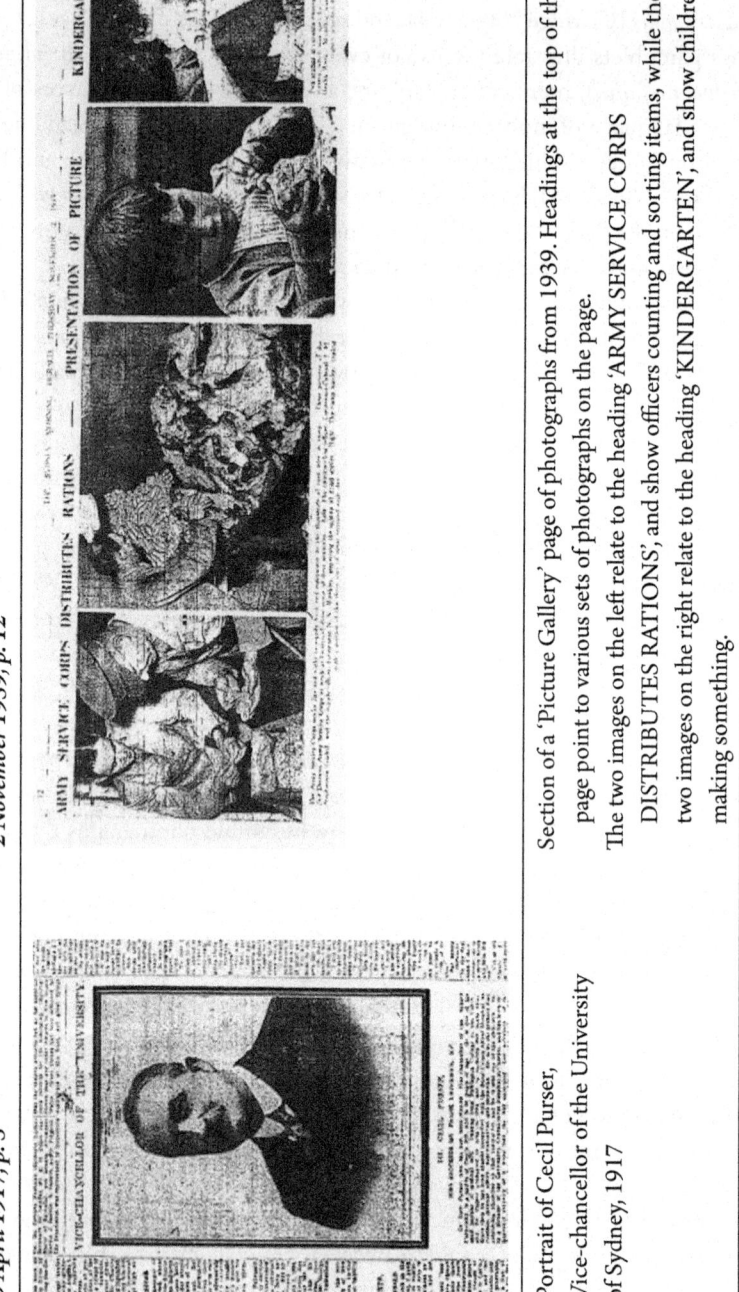

9 April 1917, p. 3	2 November 1939, p. 12
Portrait of Cecil Purser, Vice-chancellor of the University of Sydney, 1917	Section of a 'Picture Gallery' page of photographs from 1939. Headings at the top of the page point to various sets of photographs on the page. The two images on the left relate to the heading 'ARMY SERVICE CORPS DISTRIBUTES RATIONS', and show officers counting and sorting items, while the two images on the right relate to the heading 'KINDERGARTEN', and show children making something.

In sum, DNVA seems to offer a potentially interesting opportunity for research on historical news discourse, although such analysis requires consideration of how 'news' and 'newspaper' are conceptualized, developments in photojournalism and the news industry more generally, as well as variation across text types (e.g. accident, crime, court, disaster, war, shipping news), type of newspaper (e.g. 'popular' vs. 'elite'), and national context (e.g. United States vs. United Kingdom).

9.2 *El terror yihadista, Terroralarm, terrordramat*: Cross-cultural research

In this book, we examined news discourse from different countries/cultures, but mainly limited to the United States, United Kingdom, and Australia. Future research could apply and test the linguistic framework presented in chapter 4 by comparing stories from English-language newspapers in countries that are more different to each other (e.g. a comparison of reporting of a particular event in the United Kingdom or the United States compared to reporting of the same event in English-language news from Malaysia, China, Pakistan, or Vietnam). It should also be possible to apply the framework for visual DNVA introduced in chapter 5 to news photographs that appear in newspapers worldwide (English-language or not), although the cultural context in which these newspapers are published would need to be considered.

In contrast, the linguistic framework introduced in chapter 4 was developed on the basis of English-language news and there is a need to develop inventories for **other** languages to permit a fuller cross-cultural comparison (i.e. going beyond the comparison of English-language newspapers in different countries). This would enable researchers to ask questions such as:

- What news values are discursively construed in different cultures?
- How are these values typically constructed?
- Is there a *transnational* rhetoric of newsworthiness/discourse of news values?
- What are the similarities and differences in the semiotic practices used?
- How is the same topic or event constructed as newsworthy?

To illustrate the last question, table 9.3 contains an unrepresentative sample of front pages from several countries about a hostage-taking in Sydney in 2014—an event that we have already encountered in chapter 5.[9] Note that the newspapers included in this sample differ in many ways—for example, they are not all 'popular' or 'quality' newspapers and hence are not directly comparable in status and target audience. Many stories are derived from material from international news agencies which transmit news in many languages.

Table 9.3 A sample of reporting on the Sydney siege (December 2014) from around the world

Country	Argentina	Bolivia	Spain	Brazil
Paper	La Nacion [Reuters]	Página Siete [AFP]	La Vanguardia	Metro Rio de Janeiro
Page layout	En Sydney, 16 horas de terror	Secuestro fatal en Sídney		16 HORAS DE TENSÃO Rega a Sydney
Headline	En Sydney, 16 horas de terror	Secuestro fatal en Sídney	El terror yihadista llega a Sydney	16 horas de tensão
Gloss	In Sydney, 16 hours of terror	Siege fatal in Sydney	The terror jihadi arrives in Sydney	16 hours of tension
Free Translation	16 hours of terror in Sydney	Deadly siege in Sydney	Jihadi terror arrives in Sydney	16 hours of tension
Text	Fueron 16 horas de máxima tensión, que rompieron la tranquilidad habitual de Sydney. Un autoproclamado clérigo iraní irrumpió ayer en un café del centro de la ciudad tomó a 17 rehenes, a quienes obligo a mostrar una bandera con leyendas musulmanas. El secuestro, que se prolongó durante casi todo el día, mantuvo en vilo a los australianos y terminó con un gran operativo en el que dos rehenes y el atacante, un islamista que aparentemente actuó por su cuenta, terminaron muertos. El país, aliado de Estados Unidos, estaba en alerta por un posible ataque.	RESCATE En el tiroteo con la Policiá, el secuestrador, un clérigo musulmán, y dos de sus rehenes perdieron la vida.	Un clérigo musulmán mantuvo ayer secuestrados durante 17 horas a los clientes y empleados de una cafetería del centro de Sydney (Australia), hasta que la policía lanzó la operación de rescate. El balance fue de tres personas muertas—entre ellas el secuestrador, Man Haron Monis, un refugiado iraní con antecendentes penales - y otras cuatro personas heridas. En la imagen, varios rehenes huyen del café en el momento en que la policía asalta el local.	Polícia invade café em Sydney onde iraniano mantinha 17 prisoneiros. Sequestrafore 2 reféns são mortos

Gloss	It was 16 hours of maximum tension that broke the tranquillity usual of Sydney. A self-proclaimed cleric Iranian stormed yesterday in a cafe in the centre of the city took 17 hostages who he forced show a flag with words Arabic. The siege, which extended during almost all of the day, kept in suspense the Australian and ended with a big operation in which two hostages and the attacker, an islamist who apparently acted on his own, ended up dead. The country, allied with the United States, was on alert for a possible attack.	RESCUE In the gunfire with the police, the siege taker/abductor, a cleric muslim, and two of his hostages lost their lives.	A cleric muslim maintained yesterday hostages during 17 hours customers and employees of a cafe in the centre of Sydney, until the police launched an operation of rescue. The result was three people dead—among them the hostage-taker, Man Haron Monis, a refugee Iranian with background criminal—and another four people wounded. In the image, several hostages fled from the cafe in the moment that the police broke into the shop.	Police storm a cafe in Sydney where Iranian held 17 prisoners. Assailant 2 hostages were killed
Free Translation	16 hours of the highest tension shattered the usual tranquility of Sydney. A self-proclaimed Iranian cleric stormed into a cafe in the city centre and took 17 hostages forcing some of them show a flag with Arabic words on it. The siege, which lasted for most of the day, kept Australia in suspense and ended with a major offensive, which resulted in the deaths of two hostages and the attacker, who apparently acted alone. The country, a US ally, was on alert for a possible attack.	RESCUE During the exchange of gunfire with the police, the hostage-taker, a Muslim cleric, and two hostages lost their lives.	A Muslim cleric yesterday held customers and employees of a central Sydney cafe hostage for 17 hours, until police launched a rescue operation. The result was three dead—among them the hostage-taker, Man Haron Monis, an Iranian asylum seeker with a criminal record—and another four people wounded. The photo show the moment the hostages fled as the police stormed the cafe.	Police storm a Sydney cafe where an Iranian held 17 people hostage. The assailant and two hostages were killed
Other verbal elements	N/A	Image caption	N/A	Issue header [Terror na Austrália], image caption
Photo/s	yes	yes	yes	yes
Photo attribution	Reuters	AFP	Joosep Martinson/Getty	Reuters

(continued)

Table 9.3 Continued

Country	Portugal	Austria	Germany	Canada	Sweden
Paper	Publico	Die Presse [Reuters]	Süddeutsche Zeitung [SZ]	La Presse	Aftonbladet
Page layout					
Headline	Sequestro na Australia 17 refens, 16 horas de cerco e tres mortos	Sydney: Blutiges Ende nach sechzehn Stunden Geiselhaft. Terroralarm in Australien	Polizei beendet Geiselnahme in Sydney	Le siège prend fin dans le sang	Tre dog i terrordramat i Sydney. Tori, 34, ville rädda gisslan—då sköts han
Gloss	Kidnapping in Australia. 17 hostages, 16 hours of siege and three dead	Sydney: Bloody end after sixteen hours hostage imprisonment. Terror alert in Australia	Police ends hostage taking in Sydney	The siege takes an end in the blood	Three died in terrorist drama in Sydney. Tori, 34, wanted to save the hostages, then he was shot
Free Translation	*Siege in Australia. 17 hostages, 16-hour siege, three dead*	*Sydney: A bloody end to a 16-hour hostage siege. Terror alert in Australia*	*Police ends hostage siege in Sydney*	*The siege ends in blood*	*Three died in terrorist drama in Sydney. Tori, 34, wanted to save the hostages, then he was shot*
Text	N/A	Ein Flüchtling aus dem Iran hat im Lindt Chocolat Café am Martin Place in Sydney zahlreiche Menschen in seine Gewalt gebracht. Nach sechzehn Stunden stürmte die Polizei das Café. Mindestens zwei Menschen starben, darunter der Geiselnehmer, ein mutmaßlicher Islamist.	Mehr als 16 Stunden nach dem Beginn einer Geiselnahme in einem Café in Sydney hat die Polizei am Montagabend das Lokal gestürmt. Zwei Menschen, unter ihnen offenbar der Geiselnehmer, seien getötet worden, berichtete der Sender Sky News. Der Täter, ein etwa 50-jaehriger vorgeblicher Prediger aus Iran, hatte in dem Café Angestellte und Gäste in seine Gewalt gebracht. Die Polizei befürchtete zunächst ein islamistisches Motiv.	Une mère de famille et le gérant du Café Lindt, qui aurait héroïquement tente de désarmer son ravisseur, sont morts hier au terme d'une prise d'otages qui aura duré près de 17 heures, et qui s'est conclue par l'assaut des policiers. Une opération « somme toute réussie », selon un expert canadien, qui souligne que le bilan aurait pu être bien plus lourd.	N/A

Gloss	A refugee from the Iran has in Lindt Chocolate Cafe at Martin place in Sydney several people in his control brought. After sixteen hours stormed the police the café. At least two people died, among them the hostage taker, a putative Islamist.	More than 16 hours after the beginning of a hostage taking in a cafe in Sydney has the police on Monday evening the cafe stormed. Two people, among them apparently the hostage taker, had killed been, reported the broadcaster Sky news. The offender, an about 50-year-old ostensible preacher from Iran, had in the café employees and guest in his control brought. The police feared at first an Islamist motive.	A mother of family and the director of Cafe Lindt who has [subjunctive, 'is thought to have'] heroically tried to disarm his abductor are dead yesterday at the end of a taking of hostages which had taken almost 17 hours and which finished with the attack of the policemen. An operation 'in sum successful' after an expert Canadian who underlies that the balance sheet could have been well much heavier.
Free Translation	An Iranian refugee held several people against their will in the Lindt Chocolate Café at Martin Place in Sydney. After 16 hours police stormed the café. At least two people died, including the hostage-taker, a suspected Islamist.	More than 16 hours after the start of a hostage siege in a café in Sydney, the police stormed the café on Monday evening. Two people, among them apparently the hostage-taker, were killed, according to the broadcaster Sky News. The perpetrator, a 50-year-old pretend Iranian preacher had held employees and guests against their will in the café. At first, the police feared that there was an Islamist motivation.	A mother and the manager of the Lindt Café who appears to have heroically tried to disarm his captor died yesterday after a hostage siege which lasted almost 17 hours and which ended with the café being stormed by police. All in all, a 'successful operation' according to a Canadian expert who emphasized that the toll could have been much higher.
Other verbal elements	N/A	N/A	Issue header (*Prise d'otages a Sydney*): reference to comment inside newspaper (*Agnès Gruda Comme à Ottawa Page A5*)
Photo/s	yes	yes	yes
Photo attribution	Jason Reed/ Reuters	Reuters? (story attribution)	Jason Reed/ Reuters	Rob Griffith

An important caveat before we discuss these front pages: in our analysis we assume that the news values that we use in this book also apply to these nine countries and we take the English resources as a starting point to see if similar resources exist in other news discourses. For a systematic study, we would advise **not** to follow the same approach but rather to first undertake research to identify culture-specific news values if applicable—for example, through an extensive culture-specific literature review or through ethnographic research. It is not advisable to make an a priori assumption that the news values we investigate in this book are universal or equally relevant around the world; although some researchers have argued that they are indeed valid for many countries (Bell 1991: 155). Similarly, one should avoid assigning either primacy or universality to an English-language framework when undertaking cross-linguistic research. It is necessary to independently develop an inventory of linguistic resources for other languages.[10] This is particularly the case when languages are investigated that are not as closely related to English as the Germanic and Romance languages we look at here (German, Swedish, Spanish, French, Portuguese).

Having said this, table 9.3 suggests that some resources for newsworthiness that we have identified for English also occur in other news discourses, for instance, quantification (e.g. *16 horas de terror, 16 horas de tensão, sechszehn Stunden Geiselhaft, près de 17 heures*) and negative lexis (e.g. *secuestro, terminaron muertos, perdieron la vida, são mortos, blutiges Ende, Geiselnahme, in seine Gewalt gebracht, le siege, dans le sang, sont mort, sköts han*). Further, there is both similarity and difference in the construction of news values: For instance, as to be expected most of the headlines focus on Negativity. Only the headline from the *Süddeutsche Zeitung* includes less Negativity and perhaps even some potential Positivity, as it does not mention the deaths but simply reports that police ended a hostage situation. Many of the headlines also construct Superlativeness with reference to the length of the hostage taking (*La Nacion, Metro Rio de Janeiro, Publico, Die Presse*) and/or reference to the 'terror' (*La Nacion, La Vanguardia, Die Presse, Aftonbladet*). Only two headlines explicitly mention the number of dead (*Publico, Aftonbladet*), while others imply casualties through adjectives such as *fatal* (*Página Siete*) and *blutiges* (*Die Presse*) or the phrase *dans le sang* (*La Presse*). Of this unrepresentative sample, only the *Aftonbladet* headline construes Personalization by focusing on Tori (one of the hostages killed during the siege).

Six of the headlines mention Sydney and two Australia, but these place references do not construct Proximity for their non-Australian target audiences. Rather, they simply establish the location of the happening as part of establishing the reported event's who, when, where, what, how, and why (cf. chapter 4). To compare, here are some of the Australian headlines emerging from this event (not included in table 9.3):

(1)

Islamic State-linked terror grips **Sydney** (*The Australian Financial Review*)

(2)
Evil strikes **our** heart *(The Daily Telegraph)*

(3)
Terror hits **our** heart *(The West Australian)*

(4)
A nation mourns *(Herald Sun)*

(5)
Terror hits **home** *(The Sydney Morning Herald)*

In these headlines, Proximity is construed for the Australian target audience through reference to Sydney, use of the inclusive first person plural possessive determiner (*our*), and reference to the wider Australian community (*home, a nation*). To construct Proximity in such ways in news reports about 'terror attacks' may be a trope. Inclusive reference also works more generally to reinforce a shared, homogeneous national identity (Coffin and O'Halloran 2005: 161).

Going beyond the headlines and considering briefly some of the other verbal text, references to place abound (e.g. *de Sydney, del centro de Sydney (Australia), em Sydney, am Martin Place in Sydney, in Sydney*), but do not establish Proximity. The only exception is the Canadian *La Presse*, which construes Proximity by quoting a source identified as *canadien*. Similar to the headlines, there is a lot of focus on Negativity and some Superlativeness (e.g. *16 horas de máxima tensión, con un gran operativo, zahlreiche Menschen*). All texts explicitly mention the number of dead, although the phrase *mindestens zwei Menschen* ('at least two people') in the Austrian *Die Presse* seems to imply that more may have died. In relation to Eliteness, most texts only include general references to the police (e.g. *la Policiá, Polícia, die Polizei, des policiers*)—construing only 'weak' Eliteness (see chapter 3). The only exception is again *La Presse*, which quotes a source whom they establish as *un expert*.

If we consider how ordinary news actors are referred to, most texts employ nouns that can be translated as 'hostages' (*rehenes, reféns*), 'customers' (*los clientes, Gäste*), 'employees' (*empleados, Angestellte*), or 'people' (*personas, Menschen*). In other words, these news actors are referred to as a group unified through their 'role' as hostages, customers, or employees or very generally as 'people'. Numbers also occur (17, 2). Thus, functionalization and genericization (van Leeuwen 2008) prevail, which establish only a very weak kind of Personalization, if at all (cf. chapter 4). As above, the outlier is *La Presse*, which uses the personalizing *une mère de famille et le gérant du Cafe Lindt, qui aurait héroïquement tenté de désarmer son ravisseur* ('A mother and the manager of the Lindt Café who appears to have heroically tried to disarm his captor'). The Canadian newspaper also differs from the others in including some Positivity through the quoted source: *Une opération « somme toute réussie »* ('All in all, a "successful operation"'), *le bilan aurait pu être bien plus lourd* ('the toll could have been much higher').

Turning now to the images used on these front pages, very similar photographs are used across all of the texts, with only the *Süddeutsche Zeitung* not including an image with its story. These photographs centre on two key stages in the siege: when hostages managed to escape from the café and run to safety; and after the siege, when the remaining hostages (some injured) were brought out of the café with paramedics in attendance. One newspaper, Brazil's *Metro Rio de Janeiro*, presents a kind of photo gallery, with seven images covering all stages of the siege, from the first images of hostages in the windows of the café, through to the recovery of victims at the conclusion of the siege. This newspaper also includes a file photograph of the hostage taker, although somewhat separated from the photographs of the siege event by a larger black frame and by not being aligned with the other images. One story (in Sweden's *Aftonbladet*) includes a supplied photograph of one of the dead hostages. Arguably, all of the images of the siege construct Negativity, and most also construct Personalization. The represented participants are, in the main, the hostages, ordinary individuals and café employees. This is arguably the easiest way for the audiences of these non-Australian newspapers to connect with the people and events in this story: they are people who are just like them. All are represented as expressing extremely negative emotional responses. Some are depicted running with hands held high, others are carried or being held by police or paramedics. Several of the images also include the specialist heavily armed police officers, who took control of the scene, thus constructing Eliteness, as well as Negativity.

In previous chapters, we have already commented on the way in which the deceased are often portrayed in imagery. The same is true here in the image of Tori Johnson, one of the hostages killed in the siege, used on the front page of Sweden's *Aftonbladet*. The shot shows him alive and smiling. While the image represents a news actor with positive emotional expression, and thus can be said to construct Positivity, we need to be sensitive to the context in which this image is being used. As pointed out in chapter 7, just because a news story includes an image that constructs Positivity, this does not mean that the news story as a whole does the same. In this particular item, reading verbal and visual text together clearly establishes the negative nature of the reported event.[11]

While we cannot undertake a full multimodal analysis here, in many ways it seems that these news items confirm some of the findings from previous chapters, namely that the same news value can be reinforced through both semiotic modes— this is clearly the case for Negativity in these news items. In those front-page stories where the verbal text is superimposed over the images and where no further words are present, the connection between words and images is maximized. We can also see that news values are often complementary, for example, the images show readers the individuals (establishing Personalization) that are only generically referred to in the verbal text. Finally, clashes between the two semiotic modes seem to occur mainly in relation to the use of images of the deceased.

If we briefly compare our analysis of these non-Australian news reports of the Sydney siege with the analysis of the Australian news media (in this section and in chapter 5), we can tentatively conclude that the news values of Negativity, Superlativeness, and Personalization dominate in all reporting, while a key difference lies in the construction of Proximity. As already noted, the verbal resources used in the Australian news media construct Proximity both through use of references to a New South Wales location (*Sydney*) but also by creating nearness to audiences in more distant Australian states through the use of *our* and *nation*, thus constructing Proximity on a national level. The international news stories examined here tell their readers where the happening has occurred by placing the event in Sydney, but do not tend to construct Proximity for their target audiences.[12]

The similarities in the international news coverage of this event may be explained in various ways: On the one hand, they may result from the use of material distributed by international news agencies which can result in a homogenization of news. Boyd-Barrett (2015) talks about the 'hegemony of powerful news agencies' (167), arguing that mainstream media 'continue to be highly dependent on a narrow range of enterprises for print, electronic and video news whether general or specialized' (121). On the other hand, the news value construction is constrained by the event itself in its material reality (see chapter 3). Different events lend themselves to being represented in particular ways (van Dijk 1988a: 113; Bignell 2002: 87). To give the most basic example, we would not expect an event that resulted in the death of ordinary citizens to be reported in a way that constructs the news value of Positivity or an event that happened in a location quite distant from that of its target audience and did not involve any of its nationals to be covered in a way that constructs Proximity. On the other hand, the material reality of events does not fully determine news discourse. Thus, Proximity can be constructed for events that did not happen inside the territory of the target audience. Figure 9.1 shows how the German tabloid *Bild am Sonntag* uses the trope of inclusive reference (the inclusive first person plural possessive determiner *unsere*) to construct the attacks in November 2015

Figure 9.1 German tabloid headline about the November 2015 attacks in Paris, 15 November 2015, p. 1 (*Bild am Sonntag*).

in Paris as affecting not just the French nation, but targeting a shared way of life, including that of the German target audience.

In sum, DNVA seems to offer a potentially interesting opportunity for cross-linguistic and cross-cultural research on news discourse. It appears that the framework for the analysis of images (chapter 5) can already be applied to news photographs from international news organizations, although this would need to be fully tested on a much larger, and more culturally diverse data set (e.g. Ghana, Ecuador, or China) also involving a wider range of topics and text types. Other semiotic resources, such as framing, typography, and colour may exhibit more variation, as different cultural associations may apply to these resources (see, e.g., van Leeuwen 2011 on colour).

With respect to the framework for linguistic analysis (chapter 4), this should only be applied to English-language data. New frameworks and inventories need to be independently developed for other languages, which would then enable cross-linguistic DNVA. Technological change makes comparative analysis of international news particularly relevant:

> The transmission of news around the globe is happening every minute of every day and is increasing in importance with advances in technology that ensure ever greater speed of communication. . . . What we need to do now is . . . to move towards a greater understanding and awareness of how intercultural news material is created and transposed. (Bielsa and Bassnett 2009: 17)

We suggest that analysis of how news values are constructed through semiotic resources could constitute a valuable contribution to such research, with the potential to offer new insights. Such research would need to consider the role of social media and news agencies,[13] in addition to debates around globalization/localization, news translation/adaptation, the homogenization of news, and media imperialism (e.g. van Leeuwen 2006b; Bielsa and Bassnett 2009; Boyd-Barrett 2015).

9.3 Concluding remarks

While our focus in this book is both synchronic and mono-lingual, DNVA seems to offer potentially interesting opportunities for diachronic and cross-linguistic/cross-cultural research on news discourse. In this chapter, we offered some of our own thoughts on potential avenues of research in these two key areas. Since there is a clear interest in research on historical news discourse (e.g. Ungerer 2000b; Brownlees 2006b; Jucker 2009; Conboy 2010; Facchinetti et al. 2012) as well as in cross-linguistic research (e.g. Ungerer 1997; Semino 2002; Thomson and White

2008; Pounds 2010; Taylor 2014) and news translation (e.g. van Leeuwen 2006b; Bielsa and Bassnett 2009), these are both promising areas for applying and developing DNVA. As we mentioned in chapter 1, this book aims to inspire researchers to use DNVA in their own subsequent explorations as well as to develop respective frameworks for other languages. We hope that this chapter has gone some way towards fulfilling these goals. In the following and final chapter, we reflect on other avenues for future research.

Notes

1. http://www.nytimes.com/ref/membercenter/nytarchive.html, accessed 10 December 2015.
2. http://www.thetimes.co.uk/tto/archive/, accessed 10 December 2015.
3. http://www.bl.uk/collection-guides/newspapers, accessed 10 December 2015.
4. http://www.nla.gov.au/content/newspaper-digitisation-program, accessed 10 December 2015.
5. http://www.proquest.com/products-services/pq-hist-news.html, accessed 10 December 2015.
6. http://www.helsinki.fi/varieng/CoRD/corpora/CNNE/index.html, accessed 10 December 2015.
7. http://www.chinednews.com/useful-links/, accessed 10 December 2015.
8. Gotti (2006: 51) also finds that 'adjectives denoting exceptionality and unnaturalness such as *curious, dreadful, monstrous, odd, strange, unusual*' occur in seventeenth-century scientific news items from the *Philosophical Transactions of the Royal Society of London*, emphasizing novelty and rarity (Unexpectedness).
9. The table does not include datelines (e.g. SYDNEY) and section references (e.g. *Mundo, 20*).
10. We need to 'ensure that descriptive categories are not merely postulated and then assumed to have some kind of universal status but that they have to be justified in the course of description of every language' (Caffarel et al. 2004: 11).
11. In relation to the use of visuals other than photographs, two newspapers make use of a black background on top of which the images are laid out and white font colour is used for the accompanying verbal text. As suggested in chapter 5, the use of black framing in this way reinforces the negative construction of the events in the images.
12. The differences between international and local reporting of this event are also evident in the page layout of the front pages. In all of the Australian coverage, this was the only story that featured on the front page (most used a single full-page image like in *The West Australian*) and many pages inside the newspapers were devoted to coverage of the siege. For the international media this was one of many stories that featured on their front pages, with some newspapers having up to nine other stories on the front page.
13. The *Associated Press* and *Thomson Reuters* dominate the market, while other news agencies resist Western narratives (Boyd-Barrett 2015: 160–170).

10

Reflections

In this concluding chapter, we want to revisit and reflect on each of the previous chapters. A special focus of our reflection will be on the avenues for further research that these chapters may have opened up. On our website (http://www.newsvaluesanalysis.com), we have compiled further relevant information on these avenues, including some example analyses and discussion.

10.1 *From little things, big things grow* (chapter 1)

In chapter 1, we introduced readers to the key concerns of this book as well as the major terms, concepts, and tools used. We noted that our primary goal is to introduce readers to discursive news values analysis (DNVA), and our secondary goal is to promote research that brings together multimodality, discourse analysis, and corpus linguistics—that is, corpus-assisted multimodal discourse analysis (CAMDA). The topology that we introduced in chapter 1 is designed to assist researchers in situating their research projects both in relation to semiotic mode and unit of analysis—whether the analysis is multimodal or not, corpus-assisted or not. Crucially, we hope that this book has encouraged others to develop both DNVA and CAMDA further and to apply them to new areas, for instance, regarding the study of variation and audience positioning in different types of news (e.g. national, regional, alternative, citizen, 'popular', 'quality', etc.).

It would also be useful to consider more comprehensively than we have done in this book where in a news item news values are construed. For instance, Bell (1991) notes the importance of story order (80–81) as well as position within the lead paragraph (176), and Jucker (1996: 383) shows that the most explicit mentions of news actors and claims to their newsworthiness are made in the lead. Intra-textual concerns could be addressed, for instance, through combining DNVA with analysis of genre structure in the analysis of complete texts (see http://www.newsvaluesanalysis.com). It would further be interesting to explore how particular discursive constructions of newsworthiness impact on audiences, for example, using DNVA as a tool to produce different versions of news stories and test them on audiences or to analyse audience reactions to different published texts. There is also scope for more research into how the construal of news values changes with the news cycle (cf. Potts et al. 2015) and varies across both semiotic mode and medium (radio, television, print, online, mobile).

10.2 Surveying the field: *It's a jungle out there* (chapter 2)

In chapter 2, we tried to untangle the semiotic jungle of how the term *news values* has been applied and conceptualized by others before introducing our own 'discursive' perspective. From a discursive perspective, we are interested in analysing news values as *values that are established by semiotic resources in use*. As we briefly noted in chapter 2, such a perspective could be applied to different phases of the news process, although we focused on published news items in this book. Various other types of discourse could be analysed: input material (interviews, press releases, photos, videos, reports, social media posts, news agency copy, etc.), newsroom discussions,[1] reviewing complaints, impartiality reports, audience comments, and so on. Thus, we surmise that it would be possible to apply the DNVA frameworks that we introduced for linguistic/visual analysis in chapters 4 and 5 to news agency copy and media releases, including comparison with published stories that arise from them. Applying DNVA in such comparisons would allow future researchers to make a novel contribution to the study of intertextuality in the news: 'the extraction (decontextualization) of meaning from one discourse and consequent insertion (recontextualization) of that meaning into another discourse' (Catenaccio et al. 2011: 1844). However, it is clear that the frameworks that we developed for the analysis of published news items (chapters 4 and 5) cannot be applied to all phases of the news process, even if a discursive perspective can. *Meta news discourse* (discourse about the news and the news process) in particular may feature specific discursive resources, and rather than constructing news values, such discourse may cite, invoke, evaluate, or negotiate news values. In general, there is much room for a systematic analysis of the communication of newsworthiness, which could make a valuable contribution to the fairly recent use of linguistic analysis to examine news processes (e.g. Cotter 2010; van Hout and Macgilchrist 2010; Catenaccio et al. 2011; Perrin 2013).

10.3 Situating our own approach to news values: *Which corner of the jungle do we inhabit?* (chapter 3)

Chapter 3 provided further information on our discursive approach and noted that we adopt a middle ground between constructionism and realism. While events should not be denied their material reality, we maintained that there is a need to avoid the assumption that news values are simply 'inherent' in events or simply reflected in discourse and also argued for a shift in emphasis to recognize that discourse has an important role to play in constituting and reinforcing news values.

In the context of our discussion, we also suggested that it would be possible to use DNVA to study sensationalism and media panics (Fowler 1991; Molek-Kozakowska 2013), even though this is not our focus in this book. In order to do so, researchers would need to consider both the 'material' and the 'discursive' dimension of news values through analysis of the fit or match between the potential news value of an event and its discursive construction. Such research could aim to assess the extent to which events are discursively made **more newsworthy** than they appear to be. However, there are certain challenges that such research would need to address first—in particular how to define an 'event' and how to determine the appropriateness of its representation (cf. Galtung and Ruge 1965: 71; Lester 1980: 992; Geis 1987: 77; Boyd-Barrett 1994: 33–34). A common problem for analysts is that they are unable to observe events first-hand as they unfold (and even if they do, that they bring to this observation their prejudices, attitudes, etc.), and mainly deal with subsequent discursive mediations. It is hence very difficult to access an event other than through discourse. Consequently, one solution to these epistemological challenges is to focus on discourses, for example, checking original documents (reports, policy documents) and news reports from different outlets (Carvalho 2008: 171). This makes it possible to 'assess at least the relative truth and accuracy of a discourse. By comparing discourses on a sliding scale, we can attempt to assess which ones are more or less accurate, taking into account all the existing evidence and discourses' (Milestone and Meyer 2012: 26). For instance, van Dijk (1988b: 280) compares the numbers used in different newspapers and finds that they vary quite significantly. Another approach is used by Bell (1991: 217) who asks sources cited in news stories to identify inaccuracies and misreporting using a five-point scale of in/accuracy. Building on such approaches, future researchers may thus be able to use DNVA in the study of sensationalism, misreporting, and media panics.

In addition, there is room for further theoretical and empirical research into the various news values discussed in chapter 3. One area that might profit from such research is the analysis of Positivity in news discourse—for example, how often, where, and how is this constructed in today's news discourse in comparison with news discourse in the past? Can any large-scale shifts be empirically demonstrated? In general, each of the news values examined in chapter 3 is worthy of much more in-depth investigation (e.g. in relation to subcategories). There is perhaps a PhD topic in each news value, especially Positivity, Unexpectedness, Consonance, and Aesthetic Appeal.

10.4 The *discourse* of news values (chapters 4 and 5)

In chapters 4 and 5, we systematically linked each news value to verbal and visual semiotic resources that regularly construct newsworthiness in published news stories—we might call this *the discourse of news values*. Both chapters provide frameworks for subsequent discursive news values analysis, without the devices comprising a 'checklist'. As a reminder, we argue that close attention needs to be paid to the meaning potential of the semiotic resource as used in a news story as well as to the target audience and time/place of publication. As also noted (in chapter 4), the discourse of news values is one way of attracting and maintaining the interest and attention of news audiences, but it is not the only one. In relation to linguistic devices, other ways of attracting an audience include word play and allusion (e.g. *Love is in the **heir**,* [singer] *George Michael jailed ... as magistrate finally **loses the faith**),* direct address *(... this man's reaction will warm **your** heart),* the use of questions *(Was Vesna murdered with a garden tool?),* or the use of 'clickbait' headlines.[2] In relation to the use of visual resources to attract audiences, one might think of the use of well-designed infographics or pictures of scantily clad women. All of these semiotic practices may function to attract and engage audiences, but differ from resources that construct news events as negative, timely, unexpected, and so on.

With respect to the introduced frameworks, the linguistic inventory presented in chapter 4 is based on extensive analysis of manifold authentic English-language news items. As we noted in this chapter, further research could focus more on broadcast news, identifying additional resources for video and audio (e.g. sound features such as stress, intonation, prosody).[3] The study of linguistic variation between different types of news is another area worthy of future study (e.g. hard news, soft news, research news). For instance, several items in the 'shared news' corpus (chapter 8) feature opening paragraphs that are not typical summary 'hard news' leads. Examples include:

- *Emily Kraus was psyched.*
- *Let's get ready to ... mumble.*
- *An e. You can write it with one fluid swoop of a pen or one tap of the keyboard. The most commonly used letter in the English dictionary. Simple, right?*
- *Are you prepared for the impending zombie invasion?*
- *It was a scene as creepy as a Hannibal Lecter movie.*

Here, it is only partially through the construction of news values that readers are attracted to the story (e.g. Personalization: *Emily Kraus was psyched*; Superlativeness: *as creepy as a Hannibal Lecter movie*). Rather, direct audience address and questions may attract audiences to these stories. A DNVA that compares hard and soft news, combined with analysis of other linguistic features, might thus provide interesting insights into the different ways in which audiences are persuaded to consume news.

In relation to the inventory for visual resources proposed in chapter 5, the main focus is on images. We only briefly point to the work that other semiotic resources such as typography, layout, and so on do in the construction of newsworthiness and more research is clearly needed in this area. Such research could also investigate cross-cultural differences, for example, in terms of the use of capital letters or colour. In this book, we also focus on still photographs, with considerable scope for research focusing on videos, online news galleries, photo essays, or multimedia story packages (e.g. Snowfall, *The New York Times*; Firestorm, *The Guardian*). The latter are a particularly interesting recent development in journalism and constitute a fruitful, if challenging, area of investigation, especially in relation to how multiple semiotic modes combine in very complex ways.

10.5 Case study 1: 'Pedalling' a critical, topic-based approach to DNVA (chapter 6)

Chapter 6 illustrated how DNVA can be used to explore if particular topics are associated with specific news values. If certain news values are emphasized, rare, or absent, this may have ideological implications. The particular topic of reporting was cycling/cyclists. The analyses suggested that a typical way of creating newsworthy events that attract audiences in relation to news discourse about cyclists appears to be the description of their death and injury. The chapter also demonstrated the application of 'mono-modal' corpus linguistic DNVA ('Zone 2' analysis with respect to our topology) and illustrated how one can combine analysis of one general news value (Negativity) with more delicate analysis of different ways or categories in which this is discursively constructed.

In its analysis of agency and its identification of victim-blaming, chapter 6 further showed the possibility of combining DNVA with other tools used in critical discourse analysis (CDA). For reasons of scope, this book focused primarily on introducing DNVA to readers. However, our aim is not to replace existing discourse analytical tools but rather to add DNVA to the toolbox (Bednarek and Caple 2014: 139). In practice, it will often make sense to combine DNVA with other tools, especially when used in CDA. Thus, DNVA could be combined with analysis of attribution, transitivity, nominalization, modality, appraisal/evaluation, figurative speech, social actor representation, and so on.

10.6 Case study 2: DNVA and the digital disrupters of social media (chapter 7)

Chapter 7 illustrated how DNVA can be used to explore the construction of newsworthiness in images used in newsbites distributed via the social media platform

Facebook. It also pointed to the potential consequences of using stock photography in the place of news photography, especially when such images do not construct news values, but carry other ideological meanings. The chapter also demonstrated the application of 'mono-modal' visual DNVA ('Zone 2' analysis with respect to our topology). Further, chapter 7 showed how visual DNVA can be combined with analysis of other aspects of news practice, for instance, the use of captions, image attribution, or layout/templating to provide insights into emerging news practices in social media and online. This is especially important in the online environment where design, templates, and story packaging are constantly evolving. Since online audience behaviour has become so important for news organizations, visual DNVA could be combined with audience research in investigating the 'clickability' and 'shareability' of one image over another.

Importantly though, the findings from this case study can be used as a base line for future research investigating the emerging practices at Facebook and other social media platforms as they themselves become 'neo-publishers' (Bell 2015). This is particularly interesting because of new developments since we collected the data for our case study in late 2014. In May 2015, Facebook launched *Instant Article*, a service that allows the company to act as a direct publishing platform for major news media organizations (Griffith 2015).[4] Subscribers to this service include *The New York Times*, *The Washington Post*, *BuzzFeed*, and *The Atlantic*. Such news websites are also subscribing to Twitter's 'news curating' service *Moments* (launched in October 2015), designed to aggregate the main stories of the day concerning a particular 'moment' (Boorstin 2015). Essentially, these services are designed for speed and make it easier to see top stories without being an expert social media user. Crucially though, rather than funnel traffic away from these social media platforms to news websites themselves, the idea behind *Instant Article*, for example, is to keep audiences on the Facebook platform (Meyer 2015). This effectively stops social referrals and poses significant challenges to the legacy news media, not least in terms of their commercial survival. Such a development hence constitutes a further step in the digital disruption of the relationship between news media organizations and social media platforms.

10.7 Case study 3: Combining DNVA and CAMDA (chapter 8)

In including the two 'mono-modal' case studies in chapters 6 and 7, we acknowledge that a single researcher will not necessarily have the skills to undertake both visual and verbal analysis. Nor will researchers always be interested in both corpus linguistics and multimodal discourse analysis or have the time or the resources to combine these approaches. Therefore, the case studies presented in these chapters illustrated how linguistic and visual DNVA may proceed without recourse to each other. Chapter 8, however, attempted to bring these two analytical strands together to investigate the roles that both verbal and visual semiotic resources play in constructing newsworthiness. We illustrated a particular approach to corpus-assisted multimodal discourse analysis where we combined the analysis of patterns in language with analysis of patterns in images, also taking into account the construction of news values across semiotic modes. Our main focus was on the analysis of patterns across texts rather than on the development of meaning within text. As mentioned in chapter 1, we do not want to prescribe this as the only way of undertaking CAMDA, but rather encourage researchers to come up with complementary ways of doing so.

In addition to showcasing one approach to CAMDA, chapter 8 illustrated how DNVA can be used to analyse the packaging of news, showing how news values are integrated and structured in the form of consumable news products and discussing the role that different semiotic modes play—whether or not they reinforce, complement, or contradict each other. A key finding here was that visual and verbal components most often complement each other, with the multimodal news story accumulating a range of constructed news values. The case study further illustrated two different approaches to the analysis of news values—a positional approach where news values established in the headlines/opening paragraph are seen as the most emphasized, and a frequency-based approach where (de)emphasis corresponds to frequency of occurrence (which was also applied in the corpus linguistic analysis in chapter 6).

The context in which this case study was placed was the sharing of news via social media. Arguably, many of us now live in an age of data pollution, where we are constantly bombarded with streams of information that vie for our attention. In this 'attention economy' (boyd 2012) shared news can capture audience members' attention and direct them to a news organization's online presence. Our analyses of shared news in chapter 8 seemed to suggest that there is ground for some concern, for instance, in relation to the type of research news that is widely shared. Another potentially troubling finding, which we did not focus on in chapter 8, concerns the way in which news organizations seem to 'piggy-back' on the social media. They do this by posting news stories about content that has already gone viral—stories which then become widely shared themselves and which are not necessarily 'news' in the traditional sense. We did report an example of this in chapter 8: *A touching moment between a zoo worker and one of his favorite animals has gone viral*. Other instances are also present in the Shared News Corpus, with at least three further items about images, video, or tests that have gone viral on social media or blogs (Impact is usually constructed through explicit references to this fact with the phrase GO VIRAL). Another example of this occurred at the time of writing this chapter, with the *BBC* publishing a story on 22 January 2016 with the headline *Wedding haka moves New Zealand Maori bride to tears*—an item about a video from a couple's wedding that was widely shared on social media. In this way, the social media have a clear impact on the news agenda, as the heritage media are reacting to the virality of social media content by publishing related stories. Ultimately, however, the future of how sharing and other audience behaviour will affect the social and semiotic practices of journalism depends on a variety of factors such as changing algorithms and the emerging importance of metrics that measure audience engagement, such as time spent with content (Moses 2015). For example, it is now known that users who access news outlets via Facebook read fewer pages and spend less time than those who access them directly (Pew Research Center 2014). If news organizations are starting to pay more attention to time spent with content, this could result in the creation of news items that hold people's attention for longer in addition to those that are simply widely shared.

Importantly, our analyses also suggest that there is considerable variety in terms of the news values constructed in such shared news. News institutions might hence be able to focus on creating news items that are likely to be shared by particular sections of the audience (which might be valued by particular advertisers), in addition to those items that are likely to be shared by as many users as possible. Already there are technologies that allow insight into personal sharing activities, determining personalized advertising (Martin and Dwyer 2015). Perhaps personalizing news will constitute the next big development after sharing news, with apps such as Apple's News already making inroads in this area. It is not our place here to predict the future of journalism, but we do want to make a strong argument for continued engagement with news media texts by discourse analysts and media linguists. Our case study in chapter 8 focused quite deliberately on the heritage news media. Future studies could replicate this study with non-heritage news media (e.g. *BuzzFeed, Huffington Post, Vice, Crikey,* etc.). This would provide a very interesting point of comparison. Likewise, this case study could provide a useful reference point for diachronic research. In 10 or 20 years from now, the same case study could be repeated to see if and how the heritage media cope with continual digital disruption and if any shifts in newsworthiness have occurred.

10.8 *Xīnwén jiàzhí, arzeshe khabari, Khabari Iqdaar* (chapter 9)

In chapter 9 we exemplified two key avenues for further research in much more detail than this final, 'reflective' chapter would have allowed us to. We proposed that diachronic and cross-linguistic/cross-cultural researchers could further develop DNVA and apply it to answer questions such as:

- How has the rhetoric of newsworthiness emerged over time, including both differences and similarities to contemporary news?
- What news values are discursively construed in different languages and cultures and how? Is there a global discourse of newsworthiness with more similarities than differences? How is the same topic or event constructed as newsworthy?

We do not propose to have answered these questions in chapter 9; rather, its key aim was to open up research for others. What is needed most urgently is the development of inventories for other languages to allow cross-linguistic comparison, without automatically taking English as the starting point. There are many additional avenues for further research, including the need for more culturally diverse data, but since we have expounded to some extent on this in the previous chapter we will say no more about it here.

10.9 Concluding remarks

In this book, we have introduced DNVA as an approach that helps discourse analysts to examine how news organizations, metaphorically speaking, 'sell' the news to us **as news** through verbal and visual resources. We argue that the concept of news values is important because it allows discourse analysts to take into account the professional context of the news media texts that they study. Throughout the book our main focus was on how news is packaged in the form of consumable news products, with the aim of providing insights into news as social practice at the micro level of semiotic construction. In other words, our approach was to examine *news as semiotic practice*. In addition to providing specific and unique insights into the investigated data, each empirical case study demonstrated how DNVA can be used to offer insights into common practices, conventions, and clichés of news reporting. That is, it can uncover the conventionalized rhetoric of newsworthiness at particular points in time and in particular kinds of data. This is important not least because of the ideological nature of news values (chapter 2). It is also useful for the insights it can provide into journalism as professional practice and as an additional tool in CDA.

We hope that DNVA will be of use to other linguistic/semiotic researchers interested in investigating news discourse. Building on our previous publications in this area, a number of researchers are already analysing the discursive construction of newsworthiness in their own work: Makki (2014, in progress) focuses on the discourse of news values in Iranian crime news reporting, while Huan (2015) aims to combine ethnographic analysis with discursive analysis of news values in Chinese and Australian hard news stories about risk events. Dahl and Fløttum's (2014) research focuses on newsworthiness in the discursive representations of climate change in British newspapers, while Molek-Kozakowska (in press) applies our framework to examine newsworthiness in popular science journalism. Fest (2015) takes a corpus linguistic perspective in analysing 4,000 news items across different varieties of English. Perhaps this book will inspire others to contribute to DNVA research in the future.

As media educators we further hope that this book has provided new insights into journalistic texts as professional practice and that this can inform how we teach and learn about such texts in first and additional language contexts (i.e. media literacy) as well as how we teach students to create such texts (i.e. journalism education). Therefore, we see this book as a contribution to both research and teaching, offering a discursive perspective on the study of news values.

To conclude, we offer our discursive approach to news values analysis as a way of bringing our research under a single umbrella, one that accounts equally for the contribution of verbal and visual semiotic resources to the construction of newsworthiness. We hope that this will inspire future research collaborations that prove as stimulating and rewarding as we have found ours.

Notes

1. Newsroom access would be necessary for analysis of how story discussions are used to negotiate news values pre-publication (see Cotter 2010).
2. Caple (2010) argues that using word play and allusion are a way of attracting and retaining an audience. Jucker (2000) provides an overview of linguistic and pragmatic strategies for interactive communication and directly addressing the reader. 'Clickbait' headlines (Blom and Hansen 2015) associated with 'digital natives' like *Buzzfeed* or *Upworthy* are now sometimes used by 'heritage' news organizations. On a more general level, the language of news stories needs to be accessible to the audience in order to engage them, e.g. casual, colloquial, and commonsensical (Hartley 1982: 98; Fitzgerald and McKay 2012).
3. In relation to broadcast news, it is important to carefully consider whether transitions (e.g. *and now for a change of pace, here at home*), which are not part of the news item per se but rather introduce it, work to construct reported events as newsworthy.
4. This product was officially launched to all Facebook customers using the iPhone app in October 2015, following the trial launch in May.

Appendix

Table A4.1 **Inventory of linguistic devices that often construct newsworthiness in English-language news**

News value	Linguistic device	Examples
Consonance ([stereo]typical)	References to stereotypical attributes or preconceptions	Drug addict parents gave 23-month-old son methadone 'like Calpol', Most broody mothers see having a child as a wonderful gift from God, …another eventful Australia Day, which most Australians enjoyed in the best way they knew how—laying under the sun on a white-sand beach or enjoying a barbecue with friends and family.
	Assessments of expectedness/typicality	a man whose love of luxury and lavish parties is **legendary**, …as dire Diaz campaign ends in **typical** style
	Similarity with past	…as the US came to terms with **yet another** mass shooting, America is **once again** torn apart by race and police power
	Explicit references to general knowledge/traditions	In keeping with the Germans' **well-known** love of beer
Eliteness (of high status or fame)	Various high status markers, including role labels	U.S. District Court Judge Scott Skavdahl, Professor Roger Stone, Snohomish county fire district 21 chief, celebrity chef Jamie Oliver, Abba legend Björn Ulvaeus

	status-indicating adjectives	the **prestigious** Man Booker prize, the city's **top** cop, a **senior** World Bank executive, a **key** federal government minister, **long-term** industry observers, **well-placed** government sources
	recognized names	Hillary Clinton, Abba, the Olympics, the Oscars, Harvard university, the World Health Organisation
	descriptions of achievement/fame	*Ronnie Barker* **of the Two Ronnies fame**, *two people who* **were selling millions of records a year**, *The Norwegian entertainer was also* **very popular in neighbouring countries**
	use by news actors/sources of specialized/technical terminology, high-status accent or sociolect (esp. in broadcast news)	N/A
Impact (having significant effects or consequences)	Assessments of significance	a potentially **momentous** day, in a **historic** legal case, a **crucial** annual conference
	Representation of actual or non-actual significant/relevant consequences, including abstract, material, or mental effects	note that will stun the world, leaving scenes of destruction, Millions of Australian homes and businesses could be hit with bigger phone and internet bills, thousands of people may be massacred

(continued)

Table A4.1 Continued

News value	Linguistic device	Examples
Negativity/Positivity (negative/positive)	References to negative/positive emotion and attitude	**concerns** about even remote chances of Ebola exposure, **fury** as primary head takes week off in term to fly to Caribbean, a move that has **outraged** local politicians, amid signs of **panic**, 'First hydrogen bomb test' **condemned**, Pale but **smiling**, former U.S. Marine Amir Hekmati recounted Tuesday how disbelief turned to **joy**, Baltimore residents **celebrate** charges in Gray case
	Negative/positive evaluative language	Corbyn's **shambolic** reshuffle, a **violent thug** who had no interest in Islam, **shoddy** financial advice, the **brilliant** astrophysicist, the **perfect** end to another eventful Australia Day
	Negative/positive lexis	Boy, 8, one of 3 **killed** in bombings at Boston Marathon; scores **wounded**, Western black rhino declared **extinct**, Flint residents **protest** high bills for 'poison' water, 13 migrants **drown** as boat capsizes off Malaysia, Nigeria has been declared officially **free of Ebola**, Teens chase kidnapping suspect on bikes, **save** 5-year-old girl, ... a baby with HIV is deemed **cured**

	Descriptions of negative (e.g. norm-breaking) or positive behaviour/state-of-affairs	Hospitals *don't have enough beds, and there **aren't enough** ambulances*, Treasurer Joe Hockey **has broken his promise** *to balance the budget by 2019,* [Canadian Prime Minister] Trudeau, who last year **unveiled a cabinet with an equal number of men and women** *'because it's 2015'*
Personalization (having a personal/human face)	References to 'ordinary' people, their emotions, experiences	*Mike's devastated owner,* *Charissa Benjamin and her Serbian husband,* *'It was pretty bloody scary',* *But one of his victims sobbed,* *Deborah said afterwards: 'My sentence has only just begun'*
	Use by news actors/sources of 'everyday' spoken language, accent, sociolect (esp. in broadcast news)	N/A
Proximity (geographically or culturally near)	Explicit references to place or nationality near the target community	*A federal judge in the **District of Columbia** …,* *A skeleton found beneath a **Leicester** car park …,* *A **Texas** father caught a man sexually assaulting his 4-year-old daughter,* ***Australian** nurse in Ebola scare*
	References to the nation/community via deictics, generic place references, adjectives	**Homegrown** *terrorist Mohamed Elomar pledges to bring the horror* **here**, *a potential attack on **the nation**'s capital and **the country**'s highest office*

(continued)

Table A4.1 Continued

News value	Linguistic device	Examples
	Inclusive first person plural pronouns	Red alert over the plot to attack **our** nation's leaders Is this the end of **our** local newsagents?
	Use by news actors/sources of (geographical) accent/dialect (esp. in broadcast news)	N/A
	Cultural references	Teenager takes his great-grandmother to **prom**, Soldiers' farewell **haka** footage goes viral
Superlativeness (of high intensity/ large scope)	Intensifiers	The Ebola outbreak [. . .] will get **significantly** worse, A **sensational** corruption inquiry has concluded..., The US government says it is '**deeply** concerned' by reports that...
	Quantifiers	**hundreds** who flew with an infected nurse, the country's **two-week-old** political crisis, a tragedy of **epic** proportions, a ... **$356 million** loss
	Intensified lexis	U.S. forces **hammered** ISIS fighting positions, vehicles and buildings, Robbers **smash** display cases, Police seek motive in Idaho shooting **rampage** that killed 3, they were **petrified**

Metaphor and simile	... country towns in northern NSW are **battling a tsunami** of crime, a June wildfire that ... ripped through **as if the land had been doused with gasoline**
Comparison	Foxtons' stock price was rising **faster than** the cost of a Mayfair penthouse, Brad Pitt and Angelina Jolie's wedding was **so secret** Jolie's father Jon Voight did not know it had taken place, ... around 5,000 **more** suicides in Europe and North America, ... **the largest drug ring in Detroit history**, ... **one of the world's most prolific** serial killers, ... 2014 **surpassed** 2010 as the warmest year
Repetition	... with **building after building** flattened or punctured by shells
Lexis of growth	The volume of email cloaked in encryption technology is **rising**, ... adding to a **growing** list of healthcare workers in West Africa hit by the epidemic, It had sheer **scale, scope, the length and the breadth** of the evil unfolded
Only/just/alone/already + time/distance or related lexis	**Already this year** 64 clandestine ice labs have been busted and dismantled, almost a hundred foreigners ... were arrested **in one raid alone**

(*continued*)

265

Table A4.1 Continued

News value	Linguistic device	Examples
Timeliness (recent, ongoing, about to happen, new, current, seasonal)	Temporal references	A terrorist attack . . . is **now** regarded as 'likely', Labour will **today** offer, **yesterday's** flash flooding
	Present and present perfect	it **is testing** our emergency resources, INDONESIA'S Justice Ministry **is about to** isolate . . . , rescuers **have been trying** to pluck survivors
	Implicit time references through lexis (e.g. ongoing, under way, begin)	A murder investigation is **under way** in Dublin, Search **ongoing** for missing Victoria woman Karen Chetcuti
	References to:	
	current trends	'selfie'—the smartphone self-portrait—has been declared word of the year for 2013
	seasonality	. . . as Public Health England urged people to keep their homes well heated **this winter**
	change/newness/discovery	In an unexpected **development**, Bowser says **change** from GLBT to LGTB is 'in keeping with the mainstream vocabulary', Mint 1969 Shelby GT500 **found** under 40 years of dust, EU leaders pick **new** top diplomats

Unexpectedness (unexpected)	Evaluations of unexpectedness	one of the **strangest** scandals, an **unusual** case in a city where prosecutions of police for excessive [sic] are **rare**
	References to surprise/expectations	**shock** at North Cottesloe quiz night, people just really **can't believe it**
	Comparisons that indicate unusuality	Sydney's **wettest August in 16 years**, the **first time since 1958**, I've lived in Toowoomba for 20 years and I've never seen anything like that
	References to unusual happenings	British man survives 15-storey plummet, German MPs considering a return to typewriters to combat spy activity, Queensland woman fights off kangaroo with backpack

Table A5.1 **Inventory of visual devices that often construct newsworthiness in English-language news**

News value	Visual devices
Aesthetic Appeal (aesthetically pleasing)	**Content:** **Represented participants:** • The depiction of people, places, objects, landscapes culturally recognized for their beauty. **Capture:** **Composition: Balance** • Dynamic, asymmetric composition, making use of the diagonal axis; • Balanced, symmetrical images where the symmetry is momentarily interrupted. **Technical affordances:** • Movement: blurring and freezing of action; • Noise: high level of graininess; • Focus: lengthening or reducing depth of field within the image.
Consonance ([stereo]typical)	**Content:** **Represented participants/attributes:** • The depiction of people and their attributes that fit with the stereotypical imagery of a person/country etc. (e.g. beer and breasts for Germany's Oktoberfest). **Activity sequence:** • Staged/highly choreographed depictions of typical activities associated with a person/group/nation.
Eliteness (of high status or fame)	**Content:** **Represented participants:** • Showing known and easily recognizable key figures, e.g. political leaders, celebrities. **Attributes:** • Showing people in elaborate costumes, uniform, or with other regalia of officialdom; • Showing self-reflexive elements like microphones/cameras. **Activity sequence:** • Showing people flanked by military, police, or bodyguards or in a media scrum; • Showing people using the specialist equipment associated with elite professions (e.g. surgeon performing an operation). **Setting:** • Showing context associated with an elite profession, e.g. books, lab, police station.

Table A5.1 **Continued**

News value	Visual devices
Impact (having significant effects or consequences)	**Content:** **Represented participants/attributes:** • Showing the after-effects (often negative) of events, e.g. scenes of destruction, injuries, damage to property; • Showing emotions caused by an event.
Negativity (negative)	**Content:** **Represented participants/attributes:** • Showing negative events and their effects, e.g. the aftermath of accidents, natural disasters, the injured/wounded, the wreckage/damage done to property; • Showing people experiencing negative emotions. **Activity sequence:** • Showing people being arrested or (as defendant) with lawyers/barristers/police; • Showing people attempting to hide their identity, e.g. using an item of clothing to cover the head, or showing aggression towards the camera, e.g. putting a hand up in front of the lens; • Showing people engaging in norm-breaking behaviour, e.g. fighting, vandalizing, stealing, attacking. **Capture:** **Technical affordances:** • Movement/blurring involving negative content, resulting in poor quality images; • Noise: dramatizing and intensifying negative content; • Focus: where extreme circumstances mean inability to provide sharp and detailed image content, e.g. water/rain on the lens; • In moving images: blurring and movement caused by camera-people moving around, running, ducking to avoid projectiles etc. (suggesting unstable situation, i.e. danger).
Positivity (positive)	**Content:** **Represented participants/attributes:** • Showing people experiencing positive emotions. **Activity sequence:** • Showing people engaging in positively valued behaviour, e.g. being successful at red carpet events, award ceremonies; • Showing actions associated with reconciliation or praise, e.g. shaking hands, hugging.

(*continued*)

Table A5.1 Continued

News value	Visual devices
Personalization (having a personal/human face)	**Content:** **Represented participants/attributes:** • Showing 'ordinary' individuals, especially when singled out and standing in for a larger group; • People dressed in informal/everyday clothing; • Carrying items such as rucksacks, handbags, shopping bags; • Showing an emotional response. **Setting:** • In the home/domestic setting; • On the street. **Capture:** **Composition: Salience** • Positioning individuals in unequal relation (in terms of textual composition, NOT in terms of social power dynamics) to others in the image frame, e.g. singling out one individual through foregrounding or backgrounding. **Composition: Shot length** • Using a close-up shot (to focus on a person's emotion, for example). **Technical affordances: Focus** • Reducing depth of field so that the focus remains on the individual.
Proximity (geographically or culturally near)	**Content:** **Represented participants/attributes/setting:** • Showing well-known or iconic landmarks (Tower Bridge, Sydney Opera House, Golden Gate Bridge), natural features (Uluru) or cultural symbols (flags, national colours/distinctive uniforms). **[Verbal text:** • Showing verbal text indicating relevant place/cultural connection, e.g. signage.]
Superlativeness (of high intensity/large scope)	**Content:** **Represented participants:** • Showing the large-scale repetition of participants in the image frame, e.g. not just one house but an entire street affected; • Showing extreme (positive or negative) emotions in participants.

Table A5.1 **Continued**

News value	Visual devices
	Capture: **Composition: Shot length** • Use of very wide angle to exaggerate differences in size/space; • Magnification (larger than life representation) through use of extreme close-up or macro lens. **Technical affordances: Movement** • Camera movement and blurring, combined with camera-people moving around, running, ducking to avoid projectiles etc. (suggesting seriousness/high danger, etc.).
Timeliness (recent, ongoing, about to happen, new, current, seasonal)	**Content:** **Represented participants:** • Natural phenomena that indicate time, e.g. the season may be implied in flora or environmental conditions; • Inclusion of cultural artefacts, like Christmas trees that are representative of a particular time of year. **Activity sequence:** • Showing the revealing of an item, to be seen for the first time. [**Verbal Text:** • Including verbal text indicating relevant time, e.g. signage.]
Unexpectedness (unexpected)	**Content:** **Represented participants:** • Showing people being shocked/surprised; • Showing unusual happenings that would be considered outside an established societal norm or expectation. **Capture:** **Composition: Salience** • Juxtaposition of elements in the frame that create stark contrast.

Table A6.1 **Frequencies of search terms**

Query term	United Kingdom		Australia		United States	
	raw f	Per 100,000 words	raw f	Per 100,000 words	raw f	Per 100,000 words
cycling	1,003	425.6	356	313.1	152	96.8
cycled	86	36.5	15	13.2	2	1.3
cyclist*	2,085	884.8	1,109	975.4	466	296.8
bicycl*	313	132.8	545	479.4	1,020	649.7
biking*	20	8.5	6	5.3	103	65.6
bike*	2,087	885.7	1,309	1,151.4	2,676	1,704.6
"to cycle"	97	41.2	18	15.8	4	2.5
cycleway	23	9.8	124	109.1	0	0.0
cycle path*	86	36.5	25	22.0	0	0.0
cycle rac*	10	4.2	0	0.0	1	0.6
cycle rack*	9	3.8	0	0.0	1	0.6
cycle route*	77	32.7	7	6.2	0	0.0
cycle shop*	7	3.0	0	0.0	0	0.0
cycle lane*	99	42.0	9	7.9	0	0.0
cycle helmet*	13	5.5	0	0.0	0	0.0
cycle horn*	0	0.0	0	0.0	0	0.0
cycle batter*	0	0.0	0	0.0	0	0.0
cycle clip*	1	0.4	0	0.0	0	0.0
cycle shorts	1	0.4	0	0.0	0	0.0
cycle track*	19	8.1	1	0.9	6	3.8
racing cycle*	0	0.0	0	0.0	1	0.6
cycle highway*	4	1.7	0	0.0	0	0.0
cycle superhighway*	72	30.6	0	0.0	0	0.0
cycle super highway*	2	0.8	0	0.0	0	0.0

Note: Importantly, the frequencies in table A6.1 represent instances of these **exact** search terms only, e.g. any string of letters starting with *cycle helmet* without any intervening words. Thus, the fact that there are no instances of the query term *cycle helmet** in the Australian sub-corpus does not mean that there are no instances of the noun HELMET. The same applies to the other query terms. Query terms also do not correspond to lemmas—for instance, *bike** will retrieve any word beginning with the characters *bike*, including word forms of the verb BIKE, the nouns BIKE and BIKER as well as compound words such as BIKE LANE, BIKE HELMET or BIKE-FRIENDLY, etc.

Table A6.2 **Top 50 collocates of *cyclist* (sorted according to MI3, T-score, LL, and range)**

	Sorted according to association measure			Sorted according to range
	In top 50 (all three measures)	In top 50 (two measures)	In top 50 (one measure)	
Grammatical words and forms of DO, BE, HAVE	a, after, an, and, at, for, has, he, her, his, in, is, of, on, the, to, was, who, with	being, over, when (T-score and LL)	as, be, been, had (T-score)	a, after, an, and, as, at, be, been, being, by, for, from, had, has, have, he, her, his, in, is, of, on, over, that, the, to, was, when, who, with
Lexical words	accident, car, collision, crash, death, deaths, died, dies, driver, hit hospital, injured, injuries, killed, knocked, left, lorry, old, road, woman	dead, die, hurt, keen, male, suffered (MI3 and LL); year (T-score and LL)	avid, fighting, sixth, sues (MI3); family, said (T-score)	accident, bike, car, collision, crash, death, died, dies, driver, hit, injured, injuries, killed, knocked, left, lorry, old, road, said, year

Table A6.3 **Top 50 5L-5R collocates of *cyclists* (sorted according to MI3, T-score, LL, and range)**

	Sorted according to association measure			Sorted according to range
	In top 50 (all three measures)	In top 50 (two measures)	In top 50 (one measure)	
Grammatical words and forms of DO, BE, HAVE	a, about, and, are, as, at, be, being, between, by, for, from, have, in, is, it, more, not, of, on, should, than, that, the, their, to, two, were, who, will, with	—	been, or, they, would (T-score)	a, about, after, and, are, as, at, be, been, being, but, by, for, from, has, have, in, is, it, more, not, of, on, than, that, the, their, they, to, two, was, were, who, will, with
Lexical words and proper nouns	cyclist, drivers, killed, London, make, motorists, number, pedestrians, ride, road, roads, use	give, injured, involving, lights, red, safer (MI3 and LL); said (MI3 and T-score)	city, year (T-score); safety (LL)	bike, city, cyclist, drivers, killed, London, motorists, number, pedestrians, ride, road, roads, said, use, year

Table A6.4 **Variants to refer to people who use a bicycle**

	United Kingdom		Australia		United States	
Cyclists/cyclist/cyclist's	2,083	884.0	1,109	975.4	466	296.8
Bikers/biker/biker's	20	8.5	6	5.3	98	62.4
Bicyclists/bicyclist/bicyclist's	1	0.4	1	0.9	192	122.3
Bike riders/bike rider/bike rider's	10	4.2	54	47.5	22	14.0
Riders/rider/rider's	186	78.9	230	202.3	304	193.6

Table A6.5 **Analysis of patterns for *drivers/motorists and cyclists; cyclists and drivers/motorists***

Major themes	Patterns for drivers/motorists and cyclists; cyclists and drivers/motorists
Conflict	*the ongoing battle between, are at war, the war between, hostile encounters between, enmity between, fight for space, love blaming each other, called for more respect between, more needed to be done to secure harmony between vehicle drivers and cyclists, the 'two tribes' attitude displayed between some drivers and cyclists, POLICE patrols aimed at 'improving relations' between drivers and cyclists, the latest in a series of violent incidents between drivers and cyclists, no need for rudeness on the roads—and this goes for drivers and cyclists alike, residents clash with rival road petitions, ought to share the road with mutual respect, rather than increase tensions between, will reduce conflict between, the cultural clashes between, tensions between, the perceived divide between, are increasingly being involved in fiery exchanges*
Safety awareness/ campaign	*are vigilant, a four-week campaign targeting drivers and cyclists with cycle safety messages, were giving drivers and cyclists advice; As a pedestrian, you expect drivers and cyclists to give way to you; Both drivers and cyclists themselves have a role in improving safety for cyclists on the road, Drivers and cyclists caught in clampdown, are urging X to be more careful, laws affecting motorists and cyclists, a grave danger to both, make the roads safer for all users, including; thousands of fines were issued to, road rules governing cyclists and motorists were being reviewed to encourage 'safer cycling', teaching cyclists and motorists to accommodate each other on the road, warned cyclists and motorists: 'Do think of the laws of the road'.*
Infrastructure	*should be segregated, The roads were never designed for motorists and cyclists to use together, superhighway had no legal status and could be shared by motorists and cyclists, the first to attempt to keep cyclists and motorists fully segregated, the proposals were for cyclists and motorists to share road space, an urgent need to get cyclists and motorists out of each other's way, the design of the superhighway was confusing for cyclists and motorists, London gets first roundabout to segregate cyclists and motorists*

Table A6.6 **Analysis of patterns for the most frequent clusters for *cyclists and pedestrians/pedestrians and cyclists***

Major themes	Patterns for the most frequent clusters for cyclists and pedestrians/pedestrians and cyclists
Conflict and collisions	BETWEEN CYCLISTS AND PEDESTRIANS: *collisions* (3 occurrences), *crashes, constant conflict*
Safety awareness/campaign	FOR CYCLISTS AND PEDESTRIANS: *road dangers; a safer, more connected environment; friendlier, look out for, make streets safer, making the path safer, increased safety, improve safety, increased safety* FOR PEDESTRIANS AND CYCLISTS: *more dangerous, make the roads safer, improve safety, reductions in casualties . . . happening* TO CYCLISTS AND PEDESTRIANS: *alert the driver to, make . . . friendlier to, reduce the risk of HGVs to*
Infrastructure	FOR PEDESTRIANS AND CYCLISTS: *a path, path, connected, a slushy slip-and-slide*

Table A8.1 **URLs of items in the Shared News Corpus**

	URLs of items in the Shared News Corpus
1	http://www.nbcnews.com/news/world/american-student-ends-trapped-giant-vagina-sculpture-n138311
2	http://www.dailymail.co.uk/health/article-2190863/Semen-good-womens-health-helps-fight-depression.html
3	http://www.nytimes.com/2013/03/04/health/for-first-time-baby-cured-of-hiv-doctors-say.html?pagewanted=all
4	http://www.usatoday.com/story/life/music/2014/03/17/kiss-def-leppard-summer-heroes-tour/6525475/
5	http://www.cnn.com/2014/02/16/us/snake-salvation-pastor-bite/index.html
6	http://www.abc.net.au/local/stories/2013/06/06/3776327.htm
7	http://www.washingtontimes.com/news/2014/mar/24/atheist-noah-director-brags-film-least-biblical-bi/
8	http://www.cnn.com/2014/02/04/tech/social-media/facebook-look-back-video/index.html

Table A8.1 **Continued**

	URLs of items in the Shared News Corpus
9	http://www.foxnews.com/us/2014/01/26/arizona-sheriff-joe-arpaio-puts-inmates-on-bread-and-water-for-destroying-us/
10	http://www.foxnews.com/health/2014/03/21/giraffe-kisses-goodbye-dying-zoo-worker/
11	http://www.news.com.au/lifestyle/health/duke-university-scientists-find-women-need-more-sleep-than-men/story-fneuz9ev-1226596253113
12	http://www.foxnews.com/health/2014/03/17/sugars-found-in-tequila-may-protect-against-obesity-diabetes/
13	http://www.foxnews.com/politics/2012/12/31/obama-gives-congress-pay-raise/
14	http://www.telegraph.co.uk/news/uknews/1895839/Drummers-are-natural-intellectuals.html
15	http://www.cnn.com/2014/01/21/tech/social-media/facebook-like-farming/index.html
16	http://www.independent.co.uk/news/uk/home-news/british-public-wrong-about-nearly-everything-survey-shows-8697821.html
17	http://www.foxnews.com/entertainment/2014/06/27/amy-adams-gives-first-class-airline-seat-to-soldier-sits-in-coach-passenger/
18	http://www.foxnews.com/us/2014/07/09/murder-drops-as-concealed-carry-permits-rise-claims-study/
19	http://www.foxnews.com/health/2011/05/18/cdc-warns-public-prepare-zombie-apocalypse/
20	http://www.miamiherald.com/2012/05/26/2818832/naked-man-shot-killed-on-macarthur.html
21	http://www.theage.com.au/entertainment/music/leonardo-da-vincis-wacky-piano-is-heard-for-the-first-time-after-500-years-20131118-2xpqs.html
22	http://www.usatoday.com/story/news/world/2014/04/17/jews-ordered-to-register-in-east-ukraine/7816951/
23	http://www.nytimes.com/2014/02/11/world/middleeast/suicide-bomb-instructor-accidentally-kills-iraqi-pupils.html
24	http://www.foxnews.com/us/2014/02/27/court-rules-school-can-ban-american-flag-shirts-to-avoid-racial-strife/

(continued)

Table A8.1 **Continued**

	URLs of items in the Shared News Corpus
25	http://www.foxnews.com/us/2013/10/01/greatest-generation-veterans-to-face-barricades-at-memorial-in-their-honor/
26	http://www.foxnews.com/politics/2014/07/27/emily-miller-federal-judge-rules-dc-ban-on-gun-carry-rights-unconstitutional/
27	http://www.foxnews.com/politics/2013/04/26/officials-found-guilty-in-obama-clinton-ballot-petition-fraud/
28	http://www.cnn.com/2013/11/07/world/europe/pope-francis-embrace/index.html
29	http://www.washingtonpost.com/blogs/election-2012/wp/2012/10/15/charity-president-unhappy-about-paul-ryan-soup-kitchen-photo-op/
30	http://www.telegraph.co.uk/news/politics/conservative/8201521/Sex-offenders-including-paedophiles-should-be-allowed-to-adopt-Theresa-May-told.html
31	http://www.telegraph.co.uk/health/healthnews/9069276/Chocolate-cake-breakfast-could-help-you-lose-weight.html
32	http://www.foxnews.com/opinion/2014/03/03/team-obama-wins-fight-to-have-christian-home-school-family-deported/
33	http://www.theguardian.com/science/political-science/2013/may/13/stephen-hawking-boycott-israel-science
34	http://www.washingtonpost.com/blogs/capital-weather-gang/wp/2014/06/02/female-named-hurricanes-kill-more-than-male-because-people-dont-respect-them-study-finds/
35	http://www.cnn.com/2013/11/07/world/asia/philippines-typhoon-haiyan/index.html
36	http://www.foxnews.com/us/2014/03/25/girl-barred-from-school-for-shaving-her-head-to-support-friend-with-cancer/
37	http://www.foxnews.com/leisure/2014/03/25/wheres-steve-mcqueen-when-need-him-16-shelby-gt500-found-under-40-years-dust/
38	http://www.cnn.com/2014/03/27/living/student-money-saving-typeface-garamond-schools/index.html
39	http://www.nydailynews.com/entertainment/gossip/paul-walker-dies-crash-report-article-1.1533786
40	http://www.cnn.com/2012/06/11/justice/texas-abuser-killed/index.html

Table A8.1 **Continued**

	URLs of items in the Shared News Corpus
41	http://www.nytimes.com/2012/05/31/nyregion/bloomberg-plans-a-ban-on-large-sugared-drinks.html?pagewanted=all
42	http://www.foxnews.com/politics/2012/10/26/cia-operators-were-denied-request-for-help-during-benghazi-attack-sources-say/
43	http://www.washingtontimes.com/news/2013/may/2/south-carolina-house-passes-bill-making-obamacare-/
44	http://www.washingtontimes.com/news/2013/feb/10/scientists-suggest-beer-after-workout/
45	http://www.foxnews.com/health/2013/03/27/scientists-find-treatment-to-kill-every-kind-cancer-tumor/
46	http://www.cnn.com/2014/03/07/us/michigan-mummified-body-found/index.html
47	http://www.cnn.com/2014/06/05/world/europe/d-day-paratrooper-jumps-again/index.html
48	http://www.cnn.com/2014/02/05/showbiz/zimmerman-dmx-boxing-match/index.html
49	http://www.abc.net.au/local/audio/2014/03/05/3957423.htm
50	http://www.theguardian.com/business/2013/feb/09/aldi-100-percent-horsemeat-beef-products
51	http://www.foxnews.com/us/2014/01/06/george-and-barbara-bush-celebrate-6th-wedding-anniversary/
52	http://www.cnn.com/2013/05/01/us/kentucky-accidental-shooting/index.html
53	http://www.cnn.com/2013/07/15/showbiz/dave-matthews-hitches-ride/index.html
54	http://www.foxnews.com/health/2014/04/15/casual-marijuana-use-linked-with-brain-abnormalities-study-finds/
55	http://www.theguardian.com/books/2012/mar/05/five-hundred-fairytales-discovered-germany
56	http://www.bbc.co.uk/news/uk-england-leicestershire-21063882
57	http://www.cnn.com/2012/08/14/showbiz/obit-palillo/index.html
58	http://www.dailymail.co.uk/news/article-2156333/Teenager-19-battered-dog-hammer-20-times-stabbed-chest-leaving-home-sign-JobCentre.html

(*continued*)

Table A8.1 **Continued**

	URLs of items in the Shared News Corpus
59	http://www.bbc.co.uk/news/world-europe-21468116
60	http://www.dailymail.co.uk/health/article-2054393/Bad-news-dads-Babies-share-mothers-bed-age-good-hearts.html
61	http://www.dailymail.co.uk/femail/article-2320235/Why-stressful-number-children--BUT-mothers-MORE-relaxed.html
62	http://www.mirror.co.uk/news/uk-news/ukip-candidate-geoffrey-clarke-calls-1495957
63	http://www.news.com.au/entertainment/tv/tony-abbott-lambasted-on-us-tv-show-last-week-tonight-with-john-oliver/story-e6frfmyi-1226940367958
64	http://www.cnn.com/2013/07/15/justice/pennsylvania-teen-heroes/index.html
65	http://blog.sfgate.com/stew/2013/11/01/s-f-to-be-transformed-into-gotham-city-for-5-year-olds-make-a-wish/
66	http://www.theguardian.com/world/2014/jul/30/world-disgrace-gaza-un-shelter-school-israel
67	http://www.usatoday.com/story/news/nation/2013/10/04/blue-ridge-parkway-pisgah-inn/2923169/
68	http://www.nytimes.com/2014/06/03/science/whats-lost-as-handwriting-fades.html
69	http://www.dailymail.co.uk/news/article-2239087/Graham-Hughes-British-man-person-visit-201-countries-WITHOUT-using-plane.html
70	http://www.nytimes.com/2014/07/15/world/middleeast/israelis-watch-bombs-drop-on-gaza-from-front-row-seats.html
71	http://www.washingtonpost.com/news/morning-mix/wp/2014/06/03/bodies-of-800-babies-long-dead-found-in-septic-tank-at-former-irish-home-for-unwed-mothers/
72	http://www.nzherald.co.nz/nz/news/article.cfm?c_id=1&objectid=10829992
73	http://www.cnn.com/2014/02/21/us/arizona-anti-gay-bill/index.html
74	http://www.dailymail.co.uk/news/article-2288910/Worlds-oldest-horse-trots-final-furlong-Irish-draught-Shayne-51-sleep-Essex-sanctuary-reaching-120-human-years.html
75	http://www.washingtonpost.com/news/morning-mix/wp/2014/04/30/hundreds-of-kidnapped-nigerian-school-girls-reportedly-sold-as-brides-to-militants-for-12-relatives-say/

Table A8.1 **Continued**

	URLs of items in the Shared News Corpus
76	http://www.dailymail.co.uk/news/article-2271440/Burger-King-admits-selling-beef-burgers-Whoppers-containing-horse-meat.html
77	http://www.dailymail.co.uk/femail/article-2218515/Think-ready-children-Hilarious-new-parent-test-taking-mummy-blogs-storm-MIGHT-just-off.html
78	http://www.dailymail.co.uk/news/article-2154283/Cats-away-Artist-turns-dead-pet-flying-helicopter-killed-car.html
79	http://www.dailymail.co.uk/news/article-2138388/Four-Georgia-men-arrested-beating-death-ex-Marine-survived-TWO-tours-duty-Iraq.html
80	http://www.dailymail.co.uk/news/article-2153253/Drug-addict-parents-gave-23-month-old-son-methadone-like-Calpol-died-overdose.html
81	http://www.dailymail.co.uk/news/article-2273440/Teen-left-brain-damaged-blind-smoking-synthetic-marijuana.html
82	http://www.dailymail.co.uk/news/article-2273591/Chicago-mother-sheds-tears-sorrow-buries-fourth-remaining-child-fatally-shot-month.html
83	http://www.cnn.com/2013/11/30/showbiz/actor-paul-walker-dies/index.html
84	http://www.washingtontimes.com/news/2013/may/6/syrian-rebels-used-sarin-nerve-gas-not-assads-regi/
85	http://www.nytimes.com/2013/06/18/world/americas/thousands-gather-for-protests-in-brazils-largest-cities.html
86	http://www.cnn.com/2013/07/14/showbiz/glee-star-dead/index.html
87	http://ftw.usatoday.com/2014/07/tim-howard-wikipedia-united-states-secretary-of-defense
88	http://www.cnn.com/2013/11/18/justice/florida-george-zimmerman-arrest/index.html
89	http://www.usatoday.com/story/news/nation/2014/04/06/anti-vaccine-movement-is-giving-diseases-a-2nd-life/7007955/
90	http://www.washingtonpost.com/blogs/worldviews/wp/2014/02/04/journalists-at-sochi-are-live-tweeting-their-hilarious-and-gross-hotel-experiences/
91	http://www.cnn.com/2011/HEALTH/01/05/autism.vaccines/index.html
92	http://www.foxnews.com/opinion/2014/05/01/teenager-takes-his-great-grandmother-to-prom/
93	http://www.foxnews.com/opinion/2014/01/29/chick-fil-gives-free-food-to-motorists-stranded-in-southern-snowstorm/

(continued)

Table A8.1 **Continued**

	URLs of items in the Shared News Corpus
94	http://www.cnn.com/2013/10/16/travel/cn-traveler-top-cities/index.html
95	http://www.cnn.com/2013/04/15/us/boston-marathon-explosions/index.html
96	http://www.cnn.com/2011/11/10/world/africa/rhino-extinct-species-report/index.html
97	http://www.nytimes.com/2014/06/16/us/starbucks-to-provide-free-college-education-to-thousands-of-workers.html
98	http://www.cnn.com/2013/08/07/health/charlotte-child-medical-marijuana/index.html
99	http://www.washingtonpost.com/business/economy/obama-administration-pushes-banks-to-make-home-loans-to-people-with-weaker-credit/2013/04/02/a8b4370c-9aef-11e2-a941-a19bce7af755_story.html

Table A8.2 **Word forms (types) that occur across at least four Hs/OPs in the SNC**

Word forms that occur across at least four headlines in the Shared News Corpus	# [any number], *to, in, of, for, a, and, at, is, with, on, the, after, are, killed, dead, his, it, school, years, first, found, home, man, Obama, study, their*
Word forms that occur across at least four opening paragraphs in the Shared News Corpus	*the, a, of, in, to, and, that, #, on, for, with, has, was, it, his, an, as, their, at, he, is, they, after, by, from, new, who, are, be, but, had, into, up, were, world, been, children, have, her, not, old, will, about, found, home, more, out, if, Monday, one, over, people, said, school, study, year, according, American, city, could, died, its, last, make, may, most, news, officials, or, Saturday, than, this, thousands, two, which, you, against, around, being, can, car, come, federal, high, it's, night, only, outside, Paul, says, state, told, US, Wednesday, when, years*

References

Adolphs, S., and Carter, R. (2013). *Spoken Corpus Linguistics: From Monomodal to Multimodal*. London/New York: Routledge.
Ahva, L., and Pantti, M. (2014). 'Proximity as a journalistic keyword in the digital era: A study on the "closeness" of amateur news images'. *Digital Journalism* 2(3): 322–333.
Allan, S. (1999). *News Culture*. Buckingham/Philadelphia: Open University Press.
Allan, S. (2013). *Citizen Witnessing: Revisioning Journalism in Times of Crisis*. Cambridge: Polity Press.
Almeida, E. (1992). 'A category system for the analysis of factuality in newspaper discourse'. *Text* 12: 233–262.
Altengarten, J. (2004). 'Creativity and the rule of thirds'. *Photo Composition Articles*. http://photoinf.com/Golden_Mean/Jim_Altengarten/Creativity_and_the_Rule_of_Thirds.htm, accessed 20 February 2006.
Anderson, M., and Caumont, A. (2014). 'How social media is reshaping news'. *Pew Research Center Fact Tank*, 24 September. http://www.pewresearch.org/fact-tank/2014/09/24/how-social-media-is-reshaping-news/, accessed 10 April 2015.
Anthony, L. (2014). *EncodeAnt* (Version 1.1.0) [Computer Software]. Tokyo, Japan: Waseda University. Available from: http://www.laurenceanthony.net/.
Anthony, L., and Baker, P. (2015a). *ProtAnt* (Version 1.0.1) [Computer Software]. Tokyo, Japan: Waseda University. Available from: http://www.laurenceanthony.net/.
Anthony, L., and Baker, P. (2015b). 'ProtAnt: A tool for analysing the prototypicality of texts'. *International Journal of Corpus Linguistics* 20(3): 273–292.
Archer, D., Wilson, A., and Rayson, P. (2002). 'Introduction to the USAS category system'. *UCREL*. http://ucrel.lancs.ac.uk/usas/usas guide.pdf, accessed 22 July 2014.
Baker, P. (2005). *Public Discourses of Gay Men*. London/New York: Routledge.
Baker, P. (2006). *Using Corpora in Discourse Analysis*. London/New York: Continuum.
Baker, P. (2009). 'The BE06 corpus of British English and recent language change'. *International Journal of Corpus Linguistics* 14(3): 312–337.
Baker, P. (2011). 'Times may change but we'll always have money: A corpus driven examination of vocabulary change in four diachronic corpora'. *Journal of English Linguistics* 39: 65–88.
Baker, P. (2015). 'Does Britain need any more foreign doctors? Inter-analyst consistency and corpus-assisted (critical) discourse analysis'. In M. Charles, N. Groom, and S. John (Eds.). *Grammar, Text and Discourse: In Honour of Susan Hunston*, 283–300. Amsterdam/Philadelphia: John Benjamins.
Baker, P., Gabrielatos, C., Khosravinik, M., Krzyzanowski, M., McEnery, T., and Wodak, R. (2008). 'A useful methodological synergy? Combining critical discourse analysis and corpus linguistics to examine discourses of refugees and asylum seekers in the UK press'. *Discourse and Society* 19(3): 273–306.

Baker, P., Gabrielatos, C., and McEnery, T. (2013a). *Discourse Analysis and Media Attitudes: The Representation of Islam in the British Press*. Cambridge: Cambridge University Press.

Baker, P., Gabrielatos, C., and McEnery, T. (2013b). 'Sketching Muslims: A corpus-driven analysis of representations around the word "Muslim" in the British press 1998-2009'. *Applied Linguistics* 34(3): 255–278.

Baker, P., and McEnery, T. (2015). 'Introduction'. In P. Baker and T. McEnery (Eds.). *Corpora and Discourse Studies: Integrating Discourse and Corpora*, 1–19. Basingstoke/New York: Palgrave Macmillan.

Barkho, L. (2008). 'The BBC's discursive strategy and practices vis-a-vis the Palestinian-Israeli conflict'. *Journalism Studies* 9(2): 278–294.

Barnhurst, K. G., and Nerone, J. (2001). *The Form of News: A History*. New York: Guilford.

Barthes, R. (1977). *Image, Music, Text*. London: Fontana.

Bech Sillesen, L. (2014). 'Good news is good business, but not a cure-all for journalism'. *Columbia Journalism Review*, 29 September. http://www.cjr.org/behind_the_news/good_news_is_good_business_but.php, accessed 14 March 2016.

Beckett, C. (2015). 'Beyoncé, cute kittens or relentless tragedy? Is good news really news at all?' *Guardian*, 2 February. http://www.theguardian.com/media/2015/feb/01/beyone-cute-kitten-tragedy-news, accessed 14 March 2016.

Bednarek, M. (2005). 'Construing the world: Conceptual metaphors and event construals in news stories'. *Metaphorik.de*, September. http://www.metaphorik.de/09/bednarek.pdf, accessed 28 September 2015.

Bednarek, M. (2006a). *Evaluation in Media Discourse: Analysis of a Newspaper Corpus*. London/New York: Continuum.

Bednarek, M. (2006b). 'Evaluating Europe—Parameters of evaluation in the British press'. In C. Leung and J. Jenkins (Eds.). *Reconfiguring Europe—the Contribution of Applied Linguistics*, British Studies in Applied Linguistics 20, 137–156. London: BAAL/Equinox.

Bednarek, M. (2008). *Emotion Talk across Corpora*. Basingstoke/New York: Palgrave Macmillan.

Bednarek, M. (2009). 'Polyphony in appraisal: Typological and topological perspectives'. *Linguistics and the Human Sciences* 3(2): 107–136.

Bednarek, M. (2012). '"Get us the hell out of here": Key words and trigrams in fictional television series'. *International Journal of Corpus Linguistics* 17(1): 35–63.

Bednarek, M. (2014). 'Linguistic resources for constructing news values, "translated" into Systemic Functional Linguistics'. Available at: http://www.academia.edu/8607437/_2015_Linguistic_resources_for_constructing_news_values_translated_into_Systemic_Functional_Linguistics.

Bednarek, M. (2015). 'Corpus-assisted multimodal discourse analysis of television and film narratives'. In P. Baker and T. McEnery (Eds.). *Corpora and Discourse Studies*, 63–87. Basingstoke/New York: Palgrave Macmillan.

Bednarek, M. (2016a). 'Voices and values in the news: News media talk, news values and attribution'. *Discourse, Context & Media* 11: 27–37.

Bednarek, M. (2016b). 'Coding manual for the analysis of news values using UAM Corpus Tool'. Available at: http://www.newsvaluesanalysis.com.

Bednarek, M. (2016c). 'Investigating evaluation and news values in news items that are shared via social media'. *Corpora* 11(2): 227–257 [Special issue on corpus approaches to evaluation].

Bednarek, M., and Caple, H. (2010). 'Playing with environmental stories in the news: Good or bad practice?' *Discourse & Communication* 4(1): 5–31.

Bednarek, M., and Caple, H. (2012a). *News Discourse*. London/New York: Continuum.

Bednarek, M., and Caple, H. (2012b). '"Value added": Language, image and news values'. *Discourse, Context & Media* 1 [Special Issue on Journalistic Stance]: 103–113.

Bednarek, M., and Caple, H. (2014). 'Why do news values matter? Towards a new methodological framework for analyzing news discourse in Critical Discourse Analysis and beyond'. *Discourse & Society* 25(2): 135–158.

Bednarek, M., and Caple, H. (2015). 'Promotional videos: What do they tell us about the value of news?' In R. Piazza, L. Haarman, and A. Caborn (Eds.). *Values and Choices in Television Discourse*, 5–30. Basingstoke/New York: Palgrave Macmillan.

Bell, A. (1991). *The Language of News Media*. Oxford: Blackwell.

Bell, A. (1995). 'News time'. *Time & Society* 4(3): 305–328.

Bell, A. (2011). 'Leaving home: De-europeanisation in a post-colonial variety of broadcast news language'. In T. Kristiansen and N. Coupland (Eds.). *Standard Languages and Language Standards in a Changing Europe*, 177–198. Oslo: Novus.

Bell, E. (2015). '12th annual Hugh Cudlipp lecture'. *Guardian*, 28 January. http://www.theguardian.com/media/2015/jan/28/emily-bells-2015-hugh-cudlipp-lecture-full-text, accessed 28 September 2015.

Bell, P. (1997). 'News values, race and "the Hanson debate" in Australian media'. *Asia Pacific Media Educator* 2: 38–47.

Bell, P., and van Leeuwen, T. J. (1994). *The Media Interview: Confessions, Contest, Conversation*. Sydney: University of New South Wales Press.

ben-Aaron, D. (2003). 'When news isn't news: The case of national holidays'. *Journal of Historical Pragmatics* 4(1): 75–102.

ben-Aaron, D. (2005). 'Given and news: Evaluation in newspaper stories about national anniversaries'. *Text* 25(5): 691–718.

Bender, J. R., Davenport, L. D., Drager, M. W., and Fedler, F. (2009). *Reporting for the Media*, 9th edn. New York/Oxford: Oxford University Press.

Berger, J., and Milkman, K. L. (2012). 'What makes online content viral?' *Journal of Marketing Research* 49(2): 192–205.

Biber, D., Johansson, S., Leech, G., Conrad, S., and Finegan, E. (1999). *Longman Grammar of Spoken and Written English*. London: Longman.

Bielsa, E., and Bassnett, S. (2009). *Translation in Global News*. London/New York: Routledge.

Bignell, J. (2002). *Media Semiotics: An Introduction*, 2nd edn. Manchester: Manchester University Press.

Blom, J. N., and Hansen, K. R. (2015). 'Click bait: Forward-reference as lure in online news headlines'. *Journal of Pragmatics* 76: 87–100.

Boorstin, J. (2015). 'Twitter's "Project Lightning" launches as "Moments"', *CNBC*, 6 October. http://www.cnbc.com/2015/10/06/twitters-project-lightning-launches-as-moments.html, accessed 10 November 2015.

Bös, B. (2012). 'From 1760 to 1960: Diversification and popularization'. In R. Facchinetti, N. Brownlees, B. Bös, and U. Fries. *News as Changing Texts—Corpora, Methodologies and Analysis*, 91–143. Newcastle: Cambridge Scholars Publishing.

Bowers, M. (2014). 'Photography requires skill. It's sad to see good Fairfax employees being let go'. *Guardian*, 7 May. http://www.theguardian.com/commentisfree/2014/may/07/photography-requires-skills-its-sad-to-see-fairfax-let-good-employees-go, accessed 20 May 2014.

boyd, d. (2012). 'The ethics of fear and how it undermines an informed citizenry'. *MediaWire, Poynter Institute*. http://www.poynter.org/news/mediawire/192509/fear-undermines-an-informed-citizenry-as-media-struggles-with-attention-economy/, accessed 7 October 2015.

Boyd-Barrett, O. (1994). 'Language and media: A question of convergence'. In D. Graddol and O. Boyd-Barrett (Eds.). *Media Texts: Authors and Readers*, 22–39. London: Multilingual Matters.

Boyd-Barrett, O. (2015). *Media Imperialism*. London: Sage.

Brezina, V., McEnery, T., and Wattam, S. (2015). 'Collocations in context: A new perspective on collocation networks'. *International Journal of Corpus Linguistics* 20(2): 139–173.

Brezina, V., and Meyerhoff, M. (2014). 'Significant or random? A critical review of sociolinguistic generalisations based on large corpora'. *International Journal of Corpus Linguistics* 19(1): 1–28.

Bridges, J. A., and Bridges, L. W. (1997). 'Changes in news use on the front pages of the American daily newspaper, 1986-1993'. *Journalism and Mass Communication Quarterly* 74(4): 826–838.

Brighton, P., and Foy, D. (2007). *News Values*. London: Sage.
Brownlees, N. (2006a). 'Introduction'. In N. Brownlees (Ed.). *News Discourse in Early Modern Britain*, 1–14. Bern/New York: Peter Lang.
Brownlees, N. (Ed.) (2006b). *News Discourse in Early Modern Britain*. Bern/New York: Peter Lang.
Brownlees, N. (2012). 'The beginnings of periodical news (1620-1665)'. In R. Facchinetti, N. Brownlees, B. Bös, and U. Fries. *News as Changing Texts: Corpora, Methodologies and Analysis*, 5–48. Newcastle upon Tyne: Cambridge Scholars Publishing.
Bruns, A., Highfield, T., and Harrington, S. (2013). 'Sharing the news: Dissemination of links to Australian news sites on Twitter'. In J. Gordon, P. Rowinski, and G. Stewart (Eds.). *Br(e)aking the News: Journalism, Politics and New Media*, 181–209. Bern/New York: Peter Lang.
Busà, G. M. (2014). *Introducing the Language of the News: A Student's Guide*. London/New York: Routledge.
Caffarel, A., Martin, J. R., and Matthiessen, C. M. I. M. (2004). 'Introduction: Systemic functional typology'. In A. Caffarel, J. R. Martin, and C. M. I. M. Matthiessen (Eds.). *Language Typology: A Functional Perspective*, 1–76. Amsterdam/Philadelphia: John Benjamins.
Cameron, D. (1996). 'Style policy and style politics: A neglected aspect of the language of the news'. *Media Culture & Society* 18: 315–333.
Cameron, D. (2009). 'Sex/gender, language and the new biologism'. *Applied Linguistics* 31(2): 173–192.
Cap, P. (2008). 'Towards the proximization model of the analysis of legitimization in political discourse'. *Journal of Pragmatics* 40: 17–41.
Caple, H. (2009). 'Playing with Words and Pictures: Intersemiosis in a New Genre of News Reportage'. PhD thesis, University of Sydney, Australia. Available at: http://ses.library.usyd.edu.au/handle/2123/7024.
Caple, H. (2010). 'What you see and what you get: The evolving role of news photographs in an Australian broadsheet'. In V. Rupar (Ed.). *Journalism & Meaning-making: Reading the Newspaper*, 199–220. Cresskill, NJ: Hampton Press.
Caple, H. (2013a). *Photojournalism: A Social Semiotic Approach*. Basingstoke/New York: Palgrave Macmillan.
Caple, H. (2013b). 'Competing for coverage: Exploring emerging discourses on female athletes in the Australian print media'. *English Text Construction* 6(2): 271–294.
Caple, H. (2016). 'Coding manual for DNVA analysis'. Available at: http://www.newsvaluesanalysis.com.
Caple, H. (in press). 'Visual media'. In C. Cotter and D. Perrin (Eds.). *The Routledge Handbook of Language and Media*. London/New York: Routledge.
Caple, H., and Bednarek, M. (2013). *Delving into the Discourse: Approaches to News Values in Journalism Studies and Beyond*. Working Paper. Oxford: Reuters Institute for the Study of Journalism, University of Oxford. Available at: https://reutersinstitute.politics.ox.ac.uk/publications/risj-working-papers.html.
Caple, H., and Bednarek, M. (2016). 'Rethinking news values: What a discursive approach can tell us about the construction of news discourse and news photography'. *Journalism: Theory, Practice and Criticism* 17(4): 435–455.
Caple, H., and Knox, J. S. (2012). 'Online news galleries, photojournalism and the photo essay'. *Visual Communication* 11(2): 207–236.
Caple, H., and Knox, J. S. (2015). 'A framework for the multimodal analysis of online news galleries'. *Social Semiotics* 25(3): 292–321.
Carter, R. (1988). 'Front pages: Lexis, style and newspaper reporting'. In M. Ghadessy (Ed.). *Registers of Written English*, 8–16. London: Pinter Publishers.
Carter, R., and McCarthy, M. (2006). *The Cambridge Grammar*. Cambridge: Cambridge University Press.
Carvalho, A. (2008). 'Media(ted) discourse and society: Rethinking the framework of Critical Discourse Analysis'. *Journalism Studies* 9(2): 161–177.

Catenaccio, P., Cotter, C., De Smedt, M., Garzone, G., Jacobs, G., Macgilchrist, F., Lams, L., Perrin, D., Richardson, J. E., van Hout, T., and van Praet, E. (2011). 'Towards a linguistics of news production'. *Journal of Pragmatics* 43(7): 1843–1852.

Cecconi, E. (2009). 'Comparing seventeenth-century news broadsides and occasional news pamphlets: Interrelatedness in news reporting'. In A. H. Jucker (Ed.). *Early Modern English News Discourse: Newspapers, Pamphlets and Scientific News Discourse*, 137–157. Amsterdam/Philadelphia: John Benjamins.

Charteris-Black, J. (2006). 'Britain as a container: Immigration metaphors in the 2005 election campaign'. *Discourse & Society* 17: 563–581.

Chouliaraki, L. (Ed.) (2012). *Self-Mediation: New Media, Citizenship and Civil Selves*. London/New York: Routledge.

Chouliaraki, L., and Blaagaard, B. B. (Eds.) (2013). Special Issue on the Ethics of Images, *Visual Communication* 12(3).

Chovanec, J. (2014). *Pragmatics of Tense and Time: From Canonical Headlines to Online News Texts*. Amsterdam/Philadelphia: John Benjamins.

Claridge, C. (2009). '"As silly as an Irish teague": Comparisons in early English news discourse'. In A. H. Jucker (Ed.). *Early Modern English News Discourse: Newspapers, Pamphlets and Scientific News Discourse*, 91–114. Amsterdam/Philadelphia: John Benjamins.

Clayman, S. E. (1990). 'From talk to text: Newspaper accounts of reporter-source interactions'. *Media, Culture and Society* 12: 79–103.

Clayman, S. E. (2010). 'Questions in broadcast journalism'. In A. Freed and S. Ehrlich (Eds.). *"Why Do You Ask": The Function of Questions in Institutional Discourse*, 256–278. Oxford: Oxford University Press.

Coffin, C., and O'Halloran, K. (2005). 'Finding the global groove: Theorising and analysing dynamic reader positioning using appraisal, corpus and a concordance'. *Critical Discourse Studies* 2(2): 143–163.

Conboy, M. (2002). *The Press and Popular Culture*. London/Thousand Oaks/New Delhi: Sage.

Conboy, M. (2006). *Tabloid Britain: Constructing a Community through Language*. London/New York: Routledge.

Conboy, M. (2007). *The Language of the News*. London/New York: Routledge.

Conboy, M. (2010). *The Language of Newspapers: Socio-Historical Approaches*. London/New York: Continuum.

Conley, D., and Lamble, S. (2006). *The Daily Miracle: An Introduction to Journalism*, 3rd edn. Melbourne: Oxford University Press.

Cotter, C. (1999). 'Language and media: Five facts about the fourth estate'. In R. S. Wheeler (Ed.). *The Workings of Language: From Prescriptions to Perspectives*, 165–179. Westport, CT: Praeger.

Cotter, C. (2010). *News Talk. Investigating the Language of Journalism*. Cambridge: Cambridge University Press.

Cotter, C. (2011). 'Diversity awareness and the role of language in cultural representations in news stories'. *Journal of Pragmatics* 43(7): 1890–1899.

Craig, G. (1994). 'Press photographs and news values'. *Australian Studies in Journalism* 3: 182–200.

Crawford, H., Filipovic, D., and Hunter, A. (2015). *All Your Friends Like This: How Social Networks Took over News*. Sydney: Harper Collins.

Cummins, R. G., and Chambers, T. (2011). 'How production value impacts perceived technical quality, credibility, and economic value of video news'. *Journalism & Mass Communication Quarterly* 88(4): 737–752.

Dahl, T., and Fløttum, K. (2014). 'Converging or diverging messages? Verbal and visual representations of climate change in two British newspapers reporting on the IPCC's 5th Assessment Report'. *Encompassing the Multimodality of Knowledge: 5th International Conference in the 360° Conference Series*, Aarhus University, Denmark, 8–10 May 2014.

Daille, B. (1995). *Combined Approach for Terminology Extraction: Lexical Statistics and Linguistic Filtering*, UCREL Technical Papers, No. 15, Department of Linguistics, Lancaster University, Lancaster, UK.

Davies, B. (2013). 'Travelling texts: The legal-lay interface in the highway code'. In J. Conley, C. Heffer, and F. Rock (Eds.). *Legal-Lay Communication: Textual Travel in the Legal Process*, 266–287. Oxford: Oxford University Press.
Davies, B. (2015). ' "Sorry mate, I didn't see you": Representations of different road users in the Highway Code'. Unpublished manuscript.
Davies, M. (2013). *Oppositions and Ideology in News Discourse*. London/Berlin: Bloomsbury.
Davis, H., and Walton, P. (1983). 'Death of a premier: Consensus and closure in international news'. In H. Davis and P. Walton (Eds.). *Language, Image, Media*, 8–49. London: Blackwell.
Djonov, E., and Knox, J. S. (2014). 'How-to-analyze webpages'. In S. Norris and C. D. Maier (Eds.). *Interactions, Images and Texts: A Reader in Multimodality*, 171–193. Boston/Berlin: Mouton de Gruyter.
Djonov, E., and Zhao, S. (Eds.) (2014). *Critical Multimodal Studies of Popular Culture*. London/New York: Routledge.
Dondis, D. A. (1973). *A Primer of Visual Literacy*. London: MIT Press.
Donsbach, W. (2004). 'Psychology of news decisions: Factors behind journalists' professional behaviour'. *Journalism* 5(2): 131–157.
Duguid, A. (2010). 'Newspaper discourse informalisation: A diachronic comparison from keywords'. *Corpora* 5(2): 109–138.
Dunning, T. (2008). 'Surprise and coincidence—musings from the long tail'. 21 March. http://tdunning.blogspot.de/2008/03/surprise-and-coincidence.html, accessed 9 December 2015.
Durant, A., and Lambrou, M. (2009). *Language and Media: A Resource Book for Students*. London/New York: Routledge.
Facchinetti, R. (2012). 'News writing from the 1960s to the present day'. In R. Facchinetti, N. Brownlees, B. Bös, and U. Fries. *News as Changing Texts: Corpora, Methodologies and Analysis*, 145–195. Newcastle upon Tyne: Cambridge Scholars Publishing.
Facchinetti, R., Brownlees, N., Bös, B., and Fries, U. (2012). *News as Changing Texts: Corpora, Methodologies and Analysis*. Newcastle upon Tyne: Cambridge Scholars Publishing.
Fairclough, N. (1988). 'Discourse representation in media discourse'. *Sociolinguistics* 17: 125–139.
Fairclough, N. (1989). *Language and Power*. London/New York: Routledge.
Fairclough, N. (1995). *Media Discourse*. London: Bloomsbury Academic.
Fairclough, N. (1998). 'Political discourse in the media: An analytical framework'. In A. Bell and P. Garrett (Eds.). *Approaches to Media Discourse*, 142–162. Oxford: Blackwell.
Feez, S., Iedema, R., and White, P. R. R. (2008). *Media Literacy*. Surry Hills, NSW: NSW Adult Migrant Education Service.
Fest, J. (2015). 'Where to find newsworthiness—A systemic-functional approach to identifying news values'. 42nd International Systemic Functional Congress, RWTH Aachen University, Germany, 27–31 July.
Fitzgerald, R., and Mckay, S. (2012). 'Just like home: Remediation of the social in contemporary news broadcasting'. *Discourse, Context & Media* 1(1): 1–8.
Fowler, R. G. (1991). *Language in the News: Discourse and Ideology in the Press*. London/New York: Routledge.
Fries, U., Lehmann, H. M., Ruef, B., Schneider, P., Studer, P., auf dem Keller, C., Nietlispach, B., Engler, S., Hensel, S. and Zeller, F. (2004). *ZEN: Zurich English Newspaper Corpus* (Version 1.0) [Computer Software]. Zürich: University of Zürich. Available from: http://es-zen.uzh.ch/.
Fries, U., and Schneider, P. (2000). 'ZEN: Preparing the Zurich English Newspaper corpus'. In F. Ungerer (Ed.). *English Media Texts—Past and Present, Language and Textual Structure*, 3–24. Amsterdam/Philadelphia: John Benjamins.
Fuller, J. (1996). *News Values: Ideas for an Information Age*. Chicago/London: University of Chicago Press.
Gabrielatos, C., and Baker, P. (2008). 'Fleeing, sneaking, flooding: A corpus analysis of discursive constructions of refugees and asylum seekers in the UK Press 1996-2005'. *Journal of English Linguistics* 36(1): 5–38.

Gabrielatos, C., McEnery, T., Diggle, P., and Baker, P. (2012). 'The peaks and troughs of corpus-based contextual analysis'. *International Journal of Corpus Linguistics* 17(2): 151–175.

Galtung, J., and Ruge, M. (1965). 'The structure of foreign news: The presentation of the Congo, Cuba and Cyprus crises in four Norwegian newspapers'. *Journal of Peace Research* 2(1): 64–90.

Garces-Conejos Blitvich, P. (2009). 'Impoliteness and identity in the American news media: The "culture wars"'. *Journal of Politeness Research* 5: 273–303.

Garretson, G., and Ädel, A. (2008). 'Who's speaking? Evidentiality in US newspapers during the 2004 presidential campaign'. In A. Ädel and R. Reppen (Eds.). *Corpora and Discourse: The Challenges of Different Settings*, 157–188. Amsterdam/Philadelphia: John Benjamins.

Geis, M. (1987). *The Language of Politics*. New York: Springer.

Gernsheim, H. (1955). *The History of Photography*. London: Oxford University Press.

Goatly, A. (2002). 'The representation of nature on the BBC World Service'. *Text* 22(1): 1–27.

Golding, P., and Elliot, P. (1979). *Making the News*. London: Longman.

Gotti, M. (2006). 'Disseminating early modern science: Specialized news discourse in the *Philosophical Transactions*'. In N. Brownlees (Ed.). *News Discourse in Early Modern Britain*, 41–70. Bern/New York: Peter Lang.

Greatbatch, D. (1998). 'Conversation analysis: Neutralism in British news interviews'. In A. Bell and P. Garrett (Eds.). *Approaches to Media Discourse*, 163–185. Oxford: Wiley-Blackwell.

Gries, S.Th. (2008). 'Dispersions and adjusted frequencies in corpora'. *International Journal of Corpus Linguistics* 13(4): 403–437.

Griffith, E. (2015). 'Why nine publishers are taking the Facebook plunge'. *Fortune Magazine*, 13 May. http://fortune.com/2015/05/13/facebook-buzzfeed-new-york-times/, accessed 10 November 2015.

Gruber, H. (1993). 'Evaluation devices in newspaper reports'. *Journal of Pragmatics* 19: 469–486.

Grundmann, R., and Krishnamurthy, R. (2010). 'The discourse of climate change: A corpus-based approach'. *Critical Approaches to Discourse Analysis across Disciplines* 4(2): 125–146.

Guo, Q. (2012). 'Perceptions of news value: A comparative research between China and the United States'. *China Media Research* 8(2): 26–35.

Haarman, L., and Lombardo, L. (2009). 'Introduction'. In L. Haarman and L. Lombardo (Eds.). *Evaluation and Stance in War News*, 1–26. London/New York: Continuum.

Hall, S. (1973). 'The determinations of news photographs'. In S. Cohen and J. Young (Eds.). *The Manufacture of News: Social Problems, Deviance and the Mass Media*, 176–190. London: Constable.

Hall, S. (1977). 'Culture, the media and the "ideological effect"'. In J. Curran, M. Gurevitch, and J. Woollacott (Eds.). *Mass Communication and Society*, 315–348. London: Edward Arnold.

Hall, S. (1994). 'Encoding/decoding'. In D. Graddol and O. Boyd-Barrett (Eds.). *Media Texts: Authors and Readers*, 200–211. Clevedon: Multilingual Matters.

Halliday, M. A. K. (1985). *An Introduction to Functional Grammar*. London: Edward Arnold.

Halliday, M. A. K., and Hasan, R. (1976). *Cohesion in English*. London: Longman.

Halliday, M. A. K., and Matthiessen, C. M. I. M. (1999). *Construing Experience through Meaning: A Language-based Approach to Cognition*. London: Cassell.

Hansen, L. K., Arvidsson, A., Nielsen, F. Å., Colleoni, E., and Etter, M. (2011). 'Good friends, bad news: Affect and virality in Twitter'. *The 2011 International Workshop on Social Computing, Network, and Services (SocialComNet 2011)*, Loutraki, Crete, Greece.

Harcup, T., and O'Neill, D. (2001). 'What is news? Galtung and Ruge revisited'. *Journalism Studies* 2(2): 261–280.

Harrison, J. (2006). *News*. London: Routledge.

Harrison, J. (2010). 'News media'. In D. Albertazzi and P. Cobley (Eds.). *The Media: An Introduction*, 3rd edn, 246–257. London: Longman.

Hart, C. (2011). 'Force-interactive patterns in immigration discourse: A cognitive linguistic approach to CDA'. *Discourse & Society* 22: 269–286.

Hart, C. (2014a). 'Construal operations in online press reports of political protests'. In C. Hart and P. Cap (Eds.). *Contemporary Critical Discourse Studies*, 167–188. London: Bloomsbury.

Hart, C. (2014b). 'Constructing contexts through grammar: Cognitive models and conceptualization in British newspaper reports of political protests'. In J. Flowerdew (Ed.). *Discourse in Contexts*, 159–184. London: Bloomsbury Academic.

Hartley, J. (1982). *Understanding News*. London: Methuen.

Haupt, J. (2014). 'Generic and Evaluative Patterns in Science News'. PhD thesis, Masaryk University, Brno, Czech Republic.

Herdağdelen, A., Zuo, W., Gard-Murray, A. S., and Bar-Yam, Y. (2013). 'An exploration of social identity: The geography and politics of news-sharing communities in Twitter'. *Complexity* 19: 10–20.

Hermerén, L. (1986). 'Modalities in spoken and written English: An inventory of forms'. In G. Tottie and U. Bäcklund (Eds.). *English in Speech and Writing: A Symposium*, 57–91. Uppsala: University of Uppsala.

Hermida, A., Fletcher, F., Korell, D., and Logan, D. (2012). 'Share, like, recommend'. *Journalism Studies* 13(5): 815–824.

Hester, J. B., and Dougall, E. (2007). 'The efficiency of constructed week sampling for content analysis of online news'. *Journalism & Mass Communication Quarterly* 84(4): 811–824.

Hjarvard, S. (1995). *Internationale TV-nyheder* [International news on television]. Copenhagen: Akademisk Forlag.

Hoskins, A., and O'Loughlin, B. (2007). *Television and Terror: Conflicting Times and the Crisis of News Discourse*. Basingstoke/New York: Palgrave Macmillan.

Huan, C. (2015). 'Journalistic Stance in Chinese and Australian Hard News'. PhD thesis, Macquarie University, Australia.

Hundt, M., and Mair, C. (1999). '"Agile" and "uptight" genres: The corpus-based approach to language change in progress'. *International Journal of Corpus Linguistics* 4: 221–242.

Hunston, S. (2002). *Corpora in Applied Linguistics*. Cambridge: Cambridge University Press.

Hunston, S. (2011). *Corpus Approaches to Evaluation: Phraseology and Evaluative Language*. London/New York: Routledge.

Hunston, S. (2013). 'Review of: McEnery, T. and Hardie, A. 2012. *Corpus Linguistics: Method, Theory and Practice*'. *International Journal of Corpus Linguistics* 18(2): 290–294.

Iedema, R., Feez, S., and White, P. R. R. (1994). *Media Literacy*. [A report for the Write it Right Literacy in Industry Research Project]. Sydney: Disadvantaged Schools Program, NSW Department of School Education.

Ingram, M. (2015). 'Facebook has taken over from Google as a traffic source for news'. *Fortune Magazine*, 18 August. http://fortune.com/2015/08/18/facebook-google/, accessed 10 November 2015.

Jaworski, A., Fitzgerald, R., and Morris, D. (2004). 'Radio leaks: Presenting and contesting leaks in radio news broadcasts'. *Journalism* 5(2): 183–202.

Jaworski, A., Fitzgerald, R., Morris, D., and Galasiński, D. (2003). 'Beyond recency: The discourse of the future in BBC radio news'. *Belgian Journal of English Language and Literature* 1: 61–72.

Jeffries, L. (2010). *Opposition in Discourse. The Construction of Oppositional Meaning*. London/New York: Continuum.

Johnson, T. J., and Kelly, J. D. (2003). 'Have new media editors abandoned the old media ideals? The journalistic values of online newspaper editors'. *New Jersey Journal of Communication* 11(2): 115–134.

Johnson-Cartee, K. S. (2005). *News Narratives and News Framing: Constructing Political Reality*. Oxford: Rowman & Littlefield.

Johnstone, B., and Mando, J. (2015). 'Proximity and journalistic practice in environmental discourse: Experiencing "job blackmail" in the news'. *Discourse & Communication* 9(1): 81–101.

Jucker, A. H. (1992). *Social Stylistics: Syntactic Variation in British Newspapers*. Berlin/New York: Mouton de Gruyter.

Jucker, A. H. (1996). 'News actor labelling in British newspapers'. *Text* 16(3): 373–390.

Jucker, A. H. (2000). 'Adressatenbezug und Formen der interaktiven Kommunikation in den Massenmedien'. In G. Richter, J. Riecke, and B. M. Schuster (Eds.). *Raum, Zeit, Medium—Sprache und ihre Determinanten. Festschrift für Hans Ramge zum 60. Geburtstag*, 637–660. Darmstadt: Hessische Historische Kommission.

Jucker, A. H. (Ed.) (2009). *Early Modern English News Discourse: Newspapers, Pamphlets and Scientific News Discourse*. Amsterdam/Philadelphia: John Benjamins.

Kemmer, S., and Verhagen, A. (2002). 'The grammar of causatives and the conceptual structure of events'. In *Mouton Classics: From Syntax to Cognition from Phonology to Text*, Vol. 2, 451–494. Berlin/New York: Mouton de Gruyter.

Kepplinger, H. M., and Ehmig, S. C. (2006). 'Predicting news decisions: An empirical test of the two-component theory of news selection'. *Communications: The European Journal of Communication Research* 31: 25–43.

Khosravinik, M. (2009). 'The representation of refugees, asylum seekers and immigrants in British newspapers during the Balkan conflict (1999) and the British general election (2005)'. *Discourse & Society* 20(4): 477–498.

Kilgarriff, A., Baisa, V., Bušta, J., Jakubíček, M., Kovář, V., Michelfeit, J., Rychlý, P., and Suchomel, V. (2014). 'The sketch engine: Ten years on'. *Lexicography* 1(1): 7–36.

Kitis, E., and Milapides, M. (1996). 'Read it and believe it: How metaphor constructs ideology in news discourse. A case study'. *Journal of Pragmatics* 28: 557–590.

Kress, G., and van Leeuwen, T. J. (2001). *Multimodal Discourse: The Modes and Media of Contemporary Communication*. London: Edward Arnold.

Kress, G., and van Leeuwen, T. J. (2006). *Reading Images: The Grammar of Visual Design*, 2nd edn. London/New York: Routledge.

Lampropoulou, S. (2014). '"Greece will decide the future of Europe": The recontextualisation of the Greek national elections in a British broadsheet newspaper'. *Discourse & Society* 25: 467–482.

Lams, L. (2011). 'Newspapers' narratives based on wire stories: Facsimiles of input?' *Journal of Pragmatics* 43(7): 1853–1864.

Landert, D. (2014). *Personalisation in Mass Media Communication: British Online News between Public and Private*. Amsterdam/Philadelphia: John Benjamins.

Lazar, A., and Lazar, M. M. (2004). 'The discourse of the new world order: 'Out-casting' the double face of threat'. *Discourse & Society* 15(2–3): 223–242.

Ledin, P. (1996). 'The prime minister, Ingvar Carlsson, he or Ingvar? Anaphoric expressions in newspaper discourse'. *Nordic Journal of Linguistics* 19(1): 55–80.

Lee, D. Y. W. (2007). 'Corpora and discourse analysis: New ways of doing old things'. In V. Bhatia, J. Flowerdew, and R. Jones (Eds.). *Advances in Discourse Studies*, 86–99. London/New York: Routledge.

Lester, M. (1980). 'Generating newsworthiness: The interpretive construction of public events'. *American Sociological Review* 45: 984–994.

Lippmann, W. (1922). *Public Opinion*. New York: Free Press. (Reprint 1965.)

Liu, S. B., Palen, L., Sutton, J., Hughes, A. L., and Vieweg, S. (2009). 'Citizen photojournalism during crisis events'. In S. Allan and E. Torsen (Eds.). *Citizen Journalism: Global Perspectives*, 43–63. Bern/New York: Peter Lang.

Ljung, M. (2000). 'Newspaper genres and newspaper English'. In F. Ungerer (Ed.). *English Media Texts Past and Present: Language and Textual Structure*, 131–150. Amsterdam/Philadelphia: John Benjamins.

López-Rabadán, P., and Casero-Ripollés, A. (2012). 'Evolution of the Spanish media agenda (1980-2010): Longitudinal analysis of the front pages of two of the most important Spanish newspapers'. *Revista Latina de Comunicación Social* 67: 470–493.

Louw, B. (1993). 'Irony in the text or insincerity in the writer?' In M. Baker, G. Francis, and E. Tognini-Bonelli (Eds.). *Text and Technology: In Honour of John Sinclair*, 157–176. Amsterdam/Philadelphia: John Benjamins.

Lozada, C. (2014). '200 journalism cliches—and counting'. *Washington Post*, 27 February. http://www.washingtonpost.com/news/opinions/wp/2014/02/27/the-outlook-list-of-things-we-do-not-say, accessed 7 November 2014.

Luginbühl, M. (2009). 'Closeness and distance: The changing relationship to the audience in the American TV news show "CBS Evening News" and the Swiss "Tagesschau"'. *Language in Contrast* 9(1): 123–142.

Luke, D. A., Caburnay, A., and Cohen, E. L. (2011). 'How much is enough? New recommendations for using constructed week sampling in newspaper content analysis of health stories'. *Communication Methods and Measures* 5(1): 76–91.

Lukin, A. (2010). '"News" and "register": A preliminary investigation'. In A. Mahboob and N. Knight (Eds.). *Appliable Linguistics: Texts, Contexts and Meanings*, 92–113. London/New York: Continuum.

Lukin, A., Butt, D., and Matthiessen, C. M. I. M. (2004). 'Reporting war: Grammar as covert operation'. *Pacific Journalism Review* 10(1): 58–74.

Ma, L., Lee, C. S., and Gho Hoe Lian, D. (2014). 'Understanding news sharing in social media: An explanation from the diffusion of innovations theory'. *Online Information Review* 38 (5): 598–615.

Machin, D. (2004). 'Building the world's visual language: The increasing global importance of image banks in corporate media'. *Visual Communication* 3(3): 316–336.

Machin, D. (2013). 'What is multimodal critical discourse studies?'. *Critical Discourse Studies* 10(4) [Special issue on Multimodal Critical Discourse Studies]: 347–355.

Machin, D., and Mayr, A. (2012). *How to Do Critical Discourse Analysis: A Multimodal Introduction*. London: Sage.

Machin, D., and Niblock, S. (2006). *News Production: Theory and Practice*. London/New York: Routledge.

Machin, D., and van Leeuwen, T. J. (2007). *Global Media Discourse*. London/New York: Routledge.

Mahlberg, M. (2007). 'Lexical items in discourse: Identifying local textual functions of sustainable development'. In M. Hoey, M. Mahlberg, M. Stubbs, and W. Teubert. *Text, Discourse and Corpora: Theory and Analysis*, 191–218. London/New York: Continuum.

Mahlberg, M. (2009). 'Local textual functions of *move* in newspaper story patterns'. In U. Römer and R. Schulze (Eds.). *Exploring the Lexis-Grammar Interface*, Studies in Corpus Linguistics 35, 256–287. Amsterdam/Philadelphia: John Benjamins.

Mahlberg, M., and O'Donnell, M. B. (2008). 'A fresh view of the structure of hard news stories'. *Proceedings of the 19th European Systemic Functional Linguistics Conference and Workshop*, 1–19.

Maier, M., and Ruhrmann, G. (2008). 'Celebrities in action and other news: News factors of German TV news 1992-2004: Results from a content analysis'. *Human Communication* 11(1): 201–218.

Makki, M. (2014). 'Why is this "event" chosen and not that one? Analysing the register of Iranian print journalism and its notion of "newsworthiness"'. *Australian Systemic Functional Linguistics Association 2014 conference (ASFLA 2014)*, University of New South Wales, Australia, 30 September-2 October.

Makki, M. (in progress). 'The Language of Iranian News Journalism: News Values, Genres, and Reporting Styles'. PhD thesis, University of New South Wales, Australia.

Marchi, A. (2013). 'The *Guardian* on Journalism: A Corpus-assisted Discourse Study of Self-reflexivity'. PhD thesis, University of Lancaster, UK.

Marchi, A., and Taylor, C. (2009). 'If on a winter's night two researchers . . . A challenge to assumptions of soundness of interpretation'. *Critical Approaches to Discourse Analysis across Disciplines (CADAAD)* 3(1): 1–20.

Marshman, E., L'Homme, M.-C., and Surtees, V. (2008). 'Portability of cause-effect relation markers across specialised domains and text genres: A comparative evaluation'. *Corpora* 3(2): 141–172.

Martin, F., and Dwyer, T. (2015). 'How did they get here? The likable engine, dark referrals and the problematic of social media news analytics'. *IAMCR 2015*, Montreal, 12-16 July.

Martin, J. R. (2001), 'Fair trade: Negotiating meaning in multimodal texts'. In P. Coppock (Ed.). *The Semiotics of Writing: Transdisciplinary Perspectives on the Technology of Writing*, 311–338. Turnhout: Brepols.

Martin, J. R., and Matthiessen, C. M. I. M. (1991). 'Systemic typology and topology'. In F. Christie (Ed.). *Literacy in Social Processes*, 345–383. Darwin: Centre for Studies in Language in Education, Northern Territory University.

Martin, J. R., and White, P. R. R. (2005). *The Language of Evaluation: Appraisal in English*. Basingstoke/New York: Palgrave Macmillan.

Masterton, M. (2005). 'Asian journalists seek values worth preserving'. *Asia Pacific Media Educator* 16(6): 41–48. http://ro.uow.edu.au/apme/vol1/iss16/6, accessed 14 March 2016.

Mautner, G. (2000). *Der britische Europa-Diskurs: Methodenreflexion und Fallstudien zur Berichterstattung in der Tagespresse*. [The British discourse on Europe: Methodological observations and case studies on daily press reportage]. Vienna: Passagen Verlag.

Mautner, G. (2007). 'Mining large corpora for social information: The case of "elderly"'. *Language in Society* 36(1): 51–72.

McCarthy, M., and Carter, R. (2004). '"There's millions of them": Hyperbole in everyday conversation'. *Journal of Pragmatics* 36: 149–184.

McEnery, A. M., Xiao, R. Z., and Tono, Y. (2006). *Corpus-based Language Studies: An Advanced Resource Book*. London/New York: Routledge.

McEnery, T., and Hardie, A. (2001–2007). *Lancaster Newsbooks Corpus*. Available from: *The Oxford Text Archive*, http://ota.ox.ac.uk/desc/2531.

McEnery, T., and Hardie, A. (2012). *Corpus Linguistics: Method, Theory and Practice*. Cambridge: Cambridge University Press.

McQuail, D. (2005). *McQuail's Mass Communication Theory*, 5th edn. London: Sage.

Meyer, R. (2015). '72 hours with Facebook instant article'. *The Atlantic*, 23 October. http://www.theatlantic.com/technology/archive/2015/10/72-hours-with-facebook-instant-articles/412171/, accessed 10 November 2015.

Milestone, K., and Meyer, A. (2012). *Gender & Popular Culture*. Cambridge/Malden: Polity.

Mnookin, S. (2004). *Hard News: The Scandals at The New York Times and their Meaning for American Media*. New York: Random House.

Molek-Kozakowska, K. (2013). 'Towards a pragma-linguistic framework for the study of sensationalism in news headlines'. *Discourse & Communication* 7(2): 173–197.

Molek-Kozakowska, K. (in press). 'Communicating environmental science beyond academia: Stylistic patterns of newsworthiness in popular science journalism'. *Discourse & Communication*.

Montgomery, M. (2005). 'Television news and narrative: How relevant are narrative models for explaining the coherence of television news?' In J. Thornborrow and J. Coates (Eds.). *The Sociolinguistics of Narrative*, 239–260. Amsterdam/Philadelphia: John Benjamins.

Montgomery, M. (2007). *The Discourse of Broadcast News: A Linguistic Approach*. London/New York: Routledge.

Montgomery, M. (2009). 'Semantic asymmetries and "the war on terror"'. In E. Bielsa and C. W. Hughes (Eds.). *Globalisation, Political Violence and Translation*, 117–135. Basingstoke/New York: Palgrave Macmillan.

Moses, L. (2015). 'Are viral traffic's days numbered?' *Digiday*, 9 March. http://digiday.com/publishers/viral-traffics-days-numbered/, accessed 14 March 2016.

Nation, I. S. P., and Waring, R. (1997). 'Vocabulary size, text coverage, and word lists'. In N. Schmitt and M. McCarthy (Eds.). *Vocabulary: Description, Acquisition and Pedagogy*, 6–19. Cambridge: Cambridge University Press.

Newman, N. (2011). *Mainstream Media and the Distribution of News in the Age of Social Discovery*. Oxford: Reuters Institute for the Study of Journalism, University of Oxford. Available at: http://reutersinstitute.politics.ox.ac.uk/publication/mainstream-media-and-distribution-news-age-social-discovery.

Newman, N., and Levy, D. (2014). *Reuters Institute Digital News Report 2014: Tracking the Future of News*. Oxford: Reuters Institute for the Study of Journalism, University of Oxford. Available at: http://www.digitalnewsreport.org/.

Nguyen, A. (2013). 'Online news audiences: The challenges of webmetrics'. In K. Fowler-Watt and S. Allan (Eds.). *Journalism: New Challenges*, 146–161. Bournemouth: Centre for Journalism & Communication Research, Bournemouth University.

O'Donnell, M. (2007). 'The UAM Corpus Tool'. *28th ICAME conference*; Stratford-upon-Avon, UK.

O'Donnell, M. (2015). *UAM Corpus Tool* (Version 3.2) [Computer Software]. Available from: http://www.wagsoft.com/CorpusTool/download.html.

O'Donnell, M. B., Scott, M., Mahlberg, M., and Hoey, M. (2012). 'Exploring text-initial words, clusters and concgrams in a newspaper corpus'. *Corpus Linguistics and Linguistic Theory* 8(1): 73–101.

O'Halloran, K. L. (2008). 'Multimodality around the world: Past, present, and future directions for research'. *35th International Systemic Functional Congress (ISFC)*, Sydney, 21-25 July.

O'Halloran, K. L., and Smith, B. A. (Eds.) (2011). *Multimodal Studies: Exploring Issues and Domains*. London/New York: Routledge.

O'Neill, D., and Harcup, T. (2008). 'News values and selectivity'. In K. Wahl-Jorgensen and T. Hanitzsch (Eds.). *Handbook of Journalism Studies*, 161–174. London/New York: Routledge.

Olmstead, K., Mitchell, A., and Rosenstiel, T. (2011). 'Navigating news online: Where people go, how they get there and what lures them away'. *Pew's Research Center's Project for Excellence in Journalism*, 9 May. http://www.journalism.org/analysis_report/navigating_news_online, accessed 25 August 2013.

Palmer, J. (1998). 'News production, news values'. In A. Briggs and P. Cobley (Eds.). *The Media: An Introduction*, 377–391. Harlow: Longman.

Palmer, J. (2000). *Spinning into Control: News Values and Source Strategies*. London/New York: Leicester University Press.

Papacharissi, Z., and Oliveira, M. d. F. (2012). 'Affective news and networked publics: The rhythms of news storytelling on #Egypt'. *Journal of Communication* 62: 266–282.

Partington, A., Duguid, A., and Taylor, C. (2013). *Patterns and Meanings in Discourse: Theory and Practice in Corpus-assisted Discourse Studies (CADS)*. Amsterdam/Philadelphia: John Benjamins.

Perrin, D. (2013). *The Linguistics of Newswriting*. Amsterdam/Philadelphia: John Benjamins.

Peterson, K. (2015). 'Why Sports Illustrated laid off all of its photographers'. *Money Watch CBS News*, 26 January. http://www.cbsnews.com/news/why-sports-illustrated-cut-all-of-its-photographers/, accessed 11 February 2015.

Pew Research Center (2014). *State of the News Media 2014*. 26 March. http://www.journalism.org/packages/state-of-the-news-media-2014/, accessed 23 March 2016.

Pew Research Center (2015). *The Evolving Role of News on Twitter and Facebook*. 14 July. http://www.journalism.org/2015/07/14/the-evolving-role-of-news-on-twitter-and-facebook/, accessed 23 March 2016.

Pflaeging, J. (2015). '"Things that matter, pass them on": ListSite as viral online genre'. *10plus1: Advancements in Linguistics*. http://10plus1journal.com/wp-content/uploads/2015/09/12_JOU_ART_Pflaeging.pdf, accessed 7 December 2015.

Piazza, R., and Haarman, L. (2011). 'Towards a definition and classification of human interest narratives in television war reporting'. *Journal of Pragmatics* 43: 1540–1549.

Piper, T. A., Wilcox, S. J., Bonfiglioli, C., Emilsen, A., and Martin, P. (2011). 'Science, media and the public—the framing of the bicycle helmet legislation debate in Australia: A newspaper content analysis'. *eJournalist* 11(2): 125–149.

Pollard, R. (2014). 'The "lost" boy: Photo of four-year-old Marwan goes viral'. *Sydney Morning Herald*, 19 February. http://www.smh.com.au/world/the-lost-boy-photo-of-fouryearold-marwan-goes-viral-20140219-hvcxm.html#ixzz2ySkkXVzo, accessed 22 January 2015.

Potts, A., and Baker, P. (2012). 'Does semantic tagging identify cultural change in British and American English?' *International Journal of Corpus Linguistics* 17(3): 295–324.

Potts, A., Bednarek, M., and Caple, H. (2015). 'How can computer-based methods help researchers to investigate news values in large datasets? A corpus linguistic study of the construction of newsworthiness in the reporting on Hurricane Katrina'. *Discourse & Communication* 9(2): 149–172.

Pounds, G. (2010). 'Attitude and subjectivity in Italian and British hard-news reporting: The construction of a culture-specific "reporter" voice'. *Discourse Studies* 12(1): 106–137.

Pounds, G. (2012). 'Multimodal expression of authorial affect in a British television news programme'. *Discourse, Context & Media* 1: 68–81.

Präkel, D. (2006). *Composition*. London: Applied Visual Arts.
Price, V., and Tewksbury, D. (1997). 'News values and public opinion: A theoretical account of media priming and framing'. In G. A. Barnett and F. J. Boster (Eds.). *Progress in Communication Sciences: Advances in Persuasion*, 173–207. Greenwich, CT: Ablex.
Rau, C. (2010). *Dealing with the Media*. Sydney: University of New South Wales Press.
Reich, Z., and Klein-Avraham, I. (2014). 'Textual DNA: The hindered authorship of photojournalists in the Western press'. *Journalism Practice* 8(5): 619–631.
Reid, A. (2014). '10 social media tips for local news organisations'. *Journalism*, 4 June. https://www.journalism.co.uk/news/10-social-media-tips-for-local-news-organisations/s2/a556974/, accessed 10 November 2015.
Renouf, A. (2007). 'Tracing lexical productivity and creativity in the British media: The Chavs and the Chav-nots?' In J. Munat (Ed.). *Lexical Creativity, Texts and Contexts*, 61–89. Amsterdam/Philadelphia: John Benjamins.
Richardson, J. E. (2007). *Analysing Newspapers: An Approach from Critical Discourse Analysis*. Basingstoke/New York: Palgrave Macmillan.
Rissel, C., Bonfiglioli, C., Emilsen, A., and Smith, B. J. (2010). 'Representations of cycling in metropolitan newspapers—Changes over time and differences between Sydney and Melbourne, Australia'. *BMC Public Health* 10: 1–8.
Ritz, M.-E. (2010). 'The perfect crime? Illicit uses of the present perfect in Australian police media releases'. *Journal of Pragmatics* 42: 3400–3417.
Ritz, M.-E., and Engel, D. (2008). '"Vivid narrative use" and the meaning of the present perfect in spoken Australian English'. *Linguistics* 46(1): 131–160.
Robie, D. (2006). '"Four Worlds" news values: Media in transition in the South Pacific'. *Australian Journalism Review* 28(1): 71–88.
Romano, A. (2015). '9 simple composition tips to take your photos to the next level'. *Mashable Australia*, 18 March. http://mashable.com/2015/03/17/photo-composition-tips/, accessed 27 March.
Rössler, P., Bomhoff, J., Haschke, J. F., Kersten, J., and Müller, R. (2011). 'Selection and impact of press photography: An empirical study on the basis of photo news factors'. *Communications* 36: 415–439.
Rychlý, P. (2008). 'A lexicographer-friendly association score'. *Proceedings of Recent Advances in Slavonic Natural Language Processing* (RASLAN): 6–9.
Schudson, M. (1978). *Discovering the News: A Social History of American Newspapers*. New York: Basic Books.
Schultz, I. (2007). 'The journalistic gut feeling: Journalistic doxa, news habitus and orthodox news values'. *Journalism Practice* 1(2): 190–207.
Schulz, W. F. (1982). 'News structure and people's awareness of political events'. *International Communication Gazette* 30: 139–153.
Scott, M. (2015). *Wordsmith* (Version 6.0.0.235—2/08/2015). [Computer Software]. Available from: http://www.lexically.net/wordsmith/.
Semino, E. (2002). 'A sturdy baby or a derailing train? Metaphorical representations of the Euro in British and Italian newspapers'. *Text* 22(1): 107–139.
Semino, E. (2008). *Metaphor in Discourse*. Cambridge: Cambridge University Press.
Shaw, P. (2006). 'Evaluative language in evaluative and promotional genres'. In G. D. L. Camiciotti, M. Dossena, and B. C. Camiciottoli (Eds.). *Variation in Business and Economics Discourse: Diachronic and Genre Perspectives*, 152–165. Rome: Officina Edizioni.
Shoemaker, P. J., Danielian, L. H., and Brendlinger, N. (1991). 'Deviant acts, risky business and U.S. interests: The newsworthiness of world events'. *Journalism Quarterly* 68(4): 781–795.
Sidnell, J. (2010). *Conversation Analysis: An Introduction*. Malden/Oxford: Wiley-Blackwell.
Singletary, M. W., and Lamb, C. (1984). 'News values in award-winning photos'. *Journalism Quarterly* 61(1): 104–108 [continued on p. 233].
Sissons, H. (2012). 'Journalism and public relations: A tale of two discourses'. *Discourse & Communication* 6(3): 273–294.

Smith, A., and Higgins, M. (2013). *The Language of Journalism: A Multi-genre Perspective*. London: Bloomsbury.

Staab, J. F. (1990). 'The role of news factors in news selection: A theoretical reconsideration'. *European Journal of Communication* 5: 423–443.

Stenvall, M. (2008a). 'Unnamed sources as rhetorical constructs in news agency reports'. *Journalism Studies* 9(2): 229–243.

Stenvall, M. (2008b). 'On emotions and the journalistic ideals of factuality and objectivity—tools for analysis'. *Journal of Pragmatics* 40(9) [Special Issue on pragmatic and discourse-analytic approaches to present-day English]: 1569–1586.

Strömbäck, J., Karlsson, M., and Hopmann, D. N. (2012). 'Determinants of news content: Comparing journalists' perceptions of the normative and actual impact of different event properties when deciding what's news'. *Journalism Studies* 13(5–6): 718–728.

Taylor, C. (2013). 'Searching for similarity using corpus-assisted discourse studies'. *Corpora* 8(1): 81–113.

Taylor, C. (2014). 'Investigating the representation of migrants in the UK and Italian press: A cross-linguistic corpus-assisted discourse analysis'. *International Journal of Corpus Linguistics* 19(3): 368–400.

Thomson, E. A., and White, P. R. R. (Eds.) (2008). *Communicating Conflict: Multilingual Case Studies of the News Media*. London/New York: Continuum.

Thornborrow, J., and Montgomery, M. (Eds.) (2010). Special issue on Personalization in the Broadcast News Interview. *Discourse & Communication* 4(2).

Tiffen R. (2010). 'Changes in Australian newspapers 1956-2006'. *Journalism Practice* 4(3): 345–359.

Tunstall, J. (Ed.) (1970). *Media Sociology: A Reader*. London: Constable.

Tunstall, J. (1971). *Journalists at Work: Specialist Correspondents: Their News Organizations, News Sources, and Competitor-Colleagues*. London: Constable.

Tunstall, J. (1996). *Newspaper Power: The New National Press in Britain*. Oxford: Oxford University Press.

Ungerer, F. (1997). 'Emotions and emotional language in English and German news stories'. In S. Niemeier and R. Dirven (Eds.). *The Language of Emotions*, 307–328. Amsterdam/Philadelphia: John Benjamins.

Ungerer, F. (2000a). 'News stories and news events—A changing relationship'. In F. Ungerer. *English Media Texts—Past and Present*, 177–195. Amsterdam/Philadelphia: John Benjamins.

Ungerer, F. (Ed.) (2000b). *English Media Texts—Past and Present*. Amsterdam/Philadelphia: John Benjamins.

Ungerer, F. (2002). 'When news stories are no longer stories: The emergence of the top-down structure in news reports in English newspapers'. In A. Fischer, G. Tottie, and H. M. Lehmann (Eds.). *Text Types and Corpora: Studies in Honour of Udo Fries*, 91–104. Tübingen: Gunter Narr Verlag.

Ungerer, F. (2004). 'Ads as news stories, news stories as ads: The interaction of advertisements and editorial texts'. *Text* 24(3): 307–328.

Utt, S. H., and Pasternack, S. (2006). 'Front page design: Some trends continue'. *Newspaper Research Journal* 24(3): 48–61.

van Dijk, T. A. (1988a). *News as Discourse*. Hillsdale, NJ: Erlbaum.

van Dijk, T. A. (1988b). *News Analysis: Case Studies of International and National News in the Press*. Hillsdale, NJ: Erlbaum.

van Dijk, T. A. (1998). *Ideology: A Multidisciplinary Approach*. London/Thousand Oaks/New Delhi: Sage.

van Hout, T., and Macgilchrist, F. (2010). 'Framing the news: An ethnographic view of business newswriting'. *Text and Talk* 30(2): 169–191.

van Leeuwen, T. J. (1984). 'Impartial speech: Observations on the intonation of radio newsreaders'. *Australian Journal of Cultural Studies* 2(1): 84–98.

van Leeuwen, T. J. (1989). 'Changed times, changed tunes: Music and the ideology of the news'. In J. Tulloch and G. Turner (Eds.). *Australian Television: Programs, Pleasures and Politics*, 172–186. Sydney: Allen and Unwin.

van Leeuwen, T. J. (1992). 'Rhythm and social context: Accent and juncture in the speech of professional radio announcers'. In P. Tench (Ed.). *Studies in Systemic Phonology* 231–262. London/New York: Pinter.
van Leeuwen, T. J. (1999). *Speech, Music, Sound.* London: Macmillan.
van Leeuwen, T. J. (2005). *Introducing Social Semiotics.* London/New York: Routledge.
van Leeuwen, T. J. (2006a). 'Towards a semiotics of typography'. *Information Design Journal* 14(2): 139–155.
van Leeuwen, T. J. (2006b). 'Translation, adaptation, globalization: The Vietnam news'. *Journalism: Theory, Practice and Criticism* 7(2): 217–237.
van Leeuwen, T. J. (2008). *Discourse and Practice—New Tools for Critical Discourse Analysis.* New York: Oxford University Press.
van Leeuwen, T. J. (2011). *The Language of Colour—An Introduction.* London/New York: Routledge.
van Leeuwen, T. J. (2015). 'Theo van Leeuwen'. In T. H. Andersen, M. Boeriis, E. Maagerø, and E. S. Tønnesses. *Social Semiotics: Key Figures, New Directions*, 93–113. London/New York: Routledge.
Vestergaard, T. (2000). 'From genre to sentence: The leading article and its linguistic realization'. In F. Ungerer (Ed.). *English Media Texts Past and Present: Language and Textual Structure*, 151–176. Amsterdam/Philadelphia: John Benjamins.
Walker, P. (2015). 'Sabotage and hatred: What have people got against cyclists?' *Guardian*, 1 July. http://www.theguardian.com/lifeandstyle/2015/jul/01/sabotage-and-hatred-what-have-people-got-against-cyclists?CMP=share_btn_fb, accessed 25 August 2015.
Welbers, K., Atteveldt, W. v., Kleinnijenhuis, J., Ruigrok, N., and Schaper, J. (2015). 'News selection criteria in the digital age: Professional norms versus online audience metrics'. *Journalism*, first published on 28 July. DOI: http://dx.doi.org/10.1177/1464884915595474.
Westerståhl, J., and Johansson, F. (1994). 'Foreign news: News values and ideologies'. *European Journal of Communication* 9: 71–89.
White, P. R. R. (1997). 'Death, disruption and the moral order: The narrative impulse in mass "hard news" reporting'. In F. Christie and J. R. Martin (Eds.). *Genres and Institutions: Social Processes in the Workplace and School*, 101–133. London: Cassell.
White, P. R. R. (1998). 'Telling Media Tales: The News Story as Rhetoric'. PhD thesis. University of Sydney, Australia.
White, P. R. R. (2004). 'Subjectivity, evaluation and point of view in media discourse'. In C. Coffin (Ed.). *Applying English Grammar: Functional and Corpus Approaches*, 229–246. London: Arnold.
White, P. R. R. (2006). 'Evaluative semantics and ideological positioning in journalistic discourse: A new framework for analysis'. In I. Lassen, J. Strunck, and T. Vestergaard (Eds.). *Mediating Ideology in Text and Image: Ten Critical Studies*, 37–67. Amsterdam/Philadelphia: John Benjamins.
Young, S. (2010). 'The journalism "crisis": Is Australia immune or just ahead of its time?' *Journalism Studies* 11(4): 610–624.
Zelizer, B. (1995). 'Words against images: Positioning newswork in the age of photography'. In H. Hardt and B. Brennan (Eds.). *News Workers: Toward a History of the Rank and File*, 135–159. Minneapolis: University of Minnesota Press.
Zelizer, B. (1998). *Remembering to Forget: Holocaust Memory through the Camera's Eye.* Chicago/London: University of Chicago Press.
Zelizer, B. (2005). 'Journalism through the camera's eye'. In S. Allan (Ed.). *Journalism: Critical Issues*, 167–176. Maidenhead: Open University Press.
Zeller, F., O'Kane, J., Godo, E., and Goodrum, A. (2014). 'A subjective user-typology of online news consumption'. *Digital Journalism* 2(2): 214–231.
Zorger, C. (1992). 'The "lead" in American radio news: A critical study of types and techniques'. In C. Blank (Ed.). *Language and Civilization: A Concerted Profusion of Essays and Studies in Honour of Otto Hietsch*, 775–789. Bern/New York: Peter Lang.

Index

accent 79, 83, 89, 92, 261, 263, 264
activity sequence 18, 113–14, 130
additivity hypothesis 28
addressee. *See* target audience
adjectives 79, 82, 92, 94, 95, 96, 99, 100, 235, 261, 263
adverbials. *See* place, time
adverbs 94, 95, 100
aesthetics. *See* news values
affect. *See* emotion
agenda setting. *See* news agenda
allusion 67, 252
analytics. *See* audience metrics
angle. *See* camera angle, news angle
appraisal. *See* assessments, evaluation
assessments
 of expectedness 77, 79, 81, 260
 of importance/significance 77, 79, 83, 261
 negative 59, 61, 77, 79, 86, 87–8, 262
 positive 59, 61, 79, 88, 262
 of unexpectedness 77, 80, 81, 100, 267
attention economy 22, 255
attitude. *See* assessments, evaluation
attributes 17–18, 111, 113–14, 130
attributing expressions. *See* reporting verbs
attribution. *See* reported speech
audience. *See* target audience
audience metrics 41, 46n8, 68, 196, 256
audio. *See* broadcast news
authority 5, 41, 58, 59, 83

balance system 132–3n3
 and Aesthetic Appeal 110, 187
 dynamic asymmetry 19–20, 110, 132n3
 interrupted symmetry 19, 133n3
bias 61. *See also* impartiality
broadcast news 5, 6, 78, 79, 83, 86, 89, 92, 108, 120, 252, 261, 263, 264
broadsheets. *See* quality press

camera angle 19–20, 108–9, 114, 116, 130–1
causality 60, 83–4, 117
clickbait 192, 196, 252. *See also* audience metrics
clusters 16, 162, 276. *See also* n-grams
code of practice 3
collocation 14, 81, 151–64
 association measures 15, 152, 273
 collocation networks 14, 158
colour. *See* framing
comparison 80, 81, 94, 96, 100–101, 122, 124, 235, 265, 267
complementarity hypothesis 28
composition 19, 66, 110, 131, 133n7, 187. *See also* balance system
concession 101
concordances 15–16
consistency analysis. *See* range
constructed week 173, 176
constructionism 51
content analysis 28, 33, 34
context 6, 67–8, 105. *See also* place, setting, target audience, time
 socio-historical context 230
contrast 2, 66, 101, 102, 271
corpus-assisted multimodal discourse analysis (CAMDA) 8–12, 255
corpus-based discourse analysis 9
corpus linguistics 8, 12–17, 21
 similarity analysis 13, 15, 166
 typicality analysis 8, 13, 144–51
critical discourse analysis 5, 8, 9, 38, 45, 53, 57, 167–8
cropping 19, 24n17
cross-cultural research 237–46
cultural references 79, 92, 201, 264
cycling/cyclists. *See* environmental news

database 21–2, 138, 177–8, 200, 230–1
deadlines. *See* news cycle

299

Index

deixis 79, 92, 93, 98, 263
determiner deletion 82
diachronic research 229–37
dialect 79, 92, 264
digital disruption 192, 254
digital revolution 117
disaster vocabulary. *See* negative lexis
discourse 7–8
discourse structure. *See* genre, logogenesis
discursive news values analysis (DNVA)
    conceptualization 4–6, 39–43, 49–53, 55
    scope 44–5
dispersion 12, 17, 152

emotion 79, 85–6, 88, 89, 118, 119, 120, 122,
    130–1, 217, 244, 262, 263, 269, 270. *See also*
    surprise
environmental news 138
    news about cycling/cyclists 137–8
ethics 3
ethnographic approach 36, 43, 44, 242
evaluation 51, 59, 61, 77, 79, 80, 83, 100, 267.
    See also assessments
evaluative language 79, 86, 87–8, 235, 262. *See also*
    assessments, evaluation
evidentiality. *See* reported speech, sources
exaggeration. *See* intensification, media panics,
    sensationalism
expectedness. *See* assessments
eyewitnesses 55, 62, 90, 117, 120

Facebook. *See* social media
figures 41. *See also* numbers
framing 126, 127. *See also* cropping, news frames
frequency 12–13, 15, 255
front-page news 125–32, 237–46
    New York Post 126–7
    West Australian 128–31
functionalization 89, 243

Galtung and Ruge 27–31
genericization 89, 243
genre 10–11, 224n3, 249. *See also* hard news, news
    story, research news, soft news
graduation. *See* intensification, quantification
GraphColl 14, 158, 160

hard news 7, 23n5, 66, 94, 117, 186, 192, 252
headlines 127, 145, 198
    analysis of 204–11
    the language of 67, 98
    and typography 125, 130
    and visual-verbal patterns 218–23
history of news. *See* diachronic research

human interest 53
hyperbole. *See* intensification, sensationalism
hypotheticality 84

image. *See* press photographs
image gallery 124, 126, 199, 236, 244
impartiality 3
intensification 80, 93–4, 95, 264
internet. *See* digital revolution, online news
intersemiotic relations 10–11. *See also*
    corpus-assisted multimodal discourse
    analysis, verbal-visual relations
intertextual analysis. *See* corpus-assisted
    multimodal discourse analysis, verbal-visual
    relations
intrasemiotic analysis. *See* corpus-assisted
    multimodal discourse analysis, verbal-visual
    relations
intratextual analysis. *See* corpus-assisted
    multimodal discourse analysis, verbal-visual
    relations
intro. *See* lead
irony 101, 208
irrealis. *See* hypotheticality

journalistic norms. *See* values
journalists. *See* news workers

keywords 13, 145

layout 126–8, 131, 173–4, 247n12
lead 94, 103–4, 224n3
    image 221–2
localizing news 63
logogenesis 10, 11

media linguistics 4
media panics 53, 251
media release. *See* press release
metafunction 8, 108
meta news discourse 250
metaphor 80, 95–6, 162, 231, 235, 265
modal verbs 206
multimodality 7–9. *See also* verbal-visual relations

narrative. *See* news story
negation 87, 101, 158–9, 215
negative lexis 86, 87, 145
negativity. *See* assessments, news values
neutrality. *See* impartiality
new media. *See* digital revolution, online news,
    social media

newness 56, 65, 66, 80, 99, 123, 210, 215, 266
news agencies 192, 237, 245, 246, 250
news agenda 30, 32, 255
news angle 148, 164. *See also* news frames, news values angle
newsbites 172
news cycle 5, 40, 41, 65, 192, 250
news definition 6–7
news discourse, 4, 7, 9, 36, 37, 38, 39, 44, 77, 78, 89, 94, 95, 98, 105, 138, 141, 221, 231, 235, 245. *See also* discourse, news language
news event 6, 27–30, 31–2, 33, 37, 39, 42, 43, 51, 53
news factors. *See* Galtung and Ruge, news selection factors
news feeds 172
news frames 46n1, 164. *See also* news angle
news gallery. *See* image gallery
news genres. *See* genre, news story
news images. *See* press photographs
news language 37, 42, 49–50, 66–7, 72n1, 77–80, 104, 231, 235, 237. *See also* news discourse
newspaper style guides. *See* style guides
news photographs. *See* press photographs
news process 28, 32, 40, 41, 43, 250
news selection factors 41
news sharing. *See* social media
news story 78, 198. *See also* news process
news style. *See* news language
news values
    Aesthetic Appeal 66–7, 110–11
    the combination of 60, 97, 102–4, 182–6, 215
    Consonance 57, 80–2, 111–13
    delimiting the scope of 39–42
    dimensions 33, 39, 42–3
    Eliteness 58–60, 82–3, 113–17
    Impact 60, 83–5, 117–18
    lists and labels 33–4, 53–6, 58, 60, 62, 64, 66
    Negativity 60–1, 85–8, 118–20
    other approaches to 31–2, 36–9
    Personalization 61–2, 88–91, 120–1
    Positivity 60–1, 85–8, 118–20
    Proximity 62–4, 91–3, 121–2
    status of 32–3
    Superlativeness 64, 93–7, 122–3
    Timeliness 64–5, 97–100, 123–4
    Unexpectedness 66, 100–2, 124
    See also discursive news values analysis, news language, press photographs
news values angle 198
news websites. *See* websites
news workers 2, 35, 42–3, 44
newsworthiness. *See* news values
news writing. *See* news language
news writing objectives 41
n-grams 12, 203. *See also* clusters
nominal phrase 82, 91, 156, 157, 215. *See also* proper nouns
novelty. *See* newness
numbers 95, 161, 235. *See also* figures

objectivity. *See* impartiality
online news 6, 173, 196–7, 222. *See also* digital revolution, image gallery
'ordinary' people 59, 61–2, 79, 89–90, 109, 114, 116, 120, 131, 184–6, 212, 216, 221, 243–5. *See also* eyewitnesses

photo gallery. *See* image gallery
place
    of publication 6, 105
    references 63, 67, 79, 91–2, 93, 242, 243, 263
podcasts. *See* broadcast news
popular press 5, 54, 62, 67, 77, 125, 127, 230, 245
positive lexis 79, 88, 262
positive news 54. *See also* news values
preferred meaning 61, 67, 68, 105
press photographs 51–2, 72n3, 107–9, 230, 235
    and news values 10, 34–5, 244
    and stock photography 190–2, 218
    See also balance system, composition, front-page news, verbal-visual relations
press releases 42, 250
pronouns 79, 92, 264
proper nouns 83
ProtAnt 13, 144–51
puns. *See* word play

quality press 5, 77, 86, 127
quantification 80, 94–5, 264
questions 252
quotation. *See* reported speech

radio. *See* broadcast news
range 12–13, 152, 154
readership. *See* target audience
realism 51
repetition 80, 96, 107, 122, 265, 270
reported speech 89, 90
reporters. *See* news workers
reporting verbs 206
represented participants 17–18
research news 7, 88, 210, 223
role labels 79, 82, 260

salience 19–20
sampling. *See* constructed week
science news. *See* research news
semantic prosody 14, 166
semantic tagging 15, 203

semiotic mode 7, 9–12, 23n6
semiotic resources 4, 7–8
semiotics. *See* social semiotics
semiotic system 7
sensationalism 53, 251
setting 18, 52, 113
shareability 41, 196, 255. *See also* audience metrics
shot length 19–20
simile 80, 96, 265
Sketch Engine 15, 17
social media 172–3, 255
   emerging news practices 179–82
   Facebook 172–3, 175–6, 221
   impact 212, 223, 255
   as neo-publishers 193, 254
   sharing news online 197, 255
   social referrals 172, 193
   Twitter 172–3, 175
social semiotics 8
sociolect 79, 83, 89, 261, 263
soft news 7, 54, 67, 252
sources 41, 56, 58, 59, 82, 83, 206
stance. *See* assessments, evaluation, evaluative language
statistics 13, 15
stereotypes 57, 81, 102, 111–13, 202–3, 212
stop list 12
story. *See* news story
story structure. *See* news story
storytelling. *See* news story, visual storytelling
style. *See* news language
style guides 44
subjectivity 23n8, 168n5, 202, 214
surprise 80, 100, 124, 267, 271
Sydney siege 128–32, 237–46
systemic functional linguistics 80

tabloids. *See* popular press
target audience 6, 42, 44, 67–70, 105, 128. *See also* audience metrics

technical affordances 20–1, 110, 131, 132n3
television. *See* broadcast news
text-image relations. *See* verbal-visual relations
time
   of publication 6, 56, 64–5, 98–9, 123, 210
   references 80, 97–8, 99, 266
   tense 97–8
titles. *See* role labels
tokens 12
topology 8–12, 137, 171, 197
transitivity 84
Twitter. *See* social media
types 12
typography. *See* headlines

UAM Corpus Tool 21, 198
unexpectedness. *See* assessments

values 3, 42. *See also* news values
verbal-visual relations 5, 9, 71, 127–8, 131, 218–23
verbs 84, 87, 95, 99. *See also* modal verbs, reporting verbs
video 255. *See also* broadcast news
viral news. *See* social media
visualization 222
visual storytelling 107, 192
voice 5, 86, 89
vox populi 59, 89, 91, 120

websites 172–3, 176, 179, 182, 196
wire service. *See* news agencies
word cloud 12–13, 144
word play 67, 252
word sketch 15, 162–4
Wordsmith 12, 21

CPSIA information can be obtained
at www.ICGtesting.com
Printed in the USA
BVOW06s2157151017
497688BV00002B/3/P